DATE DUE

JE 9 04			
NO 16 04			
OC 2 9 09			
NO 2 5 09			

DEMCO 38-296

UNDERSTANDING CONTEMPORARY CHINA

UNDERSTANDING —————————————————————————
Introductions to the States and Regions of the Contemporary World
Donald L. Gordon, series editor

Understanding Contemporary Africa, 2nd edition
edited by April A. Gordon & Donald L. Gordon

Understanding Contemporary China
edited by Robert E. Gamer

Understanding Contemporary Latin America
edited by Richard S. Hillman

Understanding the Contemporary Middle East
edited by Deborah J. Gerner

UNDERSTANDING
CONTEMPORARY
CHINA

∎

edited by
Robert E. Gamer

LYNNE
RIENNER
PUBLISHERS

BOULDER
LONDON

Cover photo by Lu Huoye, Yunnan Zhuang Studies Association,
from Katherine Palmer, *Creating the Zhuang: Ethnic Politics in the
People's Republic of China* (forthcoming).

Published in the United States of America in 1999 by
Lynne Rienner Publishers, Inc.
1800 30th Street, Boulder, Colorado 80301

and in the United Kingdom by
Lynne Rienner Publishers, Inc.
3 Henrietta Street, Covent Garden, London WC2E 8LU

Library of Congress Cataloging-in-Publication Data
Understanding contemporary China / edited by Robert E. Gamer.
    p.   cm. — (Understanding)
    Includes bibliographical references and index.
    ISBN 1-55587-687-0 (hc. : alk. paper). — ISBN 1-55587-686-2
(pbk. : alk. paper)
    1. China. I. Gamer, Robert E., 1938– . II. Series:
Understanding (Boulder, Colo.)
DS706.U53   1999
951—dc21   98-24305
                                                        CIP

British Cataloguing in Publication Data
A Cataloguing in Publication record for this book
is available from the British Library.

Printed and bound in the United States of America

The paper used in this publication meets the requirements
of the American National Standard for Permanence of
Paper for Printed Library Materials Z39.48-1984.

5 4 3 2 1

▪ Contents ▪

▪ Maps, Tables, and Figures ▪

■ MAPS

■ TABLES

■ FIGURES

▪ Photographs ▪

▪ Preface ▪

As China's importance in the world's economy and political structure grows, so too does the number of books discussing it. For the teacher of introductory courses, that is a mixed blessing. Keeping current with the research requires increasing amounts of time, and bibliographical searches reveal that most of these works pertain to topics too particular and advanced for students with little prior knowledge of China. Few are designed especially for such students.

Understanding Contemporary China was conceived to address this problem. It brings together a group of scholars who both have published extensively on China within their varied disciplines and teach introductory courses on China. We all began this enterprise with a strong sense that such a book was missing and needed. As we have worked on it over the past three years, we have become even more aware of the important niche we are filling. We have created a single text with readable chapters that introduce China from the perspectives of a number of disciplines. These chapters not only give overviews but also emphasize issues currently being researched—complete with bibliographical citations, so students can look into those sources themselves and also find other introductory texts offering additional information on different topics—and are highlighted with facts, narratives, experiences, and observations derived from the authors' close personal contact with China. Because the chapters are designed to be complete in themselves they can be assigned individually. Yet they cover a number of complementary themes, introduced in Chapter 1, to which each succeeding chapter adds form, focus, and nuance. This makes the book useful for courses offering broad multidisciplinary coverage of China, as well as courses that approach it from the perspective of a particular discipline. Some of the topics covered—geography, history, politics, economy, family and kinship, religion, literature, and international relations—are essential components of any introduction to China. Others—such as discussions of the environment, the roles and problems of women, popular culture, sexuality, demographics, and urbanization—are important topics that are often ignored in introductory works. All chapters give historical overviews along with a discussion of the most current events and the problems and prospects facing China in the future.

Chapter 1 introduces the book's themes and how they relate to our lives and concerns in the West and to Chinese living outside of China. The next two chapters introduce China's geography and long history. Readers will find some useful reference points here to which they can return when reading later chapters of the book: the maps in Chapters 2 and 3 and the dynastic chart in Chapter 3.

The rest of the book covers topics of major interest regarding China today. Each chapter gives historical background but focuses on current behavior, issues, and trends. Chapters 4 and 5 discuss the evolution of China's political institutions and entrepreneurial traditions and how they interface with the current reforms. Chapter 6 is about four topics of special concern to China: Hong Kong, Taiwan, Tibet, and the large number of overseas Chinese. Chapter 7 gives an overview of China's foreign policy. The rapid political and economic changes in today's China have contributed to and been affected by population growth, urbanization, and environmental problems—the topics of Chapters 8 and 9.

Then we turn to an examination of China's culture. Chapter 10 looks at China's family structure and the rapid changes currently taking place in sexual behavior and family relations especially in urban China. Far more than in most countries, the family plays a central role in economic relations and political ideology, which makes these changes especially consequential. Chapter 11 focuses especially on how women are involved and affected, both positively and negatively, as the economy grows. Chapter 12 provides a historic overview of how China's indigenous religions and those of nearby neighbors shaped Chinese society and how these traditions are being challenged by Christianity and communism. Chapter 13 discusses how China's literature and performance art have always had their roots in popular culture and what people are reading and watching today. This chapter, too, elucidates the rapid changes taking place in contemporary China's social and family life.

The closing chapter on trends and prospects returns to the themes introduced in Chapter 1 and points briefly to how they may play out in the near future. It gives alternative scenarios of where China's reforms may lead and also indicates some outcomes that are unlikely to occur.

Robert E. Gamer

▪ Acknowledgments ▪

I have been the sole author of my prior books. Collaborating with others in writing one has been a new and pleasant experience. I have enjoyed passing chapters around among the authors so they could make comments to one another. With their diversity of backgrounds and wealth of experience in both teaching and research, this has been an enriching experience. E-mail has made it possible to instantly transmit chapters to one another and exchange data and comments when making revisions, even with fellow authors halfway around the world in China, Singapore, and Australia, and across the Atlantic in Britain.

During the writing of this book, People to People International, a visiting lectureship at Shanghai University, a grant from University Associates at the University of Missouri–Kansas City, and the Edgar Snow Memorial Fund have helped me make trips to keep abreast of current developments in China. As usual, I have many people there to thank for leading me to information and insights found in these pages. I have room to mention only some of them: Chen Zhenya, Chen Qiuji, and Wang Junyi at Beijing University; Chen Hui of *People's Daily* and his wife, Chen Xiuxia, of the China Society for People's Friendship Studies; Huang Hua of the Ministry of Foreign Affairs; Fan Hengshan of the State Planning Commission; Shao Lei of the Ministry of Civil Affairs; Zhu Yukun of the Ministry of Labor; Li Yanping of the China International Travel Service; Jonathan Lange, H. Y. Cheung, and Lina Ting of Hong Kong Government Services; Deans Liu Dezhong, Wang Ximei, and Jiang Yongkong in Shanghai; Guang Shi Long of the Zhuhai Nanfang International Trade and Economy College; and Li Jian of the Shenzhen Economic Trade Committee. All were generous with their time and rendered assistance beyond the call of duty.

In addition to our own exchanges of opinions on drafts of chapters, our authors benefited from several anonymous reviewers who read individual chapters and two who read the entire manuscript with great care. Along with skillfully directing that process—and creating the innovative model on which this book is based—Donald and April Gordon provided considerable help in improving the book. John Condra, David Sprick, and Jessie Johnson also contributed their skills in editing individual chapters. Cheng De and Jane Cheng helped assure consistent transliteration.

The Geographic Information Systems Lab at Miami University created the maps in the volume. At the early stages, Wang Junyi, Max Skidmore, E. Grey Diamond, Timothy Cheek, Gregory Veeck, Perry Link, and Rubie Watson gave valuable assistance in getting the ball rolling. James Durig, dean of the School of Arts and Sciences at the University of Missouri–Kansas City and department chairs Robert Evanson and Dale Neuman helped me with a reduced load during part of the project.

My friend and colleague Henry Mitchell devoted much of his life to reopening dialogue between the United States and China. I am frequently reinvigorated by his boundless energy.

My wife, May Lim Gamer, collaborated on this volume in many ways. She located many volumes and facts from libraries, shared observations from her reading and experience, maintained regular contact with a host of Chinese friends here and in China, helped me achieve cultural immersion in China (and rescued me when I did not), helped me create the index and review the manuscript, and patiently abided many long evenings when I was in the house but not of it over the past three years.

R. E. G.

▪ 1 ▪

Introduction
Robert E. Gamer

Twenty years ago China seemed very distant to most of us. That is no longer the case. The chances are great that right now you are wearing or sitting near an item made in China or Taiwan. There is probably at least one Chinese restaurant in your town. Someone you know has been studying martial arts. You have Chinese or overseas Chinese classmates. Your local mall would look bare if all the goods made in China were removed. A high school or college not too far from you may be offering courses in Mandarin. A few years ago, none of this would have been likely. But today China has the world's fastest-growing economy, a fifth of the world's population, and escalating trade and travel through its borders. It has a highly motivated populace spreading to all corners of the world, a modernized army, world-class movie makers, and competitive Olympic teams. It is a major market for Coke, Pepsi, Boeing, Avon, Butler, Sprint, Black and Veatch, Warner Brothers, and a host of other Western companies. It has become a presence in our lives.

Yet, while China has been moving in around us, our comprehension of it often remains mired in the past. We think of Mao, Red Guards waving little Red Books, water buffaloes in paddy fields, laborers wearing Dixie Cup hats, pagoda temples, the Great Wall, the Forbidden City, crowds of people riding bicycles, communist officials with red stars on their caps ordering around workers in great factories, schoolchildren singing socialist songs, and a lone student stopping a tank on Tiananmen Square. All these are true images of China past or present, but contemporary China offers other images as well: modern office buildings filled with rows of computers; village streets lined with industrial parks; shantytowns for temporary workers; urban freeways jammed with buses, Jeep Cherokees, and VW sedans; and engineering projects transforming entire valleys and islands from swamp into metropolis. All help China achieve the dubious distinction of being among the world's greatest purveyors of air and water pollution. China is also lunchtime crowds lining up in front of Pizza Hut and

1

McDonald's, businessmen talking on their cellular phones over lunch, construction workers wearing Calvin Klein jackets and Nike Air athletic shoes produced in sweat shops up the road, unemployed youth chatting or begging on street corners or running in gangs, shopping malls and skyscrapers gleaming, popular talk radio shows discussing sex and relationships, steamy novels selling at corner bookstalls, and young people dancing to rock music late at night in discos.

China is ubiquitous—its clothes, electronics, food, people, and even its air are ever-present in all places. And this presence has another unique element: China still regards the 55 million Chinese living overseas as part of China. Although many of those overseas Chinese have become loyal citizens of other countries, they are often tied to China's 1.2 billion inhabitants by custom, family, and tradition. The richest of those families in Hong Kong (now part of China), Taiwan, Southeast Asia, Australia, and North America control almost as much investment capital as Japan; much of that money is invested directly or indirectly in China and in the Pacific Rim, including the coast of North America. This investment constitutes a major bond linking China to the Americas and Southeast Asia, one that the United States can ignore only at its own peril. It is important to note that 21 million of these overseas Chinese live in Taiwan. In the words of Singapore's senior minister Lee Kuan Yew, speaking before the 21st Century Forum in Beijing, "Taiwan cannot win independence, not even if the Americans want it to. It is not possible for Taiwan to be independent against the will of a united and economically strong China" (p. 30).

Lee (1996) has stated an obvious and central truth about China. It must be understood in the context of Chinese living outside its borders. China's prosperity has depended upon the investment of overseas Chinese; their prosperity, in turn, depends upon China's prosperity. Lee warns that "any clumsy, high-handed, or apparently brutal action can arouse resentment or fear in Hong Kong or Taiwan" (p. 30) and thus seriously affect China's unity and prosperity and hence its hold on Taiwan. That, in turn, would have profound economic and strategic effects around the globe. Such interdependency explains a lot about how the communist nation of China can be as immersed in free markets as it is; those markets are embedded in the social structure of this widely dispersed Chinese community.

The dispersed community shares some attitudes and habits that have been passed from generation to generation for thousands of years. It is also quite diverse. As you read *Understanding Contemporary China,* you will see these attitudes and habits, along with social divisions, showing up in a variety of contexts. The rest of this chapter will give you an overview of those attitudes, habits, and divisions. But before we get to that, we should say a bit about something that can confuse you without a brief introduction: Chinese words.

China has no alphabet. Its written language, which is thousands of years old, consists of single characters that represent entire words. Often these began as a simple stick drawing of a man, the sun, or another object that gradually became more complex and stylized over time. People had to memorize the individual characters for thousands of words. Only the educated scholar-officials and families of merchants in cities were in positions to devote the time it took to memorize these characters and learn to create them with careful brush strokes. After the communists came to power, they created about 2,200 simplified characters that could be taught to schoolchildren and used in newspapers, so as to spread literacy. But when Westerners arrived in China during the nineteenth century, they needed to transliterate the sounds of Chinese words into their Roman alphabet (romanize them). Two English sinologists, Sir Thomas Wade and Hubert A. Giles, devised a system (Wade-Giles) to do that. For geographical names, some other romanizations fell into common usage. During the 1930s a new system, *pinyin*, came closer to replicating the sounds of the words as they are pronounced in the Mandarin (literary) Chinese used around China's capital, Beijing. In 1958 this system was adopted by the People's Republic of China for its official publications, and in 1979 *Xinhua* (the China News Agency) began using *pinyin* for all dispatches. The *New York Times* and many other newspapers and scholarly publications now use *pinyin*; we use it throughout this book, except for a few words still commonly transliterated in other spellings (e.g., Yangtze, Sun Yat-sen) and when referring to people and movements in Taiwan, where Wade-Giles is still in vogue. Some fields like history still use a lot of Wade-Giles, and it is used often in transliterating literature. So you will encounter it in other books. Table 1.1 compares the *pinyin* names of some provinces and cities with transliteration common on older maps, and the names of dynasties and some other words in *pinyin* and Wade-Giles. It includes many of the Chinese words used in this book.

It is common for Chinese words to have only one or two syllables; when there are two, they are given equal emphasis in pronunciation. Words with similar sounds (and identical transliterations) may be differentiated by inflection of the voice up, down, down-up, or flat as you pronounce each syllable; each would have a different character in written Chinese script. When looking at names, Chinese give their family name first and then their personal name; Mao Zedong's family name was Mao, and his personal name was Zedong.

■ CREATIVE TENSIONS

A rubber band's ability to stretch helps it hold things together; its elasticity actually lets it wrap tightly around objects. China has many traditions that combine those traits, pulling apart while unifying. Chapters in *Understanding Contemporary China* highlight many tensions between

Table 1.1　Romanization of Chinese Terms

Pinyin	Older Geographical Transliteration	Pronunciation
Provinces		
Fujian	Fukian	foo jian
Gansu	Kansu	gahn soon
Guangdong	Kwangtung	gwong doong
Guizhou	Kweichow	gway joe
Hainan	Hainan	hi! nanh
Hebei	Hopeh	hü bay
Hubei	Hupeh	hoo bay
Jilin	Kirin	gee lin
Shaanxi	Shensi	shahn shee
Shanxi	Shansi	shehn shee
Sichuan	Szechwan	sü chwahn
Xinjiang	Sinkiang	sheen jyang
Zhejiang	Chekiang	juh jyang
Cities		
Beijing	Peking	bay jing
Chengdu	Chengtu	chung doo
Chongqing	Chungking	chawng ching
Hangzhou	Hangchow	hong joe
Nanjing	Nanking	nahn jing
Qingdao	Tsingtao	ching daow
Tianjin	Tientsin	tien jin
Xi'an	Sian	shee ahn

Pinyin	Wade-Giles	Pronunciation
Dynasties		
Han	Han	hahn
Qidan	Ch'i-tan	chee don
Qin	Ch'in	chin
Qing	Ch'ing	ching
Song	Sung	soohng
Tang	T'ang	tahng
Xia	Hsia	shah
Names		
Deng Xiaoping	Teng Hsiao-p'ing	dung sheeaow ping
Jiang Zemin	Chiang Tse-min	jyang dze min
Mao Zedong	Mao Tse-Tung	maow dze doong
Zheng He	Cheng Ho	jung huh
Zhang Xueliang	Chang Hsüeh-liang	jang shuey lyahng
Zhou Enlai	Chou En-lai	joe un lie
Zhuang-zi	Chuang-Tzu	jwong dz
Other terms		
baojia	pao-chia	bough dja
danwei	tanwei	don weigh

(continues)

Table 1.1 continued

Pinyin	Wade-Giles	Pronunciation
Dao	Tao	dow
guanxi	kuan-hsi	gwahn shee
Guomindang	Kuomintang	gwaw min dahng
Tiananmen	T'ienanmen	tien ahn mun
Xinhua	Hsin-hua	sheen hwa
Zhong guo	Chung-kuo	djohng gwaw

- Confucianism and both petty and modern capitalism
- Confucianism, Christianity, and communism
- Popular culture and formal traditions
- Regions and the capital city
- The heartland and its global outreach

China is slightly larger than the United States but has four times the number of people. Its rivers cross high, dry plateaus to connect the world's highest mountains with enormous floodplains. Its eastern provinces are among the world's most populous, its western provinces among the world's least inhabited. It first became a unified nation 200 years before the birth of Christ, with the north conquering the south; that unity has waxed and waned ever since. At the time of Christ, China was abandoning feudal states and starting to adopt both petty capitalist trade among family-run enterprises (often associated with the south) and a Confucian ethic (coming from the north). Since that ethic emphasizes family loyalty and hard work on the one hand and interfering government bureaucracy and unquestioned loyalty to northern-based leaders on the other, it both benefits and interferes with capitalism. Daoism (deriving from folk culture) and Buddhism (from India) helped individuals cultivate their inner personal lives while conforming to the rigid social conventions associated with Confucianism and family enterprises. So did popular forms of entertainment, which at the same time provided inspiration for China's highly refined art and literature. China developed some of the world's earliest large cities, which sent Chinese to ports and oases in distant parts of Asia to establish a lively trade.

By the late eighteenth century, these cities were in contact with the emerging capitalism of western Europe, which increasingly competed with China's petty capitalist enterprises. These foreigners also brought with them Christianity and Western ideas about human freedom and progress, which competed for favor with China's established religious traditions. As large factories and cities began to widen the divide between city and countryside and among social classes, communist ideology began to compete with

Christianity and capitalism for favor among workers, urban intellectuals, and peasants. Like many previous movements, those ideologies developed some Confucian traits as they adapted to China, especially those associated with strong rule emanating from the north. Today, as China strengthens its ties with international capitalism and capitalist nations, weakens its actual and ideological ties to international communism, and experiences rapid social change, traditions of both Confucianism and popular culture help fill its spiritual void. And overseas Chinese help fill its investment coffers.

Thus, China blends many traits and traditions, which seem to pull people apart and at the same time bring them together. People are expected to give their highest loyalty to their families and friends with whom they have special *guanxi* (relationships); yet the same traditions simultaneously bid them to follow the directives of the nation's top leaders. For thousands of years, China has both encouraged and strictly controlled small manufacturers and traders. China's regions have held closely to their own traditions while sharing in a common Chinese culture. That culture viewed itself as civilized and the outside world as barbarian yet continuously absorbed civilization from the barbarians. Today China has dazzlingly modern cities short distances from peasants tilling fields with primitive plows and water buffaloes to supply those cities with food. China has vast numbers of laborers toiling with simple tools to support their families and the world's highest level of economic growth. Younger computer-literate leaders compete for power with old men in Mao jackets.

These diverse traits and traditions have come to support one another. Their distinctions and competition create tensions but do not hold back progress. That has not always been so. Between the 1839 arrival of the Christian West in the first Opium War and the introduction of communism after World War II, and during the cataclysms of the Great Leap Forward and the Great Proletarian Cultural Revolution, many millions lost their lives in conflict among contending social forces. But China has learned to use conflict as a means of adapting to change. It has a disciplined social core weakened but not basically destroyed by television, consumerism, crime, and other assaults of modern culture. Its families have shown an ability to control their size, save, work hard, engage in creative entrepreneurship, and divide labor between the sexes. China's civilization has focused on an attachment to the land that has survived amid many centuries of urbanization. People who have migrated to China's cities are welcome to return to their home regions, keeping alive rural social bonds and safety nets even as people move out to the ends of the earth. When the Central Pacific Railway found its European immigrant laborers fleeing the arduous task of building a transcontinental railway across the United States in the 1860s, it turned to Chinese laborers, who arrived already organized into disciplined work units under their own foremen. For millennia, China has used this labor and considerable scientific skills to channel its vast amounts of water, mine rich seams of coal, enclose its cities and borders with walls and towers, and manufacture a variety of goods prized for their excellence around the planet. Even when divided by ideology or temporary political division or separated by vast distances after migration, families and clans deriving from the same villages have habits of cooperation to further such enterprises by sharing capital, labor, markets, and special connections. They hold together tightly even while stretching to take on global challenges.

As a result, China can contribute to global capitalism without being absorbed by it. These traits that help make it a great producer also make it a great consumer; its enormous population produces ever-increasing amounts of goods not only for world markets but also for itself. Extensive use of low-skilled labor holds down the cost of manufacturing while providing millions of people with income to buy these new goods. Unlike many third world countries, China has not developed large trade imbalances because it can produce much of what it needs. If China continues to sustain its current rates of growth, world capitalism might increasingly have to answer the reverse question: Is it ready to be absorbed by China or at least adapt its structure and mores to those of China?

■ NEW CHALLENGES

China, however, still has great challenges ahead of it. Like many third world countries, China's traditions offer little support for democracy. With its focus on obeying family and community leaders, China has suppressed individual expression. It has never allowed independent interest groups to form. Although it has long had laws, it has no tradition of rule of law. Competing political parties clash with Chinese traditions of harmony and unquestioning obedience to authority. This lets all elements of Chinese society support movements rejecting foreign influences even as they adapt to world technology, trade, and popular culture, yet this balancing act is becoming increasingly harder to maintain.

China's development has resulted in major problems. Deforestation, removal of ground cover and wetlands, water and air pollution, and giant engineering projects pose serious threats to China's food and water supplies, health, and standard of living. Despite the "one-child" policy, a growing population increasingly moving to cities is a growing strain on resources. Women made many advances during the twentieth century; fast development enhances some of those advances but brings setbacks to others. The growing economy widens the gap between rich and poor individuals and regions and brings new opportunities for corruption; as a result, much capital that should go into development ends up in nonproductive pursuits. This inefficiency, fast economic growth, and reduction in central planning have caused inflation, resource shortages, unemployment, and declines in social services. The inefficient state industries are hard to phase out because they employ large numbers of workers and still make essential goods, but they constitute a major drain on national treasuries already depleted as political and taxation powers devolve to the provinces.

These problems are amplified by an unpredictable legal system that leaves business contracts and individual liberties unprotected and makes both foreign investors and educated Chinese uneasy. In addition, China has put inadequate resources into educating a workforce with skills to run all the new enterprises; many with education seek to leave China for higher wages abroad. Hong Kong and Taiwan, both critical to China's economic future, are especially sensitive to these concerns. The coastal provinces that have been experiencing the world's fastest economic growth resist directives from central government and party organizations. Meanwhile, ethnic minorities living in interior provinces are among those receiving the fewest benefits from economic growth; they are politically and culturally marginal. China has in the past split apart into regions controlled by warlords, and competition between China's center and regions for support from the military remains intense. Military threats to Taiwan or offshore islands and crackdowns on dissidents and ethnic minorities frighten away foreign investors. These problems challenge China as it struggles to retain its fast-paced economic growth. Can it adapt democracy or develop nondemocratic alternatives to address them? If growth slows radically, can it stay unified?

Since 1842, when China's defeat in the first Opium War opened it to European influence, China has been experiencing profound cultural crisis—a crisis has never been more intense than at present. Young people who marched in the 1989 demonstrations and elders who once fought for a worker's revolution are preoccupied with making money and enjoying consumer goods. Many younger Chinese also revel in newfound freedoms to express themselves in music, dress, sexuality, and other nonpolitical ways. Many older Chinese worry that the social trends accompanying all the new market ventures in which they are engaging will threaten the jobs, housing, and social services that their work units still guarantee them. Increasing numbers of people cannot find full-time work, and it is common for men and women to have two or three sources of income. Families worry about the rising costs of goods they purchase and how they might fare if the economy should stagnate. They are profoundly torn by whether to follow traditional Chinese ways or trends from the outside world. For many, the future looks confusing. Confusion can lead people to choose authoritarianism as a safe alternative to chaos. Confusion also creates a climate for rebellion and acceptance of change. The spread of money can have the same two effects. Will China find creative or destructive ways to deal with these tensions?

We explore all these matters in the pages ahead.

■ BIBLIOGRAPHY

Lee Kuan Yew. 1996. "China Should be Patient." *Far Eastern Economic Review* (September 19).

■ 2 ■

China:
A Geographic Preface

Stanley W. Toops

China is moving onto our horizon. Though most of us know little about it, we are increasingly aware that somehow it is going to be a big factor in our lives. With over a billion people, China has more than a fifth of the world's population (Li, 1987). Just slightly larger than the United States, covering 3.7 million square miles, it is territorially the world's third-largest country. And its economy, already among the world's ten largest, is growing faster than that of any other country; soon its overall economic output could surpass our own (Greenhouse, 1993:1). Once isolated from the outside world, China's goods, people, and culture are rapidly penetrating all corners of the globe and heavily affecting our own economy and society. The next few pages will quickly introduce you to how it connects with its neighbors, how it is inhabited, and the features of its natural environment. These facts will prepare you for an overview of its history in Chapter 3 and give you a convenient reference point when geographic places and features are mentioned in later chapters.

We start by looking at where China is located on the map and its historical connections with neighboring states. Historically, China's culture and imperial power strongly influenced its closest neighbors, Korea, Japan, and the countries of Southeast Asia; in modern times, neighboring Russia, Japan, and Southeast Asia have had a powerful effect on China's political and economic development. Then we look at China's internal divisions, north and south, and east and west. Those regions have starkly different histories, and the differences persist. Finally, we examine China's natural landscape, which contains the world's highest mountains, huge deserts, and major rivers emptying into the world's most abundant floodplains. China encompasses a great diversity of cultures and physical features (Geelan and Twitchett, 1974:vii). It consists of much more than peasants tilling rice fields.

Geographic Information Systems Lab, Miami University, 1997 M.A.

Map 2.1   Regional Map of Asia

In simplest terms, we're talking about space (Linge and Forbes, 1990:1), region (Goodman, 1989:xi), and landscape (Pannell and Ma, 1983; Tuan, 1969:6). What space do China and its neighbors occupy on the map? How do its regions vary? How does China's natural landscape affect the way its people live?

■ SPACE

Where is this place, and how is it linked to its neighbors? China is located on the eastern end of Eurasia, the planet's largest continent (see Map 2.1), but its land connections on that continent consist of poor roads over harsh terrain. To the west are expanses of Central Asian dry lands and to the north is the cold steppe of Russia (see Map 2.4). To the south are the high mountains of the Himalaya, and to the east is the Pacific Ocean. China occupies an area not easily accessible to travelers and traders. The distances are far and the physical barriers formidable (Sivin 1988: 78–79).

China's closest cultural and physical connections are with Japan and Korea. These three countries are not separated by high mountains, deserts, or long stretches of ocean. Together they constitute East Asia. Sometimes Westerners call this the Far East, but that term only refers to the distance from Europe. East Asia is a better term for this region, describing its location at the eastern end of Eurasia: It is only far from places that are far from there. Southeast Asia (from Vietnam down to Indonesia) is situated to the southeast (Kolb, 1971:21–24).

To situate China, look at the country in an East Asian context. China, Japan, and Korea have very distinct cultures, histories, and natural experiences. Their religions are quite different. Unlike China, Korea is located on a peninsula, whereas Japan occupies a series of islands. But all three have been heavily influenced by Confucianism, a philosophy that began in China and has guided its ruling elite for centuries (about which you will read much more in subsequent chapters), and by Chinese art. Though their spoken languages are radically different, both Japan and Korea used Chinese characters (discussed in a moment) to write words before they developed their own alphabets; the Japanese still use Chinese characters

Wet-rice agriculture in Zhejiang.

blended with words written in their alphabet, and many Koreans use Chinese characters for scholarly writing. This diffusion of philosophical ideas, artistic expression, and writing practices connects the people of East Asia (Kolb, 1971:531).

The connections to China's other neighbors are not as strong, but these linkages are not insignificant for China. The Buddhist religion began in India and came to China via the "Silk Roads" (see Map 2.1), which also brought China's silks and other luxury goods to other parts of the continent. Confucianism influenced bordering countries in Southeast Asia, which in turn developed the technology of wet-rice (planting seedlings in wet paddy fields) agriculture that spread throughout south China. Islam, born in the Middle East, has a stronghold in western China. From the north came historically powerful external threats, the Mongol and the Manchu (Sivin, 1988:80).

□ The Middle Kingdom

China's name has historical and geographical significance (Cannon and Jenkins, 1990:269). The Chinese call their country Z*hong guo*. In the simplified characters used in the People's Republic of China, it looks like this:

中 国

The first character *(zhong)* means middle or central. Notice how it looks like a box or cake cut through the middle. The second character *(guo)* means country or kingdom. The outside square is the wall of defense for the country. So China is the Middle Kingdom, the kingdom located at the most central position.

The very name of the country imparts an idea of centrality. China has seen itself as central to the world, both in terms of looking up and looking out. The Chinese worldview placed the emperor at the connection between heaven and earth. The emperor resided in the capital, at the center of the world, so it was natural that this should be the prime connecting place between land and sky. Around this center, other countries or dominions were far away in the periphery. Those faraway people were barbarians (Freeberne, 1992:149).

The name *China* comes from the first dynasty to unify China. The Qin (pronounced "chin") dynasty unified the country in 221 B.C. The Chinese people of that time called their country after that dynasty (Borthwick, 1992:17). The ancient Greeks knew of China as Seres, the land of silk. Silk was part of the trade across the vastness of Eurasia on the "Silk Road." Another name for China is Cathay. This comes from Khitai, an ethnic group that occupied northern China in the eleventh century. Marco

Polo wrote about Cathay. People in S lavic-speaking areas still call China Khitai (Fairbank, Reischauer, and Craig, 1973:123).

The Chinese people call themselves Han, after the Han dynasty that immediately succeeded the Qin and adopted Confucian policies as its base. The Han are the dominant group in China. Although they loosely share some common physical features, their looks and average height vary from region to region, and they come from many distinct lineages. They are united by their common acceptance of the Confucian cultural norms that emerged during the Han dynasty (Cannon and Jenkins, 1990:67). Chapters 3 and 12 discuss this further.

According to Confucius, you should look carefully at the name of a person to understand what that person's role is (Fairbank, Reischauer, and Craig, 1973:44). The same can be said for the name of a country. China or Z*hong guo,* Qin dynasty or Middle Kingdom, these two names describe a country that is unified and located at the center of civilization. Its people, the Han, grant the country loyalty on the basis of traditional values.

□ Challenging the Middle Kingdom

China and its very view of itself were both fundamentally challenged when the Pacific Ocean was opened to the fleets of Europe. China itself had sent ships as far as the Indian Ocean. But once European ships entered the Pacific in numbers, China became vulnerable militarily, culturally, and economically (Sivin, 1988:84–89). Chapters 3, 6, and 7 all have much more to say about this. When China found it could not resist those on-slaughts, many in China began to question whether they were any longer the names they had been calling themselves, the people of Han traditions living in the center of the civilized world. Their space had been invaded.

■ REGIONS

China is a land of enormous internal contrasts. It is slightly larger than the United States (Pannell and Ma, 1983:1). If a map of China were su-perimposed on one of Europe, China would stretch from the North Sea south to the southern edge of the Sahara, east from Portugal to as far as the Ural Mountains. As the United States or Europe vary regionally, so does China. It is easy to approach this subject by focusing on two major divi-sions, east-west and north-south.

□ East and West

A historical division is between China Proper and the Frontier (Leem-ing, 1993). This is a distinction between the east and the west. China Proper is east of a line from Yunnan in the southwest looping around Beijing and Hebei to the sea (see Map 2.2). As Map 2.3 helps you quickly comprehend, this region has the heaviest population densities; 90 percent of the country's population lives here. Most of those people are Han and live in a Confucian society. Much of this area is suitable for agriculture in river basins and China also focused its industrial might here. The people who live within China Proper consider themselves the center of China's civilization (Leeming, 1993:12–13).

The Frontier is west of that line bisecting the country. Western China includes Inner Mongolia, Heilongjiang, Jilin, Liaoning, Ningxia, Gansu, western Sichuan, Tibet, Qinghai, and Xinjiang (see Map 2.2). Western China has far fewer people. Much of the population—including Mongols, Tibetans, and Uygurs—does not consider itself Han. Most of them adhere to Islam or Lama Buddhism. This region consists of mountains and deserts and has low rainfall. Traditionally, people were nomadic herders or farmed in oases. There is still very little industry here, even though this is one of China's richest sources for oil and coal (Cannon and Jenkins, 1990:65–67; Goodman, 1989:164).

☐ Northeast and Southeast

Another regional difference exists within China Proper. A line following just north of the Yangtze River separates the northern and southern portions of China Proper (Borthwick, 1992:54–55). The Yellow River waters northern China (see Map 2.4). This is the cultural heart of China. Rainfall is adequate for agriculture. People raise wheat, which they eat in the form of noodles or steamed bread. Much of China's heavy industry is in the north because of the coal and oil here. The northern Mandarin dialect is the basis for the standard language (Leeming, 1993:12).

The Yangtze River and West River are the lifelines of the southern region (Map 2.4). Southern China is lush compared with the north. Paddy (wet-field) agriculture is practiced here, and rice is the main food crop. Tea is grown in the hillsides. The south focuses on light industry such as textiles; it has few fuel resources. Southern dialects of the standard language, such as Cantonese, are spoken here (Leeming, 1993:13).

Part of this regionalization is expressed in the food styles of China. Cantonese style in the Guangdong province has a delicate flavor and sensibility, a more subtle approach. Sichuan food is spicy hot and numbing because of the combination of peppercorns used in preparation. Food from Hunan, Mao's home province, is the spiciest. Shanghai style makes liberal use of seafoods and is slightly sweet. Northern China style is plainer, using onions, garlic, and cabbage but few other vegetables. Beijing style is exceptional because of the imperial dishes like Beijing duck. In the north, noodles are the staple food for people, whereas rice is the staple in the south. Except

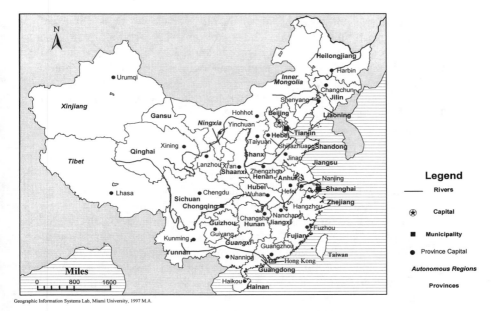

Map 2.2 Provincial Map of China

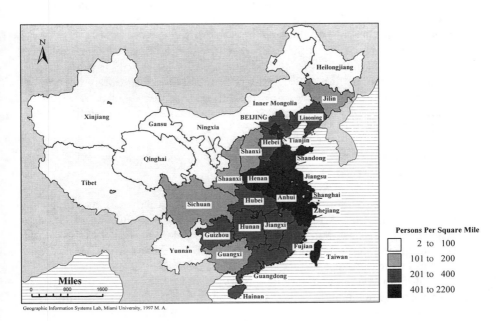

Map 2.3 Population Map of China

in Muslim areas, pork is the main meat all over China. In northwestern China, rice pilaf, spicy noodles, and lamb kebabs are common. In Tibet roasted barley flour is the staple, supplemented by some yak meat. All over China, tea is the preferred beverage (Sivin, 1988:120–121). Chinese love food and savor the specialties of their regions.

How different are the dialects? They are as different as the foods of China. *I love you* is expressed in these three characters:

我爱你

The first character means "I," the second "love," and the third "you." Anyone who can read Chinese characters knows this. But they do not all pronounce the words in the same ways. Although the Chinese use these same characters everywhere, in the north people say *wo ai ni* in Mandarin dialect. Cantonese living in Guangdong province to the south say *ngoh oi lei* in Cantonese dialect—quite a difference. Eventually, people have to write love notes to understand each other. A Cantonese writing these three characters to a lover in the north would immediately convey the meaning on paper, even though the words sound entirely different when spoken (Pannell and Ma, 1983:63–64). In Uygur, a Turkic language spoken in northwest China, *men sizni yahxi koremen* means "I love you"—quite different indeed. But since Uygur has its own written language, communication with outsiders becomes more complicated than it is among literate Chinese who can read the same characters but speak different dialects.

The regions of China are different in climate, culture, topography, agriculture, and industry (Toops and Andrus, 1993). Not only regional differences but regional identities are important. When you meet other people in China, you ask where they are from. In this fashion identity is set up: "I am a Beijing person." "I am a Sichuan person." Regional identities are strong (Cannon and Jenkins, 1990:62).

■ **THE NATURAL LANDSCAPE**

China's regional differences have their roots in physical geography. China is a land of extremes, of diverse topographies and varied landscapes. The highest point, Mt. Everest (Qomolangma) at 29,029 feet (8,848 meters) is on the border of Tibet and Nepal. The lowest point, the Turpan Depression at 505 feet (154 meters) below sea level, is in the far west of China (Geelan and Twitchett, 1974:1). The Chinese people have been working this land for 4,000 years, constantly shaping and forming it. The terraces and waterworks are a good example of this. The Chinese have sculpted the landscape, but they are not masters of it. Floods and droughts still plague China. The Chinese have not transformed fierce and austere mountains and deserts into fields of grain (Tuan, 1969:1).

The Chinese have a phrase, "vast in territory and rich in resources" *(di da wu bo)*. One perception of China is of unlimited land and resources. Another perspective of Chinese reality is that "the land is scarce and the people are many" *(di shao ren zhong)* (Leeming, 1993). Ten percent of China's vast territory is cultivated (Zhao, 1994:34); 90 percent of its 1.2 billion people live on terrain about the size of the United States to the east of the Mississippi River.

□ Three Tiers

It is easiest to approach China's physical geography by visualizing the country in three parts. As Map 2.4 shows, nature orders this landscape in three tiers, ranging from mountains to floodplains (Zhao, 1994:15). Powerful rivers have their origins high in the mountains of western China and then flow east to the sea. The rivers run through several tiers of mountains, hills, and then basins. Over two-thirds of China is mountainous, hilly, or high plateaus. This mountainous nature is a major constraint on human use of the land (Geelan and Twitchett, 1974).

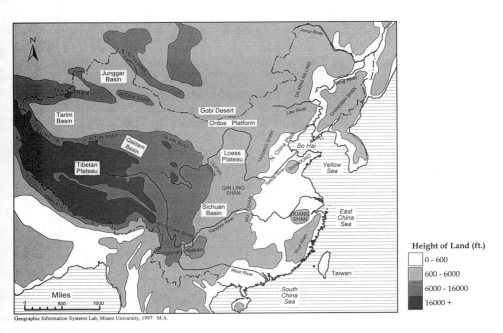

Geographic Information Systems Lab, Miami University, 1997 M.A.

Map 2.4   Physical Features of China

The highest tier is the mountains, shown on Map 2.4 with the two darkest gradations of shading, representing land ranging from 6,000 to 29,029 feet (1,829 to 8,848 meters) in elevation. Tibet lies in the heart of this region, but it also extends into Qinghai, Xinjiang, Sichuan, Gansu, and Guizhou provinces (see Map 2.2). The Himalaya range, at the southern end of this system, contains the world's highest mountains, Everest and K2. *Shan* means "mountain." You will notice several other ranges on Map 2.4 that are less familiar to you. The intermediate shading represents altitudes from 6,000 to 16,000 feet (1,829 to 4,877 meters); keep in mind that (except for 20,320-foot Mt. McKinley) the highest mountains of North America are under 15,000 feet. All the major rivers of China have their origins in these regions. Altitude is a major constraint on the habitation of people, plants, and animals (Cannon and Jenkins, 1990:85).

The middle tier is the hilly area, represented in the lightest shading— a broad expanse of basins, hills, and plateaus between 600 and 6,000 feet (183 and 1,829 meters). To the north are the Tarim and Junggar Basins and the Ordos Platform (Mongolian Plateau). Population in the northern portions of this tier (Tarim and Mongolia) is quite sparse because it is so dry. The deserts and the mountains combine to form effective barriers to the outside. Below them is the Loess Plateau, and east of Tibet are the Sichuan Basin and the Yunnan Plateau (south of the Hengduan Shan). Here there is more rainfall. The southern portion of this tier (Sichuan and Yunnan) has a dense population. Along the coast rise four ranges of hills—Changbai, Shandong, Huang, and Wuyi. Hainan Island to the south contains another range (Zhao, 1994:15).

The lowest tier (without shading), with floodplains and lowlands, is both the smallest and most populous. Notice from comparing Maps 2.3 and 2.4 how this portion of China supports the highest population densities—the land is scarce and the people are many. This segment following the coast lies lower than 600 feet (183 meters). The North China Plain follows the path of the Yellow River, while the Yangtze River and the combined paths of the Liao and Song Rivers form plains to the south and north. These plains with their many people are the agricultural and industrial heart of China. The North China Plain has less water, and the plain formed by the Liao and Song Rivers is quite cold in winter; as one moves south toward the delta of the West River the warm, wet, fertile plains provide the principal basis for China's rich agricultural output (Pannell and Ma, 1983:119).

The two highest tiers are the result of tectonic activity, the moving of the earth's plates. The Himalayas are still growing; earthquakes strike China regularly. Basins are usually not vulnerable, but the tectonic boundaries (fault lines) between plateaus and the mountain ranges have earthquakes fairly often. The most disastrous earthquakes have been those in populated areas. In 1976 an earthquake in Tianjin, near Beijing, killed over 250,000 people (Cannon and Jenkins, 1990:87–89).

☐ The Rivers Linking China

The mountains and deserts may divide China, but the river basins link it together. The natural landscape of China sometimes is summed up as *Huang He Chang Jiang,* the names for the two largest rivers, the Yellow and the Yangtze. These river systems connect the three physiographic tiers we just discussed. Over long spans of time, the rivers flowed through the mountains and plateaus carrying eroded material that washed into the sea to form and then build up the lowlands; they still break through dams and dikes during flood seasons to lay down more silt from upstream, contributing to the fertility of the soils in eastern China (Cannon and Jenkins, 1990:84).

The river of greatest historical importance is the Yellow River, since imperial China had its origins along its banks and those of its tributaries (see Chapter 3). As Map 2.4 shows, the Yellow River *(Huang He)* starts in the high mountain areas, runs north, cuts south through the Loess Plateau, and flows into the Bo Sea *(Bo Hai)* and out to the Yellow Sea *(Huang Hai).* The Yellow River and Yellow Sea gained their names from the fine fertile loess (yellow-brown soil) the river carries in its muddy waters. When the Chinese speak of "the River," it is this one. The Yellow River is also called "China's Sorrow." According to Chinese historical records, it has changed its course twenty-six times in the past 4,000 years. Since the North China Plain is very flat, people have built dikes and then more dikes to control it. Over the years, it has deposited much silt on its bottom, raising the riverbed. People in turn raised the dikes to hold up the banks. Now the riverbed is higher than the surrounding plain. When dikes break, the flood carries for miles. This is the sorrow. The river also brings joy by irrigating fields along its floodplain. When the ancient Chinese organized to build the dikes and irrigation channels, their agricultural surplus increased, and Chinese civilization developed (Pannell and Ma, 1983:27).

The longest river in China and the third longest in the world is the Long River *(Chang Jiang).* This river is also known as the Yangtze *(Yangzi* in *pinyin);* technically, this refers only to the estuary (mouth) of the river, but Europeans and Americans who were introduced to it when arriving from the ocean adopted that name—which we use in this book—to describe the whole river. As you can see on Map 2.4, the Yangtze starts in the high mountain areas not far from the headwaters of the Yellow River, but the rivers take different paths to the sea. Out of Tibet, the Yangtze passes through Sichuan and then goes through the narrow Three Gorges in Wu Shan before coming out into the Yangtze Plain. Unlike the Yellow River, this river is very important for transportation, linking the interior to the East China Sea (Zhao, 1994:110).

The Yangtze is also prone to flooding that affects millions of people, especially since this area gets plenty of rainfall. The government has built large dams and reservoirs to lessen flood damage and to generate hydroelectricity. Now the government is building the Three Gorges Dam, which will be the world's largest dam. The reservoir will fill much of the spectacular Three Gorges (Edmonds, 1992, 1994:144–150), and many people are concerned about the impact of such a dam on the environment (see Chapter 9).

The West River *(Xi Jiang)* drains southern China. As you can see from Map 2.4, this river rises out of the Yunnan Plateau and cuts through the South China Hills before it reaches the South China Sea. The Pearl River Delta, the estuary of the West River, has been an important economic area for China. Hong Kong is located there. The area is hilly, but peasants have built terraces over the years for paddy (wet-field) agriculture. This southern section of China has more than adequate moisture for wet-rice fields, and the hillsides are also good for tea. The Chinese have a saying, "when you drink water, think of the source" *(yin shui si yuan)*. These rivers are very important for China. Without water, the land is worth little (Pannell and Ma, 1983:141).

□ Climate, Soil, and Vegetation

The monsoon controls China's climate. The winter monsoon blows dry, cold air out of the northern Siberian steppes, bringing no moisture. The summer monsoon blows in hot and humid air masses from the South and East China Seas (see Map 2.4); by the time these air masses reach the interior, they have rained themselves out but are still hot. This north-south monsoon mechanism drives the climate process in China. It keeps south China warm and wet, whereas the north is cold and dry—relieved only by the Yellow River flowing from the south and winds from the East China Sea and Sea of Japan (Geelan and Twitchett, 1974:xx).

The Chinese designate their soils by color. Red soil is in the southeast, and the marshy areas of the south are blue. The loess of the north is yellow-brown, and the northeast has black soil. The deserts of the west have white soil. No soils anywhere in the world have fed so many people for so many generations (Tuan, 1969:23–31). Because of China's size and diversity, it helps to examine each region of the country to understand the linkage among climate, soils, and vegetation (Zhao, 1994:30).

The southeast, the wettest part of China, receives over 60 inches (152.4 centimeters) (sometimes nearly 80) of rain, most in the summer. The southeast portion of the United States, by comparison, has a similar climate but receives 40–60 inches (101.6–152.4 centimeters) of rain. China's southeast is subject to typhoons in the summer. Summers are extremely hot and sticky, and winters are cool and damp. In much of this part of China, people do not have heating, so the winter feels cold. Since the growing season is quite long, it is common to cultivate two crops of rice a year. On Hainan (see Map 2.2), a tropical isle, three crops are possible (Sivin, 1988:48).

Soils in the southeast are thick and sticky. This area was originally covered by broadleaf evergreen forests. Now much of the region grows rice, on fields immersed in water to nourish the young paddy shoots, and the sticky soils hold the roots firmly. They have been farmed for a long time and leached of much of their nutrients, but the farmers add night soil (human waste from outhouses and buckets) to provide humus (Pannell and Ma, 1983:33).

North of the Yangtze, the climate begins to change. The North China Plain (see Map 2.4) gains enough precipitation for crops. The yearly variability of precipitation is marked; some years may not reach 20 inches (50.8 centimeters), whereas others get closer to 40 inches. Wheat, rather than rice, dominates. Water is at a premium; some have suggested diverting part of the Yangtze's flow northward. Summers are hot and winters are quite cold. In the winter, dust storms sometimes come off the Gobi Desert, blanketing Beijing with a fine dust. Heilongjiang and Jilin (see Map 2.2) are cold indeed, especially in the long winter. Summers are short but warm, with enough moisture for crops such as corn and soybeans (Pannell and Ma, 1983:41).

The sediment left by river flooding in the North China Plain is quite fertile, though dry. This area was originally covered by forest, although now fields of wheat are most common. Some of the soils have been irrigated so much that they have become salty. Wet-field paddy cannot be formed in the dry fields of the north, and so less rice can be grown here. Heilongjiang, Jilin, and Liaoning (see Map 2.2) have poor soils except in the floodplains of the Song and Liao Rivers. Conifer forests still cover much of the mountain region.

Aridity (lack of rainfall) begins to increase in the interior of the country; half of China's territory gets less than 20 inches of rainfall a year (Cannon and Jenkins, 1990:82). The Loess Plateau and Mongolian Plateau (Ordos Platform), shown on Map 2.4, are part of the 20 percent of China that is semiarid, with 10–20 inches (25.4–50.8 centimeters) of rainfall a year. Wheat and some corn and millet are grown here with irrigation from the Yellow River. Summers are very warm and dry, and winters are quite cold and dry. The loess (the brownish-yellow soil that gives the Loess Plateau its name) is very deep and fertile, but erosion is a major problem in this area. The original vegetation was grassland and shrub; much that remains is overgrazed by cattle, and most has been plowed into fields. When the rains come, they fall hard and fast. Much of the surface loess ends up in the Yellow River (Pannell and Ma, 1983:36).

Over 30 percent of China is almost completely arid, with under 10 inches of rainfall a year (Cannon and Jenkins, 1990:82). The Takla Makan Desert in the Tarim Basin (Map 2.4) is the most extreme case, with less than 1 inch (2.54 centimeters) of rain per year. In the local language, *Takla Makan* means "if you go in, you do not come out." Turpan has recorded temperatures up to 118 degrees Fahrenheit (48 degrees Celsius). In this dry stretch of land, only the snowmelt from the mountains can give any water for sustenance. Even though the temperature is high, it is not humid, so the summers are bearable. Because Siberia, where the winter monsoons blow in, is immediately to the north, winters are severely cold. The many oases make the desert livable; they are highly productive, growing specialty crops such as melons, grapes, and cotton. In the northern portions of this arid area, steppe grasslands afford livestock grazing. The mountains have conifer forests also (Pannell and Ma, 1983:43).

The Tibetan Plateau (Map 2.4) has a unique and harsh climate. Altitude and location on the interior of a continent combine for a dry, cold climate, much like the polar extremes. Every month has temperatures below freezing. The interior of the area receives less than 4 inches (10.16 centimeters) of precipitation per year. The summer is quite short, but if you stay in the sun it is warm. Soils are poor in Tibet because there is not much plant life to decay into humus. Barley is grown in the south. The yaks, sheep, goats, and *dzo* (a cross between a yak and an ox) are the only livestock in this harsh climate. The yaks provide meat, milk, and hides for the Tibetans (Geelan and Twitchett, 1974:109). They also keep donkeys and horses, and wild asses roam the countryside.

China's 1.2 billion people have many challenges. Only 10 percent of the land will grow crops. Deserts and mountains make up much of western China. Northern China does not have enough water. Only the southeast has a climate that provides an abundance of food. Raising the economic well-being of the people will require careful management of the natural resources.

□ Economic Resources

When Marco Polo came to China, he found the Chinese burning "black rocks"; the abundance of coal and other fuel has long contributed to China's high economic output. China has several sources for energy. In the rural areas, the energy of the sun and of plants is the major source for most peasants. The burning of coal and oil provide energy for most urban areas (Smith, 1991:184). In areas with great rivers, hydroelectric power contributes increasing amounts of electricity.

Peasants use minimal amounts of oil. Coal is the fuel in the north, and people also burn rice straw, wheat straw, cornstalks, and cotton stalks to cook food and boil water. It takes a lot of straw to boil water. Since this material is burned, it is not plowed back into the ground to enrich the soil. Peasants scour the countryside looking for sticks, twigs, bark, and grass to use as fuel because so much of the natural landscape is overcut. This causes the hill slopes to erode without their natural cover. Manure piles are often used to generate methane gas for cooking and light. Small-scale hydroelectric power plants provide enough electricity for lighting in many homes (Pannell and Ma, 1983:116).

In the city a different pattern emerges. Coal supplies much energy, both for industrial and for residential use. China has the world's largest coal reserves, located mainly in northern China. Coal is processed into charcoal for cooking in urban households, and China's heavy industry relies largely on coal. Because northern China has water shortages, much of the coal is unwashed and thus burns less efficiently. Shipment of coal to other areas is a major difficulty for China. As China's industrialization increases, it will burn more coal, adding to air and water pollution (Leeming, 1993:21–23; Veeck, 1991:125). See Chapter 9 for a discussion of these problems.

China is a major producer of oil but uses most of its oil for its own industry. Much of the oil is in northeastern China; newer sites include the Bo Hai region in the northeast (Map 2.4) and Hainan Island in the southeast (Map 2.2). The biggest potential lies in the Tarim Basin of the northwest. Exploration of this desert area has been a major focus. These sites are far from industrial areas, however, so transporting the oil is a problem. As China increases its use of cars, the demand for oil products will also increase (Cannon and Jenkins, 1990:181–183).

Another energy source is hydroelectric power. Strong potential exists for electricity production on rivers of the south such as the Yangtze. Here the problems lie in moving people and in flooding large farmland areas. This power, however, will serve the needs of industry and the urban population (Cannon and Jenkins, 1990:186).

China's iron ore reserves lie mostly to the north and northeast. The Chinese have mined iron for thousands of years, and many mining operations are small scale and locally run. The reserves should be adequate in coming years if used more efficiently. China is looking for more minerals in western regions as it advances into the twenty-first century. Many of them are in out-of-the-way places to the north and west, so transportation to the heavy industry located in the north will be a problem (Zhao, 1994:45).

With better soils, water supplies, transportation, and terrain, the eastern portion of China has been more hospitable for living and economic production than the west. The northeast is well suited for heavy industry, and the southeast is ideal for agricultural production. Hence the economy of China Proper to the east has far surpassed that of Frontier China to the west. In Chapter 3 we observe that this disparity goes far back in time, and in Chapters 4 and 5 we discuss whether it might be reduced in the future. The Yangtze River can play a pivotal role in helping to move economic growth westward. The Chinese like to view the coast as a bow and the Yangtze River as an arrow that can shoot industry and economic reforms into China's interior. After all, as the next chapter says, it was the Yellow

River that shot China's imperial civilization out to the coast (Cannon and Jenkins, 1990:29).

■ BIBLIOGRAPHY

Blunden, Caroline, and Mark Elvin. 1983. *Cultural Atlas of China*. New York: Facts on File.

Borthwick, Mark. 1992. *Pacific Century*. Boulder: Westview Press.

Buchanan, Keith. 1970. *The Transformation of the Chinese Earth: Perspectives on Modern China*. London: G. Bell and Sons.

Cannon, Terry, and Alan Jenkins (eds.). 1990. *The Geography of Contemporary China: The Impact of Deng Xiaoping's Decade*. London and New York: Routledge.

Cheung, Peter T. Y., Jae Ho Chung, and David S. G. Goodman (eds.). 1996. "The 1995 Statistical Yearbook in Provincial Perspective." *Provincial China* 1:34–68.

Edmonds, Richard Louis. 1992. "The Sanxia (Three Gorges) Project: The Environmental Argument Surrounding China's Super Dam." *Global Ecology and Biogeography Letters* 4, no. 2:105–125.

———. 1994. "China's Environment." Pp. 143–170 in William Joseph (ed.), *China Briefing, 1994*. Boulder: Westview Press.

Fairbank, John King, Edwin O. Reischauer, and Albert M. Craig. 1973. *East Asia: Tradition and Transformation*. Boston: Houghton Mifflin.

Freeberne, Michael. 1992. "The Changing Geography of the People's Republic of China." Pp. 122–159 in Graham Chapman and Kathleen Baker (eds.), *The Changing Geography of Asia*. London and New York: Routledge.

Geelan, Peter J. M., and Denis C. Twitchett (eds.). 1974. *The Times Atlas of China*. London: Times.

Goodman, David S. G. (ed.). 1989. *China's Regional Development*. London and New York: Routledge.

Greenhouse, Steven. 1993. "New Tally of World's Economies Catapults China into Third Place." *New York Times* (May 20).

Institute of Geography, Chinese Academy of Sciences. 1994. *The National Economic Atlas of China*. Oxford: Oxford University Press.

Kolb, Albert. 1971. *East Asia: Geography of Cultural Region*. London: Methuen.

Leeming, Frank. 1993. *The Changing Geography of China*. Oxford: Blackwell.

Li Chengrui (ed.). 1987. *The Population Atlas of China*. Hong Kong: Oxford University Press.

Linge, Godfrey J. R., and Dean K. Forbes (eds.). 1990. *China's Spatial Economy*. Hong Kong: Oxford University Press.

Murphey, Rhoads. 1992. *A History of Asia*. New York: HarperCollins.

Pannell, Clifton, and Laurence J. C. Ma. 1983. *China: The Geography of Development and Modernization*. New York: John Wiley.

Sivin, Nathan (ed.). 1988. *The Contemporary Atlas of China*. London: Weidenfeld and Nicolson.

Smith, Christopher. 1991. *China: People and Places in the Land of One Billion*. Boulder: Westview Press.

Toops, Stanley W., and Simone Andrus. 1993. "Social Intelligence in China." *Journal of Economic & Social Intelligence* 3, no. 1:3–20.

Tuan, Yi-fu. 1969. *China*. Chicago: Aldine.

Veeck, Gregory (ed.). 1991. *The Uneven Landscape: Geographical Studies in Post Reform China*. Baton Rouge: Lousiana State University.

World Bank. 1992. *World Development Report 1992: Development and the Environment*. New York: Oxford University Press.

Zhao Songqiao. 1994. *Geography of China: Environment, Resources, Population, and Development*. New York: John Wiley.

■ 3 ■

The Historical Context
Rhoads Murphey

In Chapter 2, Stanley Toops showed how China is situated within Asia and how its people blend into the three tiers of its natural landscape. He also introduced some of the cultural diversity that has resulted from the blending. In this chapter, too, we will emphasize how nature both limits and encourages human occupancy of the land, but now our focus is on the history of human settlement, conquest, and government in China. As we begin half a million years ago and move forward to the present, another kind of blending becomes evident: China's isolation from much of the rest of the planet let it develop a unique culture that contributed extensively to civilizations elsewhere. At the same time, this culture was able to absorb conquests, technology, migrations, and religions from outside without losing its own identity. Even periods of disunity and conquests by Europeans and Japanese during the past two centuries have left China's unique culture and institutions fundamentally intact.

Chapter 2 introduced you to the distinction between Frontier China and China Proper and between southeastern and northeastern China. As we review the histories of China's imperial dynasties in this chapter it will quickly become evident that China's imperial civilization began in Frontier China but has its base in China Proper. Periodically, parts of northern China have been conquered by groups of invaders coming in from the Frontier, and the Mongols (briefly) and the Manchus (more enduringly) conquered the whole country. Yet those invaders themselves soon adopted the habits and institutions of China Proper. And China Proper itself has a long historical division; southeastern China's culture is as old and solid as that of the northeast. Those in the northeast conquered those in the southeast. That conquest has not been forgotten.

This chapter introduces a number of other themes that, like those in the prior two paragraphs, are treated more fully in subsequent chapters. China experienced feudalism and developed a centralized state long before those social and political processes came to Europe. It developed some unique relationships between government officials and merchants that often pitted

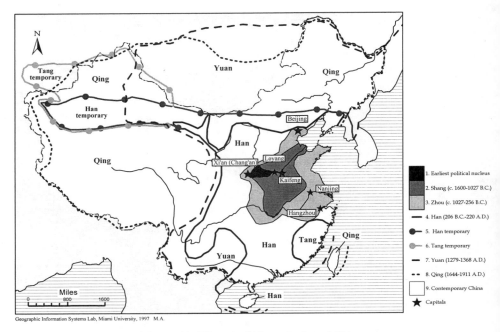

Map 3.1   Historical Boundaries of China

Note: Although the Zhou dynasty did not fall until 221 B.C., its territory was significantly decreased in 256 B.C. by the barbarian invasion.

south against north and region against region yet encouraged agriculture, commerce, and and the early growth of cities. It repeatedly tried to conquer and control people in adjoining territories. It has sometimes welcomed traders from around the world and sometimes kept them more at arm's length. The early parts of new dynasties often brought exciting growth and innovation; the latter parts often brought decline and stagnation. When the European powers first tested the empire with the 1839 Opium War, the empire was in a period of decline. That war exposed China's technological backwardness and resistance to change and opened up a century of conquest and humiliation by outside powers. Yet China has once again found the strength to rebound as it seeks to bring its technology to world levels.

■ THE PEOPLING OF CHINA

☐ Early Inhabitants

As far as we know, the ancestors of the Chinese have lived for the past half-million years in the area now covered by the modern provinces of

China Proper. China Proper is—as Chapter 2 explained—the area south of the Great Wall (which is just north of Beijing) and east of the Tibetan massif (the uplifted highlands with the two darkest shadings on Map 2.4). The earliest remains of *Homo erectus* found in China Proper are of Peking (Beijing) Man, dated approximately 500,000 B.C.; since they are fossilized, it is hard to differentiate physical characteristics from those of fossilized *Homo erectus* remains discovered elsewhere in the world. There is, however, some evidence that by about 200,000 B.C., after *Homo erectus* had merged with other humanoid species, the population, at least of northern China, had developed certain physical features associated with modern Chinese. The handheld stone choppers and knives these people fashioned were similar to those at other Paleolithic sites in East Asia but different from the stone tools made in Paleolithic Europe, India, and Africa (Chang, 1986:22–70; Gernet, 1968:19–39; Watson, 1961:22–55; Howells, 1983). This suggests that China had by then become quite isolated within its mountain and desert borders. China was to remain largely isolated from areas and cultures to the west until Portuguese adventurers arrived by sea in the sixteenth century and British naval guns finally opened China's ports to residence by foreigners in the nineteenth century. Though isolated, the Chinese borrowed extensively from neighboring regions (March, 1974:61–67), developed many inventions of their own, and united large populations and regions while central Asian and European states and empires rose and fell (Lattimore, 1940:27–39).

The Chinese have always been very conscious and proud of their long and glorious past. That consciousness and pride remain true today, and one really cannot understand contemporary China without considerable knowledge of its history.

□ North and South

China covers a huge area, larger than the United States if one includes Tibet (Xizang), Xinjiang, Inner Mongolia, and Manchuria (Heilongjiang, Jilin, and Liaoning), where cultures and physical types remain basically different from those of China Proper (Lattimore, 1940:53–80; Cheng, 1966; Pulleyblank, 1983). Even the provinces within China Proper (which itself originally contained a wide but closely related variety of cultures and physical types) cover territory large enough to hold most of the countries of western Europe. In the third century B.C., with the creation of empire under the Qin dynasty (221 B.C.), the people and culture of northern China conquered the central and southern regions of China Proper. Soon they were spreading their culture and then themselves southward.

From the time of the Han dynasty (202 B.C.–220 A.D.) and its consolidation of empire, the inhabitants called themselves "people of Han." Map 3.1 shows you how the Han dynasty moved into territory farther south and west than previous dynasties. The southernmost people conquered by the

Han were distantly related to but distinct from them. Qin and Han expansion also took place at the expense of the several more closely related but distinct peoples and cultures of central and southern China. Some of these southerners had almost certainly created what we may call "civilization"—settled agriculture, metals, writing, and cities—at least as early as or earlier than these developments in the north, where in the dry climate the evidence is better preserved (Chang, 1986:95–106, 192–242, 368–408; Li, 1985:189–221). Such early developments in the south would be a logical result of its proximity to the original sources of cultivated rice, pigs, chickens, water buffaloes, and early making of bronze, all in adjacent Southeast Asia (northern Vietnam and northern Thailand), probably well before they appeared in what is now China. Transmittal was easy, and there was probably also some movement of peoples. Before the Qin conquest forcibly united all Chinese into a single empire, the Guangdong (see Map 2.2) area was joined in a single state with what is now northern Vietnam, the state of Yueh, which spoke a common language (Meacham, 1983). But it is hard to imagine historical China without even one of the key elements derived from Southeast Asia—buffaloes for plowing the soil, rice and pigs as staples in the diet (Te-Tzu Chang, 1983:70–77), and bronze for casting (Li, 1985:265–314; Barnard, 1983; Franklin, 1983). These presumably spread in time into central and northern China, but the north was generally too dry for rice and buffaloes and only marginally hospitable for pigs and chickens.

In the course of the Qin and Han conquests, a single written language was imposed as well as a common spoken language, the ancestor of modern standard spoken Chinese, for the officials who administered the empire. Originally, northern culture overlaid the widely different cultures of the south. With the fall of the Han dynasty in A.D. 220 began the long migration of northerners southward over some 2,000 years, which, of course, added further pressures toward a national mode, in addition to the northern troops and administrators who had been operating in the south since the third century B.C. Distinct traces of different regional cultures and speech patterns remain among Han Chinese in the south, including differences in diet and cuisine as well as strong provincial identity amounting almost to clannishness. But the southward wave of Han Chinese conquest and settlement has taken all of the good agricultural land and greatly reduced the original non-Han population, who now live only in mountainous areas mainly unfit for agriculture, to which they have been driven by Han pressures. In a few subprovincial areas of this sort they constitute a majority, yet their numbers are small, and they are divided among themselves by cultural and linguistic differences. Some 91 percent of China's people are Han, with the remainder widely scattered and fragmented. As Chapter 8 explains, these percentages are somewhat inaccurate because many Han in recent years have married non-Han or asserted non-Han identity to avoid

UNDERSTANDING
CONTEMPORARY
CHINA

the one-child policy of the government, which does not apply to non-Han. Over the centuries since the Qin and Han conquest of the south, there has been widespread intermarriage as well as pressures for cultural conformity, so that the many originally quite separate and distinct cultures of central and southern China have been overlaid by a common imperial stamp. Traces of the originally wide variety of physical types as well as aspects of local or regional culture continue to be apparent beneath that stamp. Chapter 4 will tell you more about these divisions.

□ The Outer Areas

The outer areas—the Frontier, which was introduced in Chapter 2—are a separate case, originally inhabited by people only slightly related to the Han Chinese (Lattimore, 1940: 255–279; "Mysterious," 1998). The clearest cases are the Tibetans, Mongols, and Uygurs, the latter the dominant inhabitants of Xinjiang. Since 1950 the Chinese government has not only forcibly occupied these areas but promoted large-scale settlement there of Han Chinese as administrators and technicians, who now constitute the largest portion of the population of Xinjiang and a growing proportion of the population of Tibet. Outer Mongolia (Lattimore, 1940:489–510), north of the Gobi Desert, declared its independence from China in 1921 as the Mongolian Peoples' Republic, but Inner Mongolia, along the steppe frontier, was heavily occupied by Han Chinese, mainly as farmers dependent on new irrigation and road and rail lines. They now outnumber the remaining Mongols by something like 20 to 1, and the distinct Mongol culture is fading, and significant numbers of Han Chinese have also settled in Outer Mongolia as technicians. Manchuria (Lattimore, 1940: 103–150), known in China simply as "the Northeast" in an effort to soft-pedal the area's contended history as a target of Russian and Japanese ambitions (see Chapter 7), has been overwhelmed by mass Han Chinese migration since the late nineteenth century. This immigration has almost obliterated the original Tungusic, Manchu, and Mongol population as the northeast received refugees from overcrowded and drought-ridden northern China and developed its own surplus agricultural system and the largest heavy industrial complex in East Asia, thanks to its major resources of coal, iron, oil, and hydro (water) power.

The Chinese government's "solution" to the problem of non-Han minorities was to establish autonomous areas in the few pockets in the south where non-Han peoples remained a majority and in Tibet, Xinjiang, and Inner Mongolia. "Autonomous" is a bad joke, since the ruling hand of the Chinese state is omnipresent, and nearly all positions of authority are held by Han or by collaborators. In Tibet (as Chapter 6 explains), the Chinese state has tried to eradicate a separate Tibetan identity and so viciously repressed Tibetan efforts to assert it or to seek a voice in their own affairs that China has been repeatedly accused of genocide. The "autonomous" formula has convinced no one and in Chinese parlance is best referred to as "great Han chauvinism." Since minorities are such a small and fragmented percentage of the total population, often occupying strategically sensitive borders where neighboring states like to play on their discontent, the Chinese state feels free to ride roughshod over them and their interests.

■ POLITICAL PATTERNS OF THE PAST

□ Feudalism

China's recorded history begins with the Shang dynasty (ca. 1600–1027 B.C.; see Map 3.1 and Table 3.1), whose authenticity was questioned by Western scholars until excavations in the 1920s uncovered the remains of the last Shang capital, Anyang, and a great number of inscriptions giving the names of Shang kings (Li, 1957). Later excavations (Keightley, 1983; Maspero, 1978:24–33) rounded out the picture of the Shang as being dependent upon slaves captured in chronic wars with surrounding groups, already referred to as "barbarians," and as managing a productive agricultural system on the fertile loess (wind-laid, yellow-brown soil) of northern China. The chief Shang crop was millet, probably native to northern China, slowly supplemented by rice as rice moved northward. The major technological achievement of the Shang was in the working of bronze, producing objects whose technical perfection has never been equaled (Cheng, 1960; Creel, 1937:57–218; Leslie, Mackerias, and Wang, 1973:9–14; Gernet, 1968:43–66; Watson, 1961:57–101; Levenson and Schurmann, 1969:4–26). Excavations in central and southern China, where high temperatures and humidity have tended to obliterate much of the evidence, have nevertheless made it clear, as hinted at earlier, that Shang achievements were paralleled, perhaps even preceded, farther south, where writing, bronze, and a surplus-producing agriculture based mainly on rice were used (Chang, 1980; Hsu, 1995:1–32).

The Shang built large and ornate palaces whose remains can tell us a good deal about the wealth generated by agricultural surpluses, including the richly decorated chariots that were buried in the royal tombs with their horses and large numbers of followers or slaves. Writing, clearly the ancestor of modern written Chinese, slowly evolved and expanded to include abstractions; many of the characters can still be read, and the system was inherited by the next dynasty, the Zhou (Te-Tzu Chang, 1983:81–94, 107–129; Chang, 1986:295–307; Leslie, Mackerias, and Wang, 1973:15–22; Li, 1985:442–459). The Zhou's successor, the Qin dynasty, would impose this northern script on all of China, replacing the different scripts already in use farther south.

In about 1027 B.C., a great slave revolt was joined by one of the Shang feudal vassals, the Zhou who guarded the western frontiers (Hsu, 1995:33–67). Originally a "barbarian" group, the Zhou had acquired most of Shang culture and technology and used what became the traditional Chinese justification for rebellion, citing the injustices and oppression of the Shang rulers and declaring that "heaven commands us to destroy it" (Te-Tzu Chang, 1983:44–55; Maspero, 1978:86–92; Hsu, 1995:68–111). The last Shang king, alleged to have been a monster of depravity, died in the flames of his palace.

The Shang had ruled from successive capitals, frequently moved, in the central Yellow River valley, including the site of modern Zhengzhou, capital of Henan province (see Map 2.2). This was the heartland of early agriculture, but the Zhou established their new capital near modern Xi'an (see Map 3.1 and Shaanxi province on Map 2.2), their old base. Warfare continued with other groups around the fringes of the Zhou domains and periodically with groups to the south, all still called "barbarians."

The Zhou adopted the feudal solution used by the Shang, a network of supposed vassals owing loyalty to the Zhou king (Maspero, 1978:34–63; Li, 1985:460–476; Hsu, 1995:112–257). This resembled the system in medieval Europe, whereby a central state with pretensions to wider power but without the means to enforce it made alliances with local and regional groups, symbolized by ritual homage, provision of troops, and periodic gifts, in exchange for their control over their regional lands as fiefs granted by the king. For perhaps the first two or three centuries of Zhou rule, this system seemed to work reasonably well (Levenson and Schurmann, 1969:27–55; Watson, 1961:109–146; Chang, 1986:339–360; Creel, 1937:219–387). But China was changing as regional vassals increased their power and ambitions beyond the ability of the central state to control.

☐ The Decline of Feudalism

More basically, the spread of iron tools greatly increased farm production, hastened the clearing of remaining forests with iron axes as well as with fire, expedited new irrigation systems, and taken together supported a major increase in population, from perhaps 5 or 10 million under the late Shang to perhaps 20 million by mid-Zhou, spurred by rising food output, which also provided surpluses to be exchanged in trade (Li, 1985:16–58). Towns and cities began to dot the plain and the Yangtze valley, and a merchant class of some size emerged.

As in medieval Europe, none of this fit well with the feudal system based on fixed serfdom and the dominance of a hereditary aristocracy (Elvin, 1973:23–34). Serfs could escape to the new towns and begin a new life. We don't know much about the life of the common people in the first

Table 3.1 China's Imperial Dynasties and Beyond

Dynasty	In China	In the Rest of the World
Xia 2100–1600 B.C. (?)	Chinese characters developed	2700 B.C. Egyptians build Great Pyramid
Shang 1600–1027 B.C. (?)	Advanced bronze casting	1250 B.C. Moses and the exodus from Egypt 1200 B.C. Trojan War
Zhou 1027–211 B.C. Western Zhou 1027–771 B.C. Eastern Zhou 771–221 B.C.	Feudalism Emperors called "Sons of Heaven" Spring and Autumn Period 771–476 B.C. Confucius 551–479 B.C. Warring States Period 476–221 B.C.	753 B.C. Rome founded 560–483 B.C. Buddha in India 399 B.C. Death of Socrates 336–323 B.C. Alexander the Great
Qin 221–206 B.C.	China unified Great Wall unified	
Han 202 B.C.–220 A.D. Western Han 206 B.C.–A.D. 9 Eastern Han A.D. 25–220	Confucianism adopted Silk Road opens Buddhism to China Paper invented	54 B.C. Caesar invades Britain
Three Kingdoms A.D. 220–280 Eight Dynasties A.D. 265–589	Period of disunity Invasion and more division	451 A.D. Attila the Hun defeated 476 A.D. Fall of Rome
Sui A.D. 589–618	Grand Canal built	"Dark Ages" in Europe A.D. 742–814 Charlemagne
Tang A.D. 618–907	Expanding trade First dated printed book	
Five Dynasties A.D. 907–960	Period of disunity	

(continues)

Dynasty	In China	In the Rest of the World
Qidan A.D. 936–1122 Jin A.D. 1115–1234	Rule northern China	A.D. 1096 First Crusade
Song A.D. 960–1279 Northern Song A.D. 960–1126 Southern Song A.D. 1127–1279	Rule southern China Capital in Kaifeng Capitals in Nanjing, Hangzhou	Medieval Europe A.D. 1215 Magna Carta
Yuan A.D. 1279–1368	Genghis and Kublai Khan invade from Mongolia	A.D. 1300 Renaissance A.D. 1347–1351 Black Death
Ming A.D. 1368–1644	Return to rule by Chinese	A.D. 1450 Printing in Europe A.D. 1492 Columbus reaches America A.D. 1517 Reformation A.D. 1637 First British trade with Canton
Qing A.D. 1644–1911	Manchu rulers	A.D. 1776 American Revolution A.D. 1789 French Revolution
Republic A.D. 1912–1949	KMT Nationalist rule	A.D. 1917 Russia's communist revolution A.D. 1939–1945 World War II
People's Republic 1949–	Communist rule	

few centuries of Zhou rule, but it may be revealing that the arrangement mentioned by Mencius much later (third century B.C.), which he called the "well field system," included a checkerboard plan with a well in the central plot (Latourette, 1964:27, 44). Serfs were supposed to give priority to irrigating and cultivating that plot, which belonged to the feudal lord and only after that could work on the outer plots assigned to them. Serfs were bound to the lord and to his land for life, and on the lord's death could not leave but became serfs to his heir. As the economy altered and agricultural surpluses offered new opportunities for merchants and town dwellers to live and make money, such a system became increasingly hard to maintain (Li, 1985:477–490).

By this time, most writing was done with brush and ink, as in all subsequent centuries, on silk or on strips of bamboo. It was thus that the main body of the Chinese classics was originally written under the mid-Zhou: the *I-ching,* or *Classic of Change* (*Yijing*—a cryptic handbook for diviners), the *Book of Songs*, the *Book of Rituals*, and collections of historical documents (Levenson and Schurmann, 1969:56–65).

New agricultural productivity freed increasing numbers from farm labor to serve as artisans, scribes, transport workers, soldiers, officials, scholars, and merchants. Towns and cities became more important as trade centers than as centers of feudal control. At the same time, many of the original Zhou vassals were evolving toward separate statedom, as in late medieval Europe, each with its own distinctive culture. After some four centuries of Zhou rule, the political, economic, and social structure began to show strains, and eventually it disintegrated.

In 771 B.C. (the first authenticated date in Chinese history) the Zhou capital near Xi'an was sacked by rebels, and though it was rebuilt, the capital was moved to Loyang—shown on Map 3.1—in the central Yellow River valley so as to better control the Zhou domains. It was to be a vain hope, as the feudal structure continued to break up, and vassals, now emerging states, increasingly ignored Zhou authority and fought each other for dominance. The old Zhou base in the Wei valley near modern Xi'an was given as a fief to a supposedly loyal noble of the Qin clan, the new guardians of the frontier. Five centuries later, the Qin were to sweep away the crumbling remnants of Zhou pretension to found the first all-China empire (Gernet, 1968:69–84).

☐ Toward a Centralized State

The Qin were, in fact, the smallest and weakest of the major contenders among the former Zhou vassals, at least to begin with (Latourette, 1964:40–48; Li, 1985:222–239). The other rivals were various northern and central states as well as the state of Qu in the Yangtze valley and Yueh in the far south. It is still too early to speak of any of them, or of the Zhou, as "China"; each was culturally, linguistically, and politically distinct, and for some time there were also minor racial differences (Li, 1985:59–188). The 500 final years of feudalism over which they presided are known as the Spring and Autumn and the Warring States Periods. Though they shared technology, no one state dominated until the Qin conquest in 221 B.C. (Gernet, 1968:87–108; Walker, 1953:41–72; Maspero, 1978:171–268; Hsu, 1995:258–287). The state of Qu provides a good example of the differences, in that its base along the central portion of the Yangtze River led to rapid development of trade and of towns and cities. But Qu was ultimately defeated by a coalition of northern states in 632 B.C. and again in 301 B.C. (Walker, 1953:20–40). This may have been one of those contests that changes the course of history, giving the future to a peasant-based authoritarian empire, beginning with the Qin, rather than to a state where trade and merchants were prominent.

Increasing food production made it possible to field large armies of men who could be spared from farming for at least parts of the year and could be fed on surpluses. Warfare became larger in scale and more ruthless, no longer the earlier chivalric contests between aristocrats but efforts at wholesale conquest and fights for survival. The crossbow with a trigger mechanism, developed by or before this time, greatly increased firepower, range, and accuracy, and by the fourth century B.C., foot soldiers were supported by armed cavalry. All this undermined the earlier dominance of hereditary aristocrats, their chariots, and their personal retinues (Walker, 1953:73–101). Bronze and copper coins were minted by each state, standing armies proliferated, and bureaucracies began to appear. These changes offered a new range of opportunities for able commoners. For many it was a positive and welcome change, but for others the passing of the old order and the disruptions of warfare offered only chaos and moral confusion. Confucius, who lived in the Spring and Autumn Period (see Table 3.1), made it clear that his prescriptions were an effort to reestablish order and what he referred to as "harmony" following the values of an earlier "golden age." As fighting continued, Qin exterminated the remnant of Zhou power in 256 B.C., with no ceremony, and went on a generation later to overwhelm all the other states in a series of lightning campaigns ending in 221 B.C. (Levenson and Schurmann, 1969:66–78). China derives its name from Qin (Ch'in in Wade-Giles transliteration).

The chaos of the Warring States led to the growth of formulas for restoring order, like that of Confucius (551–479 B.C.) and his later disciple Mencius (372–289 B.C.), which stressed the need for order within a social hierarchy (Maspero, 1978:287–294; Martin and Shui, 1972:1–12; de Bary, Chan, and Watson, 1960:17–35, 100–111, 256–266; Schurmann and Schell, 1967:9–21, 34–66; Waley, 1939). The most important of these, after Confucianism, was Daoism, which through its cryptic text, the *Dao de jing*, or "Classic of the Way," represented a different approach to the troubles of the time (de Bary, Chan, and Watson, 1960:50–87; Maspero, 1978:305–316). The supposed author Laozi, which means simply "the old one," is a shadowy figure who was a contemporary of Confucius (Martin and Shui, 1972:13–17). Where Confucius emphasized the importance of rules for human behavior and gave advice to rulers, Daoism urged believers to relax, go with the flow, and use nature as the pattern, especially water, which flows around obstructions and seeks the lowest places. Whatever exists is natural and hence good. In practice, both Confucianism and Daoism had an appeal for most Chinese, who tended to follow both at different times, Daoism in retirement or when things went badly and Confucianism when in office; or, as has been said, they were workday Confucians and weekend Daoists. Other later philosophical schools, especially under the Qin, adopted the doctrines called Legalism, which emphasized harsh laws to control behavior instead of Confucianism's dependence on morality (Schwartz, 1985; de Bary, Chan, and Watson, 1960:136–158; Gernet, 1968:111–125; Maspero, 1978:321–328). Chapter 12 discusses these thinkers in greater depth.

The Qin conquest in 221 B.C. imposed stern measures to ensure conformity within the new empire. Primogeniture, whereby the eldest son inherits all of his father's property and status, was abolished, as a possible basis for power that might threaten the state. Land was now privately owned and freely bought and sold, which completed the end of the former feudal system. Walls had been built before to discourage raids along the northern steppe border, but these were consolidated and rebuilt under the Qin as the Great Wall, which runs east and west approximately along a line between areas to the south where normal rainfall is enough for farming and those to the north that are too dry. The Great Wall and the system of imperial roads and canals were built by forced labor, levied as part of taxes (corvée), which caused much suffering. Those who asked questions, the intellectuals, were suppressed by the new totalitarian state. Empire building is a rough business anywhere, but for all its excesses the Qin laid the groundwork for the dynasties that followed and for the modern state. These moves were doubtless popular, but the oppressively heavy set of state controls led to revolts that toppled the Qin in only fifteen years and burned the emperor's magnificent palace as rebels occupied the capital near modern-day Xi'an in 206 B.C. (Bodde, 1967; Lattimore, 1940:429–446; Latourette, 1964:66–75).

By 202 B.C. a new rebel leader emerged out of the civil war, Liu Bang, who founded a new dynasty, which he called Han (Grousset, 1959:48–53). He placed his capital on the site of modern-day Xi'an (see Maps 2.2 and 3.1). The harsher aspects of Qin rule were softened by the more humane morality of Confucianism, but many of the empire-building systems of the Qin were retained. The new dynasty emphasized the Confucian precept that government exists to serve the people and that unjust rulers must forfeit the support of the ruled while encouraging educated men to serve the state (de Bary, Chan, and Watson, 1960:172–199; Li, 1985:240–262; Chu, 1972; Wang, 1982; Loewe, 1994).

What remains of the glory of the Qin was rediscovered near Xi'an in the 1970s as excavations were begun at the massive tomb of the Qin emperor, Qin Shihuang, revealing a terra cotta (pottery) army, each of the thousands of life-size figures individually portrayed and set to guard the tomb's entrance. The idea of empire is contagious, and the Han extended their boundaries still further. In 111 B.C., emperor Han Wudi reclaimed the Qin conquests of Guangdong and into northern Vietnam and added southern Manchuria and northern Korea to the empire in 109–108 B.C. (see Maps 2.2 and 3.1). Earlier he had conquered the desert of Xinjiang, mainly to guard the "Silk Roads" westward (Map 2.1), and built watchtowers and garrison posts along it while mounting several successful campaigns against the ancestors of the Mongols in Inner Mongolia (Latourette, 1964:78–87; Grousset, 1959:54–62).

Silk caravans crossed the desert of Xinjiang by any one of three main routes and then handed over to a series of central Asian groups, who carried the silk to the shores of the Mediterranean, whence it went by ship to Rome, the biggest market, which paid for it in gold, since they had nothing to offer in exchange that the Chinese wanted (Yü, 1967). Tibet remained outside the empire. Wudi's endless campaigns and the burdens they imposed nearly caused a revolt, but following the advice of the imperial censors, he issued a famous penitential edict promising to be a better and less oppressive ruler. Han rule was briefly broken by a palace coup in A.D. 9 when the empress's nephew Wang Mang declared himself emperor of a new dynasty (Loewe, 1974:256–306; Grousset, 1959:63–67), but he was overthrown in A.D. 23 and the Han reestablished in A.D. 25, now as the Eastern Han, with its capital at Loyang (Map 3.1), where most of the dynasty's former grandeur was continued. But no political order lasts forever, and in the face of rebellion the last Han ruler abdicated in A.D. 220.

□ The Move South

There followed a confused and confusing period sometimes called the Six Dynasties where originally "barbarian" groups ruled most of the north, while the south was contested among a number of Chinese rivals (Elvin, 1973:35–53). Buddhism had come in from India during the Han, and now, in this "time of troubles," it spread widely and for a time eclipsed Confucianism while at the folk level merging with Daoism (de Bary, Chan, and Watson, 1960:279–410; Grousset, 1959:81–88). But the model of a unified empire established by the Han remained in people's minds, and after three and a half centuries of fragmentation, a new all-China dynasty, the Sui, re-created the empire of the Han. The fall of the Han dynasty had stimulated a mass movement southward of Chinese fleeing trouble in the north, a major new wave in the Han people's occupation of the south, driving most of the original non-Han inhabitants up into the mountains as the Han took the good agricultural land. This process was to continue cumulatively over the next 1,500 years or more and included the incorporation of Fujian both within the Chinese sphere and into the empires of Sui and Tang. Fujian is mountainous, and its easiest communications are by sea from the coast; its people were among the first to develop trade with Taiwan and Southeast Asia. The language of Fujian people remains different from standard Chinese but essentially the same as Taiwanese, since most of the people of Taiwan migrated from coastal Fujian beginning after A.D. 1600 (La-tourette, 1964:110–137).

The move south meant a series of adjustments to a very different environment from that in the north, where most Han had previously lived (Lattimore, 1940:469–471). New tools suited to wet-rice agriculture were developed, including the endless chain of paddles driven by two men pushing pedals on a crank, designed to move water efficiently from one paddy level to another. Rice, the dominant crop, was now transplanted from seedbeds to irrigated fields, and in the warmer and wetter southern climate yields greatly increased as a result, and two or even three crops a year became possible. Irrigation, intensive cultivation, and the creation of more or less level paddies by terracing on slopes required huge amounts of labor, provided by a growing population sustained by increased food output. In this period also began the use of human manure, or "night soil," to build the nitrogen levels that boosted yields and increased in supply as the population grew. Perhaps the clearest and most potentially destructive impact of the rising southern population was, however, the removal of most of the original forest cover to clear land for farming. As the population continued to rise, steeper and steeper slopes were invaded by terraces and the area covered by trees greatly reduced, producing, as in the north where deforestation was much older, erosion, siltation of stream and irrigation channels, and flooding. But forests harbored wild beasts such as tigers and also offered refuge for bandits, both used as peasant reasons for destroying them, often by fire.

By about the eighth century A.D., half or more of the population lived in the south, which also provided most of the imperial revenue and the food supply to feed the capital (still retained in the north because of tradition) and to guard the threatened area of the northern and northwestern frontier. But the north, the cradle of empire, had become a marginal area economically, or at least agriculturally, as the progressive removal of the forest since before Shang times led to massive erosion, siltation of streams and irrigation systems, and consequent severe and chronic flooding, especially of the silt-laden Yellow River but also of all the other streams in the north. Irrigated and cultivated land shrank disastrously, and much of the north could no longer feed itself and had to depend on southern imports of rice. The Grand Canal was built to link the north with the south for such transport.

In the south, the wetter and warmer climate meant that forests or second growth could more easily reestablish itself, especially if it was left alone, but as the population continued to increase that became less and less common, and large areas reverted to grass and brush, much less effective in retarding erosion. The growing population not only cleared more land to farm but cut from all hillsides twigs and grass for use as fuel or as fodder for penned animals. Trade, both along rivers and the sea coast, flourished in the south and supported a growing number of cities. Most places could be reached by cheap water transport, sometimes in no other way, whereas in the north most streams (including the heavily silted Yellow River) were not navigable, and goods had to be transported by pack animal, cart, and human porters at far greater cost.

The south also benefited from overseas trade in far greater volume than before, and port cities, especially along the coast from the mouth of the Yangtze River south, multiplied and prospered on the trade with Taiwan and Southeast Asia. Permanent colonies of Chinese merchants were established in the Philippines, Vietnam, Java, and elsewhere, and there was a great advance in shipbuilding, drawing its wood from near-coastal southern forests, especially in mountainous Fujian. Such developments tended to reemphasize the cultural differences of Cantonese and Fujianese from the main body of Chinese, and such differences remain. Canton (Guangzhou) and ports north of it such as Swatow (Shantou) and Amoy (Xiamen) joined Fuzhou and other Fujianese ports in generating a maritime, mercantile, seagoing world that contrasted with the inward-centered and agricultural world of the rest of China, with its imperial capital far inland and its revenue heavily dependent on the land tax. The Cantonese and Fujianese (Min) spoken languages remain distinct from standard Chinese, not mutually intelligible with it, and there is a prejudice among most other Chinese against the Cantonese, especially, as wily traders communicating with each other in their own spoken language and practicing clannishness and sharp dealing. Even their food and other customs are different. The Cantonese return the compliment by stereotyping northerners as slow-witted peasants or interfering bureaucrats. But there was a growing north-south trade as well, especially in tea, which had been adopted as the national drink during the Tang dynasty and was grown mainly in the misty hills of the south, in the mountains south of the Yangtze River, where it did not compete with rice for land and profited from the ample rainfall. To serve both domestic and overseas trade, the Chinese developed instruments of long-distance credit called "flying money" and, finally in the tenth century, paper money (Elvin, 1973:146–163).

□ Rebellion, Radiance, and More Rebellion

The Sui dynasty that reunified China in A.D. 589 did so by harsh methods and hence is often compared with the Qin. The Sui rebuilt the Great Wall and constructed the first Grand Canal, all with forced (corvée) labor. Rebellion soon spread, as in the last years of the Qin, and out of the fighting emerged a new dynasty, the Tang, which presided over an even greater empire than the Han. The Tang is considered by most Chinese the high point of their history. Elite culture flourished, and poetry achieved new richness, especially in the work of Li Bai and Du Fu, still thought to be China's greatest poets (see Chapter 13). The Tang capital, now named Chang'an (which means "Long Peace"; see Map 3.1), was again in the Wei valley on the site of modern Xi'an, which carried the aura of a great tradition because the first capital of the Han dynasty had been located there. It was a highly cosmopolitan place to which merchants and travelers came from as far as the eastern Roman empire and from most of Asia in between: Nestorian Christians (see Chapter 12), Jews, Muslims, Turks, Indians, Persians, and others thronged the streets of the capital. Tang conquests reached far into Central Asia, where they acquired horses for the imperial stables. Perhaps the best-known aspect of Tang art is their mass production of glazed porcelain figures and paintings of their beloved horses. Under Tang rule, the development of the south continued apace as more land was cleared for farming by northern migrants and as trade flourished. Renewed contacts westward revealed, as in Han times, no other civilization that could rival the Celestial Empire, and Tang China was clearly the zenith of power and sophistication. Did not all other people the Chinese encountered acknowledge this, by tribute, praise, and imitation of Chinese culture, and is that not the sincerest form of flattery (Grousset, 1959:121–177)?

Like the Han, Tang rule was briefly broken by rebellion in the mid–eighth century, and although the imperial order was restored, regional commanders continued to build their power, while rich landed families managed to slip off the tax rolls (Peterson, 1979:464–560). The civil service system begun under the Han was reestablished and strengthened but was increasingly undermined by the rich and powerful. In the mid–ninth century, the state moved against the Buddhist establishment (Weinstein, 1987) as a potential rival, confiscating the extensive temple and monastery lands and their wealth, but this was not enough to turn the tide. Total revenues fell by the end of the century, accompanied by spreading rebellion (Latourette, 1964:142–174; Elvin, 1973:54–68). In 907 one of the rebels usurped the throne and declared the Tang at an end, but fighting continued until 960, when one of the contending generals announced a new dynasty, the Song. The Song have been criticized by Chinese scholars because they gave up the wasteful and unprofitable building of empire and were ultimately overwhelmed by the hated Mongols. But the Song decision to avoid the endless wars of empire was wise and concentrated the state's energies on the provinces south of the Great Wall and east of the deserts and mountains of the west, the most productive and profitable area. The chronic struggle to hold Vietnam, Korea, Mongolia, Tibet, and Xinjiang was abandoned; these conquests had never even begun to pay their way, and the state now controlled the richest land and enterprises.

□ Southern Strategies

The Song capital was fixed at Kaifeng, on the great bend of the Yellow River (see Map 3.1), where the rebuilt Grand Canal could bring to it the rice surpluses of the Yangtze valley and where it could better administer the south, now the heart of the economy. Kaifeng became a major industrial center with a greater production of iron and steel than the whole of Europe would have in the eighteenth century and used coal as metallurgical fuel and for heating houses seven centuries before the West. China's total population passed 100 million for the first time, and Kaifeng contained over a million people. The carved wooden blocks used since the Han dynasty for printing were supplemented by movable type, which was pressed onto paper, also invented in the Han, to produce books. Literacy grew, and popular literature boomed. Paper currency issued by the state served the needs of an expanded commerce. Government officials distributed printed pamphlets to promote improved agricultural techniques; there were also ingenious new metal tools and proto-machines and new improved crop strains. It was an age of good government, with the rich landed families and regional commanders under central control for the time and revenues correspondingly healthy.

An important reason for the Song success was the re-creation of the civil service and its strengthening to new heights. Most officials were selected from among those who passed the imperial examinations (whose history is discussed in Chapter 4); imperial relatives, a plague in the past, were barred from taking those exams. Once in power, officials were regularly rated for merit and promoted or passed over accordingly. Lists of successful candidates from this time include nearly half from families who had never before produced an official—a remarkable degree of mobility and opportunity whatever one's birth. This largely civilian government tended to have a low opinion of the military, and the army did not match the efficiency of the civil service. Soldiers were recruited largely from the poorer classes, and they faced formidable opponents in the mounted warriors from the steppe, who progressively detached much of the northwest and the northeastern borderland, marginal areas to be sure, but traditionally part of the empire. There were efforts at reforming and beefing up the military, but these failed due to the rigid opposition of conservatives at the capital (Latourette, 1964:175–207; Grousset, 1959:178–194).

The price was high: the siege and capture of Kaifeng in 1126 by a mounted nomad group originally from Manchuria, the ancestors of the Manchus. The Song army regrouped and pushed the nomads north of the Yangtze but were obliged to shift their capital south to Nanjing for four years, and then to Hangzhou (see Map 3.1), where they presided over continued flourishing in the arts and technology, building on advances in the Kaifeng period, now known as Northern Song (the Hangzhou period is called Southern Song). This is thought to be the greatest period of Chinese landscape and nature painting, which together with vernacular literature and drama, blossomed in the rich urban culture of Hangzhou, which was dominated by the growing merchant group but increasingly shared with city dwellers there and in many other large southern cities. Cut off from normal trade routes through the northwest, the Song turned in earnest to developing more sea routes to Southeast Asia and India. Ports on the southeast coast flourished and became home to large numbers of resident foreign merchants, mostly Arabs. Foreign accounts agree that these were the world's largest port cities of the time.

There was a striking advance in the size and design of oceangoing ships, some of which could carry over 600 people as well as cargo, far larger than anywhere else until modern times. The earlier Chinese invention of the compass was a vital navigational aid, and these ships used multiple masts, separate watertight compartments (not known elsewhere until much later), and the stern-post rudder. In all of this, Song ships predated modern ships by many centuries. Ironically, they helped make it possible for Europeans much later, after they adopted much of Chinese ship technology, to make the sea voyage to Asia, also using the gunpowder invented in China to subdue those they visited. Hangzhou itself had a population over 1.5 million, but there were some six large cities within 300 miles and a network of smaller ones, depending like Hangzhou on the intricate system of waterways that crisscrossed the Yangtze delta and adjacent areas. Marco Polo, who actually saw Hangzhou only later under Mongol rule, marveled at its size and wealth and called it the greatest city in the world, a judgment confirmed by several other Western travelers of his period (Gernet, 1962). Chapter 8 discusses China's urban history in greater depth.

The Southern Song was also an exciting time of technological innovation and even of what seem like early steps toward the emergence of modern science. Confucian scholars like Zhu Xi pursued what they called "the investigation of things" (de Bary, Chan, and Watson, 1960:489–490), and in agriculture, manufacturing, and transport a variety of new machines and tools were developed—cultivators and threshers, pumps for lifting water, machines to card and spin and weave textile fibers, windlasses, inclined planes, canal locks, water clocks, and water-powered mills (Hommel, 1937). It all looked like eighteenth-century Europe, with commercialization, urbanization, a widening market (including overseas), rising demand, and hence both the incentive and the capital to pursue mechanical invention and other measures to increase production. Would these developments have led to a true industrial revolution in thirteenth-century China, with all its profound consequences? We will never know because the final Mongol onslaught cut them off, and later dynasties failed to replicate the details of the Song pattern. But it is tempting to think that if the Song had had just a little longer, China might have continued to lead the world, and the rise of modern Europe might not have happened as it did.

The Southern Song dynasty was far wealthier than Northern Song and had a booming economy. Unfortunately, this did not make it immune to the administrative and financial problems it inherited, but it kept functioning reasonably well until the end. Overseas trade, now a major source of revenue, was far larger than in Europe as late as the nineteenth century. Porcelain, perfected under the Tang, joined silk and lacquer as exports, and the finest pieces, called celadon, mostly made for the imperial court, have never been equaled, with their subtle bluish green or shades of white and gray glazes, exquisitely shaped. Government and private schools multiplied, to educate both the sons of the rich and the able sons of the less well-to-do. The explosion of printing and publication led to the spread of libraries and book shops and the appearance of anthologies and encyclopedias, as well as maps of the empire based on a grid of coordinates (Grousset, 1959:195–221). Mathematics was further developed, including the appearance of algebra and the use of the zero. So why did the Song succumb?

The Song were overrun in the end because the Mongols were formidable fighters who had already conquered the world's largest empire, extending even into Europe, and because of some drastic Song errors. In 1222 the Song foolishly made an alliance with the Mongols and within two years reoccupied Kaifeng, but a year later they were desperately defending their gains. For forty years the fighting raged in the north, where the heavily fortified Chinese cities were both defended and attacked with the help of explosive weapons, including cannons, which the Mongols had learned about from their great neighbor (Elvin, 1973:84–90). Song naval ships on the Yangtze mounted cannons and mortars and helped to hold back the Mongol tide, all before this devastating new technology spread to Europe, where it was quickly copied. But the Song were chronically weakened by factionalism at court, divided counsels, and inconsistent, often faulty, strategy (Murphey, 1996:113–122).

□ Unity and Cultural Continuity

By 1273 the Mongols had triumphed in the north and soon poured south, where Hangzhou surrendered in 1276. One false move against an opponent like the Mongols was usually all it took. But the Song put up a longer and more effective resistance to them than any of their other opponents—and the Mongols could never have won without the help of Chinese technicians, artillery experts, and siege engineers. Their rule in China, to which they gave the dynastic title of Yuan (see Map 3.1), lasted much less than a century and depended on many thousands of Chinese collaborators to administer the empire (Langlois, 1981). They also employed many foreigners, including Marco Polo, who served as a minor Yuan official from 1275 to 1292. His account of his experience has been dismissed by many, but on his deathbed he told his confessor, "I have not told the half of what I saw." Richard Lister (1976) and Marco Polo (1982) provide readable accounts of his travels; Frances Wood (1996) disputes his tale, but Jonathan Spence (1996b) points out reasons to believe it.

Kublai Khan, the Mongol ruler whom Marco Polo served, fixed his new capital at Beijing and became almost entirely Chinese culturally, though the welcome he extended to travelers and innovations from all over the world and the many rewards he gave to his fellow Mongols disturbed his subjects (Martin and Shui, 1972:95–107; Rossabi, 1988; Grousset, 1959:231–247). His successors were far less able, and the empire began to fall apart soon after Kublai's death in 1294, torn by rivalries among Mongol commanders and by widespread revolts among the Chinese against the exploitative Mongol rule (Murphey, 1996:121–122). By the end of the 1330s, most of China was in rebellion, and by 1350 control of the vital Yangtze valley was lost. A peasant rebel leader welded together Chinese forces, chased the remaining Mongols back into the steppe north of the Great Wall, and founded a new dynasty, the Ming, which was to restore Chinese pride and grandeur, from a new capital first at Nanjing and then at Beijing.

The imperial capital thus moved progressively eastward, from the Wei valley and Chang'an where the Zhou, Han, Sui, and Tang had ruled, to Loyang in later Han and Tang, to Kaifeng and Hangzhou under the Song, and finally north to Beijing (see Map 3.1). This migration reflected the eastward movement of the main area of threat to the imperial frontiers, from the nomads of the northwestern steppe in the Han to the Turkish tribes in the Tang to those that harried the Northern Song, then to the Mongols, and finally to the Manchus of Manchuria and their predecessors. But these northern capitals were increasingly unable to feed themselves, as the north declined ecologically and economically; hence the Grand Canal was extended to Beijing by the Mongols to bring food up from the south. Putting the capital on the exposed frontier (Beijing is only some 40 miles from the borders of Inner Mongolia) made less sense economically than establishing one in the growing southern heart of the country, such as Nanjing. The imperial tradition of locating the capital close to frontier threats exerted too strong a pull, however, and even obliged the Ming to move to Beijing from Nanjing.

Chinese history readily divides into dynastic periods and into what is called the dynastic cycle. Most post-Qin dynasties (but not the Yuan) lasted about three centuries, sometimes preceded by a brief whirlwind period of empire building such as the Qin or the Sui. The first century of a new dynasty would be one of vigor, expansion, and efficiency; the second would build on or consolidate what the first had achieved; and in the third vigor and efficiency would wane, corruption would mount, banditry and rebellion would multiply, and the dynasty would ultimately fall. A new group coming to power (again with the exception of the Mongols) would rarely attempt to change the system, only its management. Culture was continuous, even during interdynastic periods of chaos. By Tang times, most of the elements of modern Chinese culture were present. Irrigated rice was supplemented or replaced in the more arid parts of the north by wheat noodles (said to have been brought to Europe by Marco Polo or others along the Silk Roads as the origin of spaghetti) and steamed bread, or for poorer people by millet and *gaoliang* (a sorghum introduced from central Asia and, like millet, tolerant of drought).

Food was eaten with chopsticks since at least the Zhou dynasty, a model adopted early by Korea, Vietnam, and Japan, although the rest of the world ate with fingers. The Chinese cuisine is justly famous, including as it does such a wide variety of ingredients (the Chinese have few dietary inhibitions), flavors, and sauces. What went on the rice—vegetable or animal—was sliced small so that its flavors were maximized and distributed and also so it could cook quickly over a hot but brief fire. There was an increasing shortage of fuel as the rising population cut down the forests and people were reduced to twigs, leaves, and dried grasses for cooking. The universal cooking utensil was the thin cast-iron saucer-shaped pot (*wok* in Cantonese, the dialect of Guangzhou) still in use, which heats quickly but holds the heat and distributes it evenly, the technique we now call "stir-frying." Not only Cantonese words like *wok* but much of the Chinese food served in restaurants in this country and elsewhere betray their Cantonese origins, since Cantonese are the great majority of all overseas Chinese and, like many other immigrant groups, have used their native cuisine as a means of livelihood.

The Chinese landscape became converted more and more into an artificial one of irrigated and terraced rice paddies, fish and duck ponds, villages, and market towns where the peasants sold their surplus products or exchanged them for salt, cloth, tools, or other necessities not produced in

all villages. Teahouses became the common centers for socializing, relaxation, and gossip and for the negotiation of business or marriage contracts.
Fortune-tellers, scribes, booksellers, itinerant peddlers, actors or jugglers,
and storytellers enlivened the market towns and cities and the periodic
markets held on a smaller scale in most villages at regular intervals (see
Chapter 13). All this made it less necessary for people to travel far from
their native places, and most never went beyond the nearest market town.
Beyond it they would have found for the most part only more villages and
towns like those they knew, except for the provincial capital and, of
course, the imperial capital. In the dry north and the mountains of the
south, many goods moved by human porter. The wheelbarrow and the flex-
ible bamboo carrying pole were early Chinese inventions that greatly enhanced the ability to transport heavy weights, balanced as they were by
each design (wheelbarrows had their single wheel in the middle, more efficient than the Western copy) and hence enabling porters to wheel or trot
all day with loads far exceeding their unaided capacity. Most of these and
many other aspects of Chinese culture have remained essentially unchanged today, as has the deep Chinese sense of history and of the great
tradition to which they are heir.

□ The Rise and Fall of Ming

The Ming dynasty, officially founded in 1368, fit the dynastic pattern
of a first century of vigor and expansion, a second of complacency, and a
third of decline and fall (Elvin, 1973:69–83). Probably the most spectacular aspect of the first century was the expeditionary voyages of Admiral
Zheng He, seven altogether between 1405 and 1433, from ports on the
southeast coast with fleets of up to sixty ships (Martin and Shui, 1972:
109–116). They toured most of Southeast Asia, the east and west coasts of
India (where Vasco da Gama ninety years later was to make his first Asian
landfall), Ceylon (now Sri Lanka), the Persian Gulf, Aden, Jidda (from
where seven Chinese went to Mecca), and on to east Africa. Some ships
may have gone as far as the Cape of Good Hope or even around it. They
brought back giraffes, zebras, and ostriches to amaze the court and tributary agreements from a host of newly contacted states. The ships carried
export goods, mainly silks and porcelains, and brought back foreign luxuries such as spices and tropical woods. The economic motive for these
huge ventures may have been important, but the chief aim was probably
political, to show the flag and command respect for the empire. Chapter 7
says more about these missions.

Despite their size, Zheng He's ships were fast sailors with their four
decks, large crews, and cargo capacity, faster than the Spanish galleons or
Portuguese caravels of a century or two later. Their rig was designed to
take advantage of the monsoonal wind patterns; properly timed voyages

An early Chinese invention, the carrying pole,
is still commonly used in China.

could count on sailing with the wind for about half the year as far as Africa, and returning with the opposite monsoon in the other half. Like Song ships, they were built with separate watertight compartments, and despite their many encounters with storms, few were ever lost (Elvin, 1973:131–145). Such exploits of seamanship and exploration were unprecedented in the world. Their grand scale was an expression of new imperial pride, but they contributed little to the Ming economy and made no lasting impression on the Chinese mind, which continued to think of theirs as the only civilized empire and had little curiosity about foreign places. The expeditions were very expensive and, perhaps mainly for that reason, were stopped after 1433. The emperor may have felt he had made his imperial point, and it seems unlikely that trade profits even began to cover the costs. Another factor was the decision to move the capital from Nanjing to Beijing in 1421 to better command the chronically troubled northern frontier, where there was an attempted revival of Mongol power (Elvin, 1973:91–110, 203–234).

But the abandonment of the expeditions, like the move to Beijing, was a symptom of the Ming's basic conservatism and traditionalism. China's relations by sea had always been given a far lower priority than its land frontiers. Zheng He's explorations and contacts were not followed up. The Ming turned inward, rebuilt the Great Wall in the form we see today in the few parts near Beijing that have been restored, and reasserted the Chinese style in everything, partly as a reaction against the hated Mongol conquest. They devoted their energies to the development of their home base, which since Shang times they had called the Middle Kingdom, meaning not only the center of the world but one that combined the advantages of a golden mean, avoiding the extremes of desert, jungle, mountains, or cold around its borders. In whatever direction one went from China, the physical environment worsened: north (too cold), south (too hot and jungly), west (too mountainous and dry), or east into a vast and, in cultural or economic terms, empty ocean. The Chinese attributed the lack of civilization they noted in all "barbarians" to their far less favorable environment as well as to their distance from the only center of enlightenment. China was indeed the most productive area of comparable size anywhere in the world, bigger than all of Europe, more populous, and with a far greater volume of trade, domestic and foreign. The Chinese saw their interests as best served by further embellishing their home base rather than by pursuing less rewarding foreign contacts.

For some time this worked well. Prosperity increased, and with it population, trade, and cities, continuing the developments under the Song. Rice yields rose with the introduction of more productive and earlier-ripening varieties introduced from Vietnam and actively promoted by the state. In the sixteenth century, new crops from the New World, most importantly maize (corn), potatoes, and peanuts, came in via the Spanish connection in the Philippines. New irrigation and better application of manure swelled total output further (Elvin, 1973:113–130), and there was a boom in silk production as well as in cotton, introduced from India and soon the basic material of clothing for all but the rich, who often wore silk. New supplies of silver came in to pay for the exports of silk, tea, porcelain, lacquerware, and other goods, and more and more of the economy was commercialized. Merchant guilds acquired new, though unofficial, power in the growing cities and followed the luxurious lifestyle of the elite. Right through the last century of the Ming, despite political decay, technological innovation continued on Song foundations, including the development of mechanical looms. Popular literature and drama flourished, and fine porcelains, including the famous Ming blue-and-white pattern, spread beyond the court and were found in many merchant houses. Beijing was rebuilt on its Mongol foundations and filled with gorgeous palaces. The civil service system inherited from the Song also worked well until the final collapse. It was a confident and prosperous time (Struve, 1984; Hucker, 1969; Chan, 1982).

But by the end of the sixteenth century, there was a clear decline in administrative effectiveness, made worse by a succession of weak emperors and the rise of palace eunuchs to power (see Chapter 4). Banditry and piracy multiplied as government efficiency declined and poorer areas suffered increasing distress. Increased population, probably by now about 130

*The Great Wall north of Beijing, a section cleaned up for tourists (above)
and a section left unchanged since the Ming rebuilt it (below).*

million, was not accompanied by a commensurate increase in the number of officials, who were thus overworked and less effective, as well as prone to bribery to maintain their incomes. Famine and rebellion spread, and the Manchus, waiting on the northeastern border, took their opportunity to establish their own dynasty, the Qing, in 1644 (Latourette, 1964:247–274; Huang, 1981).

□ The Rise and Fall of Qing

Unlike the Mongols, the Qing successfully reproduced the Chinese pattern in all ways, and their control rested on widespread Chinese collaboration; Chinese filled about 90 percent of all official posts. The dynasty was fortunate in producing three successive able emperors, who presided over the reconquest of all of the empire and even added Tibet for the first time (see Chapter 6). The "barbarian" invaders on the steppe to the west were finally crushed for good, and Taiwan was conquered and added to the empire. The peace and order provided by the Qing and its efficient administration led to new heights of prosperity, trade, and urbanization, far beyond Ming levels, and also to a population that probably tripled between 1620 and the dynasty's end in 1911, gained another 100 million by 1950, and doubled again between 1950 and 1983 to over a billion (Chao, 1987:41; Grousset, 1959:295; Ma, 1967). By the end of the eighteenth century, production was no longer keeping pace, and in the course of the nineteenth century China fell gradually into poverty and rebellion, as Europe and the United States rode a wave of new prosperity and technological/industrial revolution. Chinese technology had long been superior, but now it fell disastrously behind, to its great loss (Elvin, 1973:285–316). Yet until as late as 1850, foreigners described China as prosperous, orderly, and admirable for its Confucian-based civil service that was open to any young man with the skill to pass the imperial examinations.

We know more about China at this period than at any before it, not only from the voluminous Chinese records but from the numerous foreign accounts, which are generally highly positive and, among other things, noted that China's foreign trade as late as the 1830s was probably larger than England's, whereas its domestic trade was many times larger. Portuguese traders had arrived at Guangzhou (Canton) early in the sixteenth century, and Jesuit missionaries were shortly thereafter at work even in Beijing. By the eighteenth century, the British became the dominant traders with China, buying silk and tea that they paid for in silver, accompanied by French, Dutch, and other European merchants and finally by Americans. From the mid–eighteenth century, all foreign traders were restricted to Guangzhou, the chief port for foreign trade, a condition they found increasingly irritating as British and European power grew while their merchants at Guangzhou continued to be treated like minor barbarians. A party sent by King George in 1793 to request wider trade privileges and diplomatic representation at Beijing was haughtily rebuffed (see Chapter 7), as was a subsequent mission in 1816 (Schurmann and Schell, 1967:104–113).

But despite the grand exterior, all was not well domestically, as population continued to outrun production in the absence of major technological change. As under the Ming, the number of administrator-officials stayed the same while the population rapidly expanded, and both efficiency and honesty suffered. China continued to protect itself against the disruptions of institutional and technological change, looking backward to its great tradition rather than forward, and was especially opposed to any ideas or innovations of foreign origin. As China declined in the nineteenth century and was wracked by increasing rebellions (Perry, 1980; Fairbank, 1992:187–232), the Qing had entered its third century. There might have been a different response from a new and vigorous administration, but the Qing were now old, rigid, fearful of change, and as originally alien conquerors, anxious not to depart in any way from their role as guardians of the ancient Chinese way in all things. The emperor Qianlong, who reigned from 1735 to 1799, was a great patron of art and rebuilt or refurbished the imperial capital inherited from the Ming in essentially the same form one can see it today. There he and other emperors received "tribute missions" from "barbarian chieftains," who knelt abjectly before the throne. China was slow to recognize that external threat now came from the "sea barbarians" instead of from its landward frontiers and looked down on them as inferior, despite their clear technological and military superiority.

Matters came to a head in 1839 over opium, which the British and Americans had begun to export from India and Persia to China in exchange for silver. The resulting drain of silver from China was worrying, and in any case the opium trade had been declared illegal. Chinese efforts to destroy the opium stored at Guangzhou led to war in which the Chinese army and navy were totally humiliated by modern British weapons. The Treaty of Nanjing, signed in 1842, granted the access the foreigners had long sought and the right to reside and trade at several coastal ports, the "treaty ports" (Fairbank, 1978). Such humiliations were destined to continue and grow in scope for over a century. A war in 1858–1860 extended foreign privileges further and opened the interior to missionaries and the rivers to foreign shipping. The empire had the help of volunteer foreign troops to put down the Taiping (see Spence, 1996a) and Nian rebellions that took over extensive territory in southern China. The Taiping rebels ruled much of Jiangsu, Anhui, and Zhejiang provinces (see Map 2.2) for eleven years. The fighting and radical social experiments (see Chapters 11 and 12) left well over 20 million casualties and formerly lush fields as barren wasteland. The Qing emperor found himself at the mercy of the foreigners and regional warlords who helped squelch the rebellions; his treasury was depleted. Foreign Christian missionaries sought converts without the traditional supervision always imposed on such activities in the past. Powerful landlords raised their own armies and collected their own taxes. In an effort to catch up, mathematics, science, and foreign languages were made part of school curricula, and sons of prominent Chinese were sent abroad for study. Still, China suffered humiliating defeat in the Sino-Japanese War of 1894–1895. Reform efforts in 1898 to improve the navy, railroads, banking, agriculture, and industry were cut short when the young emperor who endorsed them was arrested by his aunt, who took over as Empress Dowager. Chapters 6 and 7 discuss these matters further.

But China's decline into poverty was primarily the result of its own internal problems, as summarized earlier, and, indeed, one can argue that the foreign traders helped China, by widening the market and introducing railways, telegraph lines, and other aspects of "modernization," much more than they harmed it, although the psychological hurt to Chinese pride was deep.

□ Beyond the Dynasties

In 1911 the dynasty toppled or fell of its own weight; a republic was inaugurated under Sun Yat-sen, the nationalist leader, but China was soon torn by fighting among regional warlords and was partially unified only in 1927 under Chiang Kai-shek, with its new capital at Nanjing (Fairbank, 1992:279–293). There was some progress in the short decade before the Japanese attacked, burning Nanjing in 1937; killing perhaps 300,000 unarmed men, women, and children; and raping and torturing 100,000 women (Spence, 1990:447–450; Chang, 1997). The long war against Japan that followed, from a refugee capital in Chongqing in Sichuan, exhausted Chiang's Nationalist (Kuomintang, or KMT) government while it built the strength of the Chinese communists, who waged a guerrilla war in the north and captured the leadership of Chinese nationalism. Resumed civil war after the defeat of Japan ended in a total communist victory in 1949, and Chiang and his government fled to Taiwan, where his successors remain in power. Beijing was again made the capital to get in line with imperial tradition.

Hong Kong, ceded to Britain in 1841, joined the treaty ports as a major center of foreign trade and an entrepôt for trade with the rest of China; it remained a British colony until its return to China in 1997. Cut off from its hinterland in 1949, it built a profitable new structure of light industry and banking and successfully housed and employed the stream of refugees from the rest of China. Hong Kong's example of economic development was important to China as it pursued its own development, and the areas of the southeast near Hong Kong shared in its prosperity, producing goods for export as well as for domestic consumption. New industrial cities multiplied in every province, led by Shanghai, China's biggest city since about 1900, which still supports an economic and industrial boom and supplies technicians and skilled labor to other growing cities. To this extent, the semicolonial foreign period with its example of "modernization" in the treaty ports has provided a model for developing modern China, whatever its imperialist nature and its denunciation by communists and Nationalists alike (see Chapters 6, 7, and 10 for more detail).

Manchuria (the "Northeast"), its industrial plant built by the Japanese after 1905 when they wrested control from the Russians and built a dense railway network, remains the chief center of heavy industry, but many other new ones have arisen in the provinces south of the Great Wall. As one result, China is now probably the most polluted country in the world and has been stripped of forests to supply wood for its huge and still growing population, now over 1.2 billion; this has drastically increased erosion, siltation, and flooding (see Chapter 9).

■ CHINESE ATTITUDES
AND OURS ABOUT CHINA

Most Chinese still feel a deep pride in their country, not only in its modern achievements but in the long record of Chinese superiority. The record of Chinese firsts is impressive: paper and printing, porcelain, the compass, gunpowder and cannons, lacquer, distillation (during the Han, many centuries ahead of Europe), ship design, the wheelbarrow, the double-acting piston bellows, the square pallet chain pump for raising water, iron suspension bridges, canal locks, water clocks, discovery of the circulation of the blood (also during the Han, 2,000 years before Europe), breakthroughs in metallurgy, and many, many more (Needham, 1981; Hommel, 1937). Unfortunately for later centuries, these discoveries or innovations were not followed up by thoughts about how to put them to new practical uses outside the confines of low-technology agriculture. Except for the early Zhou dynasty and some later periods like the Song, there really was not a group in China one could call "scientists" (Elvin, 1973:177–199); most innovations were worked out by artisans, who were often illiterate, whereas philosophers, who dealt in abstractions, looked down on manual workers and manual work. Chinese intellectuals generally did not speculate about how changes in technology might affect society and commerce and the natural environment or devise experiments to observe the workings of the forces of nature—a key factor in the much later Western successes during the scientific revolution. They preferred to observe and speculate about human behavior and values. The general mindset of the Confucian power holders against change as disruptive doubtless also retarded the kind of scientific inquiry that led to the industrial revolution in Europe.

China did develop astronomy very early, noting and recording eclipses and sunspots in Zhou times and devising an accurate calendar. Early achievements in mathematics, mechanics, physics, and biology tended to lapse in later centuries, as did the development of instruments for predicting earthquakes, remarkable in their time. Some intellectuals in the Southern Song dynasty revived a brief interest in science, and under the Mongol Yuan dynasty Chinese scientists resumed work in mathematics and also built a large array of instruments and structures for astronomical observations. But by the time the Jesuits, carriers of the latest scientific advances in Europe, arrived at the Ming court with great curiosity about these Yuan instruments, the Chinese said they had forgotten how to use them and the mathematics that went with them. The response of the court astronomers to their realization that the ancient calculations predicting the movement of the heavenly bodies no longer fit observable reality was not that the theory needed revision but that "the heavens are out of order." Such a response could never have happened in Europe after 1600; those scientists would have sought to revise the theory so it would accord with empirical reality.

Despite such blind spots and the overriding importance of technology and science in the modern world, one cannot dismiss imperial China in any sense as a failure. For some 2,000 years it led the world in technology as in the art of government, in power as well as in sophistication, as all who encountered the Middle Kingdom acknowledged. It is difficult to measure economic well-being in the past, as it is now, but it seems likely that for most of their history until perhaps 1850, most Chinese were better off materially than most people elsewhere. As for that elusive quality we call happiness, who really knows, but China's rich literature certainly gives a picture of a generally contented populace with a strong sense of humor and a love of life. Indeed, the Chinese still value long life as the greatest of all goals, some testimony to their enjoyment of living and its pleasures. Family, and next to that food, remain the biggest values, as they have been for thousands of years. All these things are surely worth something, perhaps even more than modern technological leadership.

As Chapter 8 explains further, China has long produced more cities, and larger ones, than the rest of the world, and its urban experience is rich. European observers were impressed by it and by the huge streams of trade flowing along all China's rivers, lakes, and canals as well as in and out of its coastal ports. For all its growing technological backwardness as the nineteenth century wore on, China remained vibrantly alive; since the 1950s and the death of Mao in 1976, with his irrational utopian ideas that cost heavily in retarding economic progress as well as in lives lost, China has concentrated on maximizing its economic development and raising its technological levels toward world standards. It developed national identity and unity long before Europe and other parts of the world. Its chief failure is in denying its people anything approaching free expression, let alone a genuine democracy. It is a police state pure and simple, where all dissent is suppressed and where non-Han like the Tibetans are cruelly oppressed. It is just possible—but unlikely—that more scope may be allowed for individual freedom and initiative and for the aspirations of the many subject minorities. When one adds the record of environmental destruction since 1950, what is the best way to judge China's "success"? That depends, like so many things, on one's point of view and the topics about which one asks questions. As you read the rest of this book, with its discussion of many realms of Chinese life, this question will come to your mind more than once: What are the most important questions to ask about China's success or failure?

■ BIBLIOGRAPHY

Barnard, Noel. 1983. "Further Evidence to Support the Hypothesis of Indigenous Origins of Metallurgy in Ancient China." Pp. 237–277 in David N. Keightley (ed.), *The Origins of Chinese Civilization*. Berkeley: University of California Press.

Bodde, Derk. 1967. *China's First Unifier*. Hong Kong: Hong Kong University Press.

Chaffee, John W. 1995. *The Thorny Gates of Learning: Examinations in Sung China*. Albany: State University of New York Press.

Chan, Albert. 1982. *The Glory and Fall of the Ming Dynasty*. Norman: University of Oklahoma Press.

Chang, Iris. 1997. *The Rape of Nanking: The Forgotten Holocaust of World War II*. New York: HarperCollins.

Chang, Kwang Chih. 1980. *Shang Civilization*. New Haven: Yale University Press.

———. 1983. *Art, Myth, and Ritual: The Path to Political Authority in Ancient China*. Cambridge: Harvard University Press.

———. 1986. *The Archaeology of Ancient China*. 4th ed. New Haven: Yale University Press.

Chang, Te-Tzu. 1983. "The Origins of Early Cultures of the Cereal Grains and Food Legumes." Pp. 65–94 in David N. Keightley (ed.), *The Origins of Chinese Civilization*. Berkeley: University of California Press.

Chao Kang. 1987. *Man and Land in Chinese History: An Economic Analysis*. Stanford: Stanford University Press.

Cheng, Te K'un. 1960. *Archaeology in China: Shang China*. 3 Vols. Cambridge: W. Heffer.

———. 1966. *New Light on Prehistoric China*. Cambridge: W. Heffer.

Cheung, Kwong-Yue. 1983. "Recent Archaeological Evidence Relating to the Origin of Chinese Characters." Pp. 323–391 in David N. Keightley (ed.), *The Origins of Chinese Civilization*. Berkeley: University of California Press.

Chu, T'ung-Tsu. 1972. *Han Social Structure*. Seattle: University of Washington Press.

Creel, Herrlee Glessner. 1937. *The Birth of China: A Study of the Formative Period of Chinese Civilization*. New York: Frederick Ungar.

Dawson, Raymond S. 1972. *Imperial China*. Oxford: Oxford University Press.

de Bary, William Theodore, Wing-tsit Chan, and Barton Watson (eds.). 1960. *Sources of Chinese Tradition*. New York: Columbia University Press.

Elvin, Mark. 1973. *The Pattern of the Chinese Past*. Stanford: Stanford University Press.

Fairbank, John King. 1978. "The Creation of the Treaty System." Pp. 213–263 in John King Fairbank (ed.), *The Cambridge History of China: Late Ching 1800–1911*. Vol. 10, pt. 1. Cambridge: Cambridge University Press.

———. 1992. *China: A New History*. Cambridge: Belknap Press of Harvard University Press.

Fairbank, John King, Edwin O. Reischauer, and Albert M. Craig. 1973. *East Asia: Tradition and Transformation*. Boston: Houghton Mifflin.

Franklin, Ursula Martins. 1983. "On Bronze and Other Metals in Early China." Pp. 279–296 in David N. Keightley (ed.), *The Origins of Chinese Civilization*. Berkeley: University of California Press.

Gernet, Jacques. 1962. *Daily Life in China on the Eve of the Mongol Invasion, 1250–1276*. London: Macmillan.

———. 1968. *Ancient China: From the Beginnings to the Empire*. London: Faber and Faber.

———. 1996. *A History of Chinese Civilization*. 2d ed. Trans. John R. Foster. Cambridge: Cambridge University Press.

Goldstein, M. C. 1989. *The History of Modern Tibet*. Berkeley: University of California Press.

Grousset, Rene. 1959. *The Rise and Splendour of the Chinese Empire*. Berkeley: University of California Press.

Hansen, Valerie. 1995. *Negotiating Daily Life in Traditional China: How Ordinary People Used Contracts, 600–1400*. New Haven: Yale University Press.

Harrell, Stevan. 1995. *Cultural Encounters on China's Ethnic Frontiers*. Seattle: University of Washington Press.

Hommel, Rudolf P. 1937. *China at Work*. Cambridge: MIT Press.

Howells, W. W. 1983. "Origins of the Chinese People: Interpretations of the Recent Evidence." Pp. 297–319 in David N. Keightley (ed.), *The Origins of Chinese Civilization*. Berkeley: University of California Press.

Hsu, Immanuel Cho Yun. 1995. *The Rise of Modern China*. Oxford: Oxford University Press.

Hsu, Immanuel Cho Yun, and Katheryn M. Linduff. 1989. *Western Chou Civilization*. New Haven: Yale University Press.

Huang, Ray. 1981. *1587, a Year of No Significance: The Ming Dynasty in Decline*. New Haven: Yale University Press.

———. 1996. *China: A Macro History*. Armonk, NY: M. E. Sharpe.

Hucker, Charles O. 1969. *Chinese Government in Ming Times: Seven Studies*. New York: Columbia University Press.

———. 1975. *China's Imperial Past: An Introduction to Chinese History and Culture*. Stanford: Stanford University Press.

Keightley, David N. 1983. "The Late Shang State: When, Where, What?" Pp. 523–564 in David N. Keightley (ed.), *The Origins of Chinese Civilization*. Berkeley: University of California Press.

Langlois, John D., Jr. 1981. *China Under Mongol Rule*. Princeton: Princeton University Press.

Latourette, Kenneth Scott. 1964. *The Chinese: Their History and Culture*. 4th ed. New York: Macmillan.

Lattimore, Owen. 1940. *The Inner Asian Frontiers of China.* New York: American Geographical Society.

———. 1947. *China: A Short History.* New York: Norton.

Leslie, Donald D., Colin Mackerias, and Wang Gungwu (eds.). 1973. *Essays on the Sources of Chinese History.* Columbia: University of South Carolina.

Levenson, Joseph R., and Franz Schurmann. 1969. *China: An Interpretive History from the Beginnings to the Fall of Han.* Berkeley: University of California Press.

Li, Chi. 1957. *The Beginnings of Chinese Civilization: Three Lectures Illustrated in the Finds at Anyang.* Seattle: University of Washington Press.

Li, Xueqin. 1985. *Eastern Zhou and Qin Civilizations.* New Haven: Yale University Press.

Lister, Richard Percival. 1976. *Marco Polo's Travels in Xanadu with Kublai Khan.* London: Gordon and Cremonesi.

Loewe, Michael. 1974. *Crisis and Conflict in Han China, 104 B.C. to A.D. 9.* London: George Allen and Unwin.

———. 1994. *Divination, Mythology, and Monarchy in Han China.* Cambridge: Cambridge University Press.

Ma, Tuan-Lin. 1967. "The Population of China" and "The Unreliability of Population Figures as They Appear in Tax Registers." Pp. 236–241 in Dun J. Li, *The Essence of Chinese Civilization.* Princeton: Van Nostrand.

March, Andrew L. 1974. *The Idea of China: Myth and Theory in Geographic Thought.* New York: Praeger.

Martin, Bernard, and Shui Chien-Tung. 1972. *Makers of China, Confucius to Mao.* Oxford: Basil Blackwell.

Maspero, Henri. 1978. *China in Antiquity.* Cambridge: MIT Press.

Meacham, William. 1983. "Origins and Development of Yüeh Coastal Neolithic: A Microcosm of Culture Change in the Mainland of East Asia." Pp. 147–175 in David N. Keightley (ed.), *The Origins of Chinese Civilization.* Berkeley: University of California Press.

Meskill, John J. (ed.). 1973. *An Introduction to Chinese Civilization.* Boston: Heath.

Meyer, Milton W. 1994. *China: A Concise History.* 2d. ed. Lanham, MD: Rowman and Littlefield.

Murphey, Rhoads. 1996. *A History of Asia.* New York: HarperCollins.

———. 1997. *East Asia: A New History.* New York: Addison Wesley Longman.

"Mysterious Mummies of China." 1998. *NOVA.* PBS 2501 (January 20).

Nathan, Andrew. 1990. *China's Crisis.* New York: Columbia University Press.

Needham, Joseph. 1965–1986. *Science and Civilisation in China.* 6 vols. Cambridge: Cambridge University Press.

———. 1981. *Science in Traditional China.* Cambridge: Cambridge University Press.

Perry, Elizabeth J. 1980. *Rebels and Revolutionaries in North China, 1845–1945.* Stanford: Stanford University Press.

Peterson, C. A. 1979. "Court and Province in Mid- and Late T'ang." Pp. 464–560 in Denis Twitchett (ed.), *The Cambridge History of China: Sui and T'ang China, 589–906.* Vol. 3. Cambridge: Cambridge University Press.

Polo, Marco. 1982. *The Travels of Marco Polo.* Trans. Ronald Latham. New York: Abaris Books.

Pulleyblank, E. G. 1983. "The Chinese and Their Neighbors in Prehistoric and Early Historic Times." Pp. 411–466 in David N. Keightley (ed.), *The Origins of Chinese Civilization.* Berkeley: University of California Press.

Rossabi, Morris. 1988. *Khubilai Khan: His Life and Times.* Berkeley: University of California Press.

Schurmann, Franz, and Orville Schell. 1967. *Imperial China: The Decline of the Last Dynasty and the Origins of Modern China, the Eighteenth and Nineteenth Centuries.* New York: Random House.

Schwartz, B. I. 1985. *The World of Thought in Ancient China.* Harvard University Press.

Spence, Jonathan. 1990. *The Search for Modern China.* New York: Norton.

———. 1996a. *God's Chinese Son: The Taiping Heavenly Kingdom of Hong Xiuquan.* New York: Norton.

———. 1996b. "Marco Polo. Did He Go to China?" *Far Eastern Economic Review* 159 (August 22):37–45.

Struve, Lynn. 1984. *The Southern Ming, 1644–1662.* New Haven: Yale University Press.

Twitchett, Denis (ed.). 1986. *The Cambridge History of China.* Vol. 1: *Ch'in and Han.* Cambridge: Cambridge University Press.

Wakeman, Frederic E. 1981. *The Fall of Imperial China.* New York: Free Press.

———. 1985. *The Great Enterprise: The Manchu Reconstruction.* Berkeley: University of California Press.

Waley, Arthur. 1939. *Three Ways of Thought in Ancient China.* Stanford: Stanford University Press.

———. 1958. *The Opium War Through Chinese Eyes.* Stanford: Stanford University Press.

Walker, Richard Louis. 1953. *The Multi-State System of Ancient China.* Westport, CT: Greenwood Press.

Wang, Zhangshu. 1982. *Han Civilization.* New Haven: Yale University Press.

Watson, William. 1961. *China Before the Han Dynasty.* New York: Praeger.

Weinstein, Stanley. 1987. *Buddhism Under the T'ang.* Cambridge: Cambridge University Press.

Wood, Frances. 1996. *Did Marco Polo Go to China?* Boulder: Westview Press.

Wright, Arthur F. 1978. *The Sui Dynasty.* New York: Knopf.

Wright, M. C. 1968. *China in Revolution.* New Haven: Yale University Press.

Yü, Ying-shih. 1967. *Trade and Expansion in Han China: A Study in Structure of Sino-Barbarian Economic Relations.* Berkeley: University of California Press.

■ 4 ■

Chinese Politics

Robert E. Gamer

China has the world's oldest political system. As Rhoads Murphey explained in Chapter 3, its cultural dominance of the regions it now occupies began during the second century B.C. Its habits of governance extend to that period as well. For two millennia, those habits helped it ward off or absorb invasions from the societies that occupied central Asia. They proved vulnerable, however, when challenged during the past two centuries by the technology and institutions of Europe and a modernizing Japan.

What are China's political traditions? What has it absorbed from communism and the West? How much must China's political system change to remain unified and sustain economic growth? Can it achieve those goals? These are the questions with which this chapter deals.

First, we briefly examine some of China's political and economic traditions. In the second section, we look at the changes that took place in China's politics between the 1839 Opium War and World War II. Third, we ask how and why the communists took over China. Their consolidation of power was followed by three periods of major economic and political change; in the fourth section we try to sort out the changes that worked from those that did not. Fifth, we look at the principal challenges facing China's contemporary leaders and their chances of surmounting them. In the last two sections, we ask whether China can stay unified and what further adaptations it is likely to absorb.

■ A LEGACY OF UNITY AND ECONOMIC ACHIEVEMENT

In Chapter 3, Rhoads Murphey explained how the Qin first unified China in 221 B.C. and how the subsequent Han dynasty consolidated that conquest. One of the most significant and enduring achievements of the Han was the adoption of Confucianism, a philosophy also discussed in

Chapters 3 and 12. Confucian traditions would have a strong influence on China's subsequent ability to maintain unity and prosperity.

Confucius contended that stable governance derives from the proper performance of social obligations. The most fundamental obligation, called filial piety, is obedience of sons to fathers. Likewise, wives obey husbands, younger brothers defer to their older brothers, and subjects obey rulers. In turn, those being obeyed are to treat their cohorts with sincerity, affection, or respect, demonstrated through rituals of speech and behavior. Individuals who fail to carry out these mutual obligations disgrace themselves and those to whom they owe these obligations and destroy the foundations of the state. Citizens cannot expect to live in a stable country when they themselves fail to carry out their most basic social obligations within their families. When individual freedom or political theories conflict with one's obligation to one's family and state authorities, they must be rejected. Expressing an opinion or taking an action that shows disrespect for these mutual obligations and rituals actually destroys your own essence; you must rectify this by apologizing and changing your behavior, in order to restore your good name and come to grips with who you really are. To be true to yourself you must carry out your ritual obligations to others, to do so bonds state and society. (For excerpts from Confucius's original writings, see de Bary, Chan, and Watson, 1960:17–35.)

Furthermore, in Confucian philosophy, society is divided into greater and lesser orders (see Fairbank, 1967:36–66). The emperor and his assistants hold the highest position, yet the social hierarchy limits both them and those with wealth. Directly below the emperor in this hierarchy are the peasants and artisans, who produce the goods and whose families cleared the land and created the farms that set apart Chinese civilization from the barbarian cultures of wandering hunters and herders. Merchants, who produce nothing yet profit from the toil of others, occupy the lowest rung on the social order of Chinese civilization. All this creates a harmonious society, with emperors naturally chosen to rule, and even wealthy subjects predisposed to obey. That obedience ends only when peace and prosperity are supplanted by war, bad harvests, and natural disasters, proving that Heaven's Mandate to the emperor to govern has been withdrawn. Then a challenger may rouse popular support to overthrow the emperor. The Han dynasty itself was founded by a peasant named Liu Bang who led such a revolt against the excesses of the Qin dynasty.

Four other customs evolved that also help keep the emperor and those with wealth in line while still investing them with the power to rule and engage in business:

1. *The system of choosing emperors and their wives.* To reduce the role of the noble families that had dominated before the Qin dynasty, the sons of emperors married daughters of peasants, who were taken away

from their families when they were very young. These heirs to the throne might take several wives. Sons of the first wife were thought to have more right to the throne, but emperors had some choice in designating a successor. During most dynasties, when the emperor died, his wives and their other children would return to an obscure existence, rather than become titled nobility. Although this reduced the prestige and power of those related to the emperor, it made the stakes surrounding succession into an all-or-nothing game. That created much intrigue around the court. Many an emperor or designated heir was murdered by the mother of another heir, who might rule as an empress dowager while her young son grew up.

2. *Eunuchs.* To ensure loyalty and see to it that only the emperor had sexual access to his wives, males working within the compound of the palace were recruited at a young age from villages, castrated, and removed from their families. These eunuchs ran the compound and took care of the emperor, his wives, and their children. The eunuchs were often involved in the murders and intrigues. Public officials had to access the emperor through the eunuchs. The number and power of eunuchs grew greatly during the Ming dynasty; the Qing dynasty sought to limit their power, but it continued. (For more on their role, see Mitamura, 1970).

3. *The system of choosing public officials.* To choose its top officials, the empire held regular competitive examinations open to all boys. These exams tested the candidates' ability to write Chinese characters and their knowledge of the Confucian classics. Those who passed became "literati," or Confucian scholar-officials. They were selected and transferred as needed by the emperor to preside over justice and administration in all the regions of China. Most who passed these exams, which required extensive education and preparation, were the sons of scholar-officials, larger landowners, or wealthy merchants. But the system moving them from post to post ensured that control of administration and of a region could not automatically stay within the hands of the same local notables, as had been the case under feudalism. Sometimes a village or lineage group would help one of their brightest children prepare for these exams, allowing him to rise from the family of a humble peasant into the highest realms of the state. Ichisada Miyazaki (1981) gives an extensive introduction to this unique—and often terrifying—system for selecting public officials.

These officials had the power to regulate commerce. They sought to ensure that agriculture remained prosperous by keeping the complex system of waterways and irrigation canals working, maintaining marketplaces where goods could be bartered, and protecting private property. They also collected taxes and presided over the civil and criminal courts and local administrators.

During the twelfth century, in the Southern Song dynasty (see Chapters 3 and 5), foreign and domestic trade began to flourish. Large numbers of people engaged in the manufacture of porcelain, textiles, alcoholic beverages, ships, and other goods. Because Confucian philosophy sees agriculture as the provider of food and the supporter of the family units on which Chinese civilization is built, the scholar-officials had always encouraged invention, trade, the buying and selling of land, and other commercial pursuits that supported agriculture. These new trends disturbed them. Young people were leaving their families to seek work in the towns and cities. People were making large amounts of money creating frivolous luxuries that competed with cloth and handicrafts once produced on the farms. The richest of them could travel between regions to escape the jurisdiction of individual literati. Scholar-officials had often used their power and income to buy large amounts of land and thus ensure their high social and economic stature. Now people without land or official status, who ranked at the bottom of the Confucian social hierarchy, were in a position to become the richest in the realm.

Song Confucian philosophers thought hard about these problems. Their neo-Confucianism (see Chapter 12; de Bary, Chan, and Watson, 1960:510–581) created checks on the power of merchant acquisition by placing new emphasis on the extended family. Clans should stick together in the same villages, whose property would remain under the control of their leaders. People should be punished for moving away to set up independent households. To prevent monopolies, officials should regulate the number of looms or production facilities one person could own and the market prices. And the state would manufacture or distribute some important goods and resources. This would slow down investment in capitalist production and discourage the creation of an independent middle class. It would also encourage community leaders to assist those less fortunate in their communities (for an insightful overview, see Gates, 1996:42–61).

4. *The five Confucian relationships,* guanxi. As in the past, however, these new powers for officials were softened by *guanxi* (King, 1991; Yang, 1994; Yan, 1996). In Confucian thinking, a man's most important relationships are as father and son, as husband, between brothers, as subject of the ruler, and with certain selected neighbors, kinsmen, classmates, or other associates with whom he chooses to have special long-term relationships. These individuals exchange special favors and gifts, called *renqing* (literally, benevolence that two people owe each other; you will find more about this in Chapter 12). This exchange affirms that these individuals have "connections." Literati and merchants had always created such connections with one another; that is how many literati had acquired land. As commerce grew, these relationships helped merchants escape from over-regulation and receive clearance to engage in new business activities. Connections helped individuals make money, while assuring that it circulated back to the community. They also continued to divert investment capital into unproductive gifts.

As China approached the nineteenth century, it looked back on a long tradition of political and cultural unification combined with a vibrant market economy. It was presided over by a government that both encouraged and limited capitalist enterprise and that was itself limited by the expectations of its people that its reign bring social order and bountiful agriculture. The chief restraints on governments and citizenry lay in the expectation that people should live up to their social obligations. Communities placed limits on their own members; entrepreneurs were expected to adapt to the needs of the community. International capitalism wants social peace, but it also resists social and political restraints that hold back individual initiative. The stage was set for conflict.

■ A CENTURY OF TURMOIL

The year 1839 ushered in a century of profound challenge to these Chinese traditions (Table 4.1). In retaliation against Chinese efforts to regulate the trade in opium, British forces invaded China and forced the government to sign a treaty that was soon followed by many others (discussed in Chapters 3, 6, and 7). Foreigners gained the right to establish settlements and businesses partially free from Chinese regulation. Workers in their factories operated outside traditional associations, and their goods competed with those manufactured in Chinese workshops. They were entitled to bypass established Chinese business groups when making deals and built railways to link their coastal commerce with inland regions. Their commerce was hard for Chinese officials or local clan leaders to regulate.

In 1894, a Guangzhou native named Sun Yat-sen, who had studied in Japan and Hawaii, founded the Revive China Society (Wei, Myers, and Gillin, 1994). It advocated constitutional government for China, as did a commission created by the empress dowager. Following her death in 1908, under urging from Sun Yat-sen's movement, the imperial leaders let the provinces elect assemblies. After a series of army mutinies in 1911, China held elections for a new premier (Eto and Schiffrin, 1994, survey that dramatic year of change). Sun, the winner, returned to China from abroad to assume this post. He soon was nudged aside by Yuan Shikai, a regional leader in Beijing who had once advised the empress dowager. Sun's National People's Party, also called the Nationalist Party or Kuomintang (KMT), won the elections Yuan promised in 1913, but their victorious candidate was killed as he stepped off the train upon his arrival in Beijing. Yuan would not step down. His troops battled KMT troops, and Sun returned to exile. After Yuan's death in 1916, his successor called back Sun and the assemblies. But Yuan's successor was soon overthrown by a military coup, and Beijing's power collapsed. China fell under the control of regional warlords (Duara, 1988, offers some case studies). Because the examination system was now abolished, the old literati were no longer around to help maintain the civil bureaucracy. To make matters even worse, the 1919 Versailles Conference awarded part of the Shandong

Table 4.1 Important Dates in Modern Chinese History

1839	Beginning of first Opium War
1911	Founding of republic
1919	Founding of May Fourth Movement
1921	Founding of Communist Party
1927	KMT-communist split
1932	Japan occupies Manchuria
1934	Long March
1936	KMT-communist United Front
1937	Japan attacks China
1945	End of World War II
1949	Founding of People's Republic
1950	Collectivization of agriculture
1953	Start of first five-year plan
1957	Hundred Flowers
1958	Great Leap Forward
1963	Socialist education campaign
1966	Start of Cultural Revolution
1976	Arrest of "Gang of Four"
1978	Deng Xiaoping starts four modernizations
1989	Bloody recapture of Tiananmen Square
1992	Deng calls for expanded liberalization

peninsula (see Map 2.2 and Chapter 7) to Japan, as a reward for its support of the Allies in World War I. That began the May Fourth Movement, which Charles Laughlin introduces colorfully in Chapter 13.

In 1921, Sun met with representatives of Russia's new government, the Soviet Union, to procure help in reuniting China. That same year a small group of men (including Zhou Enlai, Deng Xiaoping, and Mao Zedong) founded the Chinese Communist Party. While they were organizing miners and textile workers into unions, Sun was using aid from the Soviet Union to create a military academy at Whampoa, just below Guangzhou (see Map 2.2). He sent his associate Chiang Kai-shek to Moscow for training, while Zhou Enlai took over as Whampoa's director. Meanwhile, Mao Zedong led Kuomintang (KMT) efforts to organize peasants.

After Sun's death in 1925, this cozy alliance dissolved. He left leadership of the KMT to Chiang Kai-shek. After defeating warlords who controlled the region around Guangzhou, Chiang recruited their troops to help attack other warlords. Soon they controlled the territory of seven provinces. But now the communists and Kuomintang disagreed on strategy for the next move. Chiang wanted to turn the offensive along the Yangtze River and up the coast to converge on Shanghai. The communist leaders preferred to head north, making alliances with warlords friendly to them there. Then they would join forces against the two most powerful warlords of the north. By then, Chiang might be pushed from leadership of the movement. The Russian advisers sided with the communists on this. In addition, many of Chiang's supporters were landlords and industrialists who feared communist demands for peasant and worker rights. Communists led powerful worker organizations in Guangzhou, Shanghai, and Wuhan (see Map 2.2; Perry, 1993; Honig, 1986). In the spring of 1927, Chiang (now leading the KMT and about to marry the sister of Sun's widow) made a secret deal with Zhang Zuolin, one of the northern warlords the communists planned to attack. Early on the morning of April 12, Chiang's men began killing all the communists they could find in Shanghai. Meanwhile, Zhang carried out a similar mission in Beijing. By year's end, the communists in Wuhan and Guangzhou had been defeated as well, but the price was heavy for the Kuomintang. Warlord forces defeated some of their troops. Out of money, Chiang used triad society (organized crime) gangs to extort money from merchants in the foreign concession areas of Shanghai.

The following year, Chiang Kai-shek broke his alliance with Zhang and headed north to defeat Zhang's armies around Beijing. The Japanese, occupying the Shandong peninsula just south of Beijing, also had designs on Zhang's territory. They blew up a train he was riding on, and he was succeeded by his son, Zhang Xueliang, who retained control of Manchuria but ceded Beijing to Chiang's KMT Nationalists. By 1931, this position had been reversed; the Japanese controlled Manchuria, and Zhang Xueliang operated from Beijing as an ally of the Nationalists. Meanwhile, Mao Zedong was organizing peasants in rural areas to the north of Guangzhou, experimenting with policies, strategies, and institutions that would improve living standards and attract followers. Having consolidated his position in the cities, Chiang sent his troops to wipe out this last remaining communist stronghold. In 1934 these communists began a Long March on foot to escape Chiang's forces; 370 days, numerous pitched battles, and 6,000 miles later, 8,000 of them (they started out with 80,000) arrived at a new base area in the hills to the north of Xi'an. Some had been members— often with little military training—of the Red Army, while others were civilian members of the Communist Party. Now, in this adversity, those lines were blurred, fitting Mao's notion that the army should be the masses directly serving the masses. Mao used the organizational methods he had pioneered farther south to help his troops aid peasants in taking control of their region, setting up farming, and patrolling the perimeters (Hinton, 1970; Snow, 1938; Thomas, 1996, on Snow). By this time, Zhang controlled Xi'an, and the Japanese in Manchuria were threatening further hostilities. Chiang Kai-shek urged Zhang to wipe out Mao's new stronghold, but Zhang was convinced that the time had come for the KMT Nationalists and the communists to make a truce and unite against the Japanese. When Chiang flew to Xi'an in 1936, he was in for a surprise. Zhang arrested him and demanded he declare a United Front with the communists. Chiang did so. Six months later, Japan attacked China.

The war against Japan was long and bloody. The Japanese troops swept from Beijing almost to Guangzhou and pushed Chiang Kai-shek's headquarters inland to Chongqing, behind the Three Gorges on the Yangtze River. Mao's forces gradually expanded their hold over the territory to the west of the Yellow River. Life was horrendous in all three areas.

• Though they refused to go along with racial extermination policies of their ally Hitler and estimates by experts vary widely, the Japanese may have killed as many as 35 million Chinese by war's end (see, for example, figures in Spence, 1990:447–448, 459–460, 464, 469; Chang, 1997). They used many people for slave labor in farms and factories and wiped out entire villages in their "three-alls" ("kill all, burn all, destroy all") campaigns.

• Warlords controlled much of the remaining territory. Impoverished peasants on their lands worked long hours producing crops to be sold elsewhere, while local people starved. In areas administered by the Kuomintang, lineage leaders often dominated their entire community, or absentee landlords exploited poor tenants. Unions were banned in the cities, and people worked for low wages under harsh conditions.

• In contrast, the communists worked with landlords to reduce their rents. They paid peasants for food and supplies used by their troops and warned their troops not to molest women. They created producer cooperatives, helped peasants pool their labor to build up fields and irrigation, and developed local industries. As a result their numbers grew rapidly, and many students left the universities to help. Peasants in Japanese or KMT areas were eager to bring their regions into communist hands or to escape into communist-held territory. By 1941, communist and Kuomintang forces were fighting one another. In 1942 Mao initiated the first of many rectification campaigns (based on the Confucian notion of rectifying your good name when you have shamed it, by apologizing and correcting your behavior), forcing people to stand before their neighbors and admit their mistakes in an effort to enforce political solidarity. The communists started letting peasants settle old scores by killing their landlords. If the land fell back into KMT control, landlords would in turn shoot peasants; the Japanese would kill them all and burn their villages. Fighting and recrimination among the three sides grew increasingly bloody.

■ UNITY NEARLY RESTORED

At war's end in 1945, much of China's countryside had been ravaged by war, deforestation, erosion, floods, and exploitative landlords. Many of its industries had been dismantled. The communists had personnel trained and eager to tackle such problems and peasants willing to work long hours to restore fields and factories. In the communist areas, inflation was low and production quickly resumed. Furthermore, Soviet leader Joseph Stalin left Manchuria to the communist forces. Many of the warlords and KMT leaders had their attention focused on other matters, and morale among their laborers was low. A portion of food that cost $1 in KMT cities in mid-1947 cost over $500 by the beginning of 1949, but strikes for higher wages were forbidden (see Spence, 1990:498–504). Against that background, KMT Nationalists battled communist forces for control of China. Morale also was low among many KMT troops, especially those who had not been paid. U.S. General Joseph Stilwell was "horrified at the campaigns of enforced conscription carried out by the Kuomintang armies, and at the sight of ragged, barefooted men being led to the front roped together, already weakened almost to death by beriberi or malnutrition" (Spence, 1990:478). Many officers fled to Taiwan before battles with communist forces ended. After Japan's surrender, Stalin occupied Manchuria and then left it to the Red Army, and the communists already occupied large pieces of terrain in northern China. Toward the end of 1948, the Red Army engaged the demoralized KMT troops to seize the railway connections linking the cities, which (except for Harbin) were still under KMT control. In January 1949, after capturing nearby Tianjin in a focused assault, the Red Army persuaded the heavily outnumbered KMT troops guarding Beijing to surrender that city, and ten days later Chiang Kai-shek resigned as president. The Red Army swept southward to take stategic cities there; by year's end, the KMT regime had retreated to Taiwan. On October 1, 1949, Mao declared formation of the People's Republic of China.

China was ready for a restoration of order. That required curbing inflation, restoring land to the peasants, rebuilding heavy industry, and creating a stable administrative structure. To accomplish this, the communists needed the skills of landlords, managers, technicians, and skilled civil servants. Many Chinese returned from abroad to help with the reconstruction. In 1950, the regime seized and redistributed about 40 percent of cultivatable land and may have killed over 2 million landlords (Dietrich, 1994:69); many friendly landlords were spared and allowed to keep their land. The government vigorously cracked down on the secret triad societies, whose corruption had been keeping urban fiscal and civil order at bay. Repeating a tactic pioneered during the Han dynasty, foreign and domestic business owners were forced to sell out for "back taxes" but then were hired to manage their former firms if they stayed. The country was divided into six military/administrative districts, each under separate command of officers of the Red Army, now renamed the People's Liberation Army (PLA). These commanders supervised both military and civil activities in their districts. The Communist Party was the "leading element" in the country but needed coordination with these military units and the civilian bureaucracy to rule. The party's top organs, the Central Committee and

Politburo (see below) contained many military officers. Extending the Qing dynasty's *baojia* approach (households grouped together under a leader; see Chapter 5) all factories, offices, schools, and other places of work were organized into work units that reported the activities of their members to those authorities *(danwei)*. A common currency was created for the entire country, and government spending was brought under tight control. Inflation declined rapidly.

The next challenge was to root out opponents of the new regime and inspire the citizenry to set aside personal gain so as to restore the nation's vitality. The animosities surrounding the Korean War (see Chapter 7), which lasted from 1950 to 1953, provided a backdrop to these efforts. As the United States Seventh Fleet patrolled the waters between Taiwan (whose regime was asserting its right to take back the mainland by force) and the mainland, and U.S. aid helped Taiwan rearm and rebuild, the communist government began a series of rectification campaigns. It wanted to be sure its citizens did not side with Taiwan and that they gave their all to promote national development and a new communist society that would be free from exploitation and that sought to better the lives of everyone rather than a select few (see Chapter 12). The 1951 "counterrevolutionary" campaign forced people to stand before their neighbors and confess that they had been disloyal to the new regime; tens of thousands of them were executed. Then the "three anti" campaigns brought managers and bureaucrats before their work units to confess waste, corruption, and activities that obstructed development. The 1952 "five anti" campaign was aimed at foreign and domestic capitalists engaged in tax evasion, bribery, theft of state property, fraud on government contracts, and theft of state economic information. The government needed their production for the Korean War and civil development and even helped pay many of their fines—making them more subservient and cautious about such practices. Few were killed. The campaigns attacked foreign enemies and called for patriotism and determination to rout those holding back China's development (Liu, 1996; and Teiwes, 1993, discuss these campaigns).

The Korean War also brought a trade blockade of China and removed it from access to foreign capital. The Soviet Union supplied capital and technical assistance for China's first five-year plan (discussed further in Chapter 5). The separate military-political units of the country were abandoned, and planning was centralized to promote frugality and growth. Government agencies were placed on tight budgets, and resources were carefully targeted. Between 1953 and 1957, agencies invested heavily in state-operated heavy industries, spread throughout the country, and in hydroelectric plants, railroads, and urban housing. Production focused on military hardware and then increasingly on machinery, construction materials, and basic consumer goods. Wages were kept low, and workers had to "contribute" heavy taxes and savings bond investments to the state, but employment was guaranteed. Little was spent on education or social welfare, but citizens were recruited for drives to wipe out pests, improve sanitation, combat common diseases, and promote literacy. Peasants were organized into mutual aid teams composed of six or seven (later, fifty) families who kept title to their land while pooling their resources. They sold the government a fourth of their grain at low prices; the government, in turn, sold flour, rice, and cooking oil to urban workers for low prices (keeping inflation low). Wealthy peasants were excluded from these teams. Agricultural output rose, but not enough to keep pace with industrial production. People's diets steadily improved, but they could buy little beyond food.

Up to that point, the government's efforts had some historical precedents in China's long history of encouraging but regulating capitalist enterprises in a successful effort to restore social and economic stability. Many people had, in fact, been pleased to see individual excesses brought under control. But now the government was ready to move beyond that, testing dangerous new waters in its efforts to ratchet up agricultural production. Capitalism would be banned, not just reformed; the state and peasant organizations would own all production enterprises. By 1955, many mutual aid teams were being incorporated into cooperatives containing 200 to 300 families, and credit was being withheld from richer families. Much of the cooperatives' land was being farmed in common, though each family retained a private plot of land.

China had pulled itself together and left the war years behind, but it was facing a baffling dilemma it still cannot solve. The Chinese people are prepared to give support to strong leaders, especially when they remember periods of disarray. They have long experience at investing in and developing farms and businesses and will devote long hours to work. But they feel strongly about carrying out their *guanxi* obligations to their own families and others with whom they have special relationships. In the 1950s, they were being asked to sacrifice living standards for their own families when they knew others were passing favors to their friends. Given a choice to spend their efforts on common fields or on their own plots, many members of cooperatives chose the latter and then lied to the tax authorities about the income they derived from selling their own livestock and vegetables (and about how small the harvest was on the common land). The most fervent communists saw this emphasis on one's own land and on jobs like hauling or hawking to earn extra money as putting capitalist family interests above those of the whole community. Communists also disliked religious practices that helped bond the community because they held back material progress by wasting resources on extravagant funerals and weddings. The communists had returned the land to the peasants but were imposing rules that ran counter to their traditional culture.

The year 1956 began on a hopeful note. According to the often-inflated reports, agricultural output seemed to be rising, so China's leaders followed Mao Zedong's guidance and rapidly pushed greater numbers of mutual aid teams into the larger cooperatives. Soviet premier Nikita Khrushchev was secretly denouncing Stalin (who had died in 1953) in the Soviet Union's party congress and openly called for peaceful coexistence. Mao and others within China's ruling circle (hoping for reconciliation with Taiwan) secretly discussed allowing greater intellectual freedom and encouraging more openness to foreigners and minorities. Some of their colleagues strongly resisted such accommodation with bourgeois elements, but this debate was short-lived. The summer brought a severe drought and disastrous harvest. Peasants resisted the imposition of the badly managed large cooperatives. In the fall, the Hungarians rose against the Soviet Union, Tibetans rioted against Chinese rule (see Chapter 6), and the Chinese communists held their first party congress since taking over China. They abruptly stopped converting mutual aid teams into cooperatives, called for greater central control of the economy, supported those who opposed a Khrushchev-style united front with bourgeois elements, and kicked Mao out of the leadership circle. For a time, neither the Soviet Union nor China suffered from a "cult of personality."

Mao (Schram, 1966; Karnow, 1972; and Li, 1994, offer interesting biographies) had been ostracized from inner party circles before. Among the party's founders, he was the only one who came from a peasant background and had not studied in Europe. The others tended to associate with intellectuals and attempted to organize among workers in the cities where they lived, whereas Mao moved into the countryside to organize peasants. His work was largely ignored by his urban comrades. In 1927, after the Kuomintang attack on the communists, Mao tried to lead a peasant uprising. The KMT quickly squelched it, and the Communist Party removed him from the Central Committee. While the KMT suppressed urban branches of the party, Mao simply continued organizing the peasants—thus providing the basis for the 1934 Long March. The survivors of that march formed the core group that would take over China. Mao was their natural leader—not the urban intellectuals.

Removed once again in 1956 from the inner circle, Mao returned to the source of his power, the peasants and workers. Early in 1957 he publicly delivered a speech drawing on one he had made privately the previous year, calling for greater intellectual freedom so that "a hundred flowers" (Spence, 1990:569–574) could bloom and "a hundred schools of thought contend (Karnow, 1972:87–90)." He said the country was now so united it could benefit from such a debate. The press, a natural ally in such an initiative, hesitated at first to print his words. When they did, criticism rushed forth. Mao had hoped the press and citizens would attack his adversaries leading the party and support his reforms. Instead, the students at Beijing University started a "Democracy Wall" and filled it with posters denouncing a wide range of Communist Party policies and even the right of the communists to rule. People around the country joined in; many were critical of Mao himself. Within weeks, Mao backed down and joined the inner circle in calling for a crackdown on the campaign and severe punishment of those making the criticisms. The antirightist rectification campaign that ensued led to 300,000 intellectuals (branded as "rightists") losing their jobs without hope of finding another and sent many of them into exile on farms. Their numbers included many of the youths who had been most zealous in supporting the initial rise to power of the communists. They would not forget this humiliation.

■ TWO DECADES OF TURMOIL

In 1957, agricultural production moved to center stage as the primary concern of China's leaders. Industrial production had been growing far more rapidly than grain production, and the income of rural workers had outpaced that of peasants. Left once again to their own devices, peasants had focused on more profitable vegetables and livestock, leaving the country with inadequate flour, rice, and cooking oil to feed its burgeoning population. Mao was determined to end this lethargy and propel China into a communist utopia by increasing agricultural and industrial output to improve the lives of everyone and surpass the capitalist West. Late in 1957 the party mobilized millions of peasants into work gangs to irrigate and terrace millions of acres of new cropland. The effort was carried out through a mass rectification campaign; units outdid themselves to show their all-out commitment to pure "red" communism by reporting huge increases in production. Encouraged by these wildly inflated figures, the following year the party announced the Great Leap Forward (see Domenach, 1995, for an alarming close-up and Dietrich, 1994:110–150, for an overview). Private plots were abolished. Work teams and cooperatives were amalgamated into gigantic communes. Families were absorbed into large crews who worked in the fields and made their meals together. These crews were even mobilized to help develop an atomic bomb and increase steel production by melting scrap metal in backyard ovens, based on Mao's ideas that committed peasants could enhance industrial output more effectively than professionals working with central planners.

In the long run, the Great Leap Forward opened much new land for agricultural production and brought new industry and agricultural capabilities to formerly remote regions (Chan, Madsen, and Unger, 1984:213–220, tells how it improved life in one small village, after a period of great pain). And it enlarged local militias, which competed with the PLA. In the short run—due to bad weather, diversion of labor to other projects, increased exports of grain to the Soviet Union based on the exaggerated output claims, layoff of skilled civil servants during the antirightist campaigns, and other mismanagement—agricultural production fell below even the disastrous levels of the prior two years. Millions of people were starving; over 20 million died (see Yang, 1996; Spence, 1990:583). Yet grain exports to the Soviet Union in payment for its aid in developing industry were increasing. Once again, the party leadership called off the campaign and removed Mao as head of state in 1959. Registration in the *danwei* was intensified to pull people back to the countryside. Private plots began to be distributed again, communes were divided among private production brigades, and rural markets reopened. Many inefficient rural industries and state enterprises were closed. Gradually, agricultural production and private entrepreneurship began to revive.

Meanwhile, the United States had begun supplying Taiwan with missiles. The Soviet Union, talking of "peaceful coexistence" with the capitalist nations, showed no signs of helping China develop an atomic bomb. Khrushchev had sent no assistance to the Great Leap Forward, which differed from his own new initiatives to provide workers with economic incentives. While China was having foreign policy disputes with India and Indonesia (discussed in Chapters 6 and 7), Khrushchev was warming relations with them. In 1960, the Soviet Union called home its technical advisers and cut off aid to China, bringing a halt to many projects.

The debate within China's inner circle of top Communist Party leaders defies simple summation. They decried the excesses that resulted from suppressing capitalist enterprises yet did not want capitalism to return. They all largely agreed that Khrushchev's policy of accommodation with capitalists was the wrong tack for China and that China's peasants and workers needed more discipline, but they disagreed on how to achieve that discipline. Mao preferred those who were "red" (a true devotee of the communist cause) to those who were simply trained experts. As evidence mounted that the efforts to instill "redness" by organizing great communes and putting peasants and workers in charge was a disaster threatening their positions as leaders of government and party organs and popular support for Communist Party rule, the leaders struggled for a way out. They chose, at this point, to restore the use of expert bureaucrats, managers, and technicians in central bureaucracy to plan allocation of resources, direct what should be grown and produced, and assist with distribution of finished products; meanwhile, they sought to give people more chance to profit from their output. Some in the party leadership felt China needed more technical expertise from the outside but feared that exposure to bourgeois capitalism would weaken people's resolve to serve their whole community.

To ensure that the renewed opportunities for profit were not at the expense of the community, national party leaders initiated a "socialist education campaign" in 1963, which attempted to reduce fraud both in accounting for grain and property and in distributing incentive pay to those who worked harder. The campaign, however, was carried out by local party leaders who themselves might have been guilty of those offenses. The communist leaders of communes, cooperatives, work teams, and state enterprises were made responsible for judging how to proceed and determining who among their own ranks was cheating; they were to discipline themselves (Siu, 1989, tells how local leaders found themselves involved in such national projects). Thus local leaders could cheat without getting caught, but ordinary people were closely supervised, without assurance of extra rewards for hard work.

To regain power, Mao took advantage of citizens' resentment over leaders' abuses of power. He applauded his model village of Dazhai for increasing production through "red" ideological fervor rather than supervision by experts, even though a party inspection team found its production was down and many of its inhabitants were undernourished. He called once again for more open debate, to let the masses—not the local party leaders—ferret out the corruption among their leaders. His position gained support among troops within the People's Liberation Army who felt that their own power was being eclipsed by the party's civilian leaders, who were calling for stricter discipline and professionalism, and by the militias that had grown in strength since the Great Leap Forward. And Mao had the ear of some groups who, ironically, were suffering from his own efforts: city people from "bourgeois" or former Kuomintang families who had lost university admissions, jobs, and party posts to individuals from the countryside who had more humble (and therefore presumably more "red") origins. He also gained support from many unemployed youth who had fled to the cities during the agricultural downturn Mao had helped create and now had been returned to the farms, where they were not always well received. Finally, the current batch of university students worried about their prospects in the wake of all the recent cataclysms.

Mao preached to these politically alienated listeners that they should assert themselves against their leaders, and they listened. In 1965, the PLA abandoned all ranks and insignia on their uniforms; officers and enlisted soldiers would be "equal" and share all work assignments. By the spring of 1966, Mao had stirred leading university campuses into protest, and protesting students began calling themselves "Red Guards." Soon they were joined by students and other supporters from throughout the country. By fall, they were dragging political leaders, teachers, bureaucrats, and others into the streets and making them confess crimes before kangaroo courts. Schools were closed, workers were stealing property from their factories, historic buildings and monuments were being destroyed, production was grinding to a halt. The Great Proletarian Cultural Revolution had begun (Schoenhals, 1996; White, 1989; Yuan, 1987; Karnow, 1972; Dietrich, 1994:205–234; Wang, 1995; Chang, 1991).

Mao had hoped to regain control of China's leadership and keep China's people focused on the good of the whole community. Instead, once again, he had roused (together with millions of people acting out of pure idealistic fervor) the anticommunist, anarchist, and disaffected citizens in the country to attack authority and seek their own personal gain—or at least disrupt community life. By February 1967, Mao was supporting efforts by the party leaders and the army to restore order. This time, it would take ten years. By the late 1960s, schools began to reopen, and Mao was seeking ties with the United States. Many more students had been sent to work in the countryside alongside those sent there earlier in the 1960s; slowly, they returned to the cities, bitter over their forced exile and long-disrupted education. Because the party's membership had expanded to include many Red Guards, a series of rectification campaigns first attacked those leading the Cultural Revolution and then those trying to bring it under control. Even top leaders of the party were subjected to beatings and imprisonment, and many were humiliated to the point of suicide.

In 1976, Zhou Enlai (who had led the restoration of party control) and Mao died. Mao's successor Hua Guofeng promptly arrested "the Gang of Four," four of the most prominent leaders of the Cultural Revolution; in their trial, they were blamed for all the excesses of that era. A new era had begun. Within four years Deng Xiaoping (for a biography see Goodman, 1994) had overcome strong challenges from his rivals to take control of the party, and the United States had extended diplomatic recognition to communist China. Mao had paved the way for reforms more in keeping with tradition—such as encouraging limited capitalism—by weakening the central bureaucracies, returning land to the peasants, and helping even small communities develop consumer industries. The United States made reforms possible by helping Hong Kong, Taiwan, Japan, and Southeast Asian countries develop strong economies and currencies to invest in China.

■ INTO THE WORLD ECONOMY

After Mao's era ended, China was free to pursue the added elements of economic strength that had eluded it before: foreign capital, technology, and markets (Naughton, 1995; Baum, 1996; Chang, 1988; Dittmer, 1994; Goodman and Hooper, 1994; Shirk, 1993). It was not free, however, to pursue democracy and pluralism. China's attempt to modernize its economy without changing its political system would confuse those in the West and would burden China with new social problems, but it would also bring China the broadest prosperity it had ever experienced.

To implement reform, Deng called for four modernizations—of agriculture, industry, defense, and science and technology—and initiated new economic policies, which are discussed in more detail in Chapter 5. The household responsibility system allowed peasants to lease plots of land

and sell their crops for profit. Groups of individuals or entire villages and townships could form cooperative enterprises to manufacture, transport, and sell goods. In addition, foreign firms could create joint ventures with firms in China. Special economic zones were created where foreign businesses could buy land and get special breaks on taxes and regulations. And state industries were authorized to fire workers, give incentive pay, and sell shares of stock to Chinese investors.

These reforms have brought China continuous economic growth at a rate surpassing 10 percent a year. As Chapter 5 explains in more detail, by 1994 China's economy was four times larger than it was in 1978; and it is likely to be eight times larger by 2002. It has become the world's third- or fourth-largest economy, behind only the United States, Japan, and perhaps Germany.

☐ Meeting the Challenges of Reform

The three groups most readily helped by Deng's reforms were the peasants, party bureaucrats in coastal provinces, and urban workers who could form cooperatives. The groups most harmed were students, intellectuals, urban youth still trapped in the countryside, central planners, and workers in state industries. To achieve power after Mao's death, Deng had to win support from factions with adherents in all these camps. Deng's successor, Jiang Zemin, faces that same challenge. This creates a dynamic in modern Chinese politics that both calls for and limits openness to the outside world.

Mao returned the land to peasant producers; Deng's responsibility system and cooperatives gave them the incentive to produce. They rapidly began bringing home profits. Intellectuals, bureaucrats, and skilled blue-collar workers with assigned jobs and fixed salaries found themselves making less than uneducated peasants and laborers. Rural workers used their incomes to build large new houses, whereas urban dwellers were crowded into small, dingy apartments. Many urban youths who had been sent to the countryside during the Cultural Revolution still could not get permission to return to the cities yet were not entitled to land or jobs where they were. The government had little money to invest in universities; students studied on drab campuses with few laboratory or library facilities, ate food ladled from buckets of gruel onto metal plates, and lived with six people in dorm rooms meant for two, without heat or air conditioning. Even graduates of the leading universities anticipated assigned jobs paying less than the income of a bicycle repairperson on a street corner or someone gathering scrap cardboard in a cart and selling it to a wholesaler. Many students had marched in demonstrations and hung posters on the "Democracy Wall" in 1976 and 1978 to help bring Deng to power and felt both unrewarded and betrayed by the arrest of Wei Jingsheng and others who had led those demonstrations.

By 1986, students were marching again, against rigged elections, their poor living conditions, low pay for university graduates, the growth in inflation and the corruption of officials who were hiring their own children and diverting resources into the pockets of their factional cohorts. In the spring of 1989, students marched once more, to raise these concerns. This time the foreign media was in Beijing to cover the historic reopening of relations with the Soviet Union as Mikhail Gorbachev flew in for a state visit, and reporters saw the students occupy and refuse to leave Tiananmen Square at the center of Beijing.

Some of the leaders felt it was time to take a more tolerant view than had ever been taken in the past toward demonstrations and suggested inviting the leaders into public dialogue about the issues the demonstrations had raised. Most, however, worried that they might get out of hand like those during the prior two decades; the students' complaints about corruption and economic disparities and their ties to political factions within the party were reminiscent of the Red Guards who started the Cultural Revolution with similar demonstrations (Benton and Hunter, 1995, present interviews with participants in such demonstrations going back to 1942). That approach prevailed, and the government responded with a bloody recapture of Tiananmen Square, arrests of and long prison sentences for demonstration leaders, a rectification campaign condemning the action, and requirements that students should serve stints in the army to remind them of the need for discipline (for inside reports, see Black and Munro, 1993; Nan, 1992; Unger, 1991; Gordon and Hinton, 1995; Gamer, 1989).

The government then took steps to defuse the anger that lay behind the demonstrations. Part of this strategy focused on the PLA. The units who ran the tanks into the square were from inland rural areas that had not benefited from the reforms; they feared and distrusted the students, who lived better than they did and were taking actions country youths would not dream of. Some soldiers lost their lives on the square, raising the level of distrust and envy. When Deng came to power he had sought to reduce the power of the PLA, which had greatly expanded during the Cultural Revolution, by separating police units from the PLA, reducing the size of military forces and budgets, and removing officers from top party posts. Now he restored officers to some of these posts and gradually increased military spending (Soled, 1995:263–282; Dreyer, 1996:205–209). The PLA was given rights to set up numerous joint ventures and sell arms abroad, which helped improve life on the bases.

Universities were mandated to start businesses, charge wealthier students tuition, and raise money in other creative ways. University campuses acquired new gardens, paint, furniture, buildings, and equipment. Mess halls began serving a variety of foods. Occupancy of dorm rooms was reduced, and more buildings were heated and air conditioned. Rather than being assigned to low paying, government jobs as in the past, students

The 1989 demonstrations took place for several weeks in cities all over China. Hangzhou saw daily scenes like this.

were now free to seek jobs with joint ventures after graduation. In 1992 Deng called for an expansion of economic liberalization. Cities all over China were allowed to set up special enterprise zones. This set off a wave of construction; new housing, roads, public buildings, factories, dams, and electrical power stations brought jobs and better living all over the country. Censors began to wink at the proliferation of pornography, foreign fiction, and rock music (in Chapter 13, Charles Laughlin elaborates on all this).

These changes, in turn, disadvantaged other groups. Peasants were upset because the government was levying higher taxes and purchasing fewer goods from them at much lower prices as it weaned urban workers off food vouchers. At the same time, both peasants and workers were paying more for purchases as high inflation continued. This combination especially harmed villagers in remote areas whose income depended largely on grain sales. Jean Oi (1989b:224–235) and Gordon White (1993:99–117) explain how village leaders, who handled grain sold to the state and still controlled the distribution of leased land when people died or moved, were in a position to enrich themselves at the expense of the poorest villagers. These leaders also led newly revived temple sects and lineage organizations, which promoted conflicts with other communities. A separate problem for workers was that many state factories could not afford to give them pay increases sufficient to compensate for inflation because these factories could not compete with joint ventures. When state employers were freed to hire and fire on the basis of merit, less educated workers felt threatened, as did the party cadres who were once largely in charge and often had little education. Inland provinces continued to lag behind those on the coast (see Goodman and Segal, 1994). Millions of itinerant workers were unwelcome in the cities where they had taken temporary residence; they and many workers in cooperatives and small businesses were without adequate social services. Peasants and workers held demonstrations and strikes that gave the government reason to accommodate their concerns. So did the fact that all these groups are tied together in networks that owe each other *guanxi*: Reform-minded bureaucrats in Beijing can work with counterparts in the provinces to counter moves of those in the capital less inclined to reform.

Toward the end of the 1990s, governments were encouraging rural communities to create village and township enterprises at a rapid pace. Inhabitants from those regions are frequently hired to work in factories of those enterprises and also flock to the cities to work on construction projects. Their remittances home help the economies there as well as those around the cities. Entrepreneurship is spreading, but it remains controlled. Personal freedoms to gamble in the marketplace are held in check by desires for personal economic security; groups work with other groups to retain privileges threatened by economic reforms.

☐ New Political Challenges

Economic development requires decentralization of control, but it also depends on national unity. It widens the gap between the rich and the poor;

bridging that gap requires help from the central government. Development not only requires some democratic reforms but also depends on some traditional social ties that interfere with democratic reforms. Economic development needs the help of foreign traders and investors; every group is likely to agree on that. But not every group can benefit from economic development at the same time. This is where disagreements arise.

Chapter 5 surveys some of the principal economic challenges with which China's leaders must grapple: inflation, the scarcity of commodities, inefficient state industries and township and village enterprises, maintenance of peasant incomes even after the elimination of government subsidies, rising unemployment, falling central government tax revenues, banking reform, the shrinking social safety net, and widespread corruption. They must deal with other problems as well, such as numerous environmental challenges, for example (see Chapter 9; Yabuki, 1994:145–151).

A host of regional rivalries and a lack of infrastructure to tie the regions together compound the difficulties. Municipalities, townships, and provinces allied with foreign multinational corporations have become the main generators of investment capital. They collect most of the tax revenues as well, including internal tariffs on goods crossing their boundaries. Cities pass "health" and "quality control" laws banning goods from other provinces. Over 1,000 disputes over internal boundary lines have sometimes led to bloodshed, as two provinces make claims on the same mines or timber. In addition, the country is divided into seven military regions whose boundaries do not correspond with provincial lines; though the central government frequently moves around senior officers, their troops have strong regional loyalties. New cars demand new roads, which often end at the city limit. China needs (and is working on) oil pipelines, a national road network, more electric generating capacity, numerous modern airfields, and other infrastructure that require national investment and coordination. Yet in the face of regional protectionism, it lacks the resources or political clout to provide them fast enough.

The PLA brought the Communist Party to power and (along with people's militias expanded during the Cultural Revolution and various layers of police forces) is the government's ultimate defense against popular uprisings and civil disorder. It wants to acquire weaponry and better living standards for its members. This creates an additional strain on government revenues. The PLA owns many joint ventures and cooperative businesses and illegally sells arms to Iran, Pakistan, and other countries. Some of its leaders advocate aggressive maneuvers against the Spratly Islands and Taiwan, which justify increasing their budgets but frighten off foreign investors.

High levels of foreign investment and trade have helped create all these problems and are also the key to solving them. A great deal of money is changing hands at many levels from market activities and from informal exchange of favors. The latter slows down the former by making investment work inefficiently, but it also provides incentives to those without whom the investment could not occur. Every phase of development has rewarded some at the expense of others. When students complained, those with the right qualifications and connections were offered job opportunities in new businesses. When peasants then complained that surrounding cities were flourishing at their expense, they were organized into owners of complexes of cooperatives and joint ventures hiring migrant workers from less prosperous villages further inland. People complain about the lack of legal reforms to stop corruption, yet many benefit directly or indirectly from the money that changes hands outside official channels. They know the absence of such reforms slows growth, but, although they may want to let that fresh air in, they also want to keep out anything that interferes with cultural reciprocities. The economic reforms have helped many with education improve their political and economic standing. Much initial profit of reform enterprises was derived from plentiful, cheap labor and land speculation: as labor becomes more expensive by world standards and the bottom falls out of speculative land prices, economic efficiency becomes a more important component of the growth needed to keep their new jobs safe. Some do not recognize this need and even those advocating it often acknowledge that moves toward economic efficiency must be cautious. Reforms like tightening legal procedures and allowing groups to register complaints threaten the very relationships that have allowed some to advance, while others fall behind or may be used by unions and cadres to block further reform. Especially since the Cultural Revolution, those with education fear that moves toward democracy might increase the political power of the masses.

The Confucian scholars living during the Song dynasty recognized the danger a free economy can pose to the rural communities that have remained the source of jobs, sustenance, and social reciprocities on which China's citizens depend. In the 1990s contemporary Chinese are learning that free land sales, market competition, and access to modern technology can destroy communities, render many peasants and workers jobless, and raise the prices of the goods produced abundantly by and for China's average citizens.

■ MAINTAINING UNITY

The decentralization accompanying economic reform has given new freedoms to China's provinces. These freedoms have largely been made possible because China is once again unified, accorded diplomatic recognition by other governments, able to ensure political stability, and able to move people and resources from one region to another for manufacturing and marketing. This strength keeps rich provinces from getting ideas about

Photo: Robert E. Gamer

*"Wall newspaper": The latest edition posted behind glass
ensures that the public has easy access to news. Papers do not criticize
the government but report on crimes and complaints.*

breaking away when they are asked to share with poor provinces, and it
gives most Chinese a strong incentive to go along with proven techniques
of maintaining unity. The isolation that China's regions experienced is
over. The center hopes that the new links they have with the outside world
and with one another will not interfere with their links to the center. It
wishes it could make provinces less independent but knows it cannot
(Kuhn, 1998).

□ Binding Together

The Communist Party has about 55 million members, with about 2
million primary organizations meeting in villages, urban neighborhoods,
danwei, and military divisions. These local branches elect a local secretary, a local party committee, and other officers, who select individuals to
serve on the county and provincial party congresses. Those bodies send
about 1,500 delegates to a National Party Congress who meet periodically;

about 300 of those delegates form the Party Congress's Central Committee. Fifteen to twenty-five of the Central Committee's members constitute its Politburo, four to six of whom belong to the Standing Committee of the Politburo, which meets regularly. That body wields the highest authority in the land.

The Standing Committee of the Politburo works closely with the party's Military Affairs Commission—the top body directing the armed forces—and with leading government ministers in the State Council. A number of individuals hold posts on more than one of these bodies: The general secretary—the highest ranking member of the party who exerts the highest authority—serves as head of both the Standing Committee and the Military Affairs Commission. He also chooses who will serve on the National Party Congress. The general secretary's post is currently held by Jiang Zemin. There are about 4 million central government bureaucrats, along with 4 million party cadres. Thus the Communist Party, the government, and the armed forces intersect to govern China.

The party's cadres, including the party secretaries, are paid functionaries of the party charged with supervising the work of the government bureaucracy, the armed forces, and other elements of government and society (Burns, 1989). Many party members and cadres were chosen during the Cultural Revolution and often have little education. Deng Xiaoping made efforts to recruit members and cadres with more professional training and motivation (Lieberthal, 1995:230–239), but this created conflicts within the party and between the party and units it supervises. Some push activities in the direction of professionalism, whereas others resist this out of fear that the needs of the masses will suffer. Party secretaries at the provincial, county, municipal, and township levels hold the highest power there and are served by dual government and party bureaucracies at those levels (Wang, 1992:73–204; Lieberthal, 1995:159–218; Shirk, 1993:55–128; Blecher and Shue, 1996).

Local leaders help choose lists of candidates for elections to party congresses and to government legislatures. *Danwei,* villages, neighborhoods, and military and cultural groups hold elections to select delegates for the local government councils and some of their own leaders from these lists. In some regions, eight small parties, which operate mostly among older city intellectuals who cooperated with the Communist Party before World War II, also select candidates for those bodies. Some 60 percent of China's 600,000 villages now hold elections with rival candidates competing for these posts. This ensures that no one may enter these races who is opposed to the government or Communist Party. It also ensures that people all over the country are involved in choosing leaders of the Communist Party and of government legislative bodies.

Periodically, meetings of the National Party Congress and the National People's Congress (the national legislature, whose Standing Committee enforces martial law during domestic disturbances) showcase that diversity. Though the main purpose of the two-week meetings is to rubber-stamp government programs, in recent years they have engaged in some lively debates about some of the divisive issues we have just discussed. Most of the time, the debate takes place behind the scenes. Many factions develop among these individuals, tying them and others together through *guanxi*. Kenneth Lieberthal and Michel Oksenberg (1988:138–168) explain how these connections, in turn, link the regions of the country with the center and one another. Lieberthal also makes a counterargument that people develop loyalty to their own *danwei*, whose leaders report to multiple bosses, causing the leaders to resist cooperation that might harm their own local interests; this results in "fragmented authoritarianism," with individual units living in "economic, social, and political cocoons" (1995:120, 169, 217–218). Combining the two points gives the complete picture. Andrew Walder (1986), looking at industries, and Vivienne Shue (1988), examining agriculture, discuss at length this battle between the state and the *danwei*—what Walder and Shue call a "honeycomb polity" of "cell-like communities."

Relations between the PLA and the government are more complex than most. Civilian ministries report directly to the State Council, which is the highest body of the government and also are supervised by the Communist Party. The PLA reports directly to the Military Affairs Commission of the Communist Party, which is headed by the general secretary of the Communist Party; it does not report to the State Council. The Ministry of Defense under the State Council has little real control over the military. So the armed forces are supervised by the party, but not by the government. PLA members serve on the party's Politburo and Central Committee, and they are well connected with party leaders at provincial and local levels as well. Many of those connections are with the old guard who developed close ties with the military in the early years of the revolutionary struggle; as the military is gradually replaced with younger troops having more professional training and civilians (like Jiang Zemin) who have no military experience take control of party affairs, those connections may diminish.

Imperial China sought a new ruler only after the prior one died. Communist China has kept that tradition. Mao was no longer in control of China's government when he died in 1976, but the struggle to succeed him did not begin until after his death. Though Deng Xiaoping gave up all his formal titles during the 1980s, the mantle of rule could not fall on anyone until his death more than a decade later. Jiang Zemin, the former leader of Shanghai, became the general secretary of the Standing Committee of the Communist Party after his predecessor was removed over the 1989 demonstrations; though he was head of the Military Affairs Commission, he was not able to visit the headquarters of the PLA without direct permission from Deng (Lieberthal, 1995:189). He worked to strengthen his position by gaining support of various elements of the army, party, and bureaucracy in all areas of the country. To do that he had to widen the spread of economic reforms while controlling the problems that arose along with them. He also had to show the networks that he was not selling out China to foreigners in any moves reminiscent of the period of foreign domination (see Chapter 7).

The new economic freedoms and the general disillusionment with the Cultural Revolution by people who had initially supported its ideology without question have lessened the value of communism as a unifying ideology (see Ding, 1994; Unger, 1996). Jiang has turned instead to nationalism (Unger, 1996) and Confucian values (see the conclusion of Chapter 12) as unifying themes. China's greatness derives from its unique culture, which gives it both unity and dynamic drive. Confucianism would preserve the family and a moral central authority, allowing for economic development and foreign trade while shielding the nation from the excesses of individualism and materialism and from foreign intrusion in China's affairs (Forney, 1996a). Jiang wants China to become powerful in the world without outside challenges to its core values. The annexation of Hong Kong in 1997 fits that theme. China's sytem would remain the same, while Hong Kong keeps its own political system with greater freedoms. Chinese leaders see this as a model for the eventual inclusion of Taiwan in a "one country with three systems" policy. Combining their advanced growth with China's can move China to the forefront among the world's economies and powers, while still resisting foreign influences that weaken it.

□ Pulling Apart

These unifying institutions and ideological strands must counter more than the independence of individual work units. They also must try to heal some broader cultural rifts.

1. Areas on the fringes of Confucian culture. Tibet was not conquered by China until 1950 (see Chapter 6). Its people are Tantric Buddhists who give their ultimate allegiances to their communities and to their religious leaders, such as the Dalai Lama. On Tibet's eastern border, many Tibetans and other inhabitants of Sichuan and Yunnan provinces share in the religion and customs of Tibet and of areas in Southeast Asia. The regions to the north and east of Tibet—now the provinces of Xinjiang, Qinghai, and Gansu (see Map 2.2)—were occasionally penetrated by Chinese armies (see Map 3.1). Tang dynasty conquests brought in Chinese culture that local people continued to absorb even after military withdrawals. The "Silk Roads" (Map 2.1) made these provinces a meeting place for many cultures and of all the world's great religions. Many of their people are

Muslim and share religious and family customs far different from those of the Han.

During the Cultural Revolution, acting on communist ideological convictions that nationality traits must be removed if bourgeois society is to wither away and the dictatorship of the proletariat flourish, Red Guard activists aggressively sought to destroy places of worship, languages, clothing, music, and all other manifestations of these cultures. During the earlier years of the People's Republic and again since the Cultural Revolution, China's communist regime has sought to retain such expressions of cultural differences, while at the same time bringing modernization to these regions. Whole provinces like Tibet, as well as individual prefectures, counties, and townships are designated autonomous areas; they cover nearly two-thirds of China's territory. Their legislatures have the right to create legislation protecting local customs. In addition, citizens registered as cultural minorities have many special privileges unavailable to those officially classified as Han. They are exempt from family planning limits (see Chapter 8) and can gain admission to higher education and cadre posts with lower qualifications.

Today, Beijing sends large numbers of Han to Tibet and cities in the outer northern arc and the southwest in the belief that it is spreading modernization and civilization. Han sent to these regions often feel exiled from the best schools, housing, and food and resent the special privileges enjoyed by inhabitants there. And local inhabitants deeply resent their destruction of old neighborhoods, hundreds of monasteries, and hillsides of timber; murders of religious leaders; insistence on communicating in Chinese rather than their native languages; cultural arrogance; and growing numbers. Non-Han residents of autonomous areas often have lower incomes and rates of literacy than their Han compatriots; some of the nation's worst pockets of poverty are to be found among them. During the 1990s numerous civil rebellions broke out in Tibet, Xinjiang, and Inner Mongolia. These regions border on countries that may even stir up unrest to help them seize disputed territories (see Chapter 7); consequently, the Chinese authorities are determined to squelch the resistance. These areas also contain some of China's most valuable natural resources. All the while, the non-Han peoples in these regions fall behind in sharing China's growing prosperity, and the growing cross-border trading increases contacts among radical groups fomenting cultural and religious separation.

2. *North-south divisions.* In Chapter 3, Rhoads Murphey pointed to numerous differences between the cultures of north and south China and the conquests of the south by the north. During the seventeenth century, the Manchus, to the northeast of China above Korea (now the eastern part of Inner Mongolia, Heilongjiang, Jilin, and Liaoning; see Map 2.2), crossed the Great Wall to conquer China; their rulers adopted the Confucian system but kept separate administrative units for Manchus. Although

they told the Han people they were imposing Confucian customs on people in the periphery, they in fact allowed those peoples much leeway in
carrying out their own cultural traditions (Rawski, 1996). In 1911, much
support for ending the empire came from Chinese who were tired of being
ruled by these alien Manchus. Once they took power, they tried to impose
their laws and customs more rigidly on those in the periphery, including
the Manchus. These peoples have strongly resisted that imposition, seeking to preserve old customs. Rank-and-file Manchus, who now constitute
less than 10 percent of the populace in Jilin and Heilongjiang provinces,
often failed to adopt Chinese ways. In addition, Edward Friedman
(1995:49, 77) points out that thousands of Mongols were tortured and
killed during the Cultural Revolution on suspicion that they were foreign
agents. And Xinjiang still experiences frequent civil unrest.

Chapter 3 also discussed the numerous peasant revolts in China's history. Many began on the Shandong peninsula at the mouth of the Yellow
River, just across the Yellow Sea from Korea (Map 2.4). This has given
Shandong residents a streak of independence, though they combine it with
longer attachment to farming and Confucian values than their neighbors to
the north. Other areas developed some independence as well. Over succeeding centuries, the inhabitants of Guangdong, Fujian, and Zhejiang (see
Map 2.1) used their access to the sea to develop trading relations with peoples throughout Southeast Asia. They also linked up with the "Silk Roads"
to sell products in the rest of Asia and Europe. During recent centuries the
capital moved to Beijing, while commerce and population expanded in the
south. Chinese like to say that the north is interested in power and the
south in money. Business activities in the south have often helped finance
military campaigns to the north. Beijing's emperors viewed with suspicion
the increasing trade contacts of the southern cities, which strengthened foreigners and made China vulnerable to foreign invasion and subversion. Periodically, they would send down edicts restricting those contacts. At the
same time, they became more dependent on the revenues that trade supplied, increasing the tax burden as commerce expanded. Southerners came
to view the northerners as people living off their money without contributing anything tangible in return beyond relief from the threat of conquest. Many of those like Sun Yat-sen, who led the fight to overthrow the
Qing dynasty, came from the south.

3. *Provincial peculiarities and urban-rural suspicion.* These southern
provinces, in turn, have different languages and cultures. The inhabitants
of Fujian, Guangzhou (Canton), and Zhejiang and along the Yangtze (not
to mention rural areas around Beijing) speak in dialects very different
from the Mandarin that Beijing enforces as the national language. They
drink different teas, eat different foods, celebrate different festivals, and
wear different clothing. Since Canton is becoming the fastest-growing commercial area, Cantonese is rapidly becoming the language of commerce.

Northerners, who speak Mandarin or still other dialects and eat foods based on wheat rather than rice, may feel especially out of place as they come down to join in commercial endeavors. In past centuries, peasants who moved south to escape the poverty of the north became known as Hakkas; Mao and Deng Xiaoping came from Hakka families. Southern inhabitants came to resent these new residents with strange habits and no land; their communities became hotbeds for secret societies and rebel groups. They also added to suspicions between urban and rural folk. During the nineteenth century, Shanghai burgeoned in size as a treaty port; many of its immigrants came from the south. They are surrounded by northern peasants, whose culture is very different (Honig, 1992). Hangzhou, the old capital, speaks dialects left over from the Southern Song dynasty period that are very different from those spoken by rural neighbors. The same is true of cities like Beijing (literally, North Capital) and Tianjin in the north. The natural suspicions that surround their cultures were enhanced in the 1980s, when rural housing and incomes were improving faster than urban, or during the 1990s, when this trend was reversed. Urbanites who have descended from families of intellectuals or merchants, which traditionally did not do manual labor and may have been sent to the countryside for this purpose during the Cultural Revolution, may feel this gulf to an especially great degree.

■ **WHAT WILL ENDURE
AND WHAT WILL CHANGE?**

China has a long tradition of limited, small-scale capitalism. Households produced crops and goods for their own use and to exchange with relatives and neighbors. They could also hire labor to produce surpluses sold in small markets or through brokers. The state taxed and regulated that trade. By combining resources of small producers, brokers could prevent large producers from monopolizing trade. Public officials could regulate the brokers and prevent the large producers from adopting technology they deemed inappropriate for maintaining the rural communities that are the ideological backbone for Confucian social relations. The introduction of guilds also gave small craftspeople the power to hold back technical innovations that might threaten their jobs. State firms produced some goods needed by other components of the economy. The *baojia* system later allowed for the organization of larger groups of people. Leaders and members of each of these units developed special relationships and exchanged favors to get others to cooperate. The basic social unit, the family, relied on the cooperation of all its members to carry out their obligations in providing labor and distributing output. Even the wealthy accepted the governmental controls that helped keep alive a peaceful and orderly business climate, let them dominate the labor force, maintained the waterways, and operated the marketplaces. They could use their wealth to help their sons become officials and respectable members of the community.

Modern China has been able to draw upon the dynamics of this system and allow the size of some of the enterprises to grow. State firms mining coal, casting steel, building locomotives, or grinding cement often employ hundreds or thousands of workers on one site using simple technology. The parts of bicycles may be produced in thousands of homes or small workshops and then collected for final assembly in a manufacturing plant. State bureaucrats and private middlemen collect crops from small farmers for distribution in urban stores and markets. Families readily grasp opportunities for their members to earn extra income; parents ensure that the members of their household work hard, if need be, to make money. Households are frugal in their expenditures and invest savings in productive activities. They will also spend large amounts of money for weddings, funerals, and special occasions—thus providing work for many small craftspeople.

The new economic reforms in 1978 initially expanded that system further. Joint ventures set up large shop floors where young women at sewing machines produced designer-label shoes, caps, shirts, and dresses. Small assembly lines fit together transistors and other simple components into television sets to be sold as "price leaders" in discount stores around the world. Auto plants built stripped-down versions of prior-model cars. The plants themselves often have scraps lying around and resemble overgrown backyard workshops.

But as modern capitalism makes greater inroads within China, the features of China's society that initially brought about growth can become impediments to further development. The newest plants are bringing with them the newest technology. Plants in Shanghai's Pudong special economic zone and other of the latest-developed areas are clean and modern; they increasingly need workers with advanced technical skills. These large firms produce economical and tempting products whose design and sophistication make them competitive with goods produced by many of the smaller firms. Indeed, they could wipe out many of these firms and the jobs of many workers. However, major impediments to such market dominance include poor transportation and the regulations that surround the older forms of capitalist enterprise. An even greater impediment to more modern capitalism is the lack of an independent middle class. The industrial revolution in Europe created a new middle class separate from the old dominating nobility; the former used political revolution to overthrow the political ascendency of the latter. China's entrepreneurs have not had to free themselves from wealthy landowning families with titles of nobility, whose dominance ended there over two thousand years ago when the Qin dynasty overthrew the feudal system of the Zhou dynasty (see Chapter 3).

They have, in fact, descended from the same social orders who ruled imperial China and include in their ranks individuals from the "Red Guard" era, who moved from being peasants to bureaucrats before becoming involved in economic enterprises. The leaders of today's joint ventures also have experience as Communist Party cadres devoted to instilling loyalty among the populace and periodically suppressing capitalist pursuits. They retain one foot in government and the other in business.

The latest generation of technically trained university graduates is taking jobs in joint ventures that pay several times what jobs in government and state enterprises offer. This gives them access to the latest consumer goods but not to great amounts of capital. To keep their jobs, they must remain loyal to their firms and the government. Those who venture into cooperatives find the same restraints that held back such enterprises in the traditional system. Many are investing in the stock market, but treacherous fluctuations in its prices make it a risky bet. The leading independent businesspeople are the business leaders in Taiwan and Hong Kong. They know that full political independence for Taiwan would endanger all their business dealings in China, so they offer support to Beijing's government in resisting that (see Chapter 6). Those businesspeople and foreign firms want to introduce enforceable civil law and open exchange of currency. But they recognize the limits on China's ability to extend such reforms even as they push for them. They seldom advocate political reforms beyond that, especially when they threaten political stability.

Fewer than 2 percent of China's youth receive higher education, and political activism does not increase one's chances for admission. China's people have been in the habit of obeying those who lead the units to which they belong. They have a long tradition of saying in public what the officials want to hear and reserving their complaints for private conversations; this conforms with the Confucian tradition that correct ritual behavior requires a socially responsible person to publicly support official ideology regardless of what one thinks of it. This tradition is a useful way to keep the public in line, but it is a powerful barrier to the organization of interest groups or to the government's learning what the public really thinks (Link, 1992).

The emperors' Mandate of Heaven was endangered by a breakdown of order and prosperity. Today, both rapid economic growth and economic slump threaten those conditions. The inflation and other side effects of rapid growth can endanger the economic well-being of many groups. An economic slump endangers the prosperity of nearly all groups. Either can lead to civil unrest. China must steer a course in between, alternately heating up and cooling down the economy, with constant attention to accommodating the problems of the groups disadvantaged by each swerve. If recent decades are any indicators, it will not always be successful, and then it will seek correction. Those maneuvers, giving waxing and waning influence to different groups and factions, help hold together the political structure and dampen economic excesses. They are likely to compel China to attempt additional innovations in civil law, banking, election processes, and administrative procedures; Susan Shirk (1993:67) makes the case that some factions will continue to oppose such change. Conceivably, a combination of those innovations and social changes could transform China into a pluralist democracy, but this process would probably take a long time (Zheng, 1998). Or these innovations may join the many others China has adopted over the centuries without radically transforming its society and politics. A serious decline in the world economy stemming from the Asian economic downturn, war emanating from central Asia or Korea or the Taiwan Straits, declining agricultural output deriving from environmental degradation, a further increase in population growth and unemployment, or other such conditions may challenge order and prosperity in ways the government cannot control, bringing internal rebellion against the regime.

For the immediate future, however, most elements of China's society will be seeking stable governance. A continuance of present patterns of growth would enhance this. It can also weaken it, however, by giving greater economic power and independence to the provinces. Beijing even talks of reducing the independence of some of the coastal cities by making them "vice provinces" reporting directly to Beijing instead of to their provincial capital. Those cities and their provinces strongly resist these suggestions.

Ultimately, China's security depends on continuing high economic growth and adjusting to the social, economic, and ecological problems that growth has produced. This requires political liberalization, whatever China's cultural reservations. In 1989, during the brief period of greater press freedom that was brutally suppressed on and after June 4, the debates among intellectuals centered around the concept of "neoauthoritarianism" (Gamer, 1994). In 1998, a new liberalization debate ensued, focusing on the concept of "civil society" and concepts of the German thinker Friedrich Hayek (1994) about the importance of rule of law to protect human rights and stable governance and freedom ("spontaneous order" emerging within society from the bottom up rather than through planning by government; "Hayek's Children," 1998). China has 200,000 "mass organizations" registered with the government, representing everything from economic interests to environmental groups. In addition, Matt Forney (1998) believes there may be an equal number of nongovernmental organizations (NGOs) that have failed to register with the government that shelter abused wives, give physical therapy rehabilitation, network divorcees and homosexuals, help the poor, stand up for women and migrant workers, preserve historic homes, help evicted tenants, and provide other educational and philanthropic services. Press reports increasingly focus on bureaucratic corruption and misbehavior, environmental degradation, and other

Tiananmen Square, 1994.

ills. Internet usage is expanding rapidly, as is viewership of foreign films and television programs. Computer-based accounting makes fraud more difficult. Workers in Hunan, Jiangxi, Fujian, Sichuan, and other provinces have held strikes, while Inner Mongolia and Xinjiang have experienced periodic rioting.

These trends divide the top leadership of the party. Some of the leaders quietly encourage most of them; others find them disturbing enough to warrant greater regulation. Between 1997 and 1998 the number of armed police has nearly doubled and a new Office on Maintaining Social Stability was created. The government's treatment of those participating in the public forums and press debate about civil society, NGOs, investigative reporting, exchanging of views on the internet, and labor activities (the most controversial of these phenomena) will provide clues as to how far liberalization can proceed. So will its handling of the label "counterrevolutionary," still officially applied to the 1989 demonstrations that led to the crackdown at Tiananmen Square. The 1976 demonstrations, which helped Deng Xiaoping take control of the party, were originally labeled "counterrevolutionary"; that label was later officially removed and those demonstrations are officially

praised for the role they played in ushering in the current economic reforms. Jiang Zemin has refrained from using the word "counterrevolutionary" to describe the 1989 demonstrations, calling them instead a "political
upheaval" or "political disturbances" and even obliquely implying at Harvard University that the government may have had "shortcomings" and
"mistakes" in handling them (Forney, 1997; Erlanger, 1997). Announcing
this change in vocabulary to be official policy would encourage these lib-
eralizing trends and test the viability of China's system in the modern
world. So will a continuance of Beijing's present policy of refraining from
overt interference in Hong Kong's policy and encouraging enforcement of
intellectual property and refining contract law procedures. As Jiang said in
his New York City debate with President Bill Clinton, "China is seeking
ways to steer a balance between social stability and political reforms
needed to adapt to new challenges ("Clinton," 1997).

■ BIBLIOGRAPHY

Bachman, David M. 1991. *Bureaucracy, Economy, and Leadership in China: The
    Institutional Origins of the Great Leap Forward.* New York: Cambridge Uni-
    versity Press.
Barnet, A. Doak. 1994. *China's Far West: Four Decades of Change.* Boulder:
    Westview Press.
Baum, Richard. 1996. *Burying Mao: Chinese Politics in the Age of Deng Xiaoping.*
    Princeton: Princeton University Press.
Benton, Gregor, and Alan Hunter (eds.). 1995. *Wild Lily, Prairie Fire: China's
    Road to Democracy, Yan'an to Tian'anmen, 1942–1989.* Princeton: Princeton
    University Press.
Black, George, and Robin Munro. 1993. *Black Hands of Beijing: Lives of Defiance
    in China's Democracy Movement.* New York: Wiley.
Blecher, Marc, and Vivienne Shue. 1996. *Tethered Deer: Government and Econ-
    omy in a Chinese County.* Stanford: Stanford University Press.
Brugger, Bill, and Stephen Reglar. 1994. *Politics, Economy, and Society in Con-
    temporary China.* Stanford: Stanford University Press.
Burns, John P. 1989. *The Chinese Communist Party Nomenklatura System: A Doc-
    umentary Study of Party Control of Leadership Selection.* Armonk, NY:
    M. E. Sharpe.
Chai, Joseph C. H. 1997. *China: Transition to a Market Economy.* Oxford:
    Clarendon.
Chan, Anita, Richard Madsen, and Jonathan Unger. 1984. *Chen Village: The Re-
    cent History of a Peasant Community in Mao's China.* Berkeley: University of
    California Press.
Chan, Anita, Stanley Rosen, and Jonathan Unger (eds.). 1985. *On Socialist Democ-
    racy and the Chinese Legal System: The Li Yizhe Debates.* Armonk, NY: M. E.
    Sharpe.
Chang, David Wen-Wei. 1988. *China Under Deng Xiaoping: Political and Eco-
    nomic Reform.* New York: St. Martin's Press.
Chang, Iris. 1997. *The Rape of Nanking: The Forgotten Holocaust of World War II.*
    New York: HarperCollins.

Chang, Jung. 1991. *Wild Swans: Three Daughters of China.* New York: Simon and Schuster.

Chen, Feng. 1995. *Economic Transition and Political Legitimacy in Post-Mao China.* Albany: State University of New York Press.

Cheng, Li. 1997. *Rediscovering China: Dynamics and Dilemmas of Reform.* Lanham, MD: Rowman and Littlefield.

"Clinton and Jiang in Their Own Words." 1997. *New York Times* (October 30).

de Bary, William Theodore, Wing-Tsit Chan, and Burton Watson (eds.). 1960. *Sources of Chinese Tradition.* 2 vols. New York: Columbia University Press.

Dietrich, Craig. 1994. *People's China: A Brief History.* 2d ed. New York: Oxford University Press.

Ding, X. L. 1994. *The Decline of Communism in China: Legitimacy Crisis, 1977–1989.* Cambridge: Cambridge University Press.

Dittmer, Lowell. 1994. *China Under Reform.* Boulder: Westview Press.

Domenach, Jean-Luc. 1995. *The Origins of the Great Leap Forward: The Case of One Chinese Province.* Boulder: Westview Press.

Dreyer, June Teufel. 1996. *China's Political System: Modernization and Tradition.* 2d ed. Boston: Allyn and Bacon.

Duara, Prasenjit. 1988. *Culture, Power, and the State: Rural North China, 1900–1942.* Stanford: Stanford University Press.

Elvin, Mark 1973. *The Pattern of the Chinese Past.* Stanford: Stanford University Press.

Erlanger, Steven. 1997. "China's President Draws Applause at Harvard Talk." *New York Times* (November 2).

Eto Shinkichi, and Harold Z. Schiffrin. 1994. *China's Republican Revolution.* New York: Columbia University Press.

Fairbank, John. 1967. "The Nature of Chinese Society." Pp. 36–66 in Franz Schurmann and Orville Schell. *Imperial China: The Decline of the Last Dynasty and the Origins of Modern China, the 18th and 19th Centuries.* Vol. 1, *The China Reader.* New York: Random House.

Feng, Jicai. 1996. *Ten Years of Madness: Oral Histories of China's Cultural Revolution.* San Francisco: China Books.

Fitzgerald, C. P. 1964. *The Birth of Communist China.* Baltimore: Penguin.

Fitzgerald, John. 1996. *Awakening China: Politics, Culture, and Class in the Nationalist Revolution.* Stanford: Stanford University Press.

Forney, Matt. 1996a. "Patriot Games." *Far Eastern Economic Review* 159 (October 3):22–29.

———. 1996b. "Trials by Fire." *Far Eastern Economic Review* 159 (September 12):62–69.

———. 1997. "Hoisted on His Own Petard." *Far Eastern Economic Review* 160, no. 6 (November 13).

———. 1998. "Voice of the People." *Far Eastern Economic Review* 161, no. 19 (May 7).

Forney, Matt, and Bruce Gilley. 1996. "In Defence of Dad." *Far Eastern Economic Review* 159 (July 25):29.

Friedman, Edward. 1995. *National Identity and Democratic Prospects in Socialist China.* Armonk, NY: M. E. Sharpe.

Friedman, Edward, Paul G. Pickowicz, and Mark Selden. 1991. *Chinese Village, Socialist State.* New Haven: Yale University Press.

Fu, Zhengyuan. 1994. *Autocratic Tradition and Chinese Politics.* Cambridge: Cambridge University Press.

Gamer, Robert E. 1989. "From Zig-Zag to Confrontation at Tiananmen: Tradition and Politics in China." *University Field Staff Reports* 10 (November).

————. 1994. "Modernization and Democracy in China: Samuel P. Huntington and the 'Neo-Authoritarian' Debate." *Asian Journal of Political Science* 2, no. 1 (June):32–63.

Gates, Hill. 1996. *China's Motor: A Thousand Years of Petty Capitalism.* Ithaca: Cornell University Press.

Goodman, David S. G. 1994. *Deng Xiaoping and the Chinese Revolution: A Political Biography.* London: Routledge.

Goodman, David S. G., and Beverly Hooper (eds.). 1994. *China's Quiet Revolution: New Interactions Between State and Society.* New York: St. Martin's Press.

Goodman, David S. G., and Gerald Segal. 1994. *China Deconstructs: Politics, Trade, and Regionalism.* London: Routledge.

Gordon, Richard, and Carma Hinton. 1995. "The Gate of Heavenly Peace." Video-recording. Brookline, MA: Long Bow Group.

Grasso, June, Jay Corrin, and Michael Kort. 1996. *Modernization and Revolution in China.* Rev. ed. Armonk, NY: M. E. Sharpe.

Grousset, Rene. 1959. *The Rise and Splendour of the Chinese Empire.* Berkeley: University of California Press.

Hayek, Friedrich A. 1994. *The Road to Serfdom.* Chicago: University of Chicago Press.

"Hayek's Children." 1998. *Far Eastern Economic Review* 161, no. 20 (May 14):82.

He, Baogang. 1996. *The Democratisation of China.* London: Routledge.

Hershatter, Gail. 1986. *The Workers of Tianjin, 1900–1949.* Stanford: Stanford University Press.

Hinton, William. 1970. *Iron Oxen: A Documentary of Revolution in Chinese Farming.* New York: Vintage.

Honig, Emily. 1986. *Women in the Shanghai Cotton Mills, 1919–1949.* Stanford: Stanford University Press.

————. 1992. *Creating Chinese Ethnicity: Subei People in Shanghai, 1850–1980.* New Haven: Yale University Press.

Hook, Brian. 1996. *The Individual and the State in China.* Oxford: Oxford University Press.

Huang, Philip C. C. 1985. *The Peasant Economy and Social Change in North China.* Stanford: Stanford University Press.

————. 1990. *The Peasant Family and Rural Development in the Yangzi Delta, 1350–1988.* Stanford: Stanford University Press.

————. 1997. *Civil Justice in China: Representation and Practice in the Qing.* Stanford: Stanford University Press.

Huang, Ray. 1996. *China: A Macro History.* Armonk, NY: M. E. Sharpe.

Itoh, Fumio (ed.). 1997. *China in the Twenty-first Century: Politics, Economy, and Society.* Washington, DC: Brookings Institution.

Jing, Jun. 1997. *The Temple of Memories: History, Power, and Morality in a Chinese Village.* Stanford: Stanford University Press.

Karnow, Stanley. 1972. *Mao and China: From Revolution to Revolution.* New York: Vintage.

Kent, Ann. 1994. *Between Freedom and Subsistence: China and Human Rights.* New York: Oxford University Press.

King, Ambrose Y. C. 1991. "Kuan-hsi and Network Building: A Sociological Interpretation." *Daedalus* (spring):63–83.

Kipnis, Andrew B. 1997. *Producing Guanxi: Sentiment, Self, and Subculture in a North China Village.* Chapel Hill: Duke University Press.

Kristof, Nicholas, and Sheryl WuDunn. 1994. *China Wakes: The Struggle for the Soul of a Rising Power.* New York: Random House.

Kuhn, Philip A. 1998. "Can China Be Governed from Beijing? Reflections on Reform and Regionalism." Pp. 149–166 in Wang Gungwu and John Wong, *China's Political Economy*. Singapore: University of Singapore Press.

Kwong, Julia. 1997. *The Political Economy of Corruption in China*. Armonk, NY: M. E. Sharpe.

Li, Zhisui. 1994. *The Private Life of Chairman Mao: The Inside Story of the Man Who Made Modern China*. London: Chatto and Windus.

Lieberthal, Kenneth. 1995. *Governing China: From Revolution Through Reform*. New York: Norton.

Lieberthal, Kenneth, and Michel Oksenberg (eds.). 1988. *Policy Making in China: Leaders, Structures, and Processes*. Princeton: Princeton University Press.

Link, E. Perry, Jr. 1992. *Evening Chats in Beijing: Probing China's Predicament*. New York: W. W. Norton.

Liu, Alan P. 1996. *Mass Politics in the People's Republic: State and Society in Contemporary China*. Boulder: Westview Press.

Lubman, Stanley B. (ed.). 1996. *China's Legal Reforms*. Oxford: Oxford University Press.

Lupher, Mark. 1996. *Power Restructuring in China and Russia*. Boulder: Westview Press.

Ma, Stephen K. 1996. *Administrative Reform in Post-Mao China: Efficiency or Ethics?* Lanham, MD: University Press of America.

MacFarquar, Roderick (ed.). 1997. *The Politics of China: The Eras of Mao and Deng*. 2d ed. Cambridge: Cambridge University Press.

Mitamura, Taisuke. 1970. *Chinese Eunuchs: The Structure of Intimate Politics*. Rutland, VT: Charles E. Tuttle.

Miyazaki, Ichisada. 1981. *China's Examination Hell: The Civil Service Examinations in Imperial China*. New Haven: Yale University Press.

Nan, Lin. 1992. *The Struggle for Tiananmen: Anatomy of the 1989 Mass Movement*. New York: Praeger.

Naughton, Barry. 1995. *Growing Out of the Plan: Chinese Economic Reform, 1978–1993*. Cambridge: Cambridge University Press.

Oi, Jean C. 1989a. "Market Reforms and Corruption in Rural China." *Studies in Comparative Communism* 22 (summer–autumn):221–233.

———. 1989b. *State and Peasant in Contemporary China: The Political Economy of Village Government*. Berkeley: University of California Press.

Park, Nancy E. 1997. "Corruption in Eighteenth-Century China." *Journal of Asian Studies* 56, no. 4 (November):967–1005.

Perry, Elizabeth J. 1993. *Shanghai on Strike: The Politics of Chinese Labor*. Stanford: Stanford University Press.

Perry, Elizabeth, and Xun Li. 1996. *Proletarian Power: Shanghai in the Cultural Revolution*. Boulder: Westview Press.

Phillips, Richard T. 1996. *China Since 1911*. New York: St. Martin's Press.

Rawski, Evelyn S. 1996. "Reenvisioning the Qing: The Significance of the Qing Period in Chinese History." *Journal of Asian Studies* 55, no. 4 (November): 829–850.

Rodzinski, Witold. 1988. *The People's Republic of China: A Concise Political History*. New York: Free Press.

Rowe, William T. 1989. *Hankow: Conflict and Community in a Chinese City, 1796–1895*. Stanford: Stanford University Press.

Schoenhals, Michael (ed.). 1996. *China's Cultural Revolution, 1966–1969: Not a Dinner Party*. Armonk, NY: M. E. Sharpe.

Schram, Stuart. 1966. *Mao Tse-Tung*. New York: Simon and Schuster.

Seybolt, Peter J. 1996. *"Throwing the Emperor from His Horse" : Portrait of a Village Leader in China, 1923–1995.* Boulder: Westview Press.

Seymour, James D., and Richard Anderson. 1998. *New Ghosts, Old Ghosts: Prisons and Labor Reform Camps in China.* Armonk, NY: M. E. Sharpe.

Shambaugh, David. 1995. *Deng Xiaoping: Portrait of a Chinese Statesman.* Oxford: Oxford University Press.

Shaw, Victor. 1996. *Social Control in China: A Study of Chinese Work Units.* Westport, CT: Praeger.

Shi, Tianjian. 1997. *Political Participation in Beijing.* Cambridge: Harvard University Press.

Shih, Chih-yu. 1995. *State and Society in China's Political Economy: The Cultural Dynamics of Socialist Reform.* Boulder: Lynne Rienner Publishers.

Shirk, Susan. 1993. *The Political Logic of Economic Reform in China.* Berkeley: University of California Press.

Shue, Vivienne. 1988. *The Reach of the State: Sketches of the Chinese Body Politic.* Stanford: Stanford University Press.

Siu, Helen F. 1989. *Agents and Victims in South China: Accomplices in Rural Revolution.* New Haven: Yale University Press.

Snow, Edgar. 1938. *Red Star over China.* New York: Random House.

Soled, Debra E. (ed.). 1995. *China: A Nation in Transition.* Washington, DC: Congressional Quarterly.

Spence, Jonathan. 1990. *The Search for Modern China.* New York: W. W. Norton.

Stranahan, Patricia. 1998. *Underground: The Shanghai Communist Party and the Politics of Survival, 1927–1937.* Lanham, MD: Rowman and Littlefield.

Sullivan, Lawrence R. (ed.). 1995. *China Since Tiananmen: Political, Economic, and Social Conflicts.* Armonk, NY: M. E. Sharpe.

Teiwes, Frederick C. 1993. *Politics and Purges in China: Rectification and the Decline of Party Norms, 1950–1965.* Armonk, NY: M. E. Sharpe.

Terrill, Ross. 1992. *China in Our Time: The Epic Saga of the People's Republic, from the Communist Victory to Tiananmen Square and Beyond.* New York: Simon and Schuster.

———. 1997a. *Madame Mao: The White-Boned Demon.* Rev. ed. Stanford: Stanford University Press.

———. 1997b. *Mao: A Biography.* Rev. ed. Stanford: Stanford University Press.

Thomas, Bernard S. 1996. *Season of High Adventure: Edgar Snow in China.* Berkeley: University of California Press.

Tong, Yanqi. 1997. *Transitions from State Socialism: Economic and Political Change in China and Hungary.* Lanham, MD: Rowman and Littlefield.

Tyson, James and Ann. 1995. *Chinese Awakenings: Life Stories from the Unofficial China.* Boulder: Westview Press.

Unger, Jonathan (ed.). 1991. *The Pro-Democracy Protests in China: Reports from the Provinces.* Armonk, NY: M. E. Sharpe.

——— (ed.). 1996. *Chinese Nationalism.* Armonk, NY: M. E. Sharpe.

Walder, Andrew George. 1986. *Communist Neo-Traditionalism: Work and Authority in Chinese Industry.* Berkeley: University of California Press.

Wang, James C. F. 1992. *China: An Introduction.* 4th ed. Englewood Cliffs: Prentice Hall.

Wang, Shaoguang. 1995. *Failure of Charisma: The Cultural Revolution in Wuhan.* Oxford: Oxford University Press.

Wang, Zheng. 1993. "Three Interviews: Wang Anyi, Zhu Lin, Dai Qing." In Tami Barlow (ed.), *Gender Politics in Modern China.* Durham, NC: Duke University Press.

Wasserstrom, Jeffrey N., and Elizabeth Perry (eds.). 1994. *Popular Protest and Political Culture in Modern China*. 2d ed. Boulder: Westview Press.

Wei, Julie Lee, Ramon H. Myers, and Donald G. Gillin. 1994. *Prescriptions for Saving China: Selected Writings of Sun Yat-sen*. Stanford, CA: Hoover Institution Press.

Wei, Pan. 1998. *The Politics of Marketization in Rural China*. Lanham, MD: Rowman and Littlefield.

White, Gordon. 1993. *In Search of Civil Society: Market Reform and Social Change in Contemporary China*. Oxford: Oxford University Press.

White, Lynn T., III. 1989. *Policies of Chaos: The Organizational Causes of Violence in China's Cultural Revolution*. Princeton: Princeton University Press.

Yabuki, Susumu. 1994. *China's New Political Economy: The Giant Awakes*. Boulder: Westview Press.

Yan, Yunxiang. 1996. *The Flow of Gifts: Reciprocity and Social Networks in a Chinese Village*. Stanford: Stanford University Press.

Yang, Dali L. 1996. *Calamity and Reform in China: State, Rural Society, and Institutional Change Since the Great Leap Famine*. Stanford: Stanford University Press.

Yang, Mayfair Mei-hui. 1994. *Gifts, Favors, and Banquets: The Art of Social Relationships in China*. Ithaca: Cornell University Press.

Yang, Xiguang. 1997. *Captive Spirits: Prisoners of the Cultural Revolution*. Oxford: Oxford University Press.

Yuan, Gao. 1987. *Born Red: A Chronicle of the Cultural Revolution*. Stanford: Stanford University Press.

Zhang, Wei. 1996. *Ideology and Economic Reform Under Deng Xiaoping: 1978–1993*. New York: Columbia University.

Zheng, Shiping. 1997. *Party vs. State in Post-1949 China: The Institutional Dilemma*. Cambridge: Cambridge University Press.

Zheng, Yongnian. 1998. "Will China Become More Democratic? A Realistic View of China's Democratisation." Pp. 167–190 in Wang Gungwu and John Wong, *China's Political Economy*. Singapore: University of Singapore Press.

■ 5 ■

China's Economy

John Wong

The prior chapters have been referring to the amazing speed at which China's economy has been growing. It is now time to brief you in greater detail on the extent of that growth, what has led up to it, and whether it can be expected to continue. The easiest way to comprehend the full extent of this phenomenon is to look at several sets of rather dramatic numbers. Then we shall briefly discuss China's economic history and look at some of the problems facing its economy.

■ CHINA'S DYNAMIC GROWTH

The Chinese economy has experienced spectacular growth since it started economic reform and the open-door policy some eighteen years ago. It chalked up an average annual growth rate of 9.8 percent during 1978–1997. Growth for 1997 was 8.8 percent, with inflation (CPI, or consumer price index) at only 2.8 percent.

When an economy grows at 7 percent, it will double its gross national product (GNP, or total economic output) in about ten years. So it is not simple for a vast economy like China to achieve such high growth for a sustained period. Japan did so in the 1960s, and the newly industrializing economies of South Korea, Taiwan, Hong Kong, and Singapore did it during much of the 1970s (see Table 5.1; Chapter 6). As these economies have matured, they have found it more difficult to continue such phenomenal growth.

Beyond the rise in GNP, China's high level of economic growth is also reflected in other statistics. Thus, in 1995, China produced 1.3 billion tons of coal (the world's number-one producer), 465 million tons of grain (number one), 94 million tons of steel (second after Japan), 20 million color TV sets, 9.3 million refrigerators, and 1.5 million automobiles ("State Statistical," 1996). Of course, we must always bear in mind that

Table 5.1 Asia Pacific Economies: Performance Indicators

Country or Region	Area (thousands of sq. km)	Population, mid-1995 (millions)	GNP Per Capita, 1995 (U.S.$)	PPP Estimates of GNP Per Capita, 1994 (current international $)	Real GDP Growth (%)						Annual Export Growth (%)		Manufacturing Export as % of Total Exports, 1993	Export-GDP Ratio, 1995 (%)	Total External Debt, 1996 (U.S.$ billions)
					1960–1970	1970–1980	1980–1990	1994	1995	1996	1980–1990	1990–1995			
China	9,561	1,200.2	620	2,900	5.2	5.8	10.2	11.8	10.2	9.7	11.4	14.3	89	21.3	126.1
Japan	378	125.2	39,640	21,110	10.9	5.0	4.0	0.7	0.8	3.3	5.0	0.4	97	8.7	—
Newly industrializing economies															
South Korea	99	44.9	9,700	11,450	8.6	9.5	9.4	8.3	8.2	6.7	13.7	7.4	93	27.5	44.5
Taiwan	36	21.3	12,400	13,200	9.2	9.7	7.1	6.5	6.4	5.5	—	—	93	38.5	—
Hong Kong	1	6.2	21,990	22,950	10.0	9.3	6.9	5.5	5.0	5.1	15.4	15.3	93	120.9	—
Singapore	1	3.0	26,730	22,770	8.8	8.5	6.4	10.1	8.2	7.0	11.0	12.2	80	141.3	—
Association of Southeast Asian Nations															
Brunei	6	0.3	21,000	—	—	—	—	—	—	7.5	—	—	—	—	—
Indonesia	1,905	193.3	980	3,800	3.9	7.6	6.1	7.4	7.5	8.5	5.3	21.3	53	22.9	108.0
Malaysia	330	20.1	3,890	9,020	6.5	7.8	5.2	8.5	9.2	8.5	10.9	12.9	65	86.8	29.0
Philippines	300	68.6	1,050	2,800	5.1	6.3	1.0	4.3	5.5	5.9	2.9	10.2	76	23.6	43.5
Thailand	513	58.2	2,740	7,540	8.4	7.2	7.6	8.5	8.8	6.5	14.3	21.6	72	33.8	75.0
Vietnam	332	73.5	240	—	—	—	—	—	8.5	9.0	—	—	—	—	30.8

Sources: World Bank, various years; *The Statistical Yearbook of the Republic of China,* 1995; and Asian Development Bank, 1997.

with over 1.2 billion people, China is such a huge country that all its statistical aggregates are inevitably in jumbo numbers. For example, China is the world's largest food producer simply because China has the world's largest number of mouths to feed!

Taking a look at China's external economic activities (which involve foreign partners and hence more reliable economic data), we find equally impressive results. China's exports in 1995 amounted to U.S.$150 billion, about six times higher than those of India. This ranks China as the world's eleventh largest exporter. On the import side, China in 1995 was a market for U.S.$132 billion worth of goods ("China," 1996). China's domestic market today is actually more open than Japan's and South Korea's at their comparable stages of economic development (Lardy, 1994).

During the past few years, China has been the world's most highly favored destination of foreign investors, with the actual amount of total foreign investment steadily rising from U.S.$11 billion in 1992 to over U.S.$47 billion in 1997 (Ministry of Foreign Trade and Economics, 1996; "Investment," 1996; "Foreign," 1997). Following successful foreign exchange reform in 1994, the Chinese currency—called "the people's currency" *(renminbi)*—appreciated some 6 percent in international currency exchanges, despite the double-digit inflation that accompanied the rapid growth and has since subsided. This in turn has led to a sharp rise in China's foreign reserves, which stood at a hefty U.S.$134 billion in September 1997. With its exports exceeding its imports (by over U.S.$40 billion in 1997), those reserves continue to grow (Wong, 1997b).

Since the Eighth National People's Congress in March 1993, China has officially become a "socialist market economy," which is conceptually devoid of meaning or just as contradictory as the journalistic term "red capitalism." But such semantics are rather insignificant. China's "socialist market economy" increasingly looks like a conventional mixed economy; government controls big industries while leaving a lot of light and consumer-oriented economic activities to a competitive marketplace.

In fact, by 1994, the prices of over 90 percent of China's consumer goods, 80 percent of raw materials, and 79 percent of agricultural produce were no longer fixed by the state but set by market forces (China Price Yearbook, 1995). This, along with the rapid decline of the state sector, has actually rendered the Chinese economy more and more capitalistic in operation.[1] In the long run, China will evolve its own brand of "market socialism."

In October 1995, the Fifth Plenary Session of the Fourteenth Central Committee of the Chinese Communist Party (CCP) adopted the Ninth Five-Year Plan (1996–2000) and the Long-Term Vision of China's Economic and Social Development for 2010. It is envisaged that China's real per capita GNP (total economic output divided by the number of people) by the year 2000 will have quadrupled from the 1980 level, despite the addition of over 300 million more people. China will then have reached the moderately affluent *(xiao-kang)* level of development, for having basically eliminated poverty and satisfied the basic needs of its people (Yabuki, 1995:229–235). From 2000 to 2010, China expects to double its per capita income so that fifteen years from now it will have developed into a moderately affluent middle-income economy.[2]

Traditionally, a five-year plan has been regarded as an integral part of a command communist economy. With the growth of the market since economic reform, the Chinese economy is no longer taking to mandatory central planning. This is very much evidenced by the grossly reduced economic role of the government over the years. The share of government expenditure declined from 32 percent of gross domestic product (GDP) in 1979 to only 13 percent in 1994; and the proportion of industrial production from the state sector had similarly declined from 73 percent to 38 percent *(Statistical Yearbook of China, 1995)*. This, along with the inevitable uncertainty that accompanies a partially reformed economy, has rendered the Chinese economy basically "unplannable." At best, a five-year plan is to serve as a kind of "perspective plan," or a rough indicator of government policy direction. As a result of the Chinese economy's dynamic growth and drastic structural changes, central planning has thus become ineffective and irrelevant. The Ninth Five-Year Plan may well be the last five-year plan to be launched by the CCP (Wong, 1995c).

■ **CHINA'S TRADITIONAL MIXED ECONOMY**

China's economy has long involved, and eluded, state planning. From the earliest dynasties, it has centered around agriculture. Already during the Qin and Han dynasties (see Table 3.1) feudalism, with serfs working the land of nobles, came to an end. Until the Song dynasty, however, large landowners controlled much of the land, expecting their tenants to furnish them with labor and loyalty; this dominance receded slowly in later centuries (see Elvin, 1973). The land produced little surplus; much of this went to enrich landowners and public officials and pay taxes. Agricultural workers were also required to devote long hours in forced corvée labor to fulfill their tax obligations to the state. The state created large factories, mines, franchises, and monopolies to produce and distribute salt, porcelain, armaments, bricks, timber, coal, gold, and copper. Periodically, reforming emperors would attempt to redistribute land or regulate interest rates; those reforms were short-lived. Merchants bought and sold goods largely for sale to public officials and wealthy landowners.

The introduction of two and three crops of rice a year during the Song dynasty, made possible by new rice strains from Southeast Asia, paved the way for major changes in China's economy and society. Gradually, the large estates gave way to smaller owner-occupied plots suitable for intensive agricultural cultivation. Greater agricultural surpluses allowed for an expanded market economy (see Shiba, 1969). Already during the Song, a fifth of China's population had moved to towns and cities, which began to produce a great variety of household products on which ordinary people came to depend (see Ma Rong's discussion in Chapter 8; Chao, 1987:56). Most such goods were produced by guilds, which regulated sales and set up apprenticeships open to new residents. In the countryside, large numbers of agricultural families sent some of their members to work in cottage industries producing silk, cotton, and other textiles. Extended families organized to control land sales and associated production.

The state issued franchises to brokers, who were authorized to witness all wholesale transactions in agricultural commodities, cotton, and silk. This let them make sure that prices were not fixed by large extended families who came to control such trade in their regions and that proper taxes were paid. These brokers, the holders of franchises for state monopolies, and the public officials to whom taxes were paid were in a position to accumulate wealth along with the many new merchants and heads of extended agricultural families. They formed a market for a growing array of luxury consumer goods. They could use their surplus capital to extend credit at high interest rates or to run pawnshops, but they failed to invest in new technologies that would spur an industrial revolution. Much of the capital was distributed among merchants and officials as *renqing,* special favors to fulfill the reciprocal obligations owed family, officials, and special friends. As a result, life did not improve for most members of the populace.

Northern China had been under control of Mongols since the tenth century; they had reduced a portion of the rural populace there to virtual serfs living on the estates of Mongol nobles. Under Kublai Khan (see Chapter 3), they tried to extend this system south. By the seventeenth century, large landowning lineages were running their own schools and charities and keeping much (though gradually declining portions) of the rural populace tied to the land as virtual serfs (Elvin, 1973:235–267; Kamachi, 1990; Huang, 1985:85–87; Naquin, 1987:146). But private urban businesses kept growing, still within a controlled atmosphere. Artisans in state-directed, guild-controlled small workshops produced an array of consumer goods. They defended themselves against excessive demands from officials and fixed wages and prices (see Rowe, 1989; Fewsmith, 1983). Nicholas Kristof and Sheryl WuDunn (1994:321) cite evidence that they also discouraged the introduction of inventions that might displace their jobs. Pawnshops and brokers extended loans and credit. As Manchu conquerors founded the Qing dynasty, they kept the Confucian system in place but added an important new social and political resource, the *baojia* system. All households were grouped together under the supervision of a headperson, who reported their activities to the authorities and organized them for activities like building dikes. All members of a *bao* were responsible if one of their members committed a criminal activity.

The Europeans who entered China via the treaty ports during the nine-teenth century brought with them the industrial revolution, but not in a form that would spur widespread economic improvement. Workers left farms to work in coastal factories for low pay. Cheap new factory-made textiles competed with textiles made in villages and thus depressed local economies (Rowe, 1984; Honig, 1986). Regions came under control of warlords who absorbed *guanxi* and taxes from the new enterprises for their own use. Lineage leaders and absentee landlords often sold goods outside their regions, where they could get higher prices. Whole regions were increasingly ravaged by warfare, often paid for by high taxes on agriculture. The state granaries, established during the Song dynasty (Will, 1991) to provide peasants with grain during times of hardship, irrigation facilities, waterways, and other public services were often not maintained. Soil exhaustion, erosion, deforestation, floods, and droughts added to the problems (Perkins, 1969; Perdue, 1987). The new republic established in 1912 tried to address these problems but, as Robert Gamer discussed in Chapter 4, found it hard to take back control from regional warlords and foreign powers and in addition found itself confronting Japanese invaders.

After the 1934 Long March, Mao Zedong succeeded in organizing peasants and soldiers to take over some of the areas facing such challenges. With or without the cooperation of landlords who remained behind, they cleared their areas of enemy forces and reestablished agricultural production for local use. Once the Japanese surrendered at the end of World War II, Mao had an ideal base from which to pursue civil war. The city areas occupied by the Kuomintang were suffering from strikes, extremely high rates of inflation, and desperate shortages of agricultural and manufactured goods.

■ FROM REVOLUTION TO REFORM

When Mao Zedong formally declared the formation of the People's Republic of China on October 1, 1949, he found himself taking over an economy poorly adapted to modern life and ravaged by a long period of war and internal strife. His first order of business was to bring down inflation and reestablish production and distribution of manufactured goods (see Spence, 1990:514–519, 541–551; and Eckstein, 1977, for a clear introduction to this period). He set in place a disciplined bureaucracy and fiscal measures that curbed inflation, and he worked with factory owners whose plants he had seized to start up production. In 1953, as the economy had completed this stage of rehabilitation, the government launched the First Five-Year Plan (FFYP), which was a typical replica of the Soviet industrialization strategy under Joseph Stalin, putting strong emphasis on the development of some key capital-intensive industries like iron and steel, railroad trains, and agricultural equipment. Large state-owned industries were created throughout China to manufacture these, employing large numbers of workers who would be housed and offered social services and lifetime employment by their employers (guarantees now dubbed the "iron rice bowl").

The FFYP was a great success, with the economy growing at the average annual rate of 8.5 percent during the plan period. But Mao was unhappy. He saw inherent "contradictions" in the Soviet development strategy, which was biased against small industry and labor-intensive technology as well as rural development. In Mao's view, the Soviet development strategy was fundamentally at odds with China's basic development conditions and resource endowment because China had started off as a much more backward economy with a huge population and a lower level of technological development.

Hence Mao started to experiment with his own developmental model. At first, he returned lands to the peasants (Eckstein, 1977:66–76; Rawski, 1972). Then he began forcing them to join production teams that became linked with larger communes to farm on a great scale. The height of this collectivization came during the Great Leap Forward in 1958–1960, which called for a simultaneous development of both agriculture and industry, both small and large industry—what Mao propagandists called "walking on two legs." In the rural areas, the "people's communes" mobilized peasants en masse for large-scale capital construction projects like building dams and irrigation systems as well as making iron and steel by native methods (the so-called backyard furnaces). Not just wasteful of resources, these mass activities also resulted in a serious neglect of farming and cultivation.

The Great Leap Forward collapsed in 1959 with disastrous economic consequences, particularly a dive in agricultural production and widespread food shortages in the countryside. The other party leaders tried to return to more traditional production methods, making industrial goods in factories and producing food on collectivized farms, but Mao was undaunted and unconvinced. As Chapter 4 explained, in 1966 he tried again by starting the Great Proletarian Cultural Revolution, which he also used as a means of getting rid of his dissenting senior party colleagues, who he considered to be revisionist. Thus, millions of students were organized as Red Guards to attack the country's power structures, including government and party establishments. Virtually all senior party leaders except Zhou Enlai had been attacked or were purged at one time or another by the Red Guards.

Unlike the Great Leap Forward, the Cultural Revolution was primarily political in nature. In the economic arena, it merely emphasized certain ideological attributes in the overall economic development strategy such as "self-reliance," "ideology and politics to take precedence over economics," or "ideological incentive to be a substitute for material incentive." Consequently, the Cultural Revolution brought much less direct disruption to economic production, though it resulted in long-term economic damage to government administration and factory management (Riskin, 1987).

However, the Cultural Revolution did leave behind at least one positive legacy. Many old guards like Deng Xiaoping emerged from this nightmare to finally realize that political and social stability is most crucial to economic development, whereas incessant class struggle and ideological contention were inimical to economic growth. Thus, when Deng finally regained power, he was determined to open a new chapter in China's modern economic history, which he did by launching economic reform and the open-door policy in December 1978 (Wong, 1993).

■ THE SUCCESSFUL TRANSITION TO A MARKET ECONOMY

China's transition to the market system since the late 1970s has been immensely successful, especially compared to the dismal performance of the economic reform programs of the former Soviet Union and Eastern European countries. Numerous books and articles have been written about the different reform experiences of China and Eastern Europe.[3] Most discussion is focused on the gradual and incremental strategy adopted by China, versus the "Big Bang" approach in Eastern Europe, where major political and economic reforms were initiated side by side. It has also been argued that the initial conditions on the eve of their respective reforms were much more favorable for China than for Russia or other Eastern European countries; China was less industrialized, its economy was much less tightly planned, and its people had a long history of individual entrepreneurship (Woo, 1994).

In a more concrete sense, the Chinese success was the product of its unique reform strategies, which were carried out with great flexibility ("taking two steps forward and—if trouble—one step back") and great pragmatism. (Deng's well-known adage is, "It does not matter if the color of the cat is black or white so long as she can catch mice.") It can also be argued that China's past reform success also owes a great deal to its entrepreneurial style, as opposed to the largely bureaucratic reform process characteristic of the Eastern European approach (Wong, 1995b).

From the start, Chinese reformers recognized that there would be no textbooks to teach them how to go about "unplanning" a socialist economy. China's reform was therefore not accompanied by any detailed plans or complicated blueprints. Since reforming a socialist economy inevitably involves a great deal of risk and uncertainty, the best strategy for Chinese reformers was to grope their way around with a gradual, trial-and-error

Photo: Robert E. Gamer

An entrepreneur in Hangzhou, Zhejiang, collects scrap metal for recycling.

approach and then to exploit opportunity for reform breakthroughs, much like true entrepreneurs making their business decisions.

Furthermore, China owed its smooth progress to the right sequencing of reform policies to suit its economic and institutional conditions. Thus, China chose to start with agricultural reform first, by instituting the "household responsibility system." The communes returned the control of land to the townships, which in turn leased it to community members (see Oi, 1989b:155–226; Zhou, 1996). They would initially sell a portion of their crops to state marketing agencies, which in turn sold basic grains and oils to urban dwellers at much lower prices (with the government subsidizing the difference). The rest they could sell privately in farmers' markets. The impact was almost immediate: a rapid growth of agricultural productivity and rural incomes. This in turn led to the mushrooming of township and village enterprises (TVEs), which subsequently became the driving force for China's economic growth (see Yabuki, 1995:53–56; Zhou, 1996; Wei, 1998; Yang, 1996). Groups of workers could join together to form these enterprises, which would create consumer goods of all kinds; they shared the profits among themselves. Private individuals could also start their own enterprises, perhaps paying a "management fee" to a village head and township government, to become a "dependent firm" *(guahu)*, with *guanxi* to a nearby TVE or state enterprise. By the mid-1990s, cooperatives, village and township enterprises, and private and *guahu* firms accounted for more than half of China's output and exports (Zhou and White, 1995:474–481).

In addition, foreign corporations can become partners with local state-owned firms to create joint ventures (Yabuki, 1995:56–59; Child, 1994; Newman, 1992). The foreign investors supply capital, technology, and international marketing organizations, and the Chinese partners supply land, workers, and the ability to obtain bureaucratic clearances and other resources. Foreign firms may also establish plants and marketing operations wholly owned by themselves; by the year 2000, half of all foreign investments will be in this form ("Multinationals," 1997). Like state industries, these ventures provide their workers with housing, health care, and other amenities. Township and village enterprises, joint ventures, and wholly foreign-owned enterprises now account for a high proportion of China's economic output, though state enterprises continue to supply most non-agricultural jobs. Some townships and villages have created numerous manufacturing, transport, or other commercial enterprises, on their own or as joint ventures with city or foreign enterprises. Profits from the village and township enterprises are shared among the villagers who participate in them, and taxes from all these concerns support local housing, schools, hospitals, and other social services to people of the community (Friedman, Pickowicz, and Selden, 1991; Kelliher, 1992; Oi, 1989b; Garnaut, Guo, and Ma, 1996; Chang, 1988:126–160; Zhou and White, 1995; Zhou, 1996; Wei, 1998).

Four cities near Hong Kong—Zhuhai, Shenzhen, Shantou, and Xiamen—were designated special economic zones in 1980. Here foreign businesses

Many small enterprises bring raw and recycled materials and manufactured pieces to and from factories. Note the workers' housing and the ramp for raising cargoes to the plant.

could get land, special tax breaks, and exemption from some regulations. Taiwan already had such zones (Howell, 1993; Chang, 1988:176–195). In 1984, fourteen more coastal cities (and in 1988 Hainan Island and parts of Shandong and Liaoning provinces) were designated as areas where foreign business was welcome; those areas have since been greatly expanded. Shanghai's Pudong Special Economic Zone was created in 1990.

Over time, central planning controls have been reduced or eliminated. As urban incomes rise, the government has ended its food subsidy programs. It has allowed all types of commodities to be bought and sold without permission from central planning agencies, and taxation is largely carried out by local authorities. It is encouraging state enterprises to reform or turn themselves into joint ventures. An increasing number of foreign firms are being allowed to operate while retaining full foreign ownership.

In putting economic liberalization ahead of political liberalization, China was better able to interface political changes with economic reform. Basically, China has followed closely the East Asian tradition of "economic growth first and political changes later" (see Wade, 1990 for an overview of this approach). Successful economic reform is used to boost the legitimacy of the political leadership, which is in turn under strong pressures to achieve good economic performance. In contrast, Russia put glasnost (political reform) before perestroika (economic reform). As a result, its vital reform measures were delayed or bogged down by politics and polemics.

However, there are disadvantages to the Chinese approach. For one thing, the Chinese way of reform, based on its weak institutional and legal framework, is apt to produce numerous rent-seeking activities and open corruption, diverting investment capital into the pockets of landlords, property speculators, and politicians (Wong, 1994). Another obvious drawback is that China's piecemeal approach has given rise to a half-reformed economy. The township and village enterprises and joint ventures have shifted control to local and provincial levels. Businesses in wealthy coastal provinces sometimes buy so much of scarce commodities like cotton that they leave shortages in inland provinces. It is harder for central authorities to slow down investment when it increases so rapidly that inflation becomes excessive. The central government still finds itself giving heavy financial support to inefficient state industries that generate employment and produce heavy equipment or household necessities that are vital but unprofitable.

The reforms did not bring free enterprise to China. Outside special economic zones, land cannot be bought and sold. Multinational corporations cannot do business in China except through a joint venture with local partners or through extensive and continual bargaining with local officials. They can buy land only in designated zones. Private, local family businesses are limited in the number of employees they can hire, the size of bank loans they can get, and the trade exhibitions they can attend, and they pay higher taxes and interest; to avoid this, they must bring local officials into their management structure by paying to become a *guahu*. Business contracts are frequently revised and overridden by bureaucrats even after they are signed. All these practices have long historical precedents. China's leaders must accommodate the Communist Party's membership (which nearly doubled during the Cultural Revolution and is still loaded with former Red Guards who have little education), the People's Liberation Army, bureaucracies ranging from Beijing to townships everywhere, farmers, urban workers, students, and intellectuals. These realities do not always square well with the modern world.

The Chinese strategy has so far worked well in reforming the agricultural and rural sector. But many critical macroeconomic reform measures like taxation, banking, finance, and foreign exchange do not effectively lend themselves to the gradualist approach by experimentation. All these reform measures are interrelated, and they have to be dealt with in one blow rather than the piecemeal strategy of the earlier phase. The recognition of this fact actually paved the way for the Third Party Plenum in November 1993 to adopt the fifty-article "Decision" for a comprehensive reform of China's economic structure, which is, in a way, the Chinese equivalent of the "Big Bang" approach to economic reform (Yabuki, 1995: 235–237). In the next section, we discuss whether a comprehensive approach to such reforms is possible.

In summary, it may be argued that China's economic reform has passed its easy "honeymoon" phase, where new development initiatives seemed to find continuous new markets open for them. The next phase of reform will be "technically, politically and socially more difficult to manage," as the World Bank chief in Beijing put it.[4]

■ IS HIGH GROWTH SUSTAINABLE?

It is clear that China has become the world's most successful "transitional economy" in terms of both dynamic growth and the reform of its economic systems. Indeed, China's economic reform has gone so far that the process cannot be reversed regardless of the outcome of the post-Deng power struggle. The next question can then be posed: Is China's dynamic economic growth sustainable?

To begin with, it is not possible for any economy to repeat a double-digit rate of growth year after year without getting overheated or running into physical and economic bottlenecks. But considering the historical pattern and structural conditions of China's past economic growth, we can easily be optimistic about its future growth potential.

Following four consecutive years of double-digit rates of growth during 1992–1995, the Chinese economy became overheated, with inflation (measured by the consumer price index) rising to a 27 percent record high in 1994 and then down to 14.8 percent in mid-1995. Since late 1995, Vice Premier Zhu Rongji, dubbed China's "economic czar," was charged with the task of bringing down the rampant inflation. Zhu introduced a number of tough macroeconomic stabilization measures, including a credit squeeze and the reimposition of control on prices of certain essential commodities. By November 1997, inflation was brought down to 1.1 percent, with only a small reduction in economic growth, which was still 9 percent for 1997 (Wong, 1997a). In common economic parlance, the Chinese economy has achieved a "soft landing." But the upshot serves to show that the Chinese economy has inherent high growth features; it keeps growing even when brakes are applied. Why?

It may be remembered that even before the reform, the Chinese economy grew at a rather fast rate of 6 percent (during 1952–1978), despite all its inherent socialist economic inefficiencies and the disruptions caused by Mao's political campaigns.[5] The reform has set free the latent dynamic economic and social forces to fuel China's further economic growth. This expansion can be easily analyzed from both demand and supply sides. To give a technical explanation, China's high economic growth on the demand side stems from its high levels of domestic investment, which are matched by equally high levels of domestic savings. According to the Asian Development Bank, China's average gross domestic investment between 1981 and 1990, when China had 13.4 percent growth, was 30.5 percent of its GDP, with its average gross domestic savings at 30.8 percent; its total gross domestic investment was 43.5 percent and gross domestic savings 41.5 percent, among the highest in the world (Asian Development Bank, 1996). The recent high growth of Hong Kong, Taiwan, South Korea, and Singapore was similarly due to their high levels of savings and investment.

China has enormous need for infrastructural investment in transportation, communications, ports, airports, and electric power plants. It is planning to build sixty new airports and upgrade twenty-five existing ones. Guangdong province alone has six new airports, either just completed or under construction. The pace of building may be moving such regions from shortages to surplus capacity, whereas other regions continue to live with inadequate infrastructure.

Apart from investment, China's future economic growth can also be boosted by rising consumption. With a moderately affluent middle class of nearly 100 million, mainly in urban areas and numerous small towns, China's appetite for consumption goods is enormous. In the rural areas, millions of peasants are buying basic household consumer durables like TVs and stereos.

Viewed from the supply side, China's economic growth can also be sustained on its own by a growing labor force and increasing productivity. As has happened already to Japan and South Korea, growth in productivity

Carrying merchandise to the retail store.

is associated with the shift of labor from low-productivity agriculture to high-productivity manufacturing. In China, the rural sector is a huge reservoir of millions of underemployed laborers (commonly known among economists as "rural disguised unemployment"). Many of these are supplying labor to fuel the continuing dynamic expansion of the TVEs in recent years and their contribution to overall growth (Wong, Ma, and Yang, 1995; Zhou, 1996; Wei, 1998).

We can, therefore, be justifiably optimistic about the overall growth prospects of China's economy over the medium and long run. Although its economy may well drop below 8 percent, it should be able to retain high levels of growth (Perkins, 1996; Wong, 1998).

The Chinese economy is in many ways developing in a manner similar to the past growth pattern of the East Asian newly industrializing economies. But unlike them, China is a vast country with a huge resource base and a huge domestic market. China has virtually the whole continent to itself to develop. At present, most growth has been concentrated on the coastal region and is yet to spread out to the vast interior. Therefore, it will take a long time for China to exhaust its total development potential.

In the long run, the Chinese economy has to grow mainly on domestic demand, quite unlike its smaller Asian neighbors, whose economic growth has to be mainly propelled by export growth or external demand. Since economic reform began in 1978, China's exports have been growing at the average annual rate of 17 percent. The world market simply cannot continue to absorb such an onslaught of export goods. But it is fortunate for China that its sheer size and diversity can provide sufficient internal dynamics to generate its own growth in the long run.

China's size is important in weathering the currency speculation that hit East and Southeast Asia in 1997. In July 1997 the value of currencies in Southeast Asia fell drastically, promoting a sharp economic downturn in the region. Seven months later the Thai baht or Indonesian rupiah would exchange for only a fifth as many U.S. dollars as before, radically raising the cost of imports or travel abroad. China and Hong Kong took measures to hold the value of their currency firm against the dollar. Only 8 percent of China's manufactures are exported or imported, but half of its exports go to Southeast Asian and, especially, East Asian countries, and much of China's economic growth has been in the export sector ("East Asia's," 1988). Half of its tourists and 80 percent of its foreign investment derive from there as well. In 1997, China's exports rose 21 percent but during the first five months of 1998 they rose only 8.6 percent over the prior year and in May declined. Foreign investment dropped by about a third (Kwang, 1998; Wong, 1998:7). Furthermore, domestic demand was soft due to overproduction of household appliances, electronics, clothing, and other consumer goods, and layoffs in state industry and bureaucracy because of Finance Minister Zhu Rongji's economic reforms. Still, during the first half of 1997 China's GDP rose 7.1 percent.

Though China cannot ignore uncertainties about future growth in the region, it does have a large internal market. It also has a consistently favorable trade balance, and its foreign reserves (at U.S.$140 billion in 1998, up from U.S.$120 billion in 1997) are the second highest in the world after Japan. Though its external debt is also about U.S.$130 billion, plus U.S.$50 billion in foreign "investments" that must be repaid, much of this is in long-term loans (in contrast, for example, to Indonesia, whose short-term debt is twice as high as its foreign exchange reserves ["On the Rocks," 1998]). It has needed to use less than 10 percent of its export earnings to repay this debt. Even with the decline in exports, this still gives it extensive resources for repayment. Since its currency is not fully convertible on international markets speculators cannot acquire enough of it to radically affect its value. Hong Kong (whose currency remains pegged to the U.S. dollar) has an additional U.S.$94 billion in foreign reserves; Chinese citizens have U.S.$665 billion in savings ("When Will," 1998). Furthermore, though most Chinese banks have lent large amounts of money to state industries unable to repay them, the economy remains controlled enough that it would be hard for individual investors to withdraw all their deposits simultaneously (as happens during banking panics in some countries). But the decline in value of currencies in neighboring states makes their textiles, shoes, and low-level electronics less expensive on international markets at a time when both world and domestic demand are declining. For example, 90 percent of China's city dwellers now own color TVs and washing machines (Yatsko, 1998). If China sustains the value of the *renminbi* while neighboring countries' currencies stay devalued, its exports will sell abroad for higher prices, making it harder for them to compete and tempting new foreign investments toward sites outside China. That competition could become fierce and intensifies the need to develop high-technology, less labor-intensive production.

■ OVERCOMING PROBLEMS AND CONSTRAINTS

The favorable pro-growth scenario described previously has to be qualified by two considerations. First, China's population growth has been slowing down considerably from the average annual rate of 1.5 percent during 1980–1990 to 1.2 percent during 1990–1994, as a result of the successful implementation of its "one-child policy" (discussed in Chapter 8). Accordingly, China's total fertility rate came down from 2.5 in 1980 to 1.9 in 1994, which is slightly below the replacement level of fertility (World Bank, 1996). This also means that China's population is not just slowing down in growth but could eventually reach zero growth after a certain time lag. But before this, the population will be rapidly aging, soon after the turn of this century. This will change its labor force structure and pose an ultimate constraint on the continuing development of labor-intensive industry in the longer run.

Second, as Table 5.2 shows, China's human resource development is among the weakest in East Asia. Only 2 percent of the relevant age group in China are receiving tertiary education compared to 42 percent in Korea

Table 5.2 Asia Pacific Economies: Social Indicators

| Country or Region | GNP Per Capita, 1995 (U.S.$) | Total Fertility Rate, 1995 (%) | Life Expectancy at Birth, 1995 (years) | Infant Mortality Rate, 1995 (per 1,000 births) | Population Per Doctor, 1993 | Adult Illiteracy, 1995 (%) | Percentage of Age Group Enrolled in Education, 1993 | | | Human Development Index, 1994[a] | |
							Primary (male)	Secondary (male)	Tertiary (all)	HDI[a]	World Ranking
China	620	1.9	69	34	645	19	120	60	4	0.626	108
Japan	39,640	1.5	80	4	609	5	102	95	30	0.940	7
Newly industrializing economies											
South Korea	9,700	1.8	72	10	855	5	100	93	48	0.890	32
Taiwan	12,400	1.5	74	5	802	8	102	95	45	—	—
Hong Kong	22,990	1.2	79	5	845	8	—	—	21	0.914	22
Singapore	26,730	1.7	76	4	722	9	—	—	30	0.900	26
Association of Southeast Asian Nations											
Brunei	21,000	—	—	—	—	—	—	—	—	—	—
Indonesia	980	2.7	64	51	7,028	16	116	48	10	0.668	99
Malaysia	3,890	3.4	71	12	2,302	17	93	56	—	0.832	60
Philippines	1,050	3.7	66	39	9,689	5	—	—	26	0.672	98
Thailand	2,410	2.0	69	36	4,420	6	98	38	19	0.833	59
Vietnam	240	3.1	68	41	2,491	6	—	—	2	0.557	121
Average of low-income countries	430	3.2	63	59	—	34	112	—	—	—	—
Average of middle-income countries	2,390	3.0	68	39	—	18	105	64	—	—	—

Sources: World Bank, 1997; Asian Development Bank, 1996; Asian Development Bank, 1994; *Taiwan Statistical Data Book 1997*; Singapore, 1997; Hong Kong, 1997.

Note: a. Human development index combines life expectancy, educational attainment, and income indicators to give a composite measure of human development.

and 45 percent in Taiwan. About two-thirds of the 220,000 or so students sent abroad for studies have not returned to China. This will in time constrain attempts to restructure and upgrade the Chinese economy into more skill-intensive and higher value-added activities. In short, China's human resource gaps, in quantitative as well as in qualitative terms, could well operate to moderate its long-term growth potential (see Watson, 1992). Of greater importance, China's pattern of growth in the longer term will critically depend on how China comes to grips with a number of specific problems and constraints.

□ Constraints from Unfinished Reform

In 1994 China carried out a comprehensive package of economic reform—an outgrowth of the 1993 Third Party Plenum discussed earlier in this chapter. In the areas of taxation and foreign exchange, the reform has been quite successful. The tax reform, aimed at unifying the tax code and simplifying the tax system and administration, came into effect on January 1, 1994.

It seems strange that a country as big as China has never had a nationwide tax administration; the bulk of its tax collection has been delegated to local governments. Thus the 1994 tax reform, by separating the tax authority between central and local governments, marks a truly significant move for Beijing. Henceforth, a new revenue-sharing arrangement between the central and local governments is to replace the complex contract-based intergovernmental revenue system, historically called "tax farming" (Ma and Luo, 1994). Whether the reform can significantly increase central tax revenues remains to be seen. If they do not increase, it will be hard for the government to support social safety net programs, reform of state initiatives, unemployment insurance, and efforts to bolster sags in the economy.

The currency exchange reform started in 1994 with unification of the dual exchange rate system that had operated from 1986 to 1993. During that period China had two currencies—foreign exchange certificates (FECs) for use by foreigners and for transactions to convert foreign currencies into Chinese currency, and *renminbi* for doing business within China. Since *renminbi* could not be converted on international exchanges, in a growing currency black market its value began to diverge sharply from that of FECs (which could be exchanged for foreign currency only through Chinese government banks at rates artificially set by them); though the two currencies officially had the same value, black marketeers operating on street corners and in back rooms could trade many *renminbi* for one FEC, showing that foreign currency was worth more to Chinese traders than the government-created exchange rate reflected. This disadvantaged businesses that had to operate on regulated current accounts (for day-to-day transactions) and capital accounts (for longer-term investments) using the legal foreign exchange currency; competitors who had connections that let them disguise their transactions more easily than was possible for most foreign investors could use *renminbi* and the black market to purchase many times more goods for the same amount of foreign exchange. That is because the black market rate of *renminbi* could "float" to the level that Chinese currency was actually worth in international trade. The exchange reform eliminated the FECs; *renminbi* now convert into foreign currencies through "managed floats." This change paves the way for China to target full *renminbi* convertibility (also free exchange on capital accounts) by the year 2000. Recently, there were official hints that China would step up the final process in order to support its entry into the World Trade Organization (WTO), though the Southeast Asian currency speculation problems could slow that down (Yee and Shan, 1996).

Progress on reforming China's 300,000 state-owned enterprises (SOEs) and the financial sector is still falling short of targets. Efforts to reform state enterprises were initially directed at improving their efficiency by restructuring management, including measures to define enterprise rights under law and to free management from government supervision. This culminated in the promulgation on July 1, 1994, of a new Company Law, which was supposed to provide the needed legal framework for the formation of "shareholding companies," which is the Chinese method of privatization.

However, progress has been very slow. A handful of state enterprises are run efficiently; the majority of them are heavily debt-ridden and cannot be easily converted into shareholding companies until they have gone through drastic financial restructuring and recapitalization. Furthermore, mere focus on ownership reform cannot ensure the efficiency and profitability of state enterprises, which eventually have to go through a fundamental management reform in order to learn how to behave like true profit-maximizing enterprises. In other words, state enterprises would ultimately have to operate under real budget constraints. Hopelessly unprofitable state enterprises would have to be shut down. China passed a bankruptcy law as early as 1986, but the government has been extremely reluctant to allow the ailing state enterprises to fold up for fear of social instability that would result from the loss of large numbers of jobs.

The problem of reforming state enterprises in all transitional economies is enormously complicated, involving larger political and social issues. For China, in particular, its large state enterprises exist like mini-welfare states, whose main objective is not confined to making profits but also includes taking care of such social responsibilities as housing, education, health care, and other services for their workers on behalf of local governments. Effective reform of state enterprises must, therefore, start with decoupling their production from their nonproduction social functions. This would ultimately entail breaking the so-called three irons—iron rice bowl, iron job position, and iron wages—which are deep-rooted social institutions, politically difficult to uproot. Thus, prior to the provision of a new social safety net or social security reform, any serious attempt to reform state enterprises by subjecting them to the necessary hard budget constraints could run the risk of throwing millions of redundant workers into the street along with creating social unrest (see Walder, 1986; Wu, 1996). By 1998, 12 million urban workers were already unemployed; only half had found new jobs. In 1998, those figures could double (Wong, 1997a:10, 1998:14; Yatsko and Forney, 1998:46; "East Asia's," 1998:37).

Beijing's latest strategy for reform of state enterprises is *zhua-da fang-xiao* (free smaller state enterprises first while hanging on to large ones). By avoiding the political risks of tackling the large state enterprises, the government is actually not attacking the main problem. A large number of state enterprises report losses year after year. In the first half of 1996, for instance, 49 percent of China's industrial state enterprises were reported to be in the red.[6] This means that the state banks had to help the ailing state enterprises, leading to the accumulation of many bad loans (Solinger, 1993; Forney, 1996). China's government vows not to continue doing that—a vow hard to keep (White, 1993:121–146). Nine-tenths of the U.S.$600 billion of bank loans outstanding in China, equivalent to 70 percent of GDP, are to state industry; half or more will never be repaid ("The Death," 1997; "East Asia's," 1998). And the problem of bad debts hinders banking reform in China.

China's TVEs, which have generated much of the growth and account for 30 percent of industrial output, also need reform. The low-value-added, labor-intensive items they make now face stiff competition from better-made goods, and these firms do not have the capital or skills to incorporate new technology. Their average growth of 30 percent a year had dropped to 12 percent in 1997 (Yatsko, 1998:52). The government is encouraging privatization of those that cannot compete.

From the standpoint of macro economic management, banking reform constitutes the most vital component of the whole economic reform package (see Huang, 1996; Kam, 1995). For the proper operation of the socialist market economy, China needs a proper financial framework for its monetary policy. In other words, the government must be able to use such key monetary instruments as money supply and interest rates in a functioning financial system for maintaining macroeconomic stabilization.

Prior to economic reform, China operated with a single bank. Since 1984 it has evolved a two-tier banking system: The People's Bank of China (PBC) became the country's central bank, and policy and commercial lending were assigned to four specialized state banks—the Bank of China, the Industrial and Commercial Bank of China, the People's Construction Bank of China, and the Agricultural Bank of China. The annual credit plan was the cornerstone of China's monetary policy; extension of credit was monopolized by these four institutions.

As economic reform took hold and the role of the market expanded, the shortcomings of such an administratively controlled annual credit plan, both in its formulation and implementation, became increasingly apparent. Many businesses in many parts of the country needed credit. When a bank gave too many bad loans, it did not have enough money left for worthy recipients who might be better able to repay. In fact, the lack of a market-based monetary policy tool has been the root cause of the violent fluctuation of the Chinese economy prior to 1993. Hence the need for banking reform.

The main thrust of the latest banking reform aims at (1) setting up a strong and independent central bank, whose primary responsibility is to maintain monetary and exchange rate stability, and (2) letting the four state-owned specialized banks operate on a purely commercial basis, leaving "policy lending" (i.e., loans of noncommercial nature) to three newly created "policy banks"—the State Development Bank, the Export and Import Bank, and the Agricultural Development Bank.

The passing of the Central Bank Act in 1994 provided the legal basis for the People's Bank of China to operate as the country's central bank, which is now supposed to have operational autonomy for conducting monetary policy. But doubt remains whether the PBC has acquired real independence to operate as a truly central bank. It is even more doubtful that the specialized banks have come near to operating like true commercial banks because most of their loans are still not based on commercial assessment, and the interest rates are still not determined by market forces. A principal concern is their huge amount of nonperforming loans (called "triangular debt") contracted by state enterprises. According to *Asia Times,* "By some estimates, about 70 percent of loans by state banks, to both industrial and other enterprises, are irrecoverable" ("How to Save," 1996). According to Standard and Poor's, those bad loans total 60 percent of GDP ("East Asia's," 1998:37). In this way, the economic woes of the near-bankrupt state enterprises translate into a major problem for the banks.

Because the crucial banking and state enterprise reforms (which are actually interdependent) have failed to achieve important breakthroughs, the government's prime objective of establishing a market-based macroeconomic management system remains unfulfilled (Wong, 1995a). This means that the Chinese economy, without the usual built-in macroeconomic stabilizers, will continue to experience violent fluctuation. Until the transition to a full market economy is completed, China will suffer from the inefficiency of a partially reformed economy.

☐ Institutional Constraints

The major challenge faced by China today is not just to *transform* its economic system but also to *modernize* its institutional structure. China's existing institutional setup and political system were developed primarily to serve the socialist economy based on central planning and dominated by the CCP. They are clearly inappropriate for a market economy.

Liberal detractors would hastily jump to the conclusion that for political reform China must necessarily call for a Western style of democracy. This is clearly unwarranted in the East Asian tradition, which has followed instead the sequence of "development first, democratization later." Furthermore, such drastic political transformation as full democratization for a big and diverse country like China is plainly unrealistic at the present stage: it will simply bring more chaos *(luan)* to China, if the democracy experiments in several Asian countries can serve as a guide. Nor will political democracy necessarily facilitate China's present economic growth and social progress. It is to be remembered that South Korea's industrial takeoff took place under a military dictatorship, Taiwan's under martial law, and Hong Kong's under colonial rule (see Chapter 6).

At the same time, however, a Marxist-Leninist state is fundamentally incompatible with a functioning market system. Market forces, operating on their own, only recognize economic signals, not the "Cardinal Principles" of the CCP dedicated to maintaining central power and guaranteeing all citizens economic rights. Either the free market process of economic development would eventually undermine the Marxist-Leninist state, or the rigid Marxist-Leninist system would resist crucial changes by giving way to a half-reformed market system, with all its inefficiencies we have just been discussing. In either case, the CCP must adapt and change.

Assuming that no ruling party is willing to share power on its own volition, the most formidable challenge for the CCP is how to skillfully manage institutional changes without losing its total political legitimacy. On the one hand, the party has to step up institutional and political reform to facilitate the development of the socialist market economy; but on the other, it has to ensure that those changes will not undermine its own rule. This is a highly delicate business, which will test the true statecraft of the future CCP leadership.

To retain power, the CCP obviously has to renew itself by attracting more younger and better-educated members. This would compromise the party's past emphasis for its membership on the class background of workers and peasants, rather than on their skills and education. In the longer run, it has got to transform itself into a modern, development-oriented political organization based on meritocracy rather than ideological dogma. An authoritarian regime dominated by a ruling party with a modern and pragmatic outlook can still foster economic development, but one with a rigid ideology cannot.

It is now clear that rapid economic and social changes in China have already brought about a decay in the CCP's local organizations, especially in the rural areas. This was inevitable once it had lost its original revolutionary ideological fervor amid the spread of prosperity and materialism. One possible scenario for the future is that after the passing of the old guard, the CCP might well split into factions. With China getting more developed and the population better educated, some CCP factions may even assume a new label such as social democrats.

For the likely shape of China's future political system, China scholars foresee the weakening of the party's authority along with the gradual erosion of the state's direct control over the economy and society. In the longer run, although the CCP will continue to be an important institution, it is not likely to retain its dominance over the overall political system. Rather, the party, the military, the provincial and municipal bureaucracies, the people's assemblies, and the central economic bureaucracies will all compete in a largely peaceful manner for supremacy. As Michel Oksenberg says, "None of these institutions is likely to emerge as a clear victor, resulting in a complex system of several overlapping yet competing centers of power, with the relative power of each institution varying over time and from place to place" (1996:2).

Whatever is the more likely scenario, political pluralism is bound to follow economic development. In the short run, however, the CCP cannot renounce its Marxist doctrines without immediately losing its own legitimacy, as happened in Eastern Europe. Therefore, it has to be extremely cautious in its political reform; initially perhaps it will focus on improving the system of government such as separating the party from the government, which in turn will pave the way for the establishment of a professional civil service. It should also reform its present cadre system, with professionals and technocrats gradually replacing the old "socialist bureaucrats," who are appointed by the CCP's organization department, not by open recruitment based on competition. The role played by technocrats in managing successful economic development in the East Asian newly industrializing economies is well known to the Chinese leadership, which has also started to stress the importance of civil service reform.

All these political reforms may weaken the CCP's monopoly on power. But at the same time, it is buying time as the resultant improvement in administrative efficiency and government performance will help it stay in power. The potential gain in popularity as a successful modernizer can offset the loss of its old legitimacy. In the process, much still depends on whether or not the top leadership retains its political skills in managing these changes.

For the immediate future, however, the other aspects of institutional changes involving legal reform are more urgently needed. All modern states have clear rules and regulations to set out the limits of authority and define the general behavior of market participants. The absence of the rule of law, due to the Chinese tradition of "rule of man," is the weakest link in the Chinese political system. Needless to say, a strong and transparent legal framework can definitely promote business and foreign investment by reducing transaction costs in the form of rent-seeking and corruption activities. So long as businesses must pay bribes to ensure that contractual obligations are met and cannot take cases to an impartial court when contractual obligations are broken, doing business in China remains highly risky.

Since economic reform, China has enacted over 160 new laws, over half of which are related to commerce. But legal reform goes beyond the simple process of making laws or setting up law courts. It has to build up an effective legal infrastructure with an independent judiciary that is free from control by the party (see Keith, 1994). Furthermore, China, as primarily a Confucian state with no Greco-Roman legal traditions, needs to undertake greater efforts to foster the necessary "legal culture."

Again, legal reform is not without its political risk to the CCP. The legal reform could lead to the weakening of the communist rule because it would mean that the party could no longer remain above the law. The climax of the legal reform will be reached when the CCP agrees to write a new constitution for China that removes all its special privileges. All in all, political and institutional changes will hasten the emergence of some kind of democracy in China.

☐ Social Constraints

As Chapters 1 and 4 indicated, the cultural tradition of Confucianism creates a "savings ethic," a "learning ethic," a "work ethic," cooperation among entrepreneurs and public officials, and other behavior patterns that can foster economic growth (Wong, 1996). Other newly industrializing economies of Asia that share this culture—Taiwan, South Korea, Hong Kong, and Singapore—have demonstrated an inherent social capability to sustain economic development (see Skoggard, 1996). These precedents should bode well for China's economic development as well.

However, China's rapid economic growth in recent years has given rise to a lot of negative social externalities, from rising social expectations and widespread social envy to rising crime, which have constantly worried the Chinese leadership. A sense of a general "moral crisis" is sweeping China. To be sure, such a moral crisis is also prevalent (or actually worse) in Russia and other Eastern European countries. How far does it represent a transitional phenomenon? Will it go away by itself once these socialist countries have completed their economic and social transitions?

Most China experts take the view that many of those negative social externalities may create frictions in the economic growth process, but they will not, on their own, be serious enough to disrupt the process. The

Chinese authorities understandably place a high priority on maintaining social order, which is crucial for economic growth and economic reform. It is often the case that the best way to deal with the by-products of rapid economic growth is to continue with rapid economic growth, which will generate more resources to deal with social problems.

For example, take the case of employment. Between 1978 and 1993, China's labor force increased by 213 million, with 75 percent employed in manufacturing and services. As a result of high economic growth since the reform, a majority of all new entrants into the labor force found productive employment outside agriculture. Now state enterprises are laying off more urban workers, and some 15 percent of the rural populace— perhaps 150 million people—are experiencing redundancy or "disguised unemployment," contributing to the 70 million "floating population" in China's cities (only 20 percent of whom have jobs) discussed in Chapter 8. If the Chinese economy continues to grow at 8 percent or 9 percent a year, problems like unemployment would be taken care of. If it does not, with the general slowdown in Asia's economy, unemployment could rise to as high as 20 percent (Wong, 1997a:11–13; Yatsko and Forney, 1998:46).

However, there are other critical problems that will create strains in Chinese society even with continuing high economic growth. First, the leadership must mobilize all its institutional resources to combat corruption, which is rampant in China today. Economic reform in all transitional economies generates opportunities for extortion, profiteering, and open graft and corruption. The problem is getting so serious that it threatens to undermine the social fabric of the country as well as the moral authority of the CCP. So far there has been a lot of rhetoric about corruption from the Chinese leaders, who have yet to demonstrate a determined political will to tackle this issue. The Chen Xitong affair, in which a top official (the mayor of Beijing) was removed for corruption, is more the outcome of high-level power struggle than a deliberate attempt by the leadership to crack down on widespread corrupt practices of its high officials.[7]

Municipalities, townships, and provinces all over China are raising a lot of revenue by selling land in special economic zones, operating joint ventures, collecting income taxes, setting up dummy corporations in Hong Kong, cooperating with smugglers, collecting port tariffs, and regulating the economy. They still depend on the central government to conduct interprovincial commerce, keep order, and run many governmental operations, which offers tremendous opportunities for those with special *guanxi* relationships to reward one another (see Oi, 1989a; Myers, 1989). These rewards help explain why a good deal of the tax money the provinces are supposed to be collecting for the central government never reaches Beijing.

More than a mere social evil, corruption hampers economic growth by increasing transaction costs and reducing efficiency. Rampant corruption also slows trade and investment. *Guanxi* retards business. Any contract provision can be circumvented by a bribe; the courts cannot be counted on to give restitution in the case of fraud or breach of contract. Intellectual property rights cannot be guaranteed for foreign enterprises that bring in patented technology (Alford, 1995; Murphy, 1996); counterfeit merchandise abounds. Investment capital gets diverted into unproductive uses, like imported Mercedes for officials to ride around in. As a result, governments do not have predictable revenues to carry out projects and pay back loans, and projects remain unfinished or go way over budget. Hong Kong, Taiwan, Korea, and Singapore have all made serious attempts to tackle the problem of corruption. China too must manage this problem properly and take care that it does not creep too deeply into Hong Kong now that it is a part of China.

A second macro social issue with serious economic and political consequences is the growing income disparity between the fast-growing coastal zones and the backward interior provinces, between urban and rural areas, or between industrial and agricultural sectors. The recent Ninth Five-Year Plan (1996–2000) has emphasized the need for a new development strategy to narrow income gaps in China, indicating that Beijing can no longer shrug off this problem. The percentage of the population earning less than U.S.$0.60 a day has declined from over 25 percent in 1978 to 7 percent. But a fourth of the populace—many, but by no means all, living in inland provinces—earn less than U.S.$1 a day (Lyons, 1994).

Many now support themselves from small sidewalk stalls.
The individuals in this photograph repair shoes and umbrellas.

Photo: Robert E. Gamer

*Being self-employed or working for a smaller enterprise can mean
the loss of day care facilities like this, offered by many larger employers.*

Underlying the regional development gaps is the deep-rooted inter-regional political rivalry and the political tension between the center and provinces. Both pose a threat to China's national unity. Some provinces have, from time to time, undertaken unilateral measures to protect their vested economic interests by obstructing the flow of resources (e.g., inter-provincial "trade wars"), and this affects the efficient operation of the Chinese economy as a single market.[8] When coastal provinces can pay more for commodities than the central government, they can corner the market and deprive other provinces of these goods (Yabuki, 1995:31–40; Shirk, 1993:144). Suffice it to say that China needs greater political and economic integration to boost its economic growth, which in turn depends on closing the regional development gaps.

Third, China has to step up the social security reform, which was actually one of the unfulfilled key areas in China's 1994 reform package. As pointed out earlier, the crucial state enterprise reform could not take off because of the lack of a new social safety net. China's old social security system is based on the *danwei* (work unit), which was developed for the highly regulated society under Mao's time (see Walder, 1986; Oi, 1989b; and Chan, Madsen, and Unger, 1984, for excellent closeup studies of these units). But the reform has since eroded the *danwei* system before a new social security system to suit the operation of market economy is in place. Millions of workers now work for township and village enterprises that do not offer full housing, health care, pensions, day care, and other employee benefits. A new social security system is needed to deal with such problems as labor mobility, the aging population, and so on. The government is experimenting with private insurance schemes and other innovative strategies to fill this gap (Nann, 1995; Forney and Yatsko, 1997). Few people have adequate income or savings to pay for these necessities themselves. Municipalities, townships, and other units of government are spending increasing amounts on building and subsidizing the operation of these facilities.

☐ Resource Constraints

China is a huge country with a vast and diverse natural resource base, but it also has a population of 1.2 billion. Continuing economic growth in the future will certainly stretch China's natural resources to their limits, giving rise to acute supply and demand imbalances.

Agriculture is now worrying the Chinese leadership, as a result of a 2.6 percent drop in grain production in 1994. Is China "starting to lose the capacity to feed itself," as the American environmentalist Lester Brown recently warned?[9] There are, at present, no concrete signs that China is heading for a full-blown food crisis. Following Brown's sensational statement, Chinese specialists have recently reassessed China's agricultural resource base and its technological foundation and concluded that by and large China will be able to feed itself (Wong, 1995d). However, the Chinese government still has cause for real concern over the current state of Chinese agriculture, not least because of rising peasant discontent.[10]

Because China is the world's largest producer of grain, it is correct to say that China's food problem can also become a world food problem. If China were to import 5 percent of its consumption needs, this would amount to the total grain trade of the European Union, and a 10 percent import would seriously disrupt the world grain market! In other words, China must maintain its high level of food self-sufficiency; it is simply too big to specialize in manufactured exports and import food, as is the case with Japan or Asia's other newly industrializing economies.

Chinese agriculture really faces a number of daunting challenges. China's 1.2 billion population will increase a further 200 million by 2010 and some 300 million by 2025. Over 200 million peasants are illiterate and unsuited for city jobs other than hard manual labor. With continuing urbanization and rising per capita income and hence changes in food consumption patterns, China will have to increase its grain production from its present level of 450 million tons to well over 600 million tons by 2020. The increased production has to be done with no substantial increase—more likely a decline—in arable land.[11] The switch to more profitable crops and environmental degradation has leveled off the wheat and rice crop (Yabuki, 1995:91–97).

For an effective long-term solution to the agricultural problem, however, the government has to properly manage agricultural development amidst rapid industrial growth—the agricultural sector is set to decline as industrialization increases. There should be a balanced agricultural development strategy that will not squeeze farmers too hard and too fast, while it promotes agricultural productivity by stepping up technological progress.

Even though energy is less important than agriculture in socioeconomic terms, ready energy resources are a necessary component of economic development. And China's energy sector is giving out early warning signals. China's present consumption of energy on a per capita basis is still very low. Its per capita energy use for 1994 was equivalent to only 647 kilograms (kg) (1,426 lb) of oil, compared to 3,825 kg (8,432 lb) for Japan and 3,000 kg (6,614 lb) for South Korea. Also, China's total energy demand grew at the annual rate of only 5.5 percent during 1980–1990, which is significantly below its GDP growth (World Bank, 1996). However, future economic growth will certainly raise China's overall energy consumption level, with serious implications for the world energy market because of China's huge demand potential. China's share in world primary energy demand will increase from 8.9 percent for 1993 to 10.9 percent for 2000 (Priddle, 1996).

Despite being the world's sixth-largest oil producer (146 million tons in 1994, or 5 percent of the world's oil output), China has become a net importer of oil since 1993. By 1998, China has begun to buy extensive oil fields in Central Asian countries. China may have to import 50 million tons of crude oil a year by 2000. Beyond 2000, the situation will depend on China's investment in oil and gas exploitation.

Similarly, China's dynamic economic growth is already exerting a lot of pressure on its existing water and land resources as well as on its environment. The Chinese themselves will mainly bear the costs of pollution: Only about 20 percent of industrial waste and 15 percent of sewage flowing into China's rivers are treated. But there is also considerable cross-border pollution due to China's heavy reliance on coal for most of its energy needs. In many parts of China, airborne levels of sulphur dioxide in winter have exceeded World Health Organization guidelines. Richard Edmonds discusses all these problems in Chapter 9.

Accordingly, the Chinese government has started to pay serious attention to the environmental issue. But its investment in pollution control is only a small fraction of government expenditure; and enforcement is lax, especially in the rural areas. In the long run, China's economic development is much like a race, whereby new resources have to be quickly created so that the government can use them to cope with the problems and by-products of development such as pollution.

■ MUDDLING THROUGH

Each of the constraints discussed earlier presents a formidable challenge to the Chinese leadership, and they all can, in varying degrees, operate to moderate China's long-term growth capability. No one can foresee exactly how the Chinese leadership will respond to them, or how long it will take to overcome those problems. Many China experts take the view that China can somehow "muddle through."

The point is that China's dynamic economic growth can be slowed but not stifled. Given continuing peace and stability, China will ultimately realize its major economic development objectives, certainly by 2025, if not by 2015. By then China will clearly be a middle-income economy in terms of its per capita income, but its total GDP will make it the world's largest economy. It is thus important for all international organizations to start engaging China now on all major global and regional issues. That is why Singapore and many other Asian countries support China's bid to join the World Trade Organization, so that China can learn to play by global rules.

■ NOTES

1. It may be noted that since the second part of 1994, the government has taken measures to recontrol the prices of certain food or important consumer items as a means to fight the rampant inflation. Such stabilization measures are not anti-reform in nature.

According to the data released by the State Planning Commission, the number of industrial products to be produced under state mandatory planning decreased from 120 in 1980 to twenty-nine in 1995 and, in value term, from 40 percent of the total industrial output in 1980 to 4.5 percent in 1995. For price control, the "overwhelming majority of commodities now (by 1995) have their prices formed by the market." By the end of 1995, only seventy-four important commodity items of heavy industry were still subjected to state control, of which fifty-one items were on "state-guided prices." *China Economic News* (Beijing), 1995.

2. For the full text of the plan in English, see *Xinhua News Agency* (Beijing) 1995. 0702 GMT (October 4).

3. See, for example, the June 1994 issue of the *Journal of Comparative Economics*, "Experiences in the Transition to a Market Economy," with Jeffrey Sachs and Wing Thye Woo as guest editors. For a more recent analysis, see Rawski, 1995.

4. German correspondent Peter Seidlitz interviewed Pieter P Bottelier, the World Bank's country representative in China. See Seidlitz, 1995.

5. This official growth rate tends to overstate China's actual growth as it was estimated by revaluing Chinese GDP at 1980 prices rather than earlier year prices and hence inflates the contribution of industry to GDP growth. A more realistic average growth should be around 4.5–5.0 percent, which is still quite a respectable growth performance, at least higher than that of India.

6. "China's Economy Was Stable in First Half." 1996. Though just over 100,000 of China's state-owned industries account for a third of China's industrial output, and 70 percent of China's industrial workers are in state-owned factories, those industries generate less than 1 percent of China's industrial profits and rely on huge grants from the national government that are seldom repaid. Forney, 1996.

7. Chen Xitong is party secretary of Beijing and a member of the Politburo. Chen is, so far, the highest official to be disgraced for corruption.

8. According to a recent World Bank study, China's economic fragmentation is very serious, as manifested in its lower degree of industrial specialization and market integration as compared to the European Union and the United States. World Bank, 1994.

9. Brown argues that with China's population growing by 14 million a year and increasing meat consumption amidst the rapid shrinkage of croplands, by 2030 China could face a serious grain shortfall of 384 million tons, or at least 263 million tons, which would exceed the world's entire grain exports of about 200 million tons in 1993. Brown, 1994a, 1994b.

10. China's agricultural economists have since made more realistic demand projections, which show that China's import demand will rise steadily. By 2000, imports are expected to reach 40 million tons, which will affect the world grain market by ending the historical decline in grain prices but will not disrupt the world grain market itself. After 2000, China's grain imports are expected to stabilize on account of China's declining population growth and increases in grain supply from higher productivity. See Lin, Huang, and Rozelle, 1996.

11. Ibid.

■ BIBLIOGRAPHY

Alford, William P. 1995. *To Steal a Book Is an Elegant Offense: Intellectual Property Law in Chinese Civilization.* Stanford: Stanford University Press.

Allee, Mark A. 1995. *Law and Local Society in Late Imperial China: Northern Taiwan in the Nineteenth Century.* Stanford: Stanford University Press.

Ash, Robert, and Y. Y. Kueh (eds.). 1996. *The Chinese Economy Under Deng Xioaping.* Oxford: Oxford University Press.

Asian Development Bank. 1994. *Human Development Report.* Manila: Asian Development Bank.

———. 1996. *Key Indicators of Developing Asian and Pacific Countries.* Manila: Asian Development Bank.

———. 1997. *Asian Development Outlook.* Manila: Asian Development Bank.

Berger, Mark, and Douglas Borer. 1997. *The Rise of East Asia: Critical Visions of the Pacific Century.* London: Routledge.

Bernhardt, Kathryn, and Philip C. C. Huang (eds.). 1994. *Civil Law in Qing and Republican China.* Stanford: Stanford University Press.

Bhalla, A. S. 1995. *Uneven Development in the Third World: A Study of India and China.* 2d ed. New York: St. Martin's Press.

Bian, Yanjie. 1995. *Work and Inequality in Urban China.* Albany: State University of New York Press.

Blecher, Marc, and Vivienne Shue. 1996. *Tethered Deer: Government and Economy in a Chinese County.* Stanford: Stanford University Press.

Brook, Timothy. 1989. *The Asiatic Mode of Production in China.* Armonk, NY: M. E. Sharpe.

Brown, Lester R. 1994a. "Question for 2030: Who Will Be Able to Feed China?" *International Herald Tribune* (September 28).

———. 1994b. "When China's Scarcities Become the World's Problem." *International Herald Tribune* (September 29).

Chan, Anita, Richard Madsen, and Jonathan Unger. 1984. *Chen Village: The Recent History of a Peasant Community in Mao's China.* Berkeley: University of California Press.

Chang, David Wen-Wei. 1988. *China Under Deng Xiaoping: Political and Economic Reform.* New York: St. Martin's Press.

Chao, Kang. 1987. *Man and Land in Chinese History: An Economic Analysis.* Stanford: Stanford University Press.

Chen, Min, and Winston Pan. 1993. *Understanding the Process of Doing Business in China, Taiwan, and Hong Kong.* Lewiston, NY: Edward Mellen Press.

Cheng, Li. 1997. *Rediscovering China: Dynamics and Dilemmas of Reform.* Lanham, MD: Rowman and Littlefield.

Child, John. 1994. *Management in China During the Age of Reform.* Cambridge: Cambridge University Press.

China Price Yearbook 1994 *[Zhongguo wu-jia nian-jian 1994].* 1995. Beijing: China Statistical Publishing House [Zhongguo Tongji Chubanshe].

China Economic News (Beijing). 1995. Vol. 48 (December 11).

"China's Economy Was Stable in First Half." 1996. *Asian Wall Street Journal* (Hong Kong) (July 22).

"China Records 11 Trade Surplus for '95." 1996. *Straits Times* (Singapore) (January 4).

Croll, Elisabeth. 1994. *From Heaven to Earth: Images and Experiences of Development in China.* London: Routledge.

"East Asia's Whirlwind Hits the Middle Kingdom." 1998. *Economist* 346, no. 8055 (February 14): 37–39.

Eckstein, Alexander. 1977. *China's Economic Revolution.* Cambridge: Cambridge University Press.

Elvin, Mark. 1973. *The Pattern of the Chinese Past.* Stanford: Stanford University Press.

Engholm, Christopher. 1994. *Doing Business in Asia's Booming "China Triangle": People's Republic of China, Taiwan, Hong Kong.* Englewood Cliffs: Prentice-Hall.

Feuerwerker, Albert. 1996a. *Studies in the Economic History of Late Imperial China: Handicraft, Modern Industry, and the State.* Ann Arbor: University of Michigan Monographs in Chinese Studies.

———. 1996b. *The Chinese Economy, 1870–1949.* Ann Arbor: University of Michigan Monographs in Chinese Studies.

Fewsmith, Joseph. 1983. "From Guild to Interest Group: The Transformation of Public and Private in Late Qing China." *Comparative Studies in Society and History* 25:617–640.

———. 1994. *Dilemmas of Reform in China: Political Conflict and Economic Debate.* Armonk, NY: M. E. Sharpe.

"Foreign Fund Tops U.S.\$47 Billion in First 11 Months of 97." 1997. *China Daily* (December 14).

Forney, Matt. 1996. "Trials by Fire." *Far Eastern Economic Review* 159 (September 12):62–69.

Forney, Matt, and Pamela Yatsko. 1997. "No More Free Lunch." *Far Eastern Economic Review* 160 (October 16):62–66.

Freeman, Duncan (ed.). *The Life and Death of a Joint Venture in China.* Hong Kong: Asia Law and Practice.

Friedman, Edward, Paul G. Pickowicz, and Mark Selden. 1991. *Chinese Village, Socialist State.* New Haven: Yale University Press.

Gao, Shangquan. 1996. *China's Economic Reform.* New York: St. Martin's Press.

Garnaut, Ross, Guo Shutian, and Ma Guonan (eds.). 1996. *The Third Revolution in the Chinese Countryside.* Cambridge: Cambridge University Press.

Gates, Hill. 1996. *China's Motor: A Thousand Years of Petty Capitalism.* Ithaca: Cornell University Press.

Gibbons, Russell. 1997. *Joint Ventures in China: A Guide for the Foreign Investor.* Melbourne: Macmillan.

Godement, Francois. 1997. *The New Asian Renaissance.* London: Routledge.

Goodman, David S. G. (ed.). 1997. *China's Provinces in Reform: Class, Community, and Political Culture.* London: Routledge.

Grub, Phillip Donald, and Lin Jian Hai. 1991. *Foreign Direct Investment in China.* New York: Quorum Books.

Ho, Samuel. 1978. *Economic Development of Taiwan, 1860–1970.* New Haven: Yale University Press.

Hong Kong. 1997. *Annual Digest of Statistics.*

Honig, Emily. 1986. *Sisters and Strangers: The Cotton Textile Workers of Shanghai.* Stanford: Stanford University Press.

"How to Save Chinese Banks Without Bringing Down the System." 1996. *Asia Times* (Bangkok) (July 30).

Howell, Jude. 1993. *China Opens Its Doors: The Politics of Economic Transition.* Boulder: Lynne Rienner Publishers.

Huang, Philip C. C. 1985. *The Peasant Economy and Social Change in North China.* Stanford: Stanford University Press.

———. 1990. *The Peasant Family and Rural Development in the Yangzi Delta, 1350–1988.* Stanford: Stanford University Press.

Huang, Yasheng. 1996. *Inflation and Investment Controls in China: The Political Economy of Central-Local Relations During the Reform Era.* Cambridge: Cambridge University Press.

Ikels, Charlotte. 1996. *The Return of the God of Wealth: The Transition to a Market Economy in Urban China.* Stanford: Stanford University Press.

"Investment to Be Steady." 1996. *China Daily Business Weekly* (Beijing) (January 28–February 4).

Kam, On Kit (ed.). 1995. *Financial Reform in China.* London: Routledge.

Kamachi Noriko. 1990. "Feudalism or Absolute Monarchism? Japanese Discourse on the Nature of State and Society in Later Imperial China." *Modern China* 87, no. 3:330–370.

Keith, Ronald C. 1994. *China's Struggle for the Rule of Law.* New York: St. Martin's Press.

Kelliher, Daniel. 1992. *Peasant Power in China: The Era of Rural Reform, 1979–1989.* New Haven: Yale University Press.

Kluver, Alan R. 1995. *Legitimating the Chinese Economic Reforms: A Rhetoric of Myth and Orthodoxy.* Albany: State University of New York Press.

Kristof, Nicholas, and Sheryl WuDunn. 1994. *China Wakes: The Struggle for the Soul of a Rising Power.* New York: Random House.

Kwang, Mary. 1998. "The 64 Million Yuan Question." *Strait Times* (Singapore) (July 2).

Lardy, Nicholas R. 1992. *Foreign Trade and Economic Reform in China.* Cambridge: Cambridge University Press.

————. 1994. *China in the World Economy.* Washington, DC: Institute for International Economics.

Lee, James. 1990. *State and Economy in Southwest China.* Stanford: Stanford University Press.

Leong, Liew. 1998. *The Chinese Economy in Transition: From Plan to Market.* Cheltenham: Edward Elgar.

Lin, Justin Lifu, Jikun Huang, and Scott Rozelle. 1996. "China's Food Economy: Past Performance and Future Trends." Paper presented at the OECD Conference on "China in the 21st Century: Long-term Global Implications," Paris, January 8–9.

Lindau, Juan D., and Timothy Cheek. 1998. *Market Economics and Political Change: Comparing China and Mexico.* Lanham, MD: Rowman and Littlefield.

Lyons, Thomas P. 1994. *Poverty and Growth in a South China County: Anxi, Fujian, 1949–1992.* Ithaca: Cornell University Press.

Lyons, Thomas P., and Victor Need (eds.). 1994. *The Economic Transformation of South China: Reform and Development in the Post-Mao Era.* Ithaca: Cornell University Press.

Lyons, Thomas P., and Wang Yan. 1988. *Planning and Finance in China's Economic Reforms.* Ithaca: Cornell University Press.

Ma, Junlei, and Luo Liqin. 1994. "Important Reforms in China's Tax System." *JETRO China Newsletter* (Tokyo) 110 (May–June).

Mann, Jim. 1997. *Beijing Jeep: A Case Study of Western Business in China.* Boulder: Westview Press.

Mann, Susan. 1987. *Local Merchants and the Chinese Bureaucracy, 1750–1950.* Stanford: Stanford University Press.

Mastel, Greg. 1997. *The Rise of the Chinese Economy: The Middle Kingdom Emerges.* Armonk, NY: M. E. Sharpe.

McCormick, Barrett L., and Jonathan Unger (eds.). 1995. *China After Socialism: In the Footsteps of Eastern Europe or East Asia?* Armonk, NY: M. E. Sharpe.

Ministry of Foreign Trade and Economics. 1996. China's Foreign Trade Yearbook 1995. Beijing: China Statistical Publishing House [Zhongguo Tongji Chubanshe].

"Multinationals in China: Going It Alone." 1997. *Economist* (April 19).

Murphy, David J. 1996. *Plunder and Preservation: Cultural Property Law and Practice in the People's Republic of China.* Hong Kong: Oxford University Press.

Myers, James T. 1989. "China: Modernization and 'Unhealthy' Tendencies." *Comparative Politics* 21:193–213.

Nann, Richard C. 1995. *Authority and Benevolence: Social Welfare in China.* New York: St. Martin's Press.

Naquin, Susan. 1987. *Chinese Society in the Eighteenth Century.* New Haven: Yale University Press.

Naughton, Barry. 1995. *Growing Out of the Plan: Chinese Economic Reform, 1978–1993.* Cambridge: Cambridge University Press.

Newman, William H. 1992. *Birth of a Successful Joint Venture.* Lanham, MD: University Press of America.

Oi, Jean C. 1989a. "Market Reforms and Corruption in Rural China." *Studies in Comparative Communism* 22 (summer–autumn):221–233.

————. 1989b. *State and Peasant in Contemporary China: The Political Economy of Village Government.* Berkeley: University of California Press.

Oksenberg, Michel. 1996. "China's Political Future." *JETRO China Newsletter* 120 (January–February).

"On the Rocks." 1998. *Economist* 346, no. 8058 (March 7).

Perdue, Peter C. 1987. *Exhausting the Earth: State and Peasant in Hunan, 1500–1850.* Cambridge: Harvard University Press.

Perkins, Dwight. 1969. *Agricultural Development in China, 1368–1968.* Chicago: Aldine.

———. 1996. "China's Future: Economic and Social Development Scenarios for the 21st Century." Paper presented at the OECD Conference on "China in the 21st Century: Long-Term Global Implications," Paris, January 8–9.

Potter, Jack M. 1968. *Capitalism and the Chinese Peasant.* Berkeley: University of California Press.

Powell, Simon. 1992. *Agricultural Reform in China: From Communes to Commodity Economy 1978–1990.* Manchester: Manchester University Press.

Priddle, Robert. 1996. "China's Long-Term Energy Outlook." Paper presented at the OECD Conference on "China in the 21st Century: Long-Term Global Implications," Paris, January 8–9.

Rawski, Evelyn Sakakida. 1972. *Agricultural Change and the Peasant Economy of South China.* Cambridge: Harvard University Press.

Rawski, Thomas G. 1995. "Implications of China's Reform Experience." Department of Economics, University of Pittsburgh Working Paper no. 295, June (to appear in *China Quarterly*).

Redding, S. Gordon. 1990. *The Spirit of Chinese Capitalism.* Berlin: Walter de Gruyter.

Republic of China. 1997. *Taiwan Statistical Data Book.* Taipei: Government Printing Office.

Rimmer, Peter J. 1997. *Pacific Rim Development: Integration and Globalisation in the Asia-Pacific Economy.* London: Allen and Unwin.

Riskin, Carl. 1987. *China's Political Economy: The Quest for Development Since 1949.* New York: Economics of the World Series.

Rowe, William T. 1984. *Hankow: Commerce and Society in a Chinese City, 1796–1889.* Stanford: Stanford University Press.

———. 1989. *Hankow: Conflict and Community in a Chinese City, 1796–1895.* Stanford: Stanford University Press.

Seidlitz, Peter. 1995. "China: On Track, But a Tricky Road Ahead." *Business Times* (Singapore) (January 13).

Shiba, Yoshinobu. 1969. *Commerce and Society in Sung China.* Trans. by Mark Elvin. Ann Arbor: University of Michigan Abstracts of Chinese and Japanese Works on Chinese History.

Shih, Chih-yu. 1995. *State and Society in China's Political Economy: The Cultural Dynamics of Socialist Reform.* Boulder: Lynne Rienner Publishers.

Shirk, Susan. 1993. *The Political Logic of Economic Reform in China.* Berkeley: University of California Press.

Singapore. 1997. *Yearbook of Statistics.* Singapore: Government Printing Office.

Skoggard, Ian A. 1996. *The Indigenous Dynamic in Taiwan's Postwar Development: The Religious and Historical Roots of Entrepreneurship.* Armonk, NY: M. E. Sharpe.

Solinger, Dorothy. 1993. *China's Transition from Socialism: Statist Legacies and Market Reforms.* Armonk, NY: M. E. Sharpe.

Spence, Jonathan. 1990. *The Search for Modern China.* New York: W. W. Norton.

"State GDP Grows 9.8 Per Cent in Past Six Months." 1996. *China Daily* (Beijing) (July 20).

Statistical Yearbook of China. Beijing: China Statistical Publishing House. [Zhongguo Tongji Chubanshe]. State Statistical Bureau. 1995.

"State Statistical Bureau's Statistical Communique of China's Economic and Social Development in 1995." 1996. *Renmin Ribao* (People's Daily, Beijing)
(March 7).

Tam, On Kit. 1995. *Financial Reform in China*. London: Routledge.

Taylor, Robert. 1996. *Greater China and Japan: Prospects for Economic Partnership in East Asia*. London: Routledge.

"The Death of Gradualism." 1997. *Economist* 342 (March 8):8007.

Wade, Robert. 1990. *Governing the Market: Economic Theory and the Role of
Government in East Asian Industrialization*. Princeton: Princeton University
Press.

Walder, Andrew G. 1986. *Communist Neo-Traditionalism: Work and Authority in
Chinese Industry*. Berkeley: University of California Press.

Walder, Andrew G. (ed.). 1996. *China's Transitional Economy*. Oxford: Oxford
University Press.

Watson, Andrew (ed.). 1992. *Economic Reform and Social Change in China*. London: Routledge.

Wei, Pan. 1998. *The Politics of Marketization in Rural China*. Lanham, MD: Rowman and Littlefield.

"When Will the Good Times Roll Again?" 1998. *Far Eastern Economic Review*
161, no. 7 (February 12):51–54.

White, Gordon. 1993. *The Politics of Economic Reform in Post-Mao China*. Stanford: Stanford University Press.

———. 1996. *In Search of Civil Society: Market Reform and Social Change in
Contemporary China*. Oxford: Oxford University Press.

White, Lynn T. III. 1998. *Unstately Power: Local Causes of China's Economic Reform*. Vol. 1. Armonk, NY: M. E. Sharpe.

Will, Pierre-Etienne. 1991. *Nourish the People: The State Civilian Granary System
in China, 1650–1850*. Ann Arbor: Center for Chinese Studies, University of
Michigan.

Wong, John. 1993. *Understanding China's Socialist Market Economy*. Singapore:
Times Academic Press.

———. 1994. "Power and Market in Mainland China: The Danger of Increasing
Government Involvement in Business." *Issues and Studies* (Taipei) 30, no. 1
(January).

———. 1995a. "Assessing China's Economic Reform Progress in 1994." *JETRO
China Newsletter* (Tokyo) 112 (January–February).

———. 1995b. "China's Entrepreneurial Approach to Economic Reform." *IEAPE
Internal Study Paper* (Singapore) 8 (February 16).

———. 1995c. "China's Ninth Five-Year Plan: Economic Agenda of the Fifth
Party Plenum." *IEAPE Commentaries* (Singapore) 17 (October).

———. 1995d. "Why Is the Chinese Government So Concerned About Agriculture?" *IEAPE Background Brief* (Singapore) 87 (May 18).

———. 1996. "Promoting Confucianism for Socioeconomic Development: The
Singapore Experience." In Tu Wei-ming (ed.). *Confucian Traditions in East
Asian Modernity*. Cambridge: Harvard University Press.

———. 1997a. "China's Economy in 1997." *EAI Background Brief* (Singapore) 6
(December 29).

———. 1997b. "Will China Be the Next Financial Domino?" *EAI Background
Brief* 4 (December 11).

———. 1998. "Interpreting Zhu Rongji's Stategies for the Chinese Economy." *EAI
Background Brief* (Singapore) 11 (March 31).

Wong, John, Rong Ma, and Mu Yang. 1995. *China's Rural Entrepreneurs: Ten
Case Studies*. Singapore: Times Academic Press.

Woo, Wing Thye. 1994. "The Art of Reforming Centrally Planned Economies: Comparing China, Poland, and Russia." *Journal of Comparative Politics* 18, no. 3 (June).

Woodruff, John. 1989. *China in Search of Its Future: Years of Great Reform.* Seattle: University of Washington Press.

World Bank. 1994. *China: International Market Development and Regulation.* Washington, DC: World Bank.

———. 1996. *World Development Report.* New York: Oxford University Press.

———. 1997. *World Development Report.* New York: Oxford University Press.

———. various years. *World Development Report.* New York: Oxford University Press.

Wu, Yanrui. 1996. *Productive Efficiency of Chinese Enterprises: An Empirical Study.* St. Martin's Press.

Wu, Yu-Shan. 1994. *Comparative Economic Transformations: Mainland China, Hungary, the Soviet Union, and Taiwan.* Stanford: Stanford University Press.

Xia, Mei, Lin Jian Hai, and Phillip Donald Grub. 1992. *The Reemerging Securities Market in China.* New York: Quorum Books.

Yabuki, Susumu. 1995. *China's New Political Economy: The Giant Awakes.* Boulder: Westview Press.

Yang, Dali L. 1996. *Calamity and Reform in China: Rural Society and Institutional Change Since the Great Leap Famine.* Stanford: Stanford University Press.

Yatsko, Pamela. 1998. "New Owners." *Far Eastern Economic Review* 161, no. 6 (February 5):52–53.

Yatsko, Pamela, and Matt Forney. 1998. "Demand Crunch." *Far Eastern Economic Review* 161, no. 3 (January 15):44–47.

Yee, Dany, and Shan Li. 1996. "Transparency Is Key to Convertibility." *Asian Wall Street Journal* (Hong Kong) (July 15).

Yi, Gang. 1993. *Money, Banking, and Financial Markets in China.* Boulder: Westview Press.

Young, Susan. 1995. *Private Business and Economic Reform in China.* Armonk, NY: M. E. Sharpe.

Zhou, Kate Xiao. 1996. *How the Farmers Changed China: Power of the People.* Boulder: Westview Press.

Zhou, Kate Xiao, and Lynn T. White III. 1995. "Quiet Politics and Rural Enterprise in Reform China." *The Journal of Developing Areas* 29 (July):461–490.

▪ 6 ▪

China Beyond the Heartland

Robert E. Gamer

We have now had an overview of China's geography, history, politics, and economy. In this chapter, we take a closer look at four special topics: overseas Chinese, Hong Kong, Taiwan, and Tibet. These elements are all part of China, and yet not. They figure prominently in China's defense, foreign policy, economy, and culture. Even before reading this book, you were probably already aware that Hong Kong reverted to China in 1997, that Taiwan and China are engaged in vigorous diplomatic and military competition, and that Tibetans have resisted China's presence in their territory. The outcome of these issues will have enormous consequences in determining China's future. We look at some historical background on each and then examine present and future trends. But we begin with another topic, perhaps less familiar to you, that will help you comprehend China's extraordinary economic growth and some of the threads that tie together China, Hong Kong, and Taiwan: overseas Chinese. As Chapter 1 indicated, there are 55 million Han who have left or whose ancestors left China, including those in Taiwan and Hong Kong. The richest among them control nearly as much investment capital as Japan (Seagrave, 1995:285). As you will see, most of China's direct foreign investment comes from them. Hong Kong alone accounted for 16 percent of all Asia's trade in 1995 (Gilley, 1997). How have they become so wealthy? How have they come to figure so prominently in China's affairs?

▪ OVERSEAS CHINESE

For thousands of years, Chinese merchants have been trading in Indochina (Vietnam), Cambodia, Siam (Thailand), Malaya (mainland Malaysia), and Java (part of Indonesia)—all in Southeast Asia (see Map 2.1)—and in

Korea and Japan. Their trade brought great prosperity to China's leading families during the Tang, Song, Yuan, Ming, and Qing empires (Table 3.1). Most simply traveled there on business trips; a few settled, married native women, and became absorbed into local society. When the Europeans arrived in the sixteenth century, they created or captured Macao (across the bay from Hong Kong), Manila in the Philippines (the big island group north of Indonesia; see Map 2.1), Melaka (Malacca) in Malaya, and Batavia (Jakarta) and other ports in Java and encouraged Chinese merchants and artisans (largely from the southern provinces of Fujian, Guangdong, and Zhejiang; see Map 2.2) to move there. These settlers brought Chinese wives and established or expanded Chinese communities; many became prosperous from their trading activities (Wang, 1991). As China's population burgeoned during the nineteenth century, relatives from their home provinces and unemployed urban youth moved to those communities and to the newly founded ports of Penang and Singapore in Malaya. They filled jobs as laborers, miners, plantation workers, teachers, journalists, traditional opera performers, house servants, and retailers. Others went to the Americas and Australia to construct railroads and work on farms. Some settled in Tokyo, smaller Pacific islands, Sydney, Calcutta, Paris, London, Vancouver, the West Indies, and Lima. Those working on farms, plantations, mines, and railroads often experienced cruel treatment and harsh conditions. Those who did not perish or return home stayed to set up laundries or small shops or work for other Chinese in "Chinatowns," which began to emerge even in cities beyond the port of original entry into the country.

The principal source of income for overseas Chinese communities was trade with China. The wealthiest families made their fortunes serving as middlemen in trade transactions between China and non-Chinese in Asia, Europe, or the Americas. They became patrons to Chinese-language schools, newspapers, temples, festivals, and other cultural activities; welfare and legal aid societies; and cemeteries. Siam and the Philippines encouraged Chinese to intermarry and mingle with indigenous people in places of work; elsewhere, they met with greater wariness and prejudice. The British in Malaya and Singapore hired Chinese and other ethnic groups for some bureaucratic posts; most of the remaining Chinese in these settlements worked for themselves or for other Chinese. Most Chinese sent money home to poorer relatives in China.

In the second half of the nineteenth century, prominent Chinese families began sending some of their children abroad to study. Those students discovered that except in the Philippines, where the Spanish had established schools and universities for native inhabitants, few Chinese born overseas were studying outside their own communities. Most who attended school were taught in Chinese dialects. In contrast, U.S. missionary schools in China introduced their students to English and a modern Western

Chinese sampans and shophouses in Singapore, 1964.

curriculum; their best graduates were welcomed into leading U.S., British, and European colleges and universities. Japan, too, welcomed students from China. Upon their return home, many of these graduates became prominent in China's government, commerce, and cultural life. Their exposure to Japanese, U.S., and European languages and cultures was far deeper than that of most Chinese living abroad.

The Chinese studying abroad returned home wanting to introduce China to techniques and ideas they had learned on their sojourns—to change Chinese culture. In contrast, leaders of Chinese communities abroad wished to preserve Chinese traditions among their families, workers, and neighbors. In exchange for cash remitted to their families in China, they asked China's leaders for assistance in dealing with the governments and societies of their adopted lands. Both these responses were very new. Until the second half of the nineteenth century, educated Chinese did not venture abroad to study, and China did not concern itself with the needs of Chinese who had moved abroad. To control piracy and rebels, the Ming and Qing governments had forbidden emigration under penalty of death. The treaties imposed after the Opium Wars (discussed below and in Chapter 7) changed that. They forced the emperors to allow emigration, while giving China the right (as a new participant in European-created international law) to protect its subjects living abroad. For the first time, China sent ambassadors and consuls to foreign capitals and trading cities. There they discovered the great prosperity of the overseas Chinese. The Qing government began to support schools for Chinese in Southeast Asian countries and conferred citizenship on overseas Chinese and their children. Chinese consular officials were available to assist Chinese when they encountered problems in their adopted countries and to intercede against abuses of laborers. After centuries of being cut off from their homeland, under threat of the death penalty imposed since the Ming dynasty for being illegal emigrants, overseas Chinese were being treated as compatriots. In exchange, the Qing government encouraged them to send money home to relatives.

This created precedents that continue to affect China's foreign relations and the lives of overseas Chinese. It encouraged the predisposition of overseas Chinese to isolate themselves from the social and political life of their adopted lands and to interest themselves in the politics and economy of China. It reinforced the inclination of China's governments to treat the overseas Chinese as continuing subjects of China and the lands where some of them reside as part of China's domain. Most important, it also helped end the Qing dynasty. The Kuomintang and the Republican movements were born among Chinese studying abroad and benefited from substantial financial contributions from overseas Chinese.

After the Qing dynasty was overthrown in 1911, all political factions in China sought financial and moral support among overseas Chinese, who helped set up schools for their children. The Kuomintang government promoted equal treatment for overseas Chinese in their countries of residence, helped them send their children to China for study, and gave special incentives to overseas Chinese for establishing businesses in China. It focused heavily on establishing schools, training teachers, and setting standards for the children of overseas Chinese and criticized the governments of those countries for "interfering" in this education, which was conducted entirely in the Chinese language, when they sought assurance that it would help integrate pupils into their adopted lands (Fitzgerald, 1972:8).

From 1921 to 1927, the communists and Nationalists cooperated in a "united front" in China; after that, they vied with each other and with the warlords for control of territories. All these factions sought financial and moral support from the overseas Chinese. In 1936, to counter the Japanese, they once again declared a "united front," with both the Kuomintang and the communists proclaiming that overseas Chinese were included in their efforts to cooperate. By giving their attention and resources variously to the Kuomintang and the communists, overseas Chinese remained within China's orbit and roused suspicions among their new compatriots that they were not entirely loyal to their adopted lands. They also found themselves caught up in the ideological battle between communism and the Western democracies, even though many of them had thought little about such issues.

As you will see in Chapter 7, that problem of divided loyalties would continue after War War II. Both China and Taiwan, now ruled respectively by the communists and the Kuomintang Nationalists, would need the deep pockets and the economic connections of these overseas Chinese as they sought to spread their economic and political influence in the region. And an island that was barren when China sought to control the opium trade in 1839 would play a pivotal role in this. So we fit it into the story here.

■ HONG KONG

□ Beginnings

In 1839, the Qing emperor appointed Lin Zexu as special commissioner in Guangzhou, the only port open to foreign trade (as Chapter 7 explains), and ordered him to stamp out the opium trade. Thus began China's humiliation by foreign powers. Guangzhou (Canton) is located on the West River near the Pearl River delta of the West River (see Maps 2.2 and 2.4), just upstream from the Portuguese-founded city of Macao. Lin sent troops to the foreign wharves where trading took place and refused to let anyone leave until they surrendered the opium inside and promised not to import more. Among those in attendance was Captain Charles Elliot, Britain's trade representative. After six weeks of standoff, Elliot surrendered 3 million pounds of opium to Lin, who had it flushed into the sea. Elliot retreated downstream to Macao, where the Portuguese did not wish to become involved. Hence he headed across the Pearl River delta to a sparsely inhabited island called Hong Kong. It contained an excellent protected harbor, where he and his companions stayed on board ship. When some Chinese war junks tried to expel his crews from the harbor, Elliot's ships sank them. The following summer, the British sent a fleet commanded by Elliot's cousin, Admiral George Elliot, to avenge the action. Because they would not sign pledges declaring they would no longer trade in opium, Lin had them all expelled from Macao. They, too, headed across the bay where, by now, Captain Elliot had established a village on Hong Kong harbor. Though the British had declared an embargo on trade with China, the Americans were acting as intermediaries for the British and signed bonds promising to obey the Chinese laws.

Admiral Elliot blockaded Guangzhou's harbor, headed north to blockade the mouth of the Yangtze River, and then entered the city of Tianjin unopposed (see Map 2.2). This was the first Opium War. In the negotiations that followed, China ceded the island of Hong Kong to Britain and offered to pay some war indemnity and reopen Guangzhou's trade with Britain. When the word reached Britain, foreign secretary Lord Palmerston was furious about these terms; the only real concession of the Chinese was modified rights to "a barren island with hardly a house on it." He dismissed Elliot, refused to sign the treaty, and sent another expedition that reopened hostilities, decisively defeating Qing forces and leading to the 1842 Treaty of Nanjing (Hibbert, 1970:73–182).

This treaty became the basis for all China's relations with foreign powers. It opened Guangzhou, Fuzhou and Xiamen in Fujian province, Ningbo in Zhejiang province, and Shanghai for residence by British subjects, created British consulates there, and let British merchants carry on trade with whomever they chose and not merely with official trading organizations (*cohongs;* see Chapter 7). It let Chinese subjects reside with and work for the British and promised to protect British living in China, along with their property. It limited taxation on imported goods to "a fair and regular tariff" at customs halls in the five "treaty ports" and stipulated that foreigners need no longer use terms like "I beg you" in correspondence with Chinese officials (Spence, 1990:159–160). Deviating from his instructions, the British negotiator also forced the Chinese to cede Hong Kong island to Britain "in perpetuity." Further treaties would increase the number of treaty ports, extend these privileges to other nations, and allow missionaries to come to China and foreigners to learn Chinese. Foreign countries would also be able to establish embassies in Beijing. And the treaties would expand the principle of *extraterritoriality,* that any foreigner accused of a crime should be turned over to officials of his or her own government for punishment. Chapter 7 will tell you still more about all this.

Among the treaty ports, only one would maintain prominence: Shanghai.[1] Its chief rival was that "barren island," Hong Kong. Immediately after Elliot's arrival, operators of trading ships like Alexander Matheson, Lancelot Dent, and William Jardine began to build warehouses there, where they could store opium and other goods they traded with China, away from the reach of Chinese officials. Soon a frontier community, composed of Chinese and a few British subjects, was growing along the harbor. The many islands on the seacoast north of the Pearl River delta had provided refuge for pirates and smugglers, who had plied these waters for centuries. During the decades following establishment of Hong Kong, the island community became a neutral place where British and Chinese traders, pirates, bankers, and officials could meet to do business. More wars and skirmishes were to ensue before diplomatic and trade relations with China stabilized; even when they were at their most intense, ships moved in and out of Hong Kong harbor carrying goods between China and the rest of the world. Crowded streets emerged on the hillsides that rise steeply from the harbor.

☐ Rising Stature

In 1860, the British received a lease on Kowloon, the small, flatter peninsula on the mainland just across from Hong Kong harbor. There they had room to lay out military barracks. In 1896, the Chinese (smarting from the Treaty of Shimonoseki after their defeat by Japan in the Sino-Japanese War; see Chapter 7) signed a secret agreement with Russia, agreeing to take common action against the Japanese in case of attack and allowing Russian ships to use any Chinese port. The Germans then used the murder of two missionaries as an excuse to send in warships and force China to lease them the port of Qingdao on the Shandong peninsula (Map 2.2) for ninety-nine years. Across the bay, the Russians seized Lushun in Manchuria and negotiated a treaty ceding it to them (they renamed it Port Arthur) for twenty-five years. South of the Pearl River on Hainan Island (Map 2.2), the French signed a lease ceding France a harbor for ninety-nine years. Feeling the need for more land to defend Kowloon harbor from the Russian and French warships now plying Chinese waters, in 1898 the British obtained a ninety-nine-year lease for the New Territories—365 square miles of land north of Kowloon and 235 surrounding islands. The Kowloon-Canton railway, completed in 1912, linked Kowloon with the New Territories and China. It helped encourage more of Hong Kong's expanding populace (now surpassing a quarter million) to move across into Kowloon.

Hong Kong's unique position as a meeting place between China and the outside world was maturing. The 90,000 inhabitants of the New Territories had a history of independence from China—there is little record of them being under Chinese rule before the eleventh century. Since many had been engaged in smuggling activities and rebelled fiercely against the new Qing dynasty, the emperor forced them to move inland from the sea in 1662. Later on, coastal fishermen and farmers from farther north joined them. By the end of the nineteenth century, other rebels had gravitated to the area. Hong Kong had already become a place where China and the outside world could meet. The Hong Kong and Chinese Bank, founded in 1865, had grown into the biggest bank in China by the end of the century. Hong Kong and Macao facilitated contact, remittances, investment, and trade with overseas Chinese in countries that did not have diplomatic relations with China. Hong Kong's non-Chinese populace still did not exceed 20,000; fewer than 1,500 were British. Chinese in Hong Kong could study and discuss new ideas without worrying about political consequences; they could learn about parliamentary government and speak English as their principal language. The Red House, located in the New Territories, became the center where several coups against the Qing dynasty were planned. Hundreds of individuals involved in those aborted attempts sought refuge there. Sun Yat-sen studied medicine at Hong Kong's College of Medicine for the Chinese, which would expand into Hong Kong University in 1911, the year he founded the republic (see Chapter 4).

The Suez Canal opened in 1869, making the voyage from western Europe to India and the Far East much shorter. Between 1880 and 1890, Britain's foreign investment rose to three-quarters of its domestic investment.

Its foreign trade was greater than that of France, Germany, and the United States combined. Still, by the end of the century British exports to China constituted only 1.5 percent of its total exports; Britain and all its colonies combined exported less to China than to Holland (Welsh, 1993:282, 318). This would not change markedly before the end of World War II. Hong Kong's trade in opium and other goods made it basically profitable, but not among Britain's greatest sources of colonial income. Britain decided to concentrate its military forces in Singapore, rather than Hong Kong. Shanghai's volume of trade came to match that of Hong Kong.

Many Chinese became wary of Britain's imperialism and the strict social segregation it maintained between Chinese and white inhabitants of its colonies. The Whampoa Military Academy just outside Guangzhou became the launching ground in 1925 for Chiang Kai-shek's attempt to take China back from the warlords, who had removed power from Beijing. Using weapons and advisers supplied by the Soviet Union, he swept out from Guangzhou to take territory from the warlords. This was accompanied by strikes and student demonstrations. On May 30, 1925, British troops fired on some demonstrators in Shanghai, killing and wounding several, and this precipitated strikes against the British in many cities. During one of those strikes in Hong Kong, British troops killed over fifty Chinese and wounded a hundred more. For sixteen months China boycotted Hong Kong ships and goods, crippling its economy. Soon China's united front had split apart, Japanese aggression grew, and the republic sought aid from the United States and Britain. Hong Kong's trade resumed.

When Japan occupied Hong Kong in 1941 after a short battle, it had 1.6 million inhabitants. Britain returned to liberate the island in 1945 and quickly restore law and order, a stable currency, public utilities, adequate supplies of food, and a stable business climate. This contrasted sharply with the situation in Chinese cities. And Britain's policy of continuing good relations with the Kuomintang while establishing early diplomatic relations with the new communist regime contrasted with the behavior of other Western powers in the region. That set the stage for a new and important phase in Hong Kong's history. As civil war erupted in China hundreds of thousands of refugees poured across Hong Kong's border, until both sides shut off the flow by 1950. Many of these refugees, fleeing Shanghai and other former commercial centers, were experienced in business. The immigration created a huge housing problem, spurring Hong Kong's government into a massive housing construction program. Thousands of small industries employed many of the new workers.

□ Living with the People's Republic

China contended that Hong Kong had been the result of treaties imposed on China and was therefore a part of China temporarily under foreign occupation. There was always a conflict between the new Chinese

Hong Kong boat dwellers, 1964.

Republic's anti-imperialism and its relations with Britain (Jain, 1976:158–183). Although the People's Republic of China (PRC) was slow to create full diplomatic links with Britain due to Britain's refusal to break off relations with Taiwan, it never broke the relations it established early on. Britain reluctantly went along with the United States' call for an embargo of China; yet trade continued through Hong Kong (Boardman, 1976). The Bank of China building in Hong Kong housed the New China News Agency; in the absence of formal diplomatic relations, it acted as the representative of the PRC for relations with Britain. The American consulate in Hong Kong became the largest in the world, gathering intelligence on China and seeking to keep communist goods from reaching the United States through Hong Kong. The consulate's presence helped encourage cooperation between smugglers and Hong Kong revenue officers. Meanwhile, many prominent Shanghai businesspeople opened small workshops producing clothing and small consumer goods. In contrast to Britain and China, they were free to make purchases in stable U.S. dollars. Taxes were low, wages were rising, and profits could be sent out of the colony freely. The civil disturbances of the Cultural Revolution (see Chapters 4 and 7) spread into Hong Kong in 1967 and disrupted the economy briefly. The island gradually increased its exports to the outside world and remained the easiest point of entry for visitors to China. Hong Kong manufacturers, seeking more cheap labor, began to establish factories in the nearby province of Guangdong.

When China's opening to the world began in 1978, Hong Kong was perfectly positioned to become the hub of the reforms taking place in the special economic zones discussed in Chapters 4 and 5. Two of the first four zones to be established—Shenzhen and Zhuhai (adjoining Macao)—are close to Hong Kong. A Hong Kong resident who had made billions on the Hong Kong real estate market, Gordon Wu, immediately began construction on a six-lane turnpike linking Shenzhen to Hong Kong, using his own money. At that point, Shenzhen was just a farming village. The colossal gamble spurred colossal growth. Today Shenzhen is filled with factories, skyscrapers, amusement parks, hotels, and office buildings. Hong Kong's new U.S.$7 billion airport includes highways, bridges, tunnels, and new towns. Guangdong's government is building roads, bridges, airports, and vast swamp reclamation projects. Hong Kong and Kowloon are packed with new luxury office complexes, hotels, convention centers, wharves, and shopping malls. The Pearl River delta and the Yangtze River delta around Shanghai, farther north, are the fastest growing economic regions in the world, often surpassing 20 percent increases in gross domestic product (GDP) a year (see Lyons, 1994). Hong Kong has become the world's eighth-largest trading economy, accounting for about a sixth of China's total GDP (Patten, 1997). Hong Kong is the largest foreign investor in the Philippines, the second-largest in Vietnam, and third-largest in Indonesia, Thailand, and Taiwan (Gilley, 1997).

Between 1970 and 1993, Hong Kong's economy quadrupled in size (its per capita GDP surpasses those of Britain, Australia, Canada, and Italy), but the percentage of its GDP deriving from manufacturing dropped from 31 to 11 percent. Over 80 percent of Hong Kong manufacturers have set up production facilities elsewhere in China, where they employ some 5 million people (more than double Hong Kong's workforce).[2] Hong Kong's trade in goods expanded thirty-seven-fold since 1970 (*Hong Kong,* 1995: 65–66).[3] Eighty percent of its exports are either to or from the rest of China; more than half of China's exports are handled through Hong Kong.[4] Over half of China's foreign investment comes from or through Hong Kong; China is the third-largest investor in Hong Kong (U.S.$149 billion in 1996).[5] Hong Kong's airport is the world's second busiest in terms of cargo tons carried and the third busiest in terms of passengers, and Hong Kong harbor is the world's busiest container port; with 1998, airport traffic grew 10 percent a year and harbor cargo by 20 percent.

To adapt to its new roles as China's financier, marketer, raw materials supplier, quality controller, packager, and shipper, Hong Kong's government has invested heavily in developing harbor and airport facilities, office and convention space, education, housing, and health care.[6] Between 1963 and 1995, the portion of government expenditures devoted to health, education, housing, and social welfare grew from 21 percent to 48 percent. Since 1970, expenditures on public housing have grown over 6 percent a year (Welsh, 1993:478; "The Importance," 1997); over half the populace lives in subsidized public housing, paying low rent or purchase fees (*Hong Kong,* 1995:209). Health care at family planning, child and maternal

Hong Kong harbor, 1964.

Hong Kong harbor, 1996.
The buildings are much taller and the air pollution much heavier.

health centers, social hygiene clinics, tuberculosis clinics, and emergency wards is provided free of charge, and other health services are heavily subsidized by the government (*Hong Kong,* 1995:176).[7] The government spends 21 percent of its recurrent budget and 5 percent of its capital budget on education to ensure that the workforce adapts to the new demands of technology and the service economy. Students with inadequate means receive grants to pay for school fees, travel, and textbooks from primary school through university. Hong Kong had one university at the end of World War II; six have been founded since (four since 1985), specializing in business, technical, and adult education. Secondary schools offer many technical, industrial, and business courses, with apprenticeships and training for the disabled. Buildings and equipment are modern and advanced. In 1987, only one young person in thirty-three pursued a higher education; by 1997, one in four did (Patten, 1997).

More than half the revenues for this derive from a corporate profits tax, income taxes, and the tax on land sales. Seven percent come from taxes on bets at the Hong Kong Jockey Club (which generates twice the revenue of all U.S. race tracks combined). The rest come from various stamp duties, fees, duties on imports (cars, gasoline, cigarettes, liquor), utilities, hotel rooms, airport use, motor vehicles, estates, and many other transactions. There is no capital gains tax. Still, government expenditures account for only 16 percent of GDP, compared with 42 percent in Britain and 68 percent in Sweden (McGurn, 1996).

Hong Kong is a useful place to evade authority. Officers of Chinese state-owned firms use assets derived from listing on the Hong Kong stock exchange to buy their parent companies at deep discounts—avoiding Chinese taxation and secretly diverting funds to their own pockets. When exporting through Hong Kong, they leave profits behind in Hong Kong firms they control by undervaluing the exported good as it enters Hong Kong and is sold to their puppet firm. Over a thousand Chinese state-owned firms have created such Hong Kong "joint ventures"; many relatives of China's senior government ministers sit on the boards ("The Chinese," 1994).[8] This gives them an especially strong personal, as well as political, incentive to keep Hong Kong's economy healthy, but it also puts them in a position to harm China's economy. Some of these companies, like Everbright, have been sending cadre officials from the mainland to manage firms they have come to control in Hong Kong; others, like Citic Pacific, have largely left Hong Kong managers in charge of the business. The former approach has proven disastrous (Sender, 1996; McGurn, 1996). As increasing numbers of companies sell shares to members of China's State Council, this problem grows.

□ The Transition to Chinese Rule

Hong Kong was ruled by a governor appointed by Britain from 1841 to 1997. Initially, he was assisted by a Legislative Council also composed of appointed individuals. In 1884, one Chinese was appointed to the council; the number grew to three (out of eighteen) in 1929. In 1984, the British and Chinese governments issued a joint declaration on the future of Hong Kong. At that point, all members of Hong Kong's Legislative Council were still appointed (though elections for some members of a sanitary board, later broadened into an urban council, had been held since 1883).

The Sino-British Joint Declaration agreed to return Hong Kong to China on July 1, 1997. Never in modern history has a handover of territory been agreed on so far in advance. Hong Kong would be a special administrative region guaranteed an "open and free plural society" with its own laws, institutions, and freedoms for fifty years (Bueno de Mesquita, Newman, and Rabushka, 1996). It could maintain its liberal policies on exchange controls; join international trade and cultural organizations; collect its own taxes and use them for its own purposes; and determine its own policies on international air travel, land rights, passports, and shipping rights. Hong Kong would be part of China but would maintain a separate system—"one country, two systems." A joint liaison group would conduct consultations to prepare for the turnover.

In 1985, for the first time in Hong Kong's history, the governor agreed to hold elections for some seats on the Legislative Council (twenty-four of its fifty-six members; by 1991, fifty of sixty). Some other members were appointed by newly created district boards and regional councils as well as the urban councils; a majority of members of the district boards and a minority of the members of the regional and urban councils were chosen by elections. The governor did not get approval from the joint liaison group, and Chinese leaders were angered by the move. They remembered that the 1898 lease on Kowloon and the New Territories had provided for Chinese to retain control of local government there; the following year the British voided that part of the agreement and took direct control of local government. And the 1984 offer of "one country, two systems" in the Sino-British Joint Declaration, as with the similar offer to Taiwan in 1981 discussed shortly, had assumed that both systems would restrain democracy. In 1994 China's government indicated that, after the transfer in 1997, it would ignore Hong Kong's reforms. In 1996 China appointed a preparatory committee to choose the governor's replacement; a third of the members were owners of major Hong Kong companies, and another third were Hong Kong professional people, while the rest came from China. The committee chose the owner of a major shipping company to replace the governor and endorsed Beijing's plan to cancel all the new changes in the legislature, but to elect a new one the following year on its own terms. That election in 1998 brought a record 53 percent of the electorate to the polls to directly elect twenty of the new body's sixty members; thirty more were indirectly elected by corporate and professional voters. Parties critical of the government won over two-thirds of the votes (and a third of the legislature's seats under complex voting rules) and called for a speedup of electoral reform.

Under Hong Kong's Basic Law, it will hold direct elections for a majority of legislative seats and for its chief executive by 2007 ("Unintended Consequences," 1998). A new Court of Final Appeals was created in Hong Kong to replace the British High Court in London, which had formerly been the highest court of appeals, though China's National People's Congress retains the ultimate right to amend Hong Kong's Basic Law should it wish to do so. The Committee of Twelve (with six members chosen by Beijing and six by Hong Kong) will review the constitutionality of legislation passed by Hong Kong's legislature. British troops garrisoned in Hong Kong were replaced by troops from the PRC. Hong Kong's professional civil servants, who had been running the government, retained their jobs so long as they declared loyalty to the new regime. Over half of Hong Kong's citizens hold British passports; they are technically violating China's citizenship laws, but in 1996 the Chinese government announced a "don't ask; don't tell" policy toward them. Many of those British passport holders also have passports, houses, apartments, and investments in Vancouver, the United States, Australia, Britain, and elsewhere and can therefore move their money at will.

China has succeeded in attaching Hong Kong to China. However, China has had difficulty controlling the behavior of other provinces and special economic zones, and Hong Kong, with a long history of independence and many wealthy leaders, may be even more difficult to control. Although the government in Beijing obviously has a strong interest in letting Hong Kong fulfill functions that have been essential to China's growing prosperity, it is also wary of how political activities by Hong Kong's citizens might affect groups elsewhere in China. During the opening months of Hong Kong's absorption into China, however, Beijing resisted any temptations to overtly interfere in Hong Kong's affairs. The 1997 Asian economic turndown brought a sharp drop in Hong Kong's real estate prices, exports, and tourism. In places like Shanghai's Pudong special economic zone, mainland China is increasingly developing the infrastructure and talents to bypass Hong Kong when doing business with foreigners. While Hong Kong's trade and assets remain formidable, these phenomena provide warning that it will need to develop new economic strategies, such as working with firms on the mainland to develop communication systems and other high-technology applications.

■ **TAIWAN**

We turn now to the other focal point for overseas Chinese—Taiwan, formerly Formosa (Map 2.2). At the end of World War II, overseas Chinese took power there. Like Hong Kong, it is heavily involved in China's economy. But is it a part of China or a separate nation? Why does this small island figure so prominently in Chinese and world affairs?

China has never succeeded in establishing cultural or political dominance over the island of Formosa. In the seventeenth century, Chinese traders from Guangdong and Fujian began crossing the straits to Formosa, purchasing deer hides and horns from hunters and traders there (Rubinstein, 1997). These Chinese established some small settlements along Formosa's southwest coast. Chinese and Japanese pirates and Spanish traders also sought refuge in nearby harbors, and in 1624 Dutch traders established the fort of Zeelandia on one of them. Chinese settlers moved to these towns. During the following two decades, the Ming dynasty was falling to Manchu invasion. A Fujian pirate with a trading empire extending to Japan had a son, Koxinga, by a Japanese wife. Koxinga turned his father's home of Xiamen (in Fujian; see Map 2.2) into a major trading port, but as the Qing armies moved toward his city, he set his eyes and guns on Zeelandia. Although the Dutch resisted his assault for several months, in 1662 they surrendered. When the Qing conquerors pursued their policy of removing coastal Chinese of Fujian and Guangdong inland to cut off their independent trading activities, tens of thousands of them fled to Zeelandia. In 1683 a large Qing fleet finally brought it under submission.

The Qing established a new city, Tainan, near Zeelandia, and declared it the capital of the island, which would now be a part of Fujian province. They largely left it alone, restricting further Chinese immigration and declaring that the lands belonging to the native Formosans should be retained by them. After a revolt during the eighteenth century, hoping to make it less of a frontier society, the emperors allowed wives and children to join the Chinese men on the island and the Chinese to rent land from the native islanders. In 1858 an "unequal treaty" (see Chapter 7), the Treaty of Tianjin, opened additional treaty ports, including two on Formosa. By that time, numerous Chinese were crossing the straits to settle cities and farms there. In 1871, Formosan aborigines killed fifty-four shipwrecked Ryukyu sailors (the Ryukyu Islands are located between Taiwan and Japan; see Map 2.1). Japan asserted its right to seek justice for the Ryukyuans. The Ryukyu Islands had been paying tribute to China since 1372 but had also been paying tribute to Japan since 1609 (without China's knowledge). The Japanese sent a fleet to Formosa in 1874. The Chinese fleet defending Formosa contained guns for firing salutes that would burst if real shells were fired; it could not mount a defense. The treaty that followed gave Japan the right to build barracks on Formosa, paid for by China (Welsh, 1993: 315–317; Hsu, 1980:84–88). The Japanese then occupied Formosa but, after protests from the British, retreated. In 1879, they annexed Okinawa and the other Ryukyus. In 1885, China declared Formosa a full province. Within a decade, the Japanese soundly defeated the Chinese navy in the Sino-Japanese War. The Treaty of Shimonoseki (Cameron, 1975:155–162), signed in 1895, forced China to give Japan Formosa (which they renamed

Taiwan), the Pescadores Islands (in the straits between Formosa and the mainland), and the Liaodong peninsula of Manchuria (the southern tip of Liaoning; see Map 2.2).

The Japanese forced the Chinese inhabitants of Taiwan to learn the Japanese language and customs. They used the island to supply Japan with food, wood, minerals, and chemicals; its economy prospered as Japan's Co-prosperity Sphere took over Asia. At the Cairo Conference in 1943, anticipating Japan's defeat, Franklin D. Roosevelt and Winston Churchill agreed to the demand of Chiang Kai-shek that Taiwan be awarded to his Kuomintang Nationalists. Nationalist troops entered the island in 1945, but their corruption and inefficiency soon eroded its stability and economy. When riots erupted in 1947, they suppressed them brutally, executing thousands of intellectuals and prominent citizens and contributing to enduring resentment of the Nationalists by the native Formosans. By 1949, the communists were overwhelming the Nationalist troops on the mainland (see Chapter 4); 2 million of them fled to Taiwan, where Chiang Kai-shek set up his government in exile. Having cleared him and his armies from the mainland, the communists vowed to take Taiwan as well and complete their victory. The Nationalist base closest to mainland was on the island of Quemoy, part of a group of fourteen islands just outside Amoy Bay, outside the old Chinese treaty port of Xiamen. Just beyond Quemoy lies the Taiwan Straits that separate Taiwan from the mainland. The communists began shelling that island group in October 1949 but did not have the military capability to mount an immediate invasion of those islands or of Taiwan. In the months that followed, both the communist and Nationalist forces ceased hostilities while they assessed their options. The U.S. secretary of state, Dean Acheson, gave a speech outlining U.S. strategic interests in the area without mentioning South Korea and Taiwan.

Then, on June 25, 1950, North Korea attacked South Korea. Two days later, the United States extended protection to Taiwan. It gave Taiwan military assistance and patrolled the straits between Taiwan and the mainland (Accinelli, 1997; Cheng, Chi, and Wu, 1995; Tucker, 1994). In 1954 China shelled islands in the Taiwan Straits; in response, the United States signed a treaty with Taiwan guaranteeing to defend it and the Pescadores Islands just to the west of it within the straits from invasion, in exchange for a pledge that Taiwan would not attack the mainland without approval by the United States. Six months later, China pledged it would use only peaceful means to liberate Taiwan and declared that Kuomintang members were even welcome to visit China. Until the Cultural Revolution began, China gave official receptions for all visiting groups of overseas Chinese, but this did not stop further hostilities. When China began bombarding the offshore islands of Quemoy and Matsu in 1958, the United States sent in troops (Hinton, 1972:67–92; Jain, 1976:82–111). In 1962, Chiang Kaishek threatened to invade the mainland; the United States restrained him, and the Soviet Union threatened to support China against an invasion.

Photo: Robert E. Gamer

The old European treaty port enclave on Gulangyu island (foreground), Xiamen (upper left), and Amoy Bay and the Quemoy islands (upper right).

The United States initiated a massive program of military and civilian aid to Taiwan (Tucker, 1994). Chiang Kai-shek initiated land reforms to give land to native Formosan farmers, restricted imports, and helped foreign industries in a special economic zone obtain credit and avoid taxes and regulations on exports. (This zone, created in the 1960s, would become a model for mainland China's special zones after 1978, which were discussed in Chapters 4 and 5.) With exports of manufactured goods surging, Taiwan's gross national product (GNP) quadrupled between 1950 and 1980 (Marsh, 1996; Gold, 1986). When U.S. president Richard Nixon visited Beijing in 1972, he agreed to leave how to work out the integration between Taiwan and the mainland up to both sides. When the United States resumed full diplomatic relations with China in 1979, it broke off formal relations and its defense treaty with Taiwan. Taiwan also lost its seats on the International Monetary Fund and the World Bank. Since Taiwan claims to represent all of China (calling itself the Republic of China, not the Republic of Taiwan), and mainland China also claims Taiwan as one of its provinces, the bodies had to choose which regime represented China. Recognizing the People's Republic of China as the government of China required breaking off formal relations with the Republic of China. This was a dramatic switch.

By 1979, Taiwan's per capita GNP was six times that of mainland China.[9] But discontent was growing on the island. Riots in 1971 and 1972 had protested Taiwan's loss of its United Nations seat and special relationship with the United States, as the United States and the People's Republic of China warmed relations. People were angry over corruption and lack of freedoms under Kuomintang rule, and native Formosans were expressing resentment over the takeover of their island by Chinese from the mainland; many of them wanted Taiwan to declare itself independent of the mainland, with no aspirations to become a part of or to take over China. Then it could gain diplomatic recognition and join international bodies like any other nation. The Kuomintang claimed the right to put down these demonstrations with strict military measures because it was still engaged in a civil war to regain the mainland. In 1975, Chiang Kai-shek died and was succeeded by his son, Chiang Ching-kuo. He, in turn, died in 1988.

Meanwhile, investment continued to pour into Taiwan, and its trade rose markedly. Two of China's first four "special economic zones" created in 1980, Shantou (in Guangdong) and Xiamen (in Fujian), are on the coast opposite Taiwan. The initial investment response was slow, but by the end of the decade it was picking up speed rapidly. Due to the political tensions, Taiwanese trade and investment on the mainland had to be done quietly through Hong Kong. In 1987, just before his death, Chiang Ching-kuo lifted the ban on travel to the mainland, opening a flood of Taiwan investment and tourism there. He also lifted the strict martial law that had tightly restricted civil liberties for years, which allowed opposition parties to form and the press to print opposing views; for the first time, native Formosans could win legislative seats. Many of them backed the Democratic Progressive Party. Chiang's successor to the presidency and control of the Kuomintang, Lee Teng-hui, was born and raised in Taiwan. He held the first open elections for a fully elected national legislature, which left the Kuomintang with a slim majority of seats, and later (as discussed in Chapter 4 and later in this chapter) held elections for president.

One of the most controversial issues raised by a number of leaders of the Democratic Progressive Party, now the principal opposition party, is a call for total independence for Taiwan. Even the new legislature contains seats for districts on the mainland and for overseas Chinese in Southeast Asian countries—a strange phenomenon discussed further in Chapter 7. Those seeking independence would simply declare Taiwan a sovereign nation, with no formal links to overseas Chinese and no claim over the mainland. In 1991, President Lee sought to defuse this issue by putting the shoe on the other foot. He called on Beijing to recognize Taiwan as a separate, independent nation. Then Taiwan would negotiate with China over reunification, providing it renounces the use of military force against Taiwan and introduces democracy and free enterprise on the mainland (terms Lee knows are not acceptable to the communist regime). First there would be informal contacts, then official governmental contacts, and finally steps toward reunification.

In 1981, Beijing suggested that Taiwan might become a special region of China with its own system of government (continuing under Kuomintang rule) and military forces. Beijing is not inclined to retreat from that position, though it may accept a greater Taiwanese presence within international economic and trade bodies. Meanwhile, millions of Taiwanese visit relatives on the mainland, and billions of dollars of investment capital flow across the straits. Billions of dollars in indirect trade flows between the two places through Hong Kong. Nine percent of direct foreign investment in China comes from Taiwan, making it the second-largest foreign investor in China; two-thirds of foreign investment in China comes through Taiwan and Hong Kong ("The Importance," 1997).[10] Nongovernmental organizations have been created to consult on repatriation of mainlanders who have illegally migrated to Taiwan, youth exchanges, protecting investments, control of smuggling and fishing, intellectual property rights, and other issues.

Still, Taiwan persists in seeking recognition by international bodies as the legitimate government of China. It has sought readmission to the United Nations, formal visits by its president to other nations, admission into international trade organizations, and unofficial and informal relations with as many countries as possible. Only twenty-nine countries (largely poor nations from Central America and Africa) still maintain diplomatic relations with it rather than with the PRC. It has offered economic aid to those poor nations in exchange for diplomatic relations. The most prosperous among them, South Africa, switched recognition to Beijing in 1998. Beijing strongly resists all moves by other countries to maintain relations with Taiwan. When the president of the United States invited President Lee to visit the United States for an informal, unofficial visit in 1995, Beijing raised the level of tension. It sent its fleet into the Taiwan Straits shortly before Taiwan's first presidential election in 1996 and talked of threatened invasion. These actions may have dampened enthusiasm for independence, but they also frightened foreign investors, brought denunciations from governments around the world, and failed to prevent Taiwan's voters from returning President Lee to office. A week later, Beijing—still trying to show toughness—announced that Hong Kong's legislative reforms would be abandoned after 1997 and that the popular chief secretary of Hong Kong's civil service would be removed for opposing this move (she was later asked to stay). China had indicated two years earlier it would abandon the reforms, so that came as no surprise; but the timing and tone of the formal announcement and accompanying dismissal (flying in the face of its assurances that Hong Kong's civil service would remain independent and coming immediately after the crude attempts to influence

Taiwan's election) pushed panic buttons. During the week that followed, as many people applied for British passports as had applied during the five previous years combined; sports arenas were hastily requisitioned to hold the lines of applicants. This gave over half of Hong Kong's populace these escape documents (Gilley, 1996a). Taiwan, whose president and legislature were now democratically elected, weighed in with an announcement that it would give refuge to political dissidents after 1997.

Shortly thereafter, Beijing demanded that some judges it did not like step down and handed Hong Kong's government a list of "ten demands" it must carry out before the turnover; when asked to compromise, it refused to do so. It threatened to reimpose British laws passed before the agreement to turn over Hong Kong, including those allowing severe repression of political dissidence and censorship of the media. It called the Hong Kong Alliance in Support of Patriotic Democratic Movements, whose members include legislators, "subversive" and implied that its members could not serve in future legislatures (Gilley, 1996b). The fact that Hong Kong's new Court of Final Appeals and its Committee of Twelve's power to review the constitutionality of legislation passed by Hong Kong's legislature can be overruled by China's National People's Congress underscores the seriousness of those demands.

Younger residents do not respond cordially to such uses of blunt military and political instruments; Beijing did not return to such tactics after Hong Kong became a special administrative region in July 1997, adopting instead a deliberate policy of remaining publicly silent on Hong Kong issues. Efforts to undermine the independence of Hong Kong's bureaucracy and courts would frighten the business community and bring a flight of capital. The many banks maintaining headquarters in Hong Kong can move to Singapore and elsewhere. Since Hong Kong has been the principal provider of capital to fuel China's reforms, such flight could threaten the entire reform process.

The issue of Taiwan's relationship with China inextricably enmeshes the 55 million overseas Chinese, most of whom live in Hong Kong, Taiwan, and Southeast Asia. Some of them are billionaires, leading guilds and trading associations that dominate the economies of Indonesia, Singapore, Malaysia, Thailand, the Philippines, Burma, and China itself. They can move themselves and their money at will. They have intimate connections with the leaders and bureaucracies of all these governments. As mentioned earlier, together they may hold almost as much investment capital as Japan (Seagrave, 1995:285). Even Chinese living in other Southeast Asian countries who are seeking to assimilate as citizens must face the hatred of many fellow citizens who resent Chinese dominance of their economies; Chapter 7 pursues this issue further. The lives of all expatriate Chinese are tied together (see Suryadinata, 1985; Lever-Tracy, Ip, and Noel, 1996; Robison and Goodman, 1996). Leaders of both mainland China and Taiwan know they cannot go it alone without the full input from this overseas Chinese community; their prosperity depends on the investment capital and trading links of that widely dispersed community. Any political disintegration of mainland China would also divide the loyalties of the overseas Chinese, and any civil war there would spread to Taiwan. Overseas Chinese would be asked to choose sides, further endangering their positions in their own adopted lands. In an incident that highlights this interdependence, a week after Taiwan's presidential election, President Lee and Premier Jiang Zemin reestablished informal contacts. Taiwan's business community, with ever-increasing indirect investment in China via Hong Kong and other ports, encourages such dialogue and an end to Taiwan's ban on direct investment and trade (Baum, 1997). And as the Democratic Progressive Party shows increasing strength (winning twelve of twenty-three local government seats in 1997 elections), Beijing has opened dialogue with its leader, Hsu Hsin-liang; he talks of creating better business links with China, softening the message of those in his party who demand complete independence.

■ TIBET

China, Hong Kong, and Taiwan carry out a shadow play with thrusts and parries of defiance, although they in reality share many cultural ties and commercial transactions. Tibet represents a sharp contrast: It is an area without such cultural or economic ties to China. Here the thrusts and parries are far more real. Tibet's ties to China are complex, as are the animosities that separate them.

The Tibetans are a people living on a high, sparsely settled plateau (see Chapter 2, especially Map 2.4). Along the drier northern portions of the plateau—in Kham, Amdo, and Chantang—they made their living by herding sheep and yak. Along the river valleys and mountain passes to the south, a feudal nobility and the king parceled out lands in exchange for rent and labor services. The king presided over the region, while Bonpos, storytellers and singers of riddles, propagated religious beliefs associated with totemism, animism, and occultism (see Chapter 12).

The seventh to tenth centuries A.D. brought power and culture to Tibet (Stein, 1972:56–75). In the seventh century, Buddhism (also examined in Chapter 12) was introduced to Tibet from India. The country developed a written alphabet, based on the script of Kashmir. Tibetan kings, beginning with the legendary Songsten Gampo, conquered territory in Nepal, Turkestan, and far north and east into what is now Yunnan, Sichuan, Xinjiang, Qinghai, Gansu, and Shaanxi (Map 2.2); married daughters of Chinese emperors and of rulers from other surrounding principalities; and welcomed scholars from Iran, China, and elsewhere. They signed peace treaties delineating borders with China in A.D. 734 and 822.

In about A.D. 775 the king presided over the construction of a great Buddhist monastery at Samye, brought in a monk from Nepal to be its abbot, ordained several noblemen as monks, and arranged for monks from China to come in and preach. In 791 he decreed Buddhism to be the official state religion. Monks would have special privileges and were to receive gifts. Several hundred people took religious vows. In the succeeding centuries, disputes severely weakened the power of the kings. Some nobility resisted the adoption of Buddhism, whereas others (sometimes claiming divine descent) took charge of the monasteries that sprouted up all over Tibet and surrounding regions, passing the post of abbot from uncle to nephew. Many people joined these monasteries, which began to acquire much land and wealth. Doctrinal disputes arose among the monks; some became morally decadent. Traditional Bonpo religious practices continued and were absorbed into Buddhism.

At the start of the thirteenth century, Genghiz Khan, who was to conquer China (see Chapter 3), sent his troops deep into Tibet, whose leaders agreed to send him tribute and thus symbolically recognized his power. Genghiz Khan, in turn, invited the Tibetan scholar Sakya Panchen to Mongolia, where he helped him devise an alphabet. In 1270 Kublai Khan granted Sakya's followers rulership of all Tibet; meanwhile, Genghiz's descendants were fighting among themselves for control of Mongolia, and various Tibetan monasteries allied with some of them to contest for power, often joining in with their own fighting forces. Two orders, the Black Hats and Red Hats, started looking in villages shortly after the death of a holy individual (a bodhisattva, which we discuss more later) to seek a baby into which his soul had been reborn, or reincarnated; those individuals were brought into monasteries to be raised as lamas (superior ones). In 1283 the Red Hats declared one of these lamas ruler of Tibet. In keeping with Tantric traditions popular at the time in India, these orders used mantras (repetition of mystical words and revolutions of prayer wheels) and mandalas (sacred diagrams) in rituals and meditations.

Concerned with these two orders' emphasis on worldly power and wealth, in 1403 a monastic scholar founded the Geluk-pa (Yellow Hat) order that also emphasized the need for monastic discipline, personal morality, and good works as part of the search for total liberation from the world. Armed with this reforming zeal, armies from its monasteries fought with the Red Hats, the followers of Sakya and the remaining Bonpo orders, and the weak kings and princes for political control.

In 1578 the Mongol ruler Altan Khan, seeking an ally among the contending forces, declared the head of the Yellow Hats to be the Dalai (oceanwide, all-embracing) Lama; Altan's influence was extended further upon the death of this Dalai Lama, when the monks found his reincarnated successor to be none other than a great-grandson of Altan Khan! But this did not stop the bitter fighting for control among the various sects and the

Photo: Robert E. Gamer

Tibetan monk with prayer wheel.

kings, who in turn allied with rival Mongol princes. In the seventeenth century, a Mongol ruler sent his armies into Tibet, killed the king, helped the fifth Dalai Lama build the great Potala palace that still dominates the valley above the capital of Lhasa, and in 1641 declared him the sovereign of Tibet (with a governor nominated by the Mongols to assist him). The

Manchu ruler who founded the Qing dynasty in 1644 also was his ally. After his death, bitter fighting broke out among various Tibetan factions, Mongol princes, and Chinese emperors over his successors and who should choose them. When Dzungar Mongol forces invaded Tibet in 1717 to drive out another Mongol prince who had killed the sixth Dalai Lama and was trying to replace him with his own candidate, China attacked Tibet and established small military garrisons there.

The Dalai Lama ruled with assistance from ministers, a council composed of monks and nobles, another monastic council, and a National Assembly composed of high officials; important decisions required the approval of all these bodies (Rahul, 1969:22–72; Richardson, 1984:14–27). Between the death of a Dalai Lama and the growth into manhood of the next, regents were chosen to assume his office. Nobles held power and supervised administration in various regions of Tibet; Kham and Amdo to the northeast remained under Mongol control. China sent to Lhasa two formal representatives *(ambans)*, who exerted influence over governance of the kingdom; when they killed a Tibetan official in 1750, Tibetans massacred Chinese living there (Hoffman, 1971:59–63). Chinese troops intervened to restore order. Chinese troops also helped Tibet repel an invasion by Gurkhas (from Nepal) in 1788 to capture Ladakh (east Kashmir, on Tibet's western border), dictated the peace terms, and closed the borders to the British—who may have instigated the invasion. The Chinese also successfully helped the Tibetans resist invasions from Dogras (out of Kashmir) in 1841. In 1847, despite that loss, the British marked the boundaries between Tibet and Dogra; the Chinese did not recognize that boundary, which later became the focus of China's dispute with India. But another Gurkha attack in 1855 was more successful, forcing Tibet to give them trading rights.

The Dalai Lama is believed (along with Songsten Gampo, Tibet's first centralizing Buddhist king) to be the indirect reincarnation of Avalokitesvara, Tibet's patron bodhisattva (one who has achieved a degree of enlightenment but has returned to earth to help living mortals achieve spiritual progress). Tibet's second great lama is the Panchen Lama, abbot of one of the great monasteries, who is the reincarnation of Amitabha, before whom Avalokitesvara took his original bodhisattva vow to return to Tibet and help all beings (Richardson, 1984:38–60). In exchange for helping repulse the 1788 Gurkha invasion, China demanded the right to dictate the candidates from whom the Dalai Lama and Panchen Lama would be chosen. They also allowed those two worthies to open new monasteries in Mongolia and China and welcomed lamas in the imperial court at Beijing. Panchen Lamas began to make that trek, developing ties to China's emperors. The Tibetans continued to ignore the Chinese when choosing Dalai Lamas.

The thirteenth Dalai Lama, who lived from 1875 to 1933, befriended a Russian lama who put him into contact with the Russian czar (Richardson,

1984:73–90, 268–273). This frightened the British, who tried to enter into negotiation with China and Tibet to define Tibet's western and southern borders. When this failed, they sent a military expedition that captured Lhasa in 1904. The Dalai Lama fled to Mongolia, but the British government (before withdrawing its troops) forced his officers to sign a convention delineating the borders it preferred and opening Tibet to trade with Britain. Two years later the British signed a treaty with China, to which Tibet was not a party, recognizing the 1904 treaty and China's suzerainty (see Chapter 7) over Tibet, and in 1907 Britain concluded a similar treaty with Russia. Then in 1910 a Chinese general began to conquer territory in eastern Tibet and then Lhasa itself, forcing the Dalai Lama to flee to India. When the new republic was formed in China in 1911, it declared that Tibet was now an integral part of China, but it could not control or defend China's troops there, now under attack from Tibetan forces. China withdrew its troops, and the Dalai Lama expelled the Chinese *ambans* and renounced all Chinese connections with Tibet. In 1914 Sir Henry McMahon obtained a Tibetan, but not a Chinese, signature on a convention signed in Simla, India, which defined boundaries and still—over Tibet's continuing objections—declared China suzerain over Tibet and even declared large portions of former Tibetan territory to be a part of China (Shakabpa, 1967: 246–259).

Except for the continuing British representative in Lhasa, who had a radio transmitter, Tibet largely cut itself off from the outside world. This isolation was enforced by a ban on selling food to outsiders and reinforced by the absence in Tibet of any roads or wheeled vehicles; only about twenty Europeans and Americans are known to have entered Tibet during this entire period. In 1915 the Khams rose in revolt and captured back some of the terrain taken from them by Chinese troops in 1910. Tibet created no ministry of foreign affairs and exchanged no ambassadors. Few Tibetans spoke any foreign language. Four students were sent to study in England, and in 1948 a few more were selected to study in India. An English school begun in Lhasa in 1945 had to close when the monasteries objected that it might interfere with religious beliefs. Tibet did not issue a passport until 1948, when it sent out a trade delegation in an attempt to alert the world to its pending troubles (Shakabpa, 1967:289–290).

After the death of the thirteenth Dalai Lama in 1933, China sent an informal delegation to Lhasa with a radio transmitter. They stayed until the Tibetan council seized the radio transmitter and expelled them in 1949, after the leader of the Sera monastery, which had ties to the Chinese, attempted a coup to overthrow the young Dalai Lama's regent (Shakabpa, 1967:290–294; Harrer, 1954:222–231), and after the new communist regime in China declared again that Tibet was a province of China. In 1950, with some assistance from Kham rebels who resented Lhasa's rule, Chinese troops entered Tibet, defeated the Dalai Lama's troops, and forced his government to sign a 1951 agreement on "the peaceful liberation of Tibet," declaring it an integral part of China. The Dalai Lama and the "existing political system in Tibet" would stay in place and freedom of religion would be guaranteed, but foreign affairs would be handled by Beijing (Richardson, 1984:290–293). El Salvador wanted the topic placed on the agenda of the United Nations, but other countries—following India's lead in contending that China's right to suzerainty over Tibet was already established—refused to allow such a debate (Richardson, 1984:186).

China's new government wished to repudiate the treaties imposed on China's emperors by Britain and other imperial powers (see Chapter 7). The 1914 Simla convention had declared that the Dalai Lama had spiritual authority over all believers in his faith but removed his political authority from Nepal, Ladakh, Bhutan, and Sikkim; the Dalai Lama had been reluctant to accept that latter provision, and China had refused to sign the convention. When India achieved independence in 1947, its government, led by Pandit Jawaharlal Nehru, moved quickly to establish good relations with China (Moraes, 1960:117–143; Patterson, 1960; Rahul, 1969:88–100). After initial objection, it acquiesced in the agreement signed between China and Tibet in 1951 and signed an agreement in 1954 giving up rights British India had claimed in Tibet, contending that China had long had suzerainty over Tibet. This treaty, however, did not precisely define the border between Tibet and India. Nehru was somewhat disturbed when he discovered that Chinese maps still showed large portions of India and those border states within Chinese territory; China's foreign minister Zhou Enlai assured him the maps were simply old (Richardson, 1984:199, 215).

Under Tibet's traditional social system, about a third of the land had belonged to the state, a third to the nobility, and a third to the monasteries who parceled these out to families (Stein, 1972:93–163; Hoffman, 1971:175–192; Carrasco, 1959; Cassinelli and Ekvall, 1969). Commoners (i.e., those not monks, nuns, or nobility) turned over portions of their agricultural output for rent and taxes and were asked to contribute labor to civic projects; otherwise they were free to move about Tibet and engage in commerce with the traders who regularly traversed the kingdom. They could also serve as administrators or rise within the hierarchy of the monasteries, though top positions usually went to nobility. Local administrators settled civil disputes and tried criminal cases, often with an ear to local public opinion; severe punishments were rare (Cassinelli and Ekvall, 1969:153–185; Richardson, 1984:16–17; Stein, 1972:134–138; Harrer, 1954:88–90). Though people lived on meager diets, starvation was uncommon because granaries and seed supplies were maintained by public authorities for distribution in time of need or emergency (Cassinelli and Ekvall, 1969:98, 115; Stein, 1972:109–125; Harrer, 1954:234). Although the Dalai Lama was both the chief sovereign and leader of his own religious order (the Yellow Hats), many monasteries belonged to other Buddhist orders or followed traditional Bon practices, and some adhered to Islam, Hinduism, and other religions, which they were free to do. Many regions were headed by nobility or monasteries that did not belong to the Yellow Hat order (Cassinelli and Ekvall, 1969:65–72; Harrer, 1954:179). The monasteries, which subjected nuns and monks to stern discipline, maintained their own militias and stored large quantities of weapons (Harrer, 1954:246–247). Young men were conscripted to serve in the army and monasteries (Cassinelli and Ekvall, 1969:294–301). The vast majority of people inside and outside the monasteries were illiterate. The monasteries resisted the introduction of modern medicine, fearing it would endanger their hold on power; infant mortality in Tibet was among the highest in the world. They also resisted introducing motor vehicles, electricity, and industry. People moved from village to village on foot or horseback and carried goods on the backs of yaks.

Around Lhasa and along the southern river valleys of Tibet, China initially left this social system largely intact, though it immediately began demanding the appointment of its supporters within the administration (Richardson, 1984:191–192). It opened new clinics and schools and rapidly proceeded to build Tibet's first road, through the Amdo and Kham regions of eastern Tibet. The road soon brought in new settlers from other parts of China as well as reforming communists. In the regions along the road, China began to take traditional grazing lands and pastures from monasteries and nobility for redistribution to commoners and new settlers. Chinese leaders talked about rescuing serfs from exploitation by feudal lords and corrupt and cruel religious leaders and returning land to the people (Strong, 1976). The Kham and Amdo people have a history of fierce independence and rebellious behavior and resented these attacks on their religion and traditional way of life (Harrer, 1954:109–131). They began physically and verbally attacking Chinese troops sent to their outposts (Patterson, 1960:125–128; Richardson, 1984:200–205). By 1954 the road reached Lhasa, and the signing of the treaty between China and India proved that Nehru would not come to Tibet's rescue.

In 1955, Beijing established a Preparatory Committee for the Autonomous Region of Tibet, headed by the Dalai Lama, to plan for new administrative procedures in Tibet; many traditional leaders feared this meant a further weakening of their powers. By 1956 open rebellion had broken out among the Kham and Amdo; Chinese troops struck back with brutal force, shelling monasteries and jailing and killing rebels. Little mercy was shown by either side (Patt, 1992:50–53; Patterson, 1960:125–135). Guerrilla forces and stockpiles of arms grew in number and strength. In 1959 came a final showdown; the Dalai Lama fled to India (Patterson, 1960:148–191; Richardson, 1984:199–214, 242; Moraes, 1960:1–31; Strong,

1976:57–86; Patt, 1992:143–166; Shakabpa, 1967:322–363). From his new exile home in India, the Dalai Lama announced that 65,000 Tibetans had died in the fighting and 1,000 monasteries had been destroyed.

The repression extended into war between China and India. China was displeased that India offered asylum to the Dalai Lama and growing numbers of Tibetan exiles. China contended, probably on good evidence (see U.S. Department of State, 1996) that Indian intelligence officers cooperated with the Central Intelligence Agency and Taiwan's Special Operations unit to encourage and arm the Tibetan rebels, and complained that Tibetan guerrillas still were receiving supplies from Nepal and India. Chinese authorities declared that Ladakhi residents of Tibet were there illegally and had to return to India; China wanted territory from Ladakh, in order to build a new road between Beijing and Lhasa. India insisted on sticking to the border defined in the 1914 Simla treaty. India withdrew trade with China. In 1962 heavy fighting broke out between India and China on the Ladakh border. China came away with minor territorial gains of land it had claimed (North, 1974:93–96; Ojha, 1969:146–173; Richardson, 1984:224–243).

Large numbers of monks, lamas, members of the nobility, and other educated people were imprisoned, executed, and subjected to brutal treatment (Patt, 1992:205–209). Most monks were removed from monasteries, the monasteries' wealth was taken, and the people were discouraged from religious practices. Public rectification campaigns forced people to attack

Tibetan monastery at Bodnath in Nepal. Mt. Everest is in the background.

their family members and village notables. Tibetans were restricted to their villages and organized into communes and into teams to carry out public works projects. Food was strictly rationed, and many suffered from hunger and starvation. Large numbers of Chinese troops were stationed throughout Tibet. Despite all this, resistance activities continued (Richardson, 1984:194, 237–258; Patt, 1992:210; Barnett, 1994; Dawa, 1987). In 1965 the Preparatory Committee for the Autonomous Region of Tibet changed Tibet's administration: The new Tibetan Autonomous Region (TAR) would be divided into eight military zones. The Panchen Lama, who had previously been used to counter the Dalai Lama, refused to cooperate further and was placed in custody. The onset of the Cultural Revolution in 1966 brought in the Red Guards, who looted and razed thousands of the remaining monasteries (there had been 2,700 in Tibet and 3,800 more in Sichuan, Qinghai, Gansu, and Yunnan) and dismissed the military government. They finally turned on themselves in factional fighting, and the People's Liberation Army tried to restore order. Some nobility and former Tibetan officials were called back to positions of prominence and some monasteries and holy places restored.

In 1987, Tibetans staged another uprising (Schwartz, 1994). China declared martial law, which it has continued with varying degrees of intensity since that time. News and travel from the outside world are strictly censored and controlled. The Dalai Lama travels throughout the world urging support for Tibet, and many socially prominent individuals support his cause. Heads of state (including the prime minister of Mongolia) continue to support China's claims over Tibet while urging China's leaders to show restraint in their treatment of Tibetans and a reopening of dialogue with the Dalai Lama. They are under pressure from some constituents to press Tibet's case for independence more firmly. China contends that Tibet is its internal affair, not the business of foreign nations that have sought to dominate Tibet themselves in the past or have asserted the right to impose their authority on Alsace-Lorraine, Scotland, Wales, Ireland, Quebec, Newfoundland, Inuit, American Indians, Hawaii, or the rebelling confederacy in the U.S. South. In 1988, China and the Dalai Lama began using informal channels to explore ways to resume dialogue.

Meanwhile (except for the Potala of the exiled Dalai Lama looming above the city as an empty monument, the Jokhang temple, and some ruins of monasteries destroyed in the Cultural Revolution and after the uprising), nearly all the original structures of Lhasa have been torn down and replaced with dull new office buildings and apartments. To maintain dominance, China has steadily increased Han immigration into Lhasa. Nearly all the shops, hotels, and offices there and in other Tibetan towns and cities are run by immigrant Han, who now constitute a majority of the capital's inhabitants. They have come far from their home provinces to this harsh land for the traditional reasons Chinese have always migrated overseas:

They can make far more money, with fewer taxes and political restrictions on their commerce. Meanwhile, many Tibetans, unable to adapt to the new economy, are reduced to permanent unemployment. Before 1959, high percentages of the male populace were monks; now very few boys become monks, and they often do not progress far in school. Religious practices are once again allowed but discouraged; it is unlawful to display a picture of the Dalai Lama. The Chinese complain that their religion leaves Tibetans with attitudes not conducive to discipline and economic endeavor; without liberation, the monks would have denied modernization to Tibet. Most of Tibet's people live outside Lhasa, away from the economic boom. Many are among China's poorest inhabitants.

■ CONCLUSION

The new Han inhabitants of Lhasa are a new breed of overseas Chinese, this time living in their own land. They bring with them economic skills and networks and tremendous personal drive. They foment vast economic change, but they also leave in their wake resentments from local peoples. Since they often make little attempt to mingle with or understand those whose cultural zones they have entered, the source of that resentment is hard for them to comprehend. In Chapter 7 we explore this further while examining China's foreign policy in Southeast Asia.

In this chapter, we have noted similar tensions in the relations of Taiwan's Han rulers with the native Formosans, whose land was conquered by the Japanese and then handed over to the Han by the victorious Allies. Much of Taiwan's economy depends on investments in and by other regions of Asia and on selling goods on the world market; however, this helped the Han immigrants more than the native Formosan farmers, until they revolted and received U.S. aid. Lhasa's new economy, too, depends heavily on the world market of tourism and precious metals; this money flows more to Han immigrants than to native Tibetans. Once established, this inherent economic dependence on the outside world can help restrain the harshest behavior and parochial instincts of Han rulers; it is hard, for example, to maintain the strictest martial law while increasing tourism. But such economic growth also widens the gap between rich and poor, Han and native.

Hong Kong provides a unique environment for interaction between Han and outsider. Largely uninhabited until recent times, lying on the shores of China, and provided with a large and secure harbor area, it was able to develop its own culture. From the beginning, its entire economy revolved around entrepôt trade, selling goods to the outside world. It was outside China and smoothly connected with the world beyond. It contains no hostile natives whose economy once depended on something else; most of its immigrants came because they wanted more freedom to carry out such commerce. Still, its prosperity has depended on remaining apart from the rules and relationships that restrict commerce in China. For thousands of years, China has depended on merchants who would venture outside its shores, using their cultural skills to make deals and connections for the homeland. Its own culture zone has encouraged investment and trade but also confined it within a regulatory grid and circle of obligations that limits their size and scope (see Chapters 4 and 7). The real money can be made in places where those regulations and obligations are not in force. Pulling Hong Kong inside the orbit endangers that arrangement. It is essential that the "one country, two systems" formula in the Sino-British Joint Declaration of 1984 work.

In Chapter 7, we shall take a broader look at China's connections with the outside world as we survey its overall foreign policy. A similar question persists. Is China seeking to take economic, political, and strategic control of this outside environment? Or is it seeking to join a community of nations that encourages both individual and national competition, with respect for the sovereignty of other nations? The fight between the PRC and the Republic of China over who represents all of China and (as we will examine more in Chapter 7) all the overseas Chinese highlights this dilemma. Do China and the overseas Chinese insist on being one cultural and political zone, with a giant grid of interlocking economic connections? Or can the economic grid coexist among competing sovereign nations, be they China and Taiwan, or China and the United States and Russia? This debate is in progress.

■ NOTES

1. Shanghai, at that time a fishing village, is today China's largest city with 1 percent of its population producing 4.3 percent of its GDP, 12 percent of its industrial output, and 11 percent of its financial services. "Good Fences Make Good Neighbors." 1997. *Far Eastern Economic Review* 160, no. 6 (February 6):36.
2. Research Department. 1995. The 132,000 enterprises in China backed by Hong Kong money account for two-thirds of foreign-funded enterprises there.
3. In 1970 manufacturing provided 47 percent of jobs; in 1994, 20 percent (Research Department, Hong Kong Trade Development Council, 1995).
4. When a firm ships components of goods through Hong Kong before they are manufactured elsewhere and then brings the finished goods through Hong Kong, this classifies as a re-export. Eighty percent of Hong Kong's exports consist of such re-exports, 92 percent of which are to or from China. Fifty-six percent of Hong Kong's re-exports are of Chinese origin, and a third are destined for sale in China. Research Department, 1995.
5. Japan (U.S.$191 billion) is first, Britain (U.S.$166 billion) second, and the United States (U.S.$94 billion) fourth. Many township and village enterprises send money to Hong Kong so they can bring it back as "foreign capital"; this may account for a fourth to a third of Hong Kong's investment in China. The Bank of

China and its twelve sister banks are the second-largest banking group in Hong Kong. Research Department, 1995; Gilley, 1997.

6. More than half the revenues for this derive from a corporate profits tax, income taxes (with a top rate of 17.5 percent), and the tax on land sales. The rest come from various stamp duties, fees, duties on imports (cars, gasoline, cigarettes, liquor), taxes on bets at the race track, utilities, hotel rooms, airport use, motor vehicles, estates, and many other transactions.

7. Hospital ward patients pay a flat U.S.$7 a day for all services, including surgery; fees may be waived for those without funds. Outpatient services at the 291 clinics generally cost under U.S.$4. Home visits by community nurses and sessions at psychiatric or geriatric centers cost less than U.S.$6.

8. Of the 10,000 firms the People's Liberation Army admits owning, about a tenth are in the Shenzhen special economic zone, just across the border from Hong Kong.

9. Taiwan's per capita income rose from U.S.$200 in 1952 to U.S.$10,000 in 1993 (Bellows, 1994:119) China's 1992 per capita income was U.S.$1,900, and Hong Kong's was U.S.$20,000 (Noland, 1995).

10. Nearly 59 percent of foreign investment comes through Hong Kong and Macau and 8.7 percent from Taiwan (which largely enters through Hong Kong). The United States contributes 8.1 percent and Japan 7.8 percent.

■ BIBLIOGRAPHY

□ The Pacific Rim and Overseas Chinese

Aguilar-San Juan, Karin (ed.). 1994. *The State of Asian America: Activism and Resistance in the 1990s.* Boston: South End Press.

Bell, Daniel, David Brown, Kanishka Jayasuriya, and David Martin Jones. 1995. *Towards Illiberal Democracy in Pacific Asia.* New York: St. Martin's Press.

Cameron, Nigel. 1975. *From Bondage to Liberation: East Asia 1860–1952.* Hong Kong: Oxford University Press.

Chan, Sucheng. 1991. *Asian Americans: An Interpretive History.* Boston: Twayne.

Chin, Ung-Ho. 1997. *Chinese Politics in Sarawak: A Study of the Sarawak United People's Party.* Oxford: Oxford University Press.

Dirlik, Arif (ed.). 1997. *What Is in a Rim? Critical Perspectives on the Pacific Region Idea.* 2d ed. Lanham, MD: Rowman and Littlefield.

———. 1998. *Chinese on the American Frontier.* Lanham, MD: Rowman and Littlefield.

Engholm, Christopher. 1994. *Doing Business in Asia's Booming "China Triangle": People's Republic of China, Taiwan, Hong Kong.* Englewood Cliffs: Prentice-Hall.

Fitzgerald, Stephen. 1972. *China and the Overseas Chinese: A Study of Peking's Changing Policy 1949–1970.* Cambridge: Cambridge University Press.

Garth, Alexander. 1973. *The Invisible China: The Overseas Chinese and the Politics of Southeast Asia.* New York: Macmillan.

Gibney, Frank. 1992. *The Pacific Century: America and Asia in a Changing World.* New York: Charles Scribner's Sons.

Karnow, Stanley. 1984. *Vietnam: A History.* New York: Penguin.

Lever-Tracy, Constance, David Ip, and Tracy Noel. 1996. *The Chinese Diaspora and Mainland China: An Emerging Economic Synergy.* New York: St. Martin's Press.

Naughton, Barry. 1997. *Economics and Technology in the PRC, Taiwan, and Hong Kong*. Washington: Brookings Institution.

Noland, Marcus. 1995. "Implications of Asian Economic Growth." *Working Paper Series No. 94–95*. Washington, DC: Institute for International Economics.

North, Robert C. 1974. *The Foreign Relations of China*. 2d ed. Encino, CA: Dickenson.

Ojha, Ishwer C. 1969. *Chinese Foreign Policy in an Age of Transition: The Diplomacy of Cultural Despair*. Boston: Beacon.

Reid, Anthony (ed.). 1997. *Sojourners and Settlers: Histories of Southeast Asia and the Chinese*. London: Allen and Unwin.

Robison, Richard, and David S. G. Goodman (eds.). 1996. *The New Rich in Asia: Mobile Phones, McDonalds, and Middle Class Revolution*. London: Routledge.

Seagrave, Sterling. 1995. *Lords of the Rim*. New York: G. P. Putnam.

Simon, Denis. 1995. *The Emerging Technological Trajectory of the Pacific Rim*. Armonk, NY: M. E. Sharpe.

Suryadinata, Leo. 1985. *China and the ASEAN States: The Ethnic Chinese Dimension*. Singapore: Singapore University Press.

Takaki, Ronald. 1989. *Strangers from a Different Shore: A History of Asian-Americans*. New York: Little, Brown.

Wang, Gungwu. 1991. *China and the Overseas Chinese*. Singapore: Times Academic Press.

Yahuda, Michael. 1996. *The International Politics of Asia-Pacific, 1945–1995*. New York: Routledge.

☐ Hong Kong

Berger, Suzanne, and Richard K. Lester (eds.). 1997. *Made by Hong Kong*. Oxford: Oxford University Press.

Boardman, Robert. 1976. *Britain and the People's Republic of China, 1949–74*. London: Macmillan.

Brown, Judith M., and Rosemary Foot. 1997. *Hong Kong's Transitions, 1842–1997*. New York: St. Martin's Press.

Bueno de Mesquita, Bruce, David Newman, and Alvin Rabushka. 1996. *Red Flag over Hong Kong*. Chatham, NJ: Chatham House.

Chan, Kam Wah. 1997. *Social Construction of Gender Inequality in the Housing System: Housing Experiences of Women in Hong Kong*. Brookfield, VT: Ashgate.

Chan, Ming K., and Gerard A. Postiglione (eds.). 1996. *The Hong Kong Reader: Passage to Chinese Sovereignty*. Armonk, NY: M. E. Sharpe.

Chan, Ming K., and John D. Young. 1994. *Precarious Balance: Hong Kong Between China and Britain, 1842–1992*. Armonk, NY: M. E. Sharpe.

Chan, Raymond K. H. 1996. *Welfare in Newly-Industrialized Society: The Construction of the Welfare State in Hong Kong*. Brookfield, VT: Ashgate.

Chang, David Wen-Wei Chang, and Richard Y. Chuang. 1997. *The Politics of Hong Kong's Reversion to China*. New York: St. Martin's Press.

Chung, Stephanie P. Y. 1997. *Chinese Business Groups in Hong Kong and Political Changes in South China, 1900–1920s*. New York: St. Martin's Press.

Cohen, Warren I., and Li Zhao (eds.). 1997. *Hong Kong Under Chinese Rule: The Economic and Political Implications of Reversion*. New York: Cambridge University Press.

Enright, Michael, Edith Scott, and David Dodwell (eds.). 1997. *The Hong Kong Advantage*. New York: Oxford University Press.

Flowerdrew, John. 1997. *The Final Years of Hong Kong*. New York: St. Martin's Press.

Gilley, Bruce. 1996a. "Darkness Dawns." *Far Eastern Economic Review* 159 (April 11):14–15.

———. 1996b. "The Sound of Silence." *Far Eastern Economic Review* 159 (April 18):26.

———. 1997. "Regional Politik." *Far Eastern Economic Review* 160 (May 29): 22.

"Good Fences Make Good Neighbors." 1997. *Far Eastern Economic Review* 160, no. 6 (February 6):36.

Hibbert, Christopher. 1970. *The Dragon Awakes: China and the West 1793–1911*. New York: Harper.

Hong Kong 1995: A Review of 1994. 1995. Hong Kong: Government Printing Department.

Jain, J. P. 1976. *China in World Politics: A Study of Sino-British Relations 1949–1975*. New Delhi: Radiant Press.

Kwok, Reginald Yin-Wang, and Alvin Y. So (eds.). 1995. *The Hong Kong–Guangdong Link: Partnership in Flux*. Armonk, NY: M. E. Sharpe.

Lo, Shui-Hing. 1997. *The Politics of Democratization in Hong Kong*. New York: St. Martin's Press.

Lyons, Thomas P. 1994. *Poverty and Growth in a South China County: Anxi, Fujian, 1949–1992*. Ithaca: Cornell University Press.

Lyons, Thomas P., and Victor Need (eds.). 1994. *The Economic Transformation of South China: Reform and Development in the Post-Mao Era*. Ithaca: Cornell University Press.

McGurn, William. 1996. "Diminishing Returns." *Far Eastern Economic Review* 159, no. 24 (June 13):62–68.

Miners, Norman. 1996. *The Government and Politics of Hong Kong*. 5th ed. Oxford: Oxford University Press.

Morris, Jan. 1997. *Hong Kong*. Rev. ed. New York: Vintage.

Patten, Christopher. 1997. "Farewell to My Hong Kong." *Newsweek* (March 3).

Research Department, Hong Kong Trade Development Council. 1995. "Hong Kong Economy Profile no. 188" (June 6).

Sender, Henny. 1996. "Tarnished Luster." *Far Eastern Economic Review* 159, no. 21 (May 16).

Skeldon, Ronald (ed.). 1994. *Reluctant Exiles? Migration from Hong Kong and the New Overseas Chinese*. Armonk, NY: M. E. Sharpe.

Spence, Jonathan. 1990. *The Search for Modern China*. New York: Norton.

Sung, Yung-wing. 1991. *The China–Hong Kong Connection: The Key to China's Open-Door Policy*. Cambridge: Cambridge University Press.

"The Chinese Takeover of Hong Kong Inc." 1994. *Economist* (May 7).

"The Importance of Foreign Devil Money." 1997. *Economist* 342, no. 8007 (March 8):10.

Tsai, Jung-fang. 1993. *Hong Kong in Chinese History*. New York: Columbia University.

"Unintended Consequences." 1998. *Economist* 347, no. 8070 (May 30):41.

Wang, Enbao. 1995. *Hong Kong, 1997: The Politics of Transition*. Boulder: Lynne Rienner Publishers.

Wang, Gungwu. 1996. *Hong Kong's Transition: A Decade After the Deal*. Oxford: Oxford University Press.

Welsh, Frank. 1993. *A History of Hong Kong*. London: HarperCollins.

Yahuda, Michael. 1996. *Hong Kong: China's Challenge.* London: Routledge.

□ Taiwan

Aberbach, Joel D., David Dollar, and Kenneth L. Sokoloff (eds.). 1994. *The Role of the State in Taiwan's Development.* Armonk, NY: M. E. Sharpe.

Accinelli, Robert. 1997. *Crisis and Commitment: United States Policy Toward Taiwan, 1950–1955.* Chapel Hill: University of North Carolina Press.

Baum, Julian. 1997. *Far Eastern Economic Review* 160, no. 45 (November 6):22–26.

Bellows, Thomas J. 1994. "Politics, Elections, and Political Change in Taiwan." *Asian Journal of Political Science* 2, no. 1 (June):114–148.

Chang, David W. 1994. "Taiwan's Unification with Mainland China: Problems and Prospects." *Asian Journal of Political Science* 2, no. 1 (June):149–168.

Chang, Parris H., and Martin L. Lasater (eds.). 1993. *If China Crosses the Taiwan Strait.* Lanham, MD: University Press of America.

Cheng, Tun-jen, and Stephan Haggard (eds.). 1992. *Political Change in Taiwan.* Boulder: Lynne Rienner Publishers.

Cheng, Tun-jen, Chi Huang, and Samuel S. G. Wu. 1995. *Inherited Rivalry: Conflict Across the Taiwan Straits.* Boulder: Lynne Rienner Publishers.

Chiou, C. L. 1996. *Democratizing Oriental Despotism: China from 4 May 1919 to 4 June 1989 and Taiwan from 28 February 1947 to 28 June 1990.* New York: St. Martin's Press.

Clough, Ralph N. 1993. *Reaching Across the Taiwan Strait: People to People Diplomacy.* Boulder: Westview Press.

Copper, John F. 1995. *A Critique of Beijing's "White Paper" on China's Reunification.* Lanham, MD: University Press of America.

———. 1996. *Taiwan: Nation-State or Province?* 2d ed. Boulder: Westview Press.

———. 1997. *The Taiwan Political Miracle: Essays on Political Development, Elections, and Foreign Relations.* Lanham, MD: University Press of America.

Dickson, Bruce. 1997. *Democratization in China and Taiwan: The Adaptability of Leninist Parties.* Oxford: Oxford University Press.

Gold, Thomas B. 1986. *State and Society in the Taiwan Miracle.* Armonk, NY: M. E. Sharpe.

Harrell, Stevan, and Huang Chun-chieh (eds.). 1994. *Cultural Change in Postwar Taiwan.* Boulder: Westview Press.

Hickey, Dennis Van Vranken. 1997. *Taiwan's Security in the Changing International System.* Boulder: Lynne Rienner Publishers.

Hinton, Harold C. 1972. *China's Turbulent Quest: An Analysis of China's Foreign Relations Since 1949.* New York: Macmillan.

Hood, Steven J. 1996. *The Kuomintang and the Democratization of Taiwan.* Boulder: Westview Press.

Hsing, You-tien. 1997. *Making Capitalism in China: The Taiwan Connection.* New York: Oxford University Press.

Hsu, Immanuel C. Y. 1980. "Late Ch'ing Foreign Relations, 1866–1905." Pp. 70–141 in John K. Fairbank and Kwang-Ching Liu, *The Cambridge History of China, Volume 11, Late Ch'ing, 1800–1911, Part 2.* Cambridge: Cambridge University Press.

Hughes, Christopher. 1997. *Taiwan and Chinese Nationalism: National Identity and Status in International Society.* London: Routledge.

Klintworth, Gary. 1995. *New Taiwan, New China: Taiwan's Changing Role in the Asia-Pacific Region.* New York: St. Martin's Press.

Leng, Tse-Kang. 1996. *The Taiwan-China Connection: Democracy and Development Across the Taiwan Straits.* Boulder: Westview Press.

Marsh, Robert. 1996. *The Great Transformation: Social Change in Taipei, Taiwan, Since the 1960s.* Armonk, NY: M. E. Sharpe.

Metzler, John J. 1996. *Divided Dynamism: The Diplomacy of Separated Nations— Germany, Korea, and China.* Lanham, MD: University Press of America.

Rubinstein, Murray A. (ed.). 1994. *The Other Taiwan, 1945 to the Present.* Armonk, NY: M. E. Sharpe.

——— (ed.). 1997. *Taiwan: A History.* Armonk, NY: M.E. Sharpe.

Simon, Denis F., and Michael Kau Ying-mao. 1992. *Taiwan Beyond the Economic Miracle.* Armonk, NY: M. E. Sharpe.

Skoggard, Ian A. 1996. *Dynamic in Taiwan's Postwar Development: The Religious and Historical Roots of Entrepreneurship.* Armonk, NY: M. E. Sharpe.

Syu, Agnes. 1995. *From Economic Miracle to Privatization: Initial Stages of the Privatization Process in Two SOEs on Taiwan.* Lanham, MD: University Press of America.

Tien, Hung-mao. 1989. *The Great Transition.* Stanford: Hoover Institution Press.

——— (ed.). 1995. *Taiwan's Electoral Politics and Democratic Transition: Riding the Third Wave.* Armonk, NY: M. E. Sharpe.

Tucker, Nancy Bernkopf. 1994. *Taiwan, Hong Kong, and the United States, 1945– 1992.* New York: Maxwell Macmillan.

Wachman, Alan M. 1994. *Taiwan: National Identity and Democratization.* Armonk, NY: M. E. Sharpe.

Wu, Jausheih Joseph. 1995. *Taiwan's Democratization: Forces Behind the Momentum.* Oxford: Oxford University Press.

☐ Tibet

Avedon, John F. 1994. *In Exile from the Land of the Snows: The Definitive Account of the Dalai Lama and Tibet Since the Chinese Conquest.* New York: Harper-Perennial.

Barnett, Robert (ed.). 1994. *Resistance and Reform in Tibet.* Bloomington: University of Indiana Press.

Beckwith, Christopher I. 1987. *The Tibetan Empire in Central Asia: A History of the Struggle for Great Power Among Tibetans, Turks, Arabs, and Chinese During the Early Middle Ages.* Princeton: Princeton University Press.

Bell, Charles. 1924. *Tibet, Past and Present.* Oxford: Clarendon Press.

Carnahan, Sumner. 1995. *In the Presence of My Enemies: Memoirs of Tibetan Nobleman Tsipon Shuguba.* Santa Fe: Clear Light, 1995.

Carrasco, Pedro. 1959. *Land and Polity in Tibet.* Seattle: University of Washington Press.

Cassinelli, C. W., and Robert B. Ekvall. 1969. *A Tibetan Principality: The Political System of Sa sKya.* Ithaca: Cornell University Press.

Craig, Mary. 1997. *Kundun: A Biography of the Family of the Dalai Lama.* Washington, DC: Counterpoint.

Dawa, Norbu. 1987. *Red Star over Tibet.* 2d ed. New York: Envoy Press.

Feigon, Lee. 1996. *Demystifying China: Unlocking the Secrets of the Land of the Snows.* Chicago: I. R. Dee.

French, Rebecca Redwood. 1995. *The Golden Yoke: The Legal Cosmology of Buddhist Tibet.* Ithaca: Cornell University Press.

Ginsburgs, George. 1964. *Communist China and Tibet: The First Dozen Years.* The Hague: M. Nijhoff.

Goldstein, M. C. 1989. *The History of Modern Tibet*. Berkeley: University of California Press.

Grunfeld, A. Tom. 1996. *The Making of Modern Tibet*. Rev. ed. Armonk, NY: M. E. Sharpe.

Gyatso, Palden. 1997. *The Autobiography of a Tibetan Monk*. New York: Grove Press.

Harrer, Heinrich. 1954. *Seven Years in Tibet*. Trans. Richard Graves. New York: E. P. Dutton.

Hoffman, Helmut. 1971. *Tibet: A Handbook*. Bloomington, IN: Asian Studies Research Institute.

Karan, Pradyumna P. 1976. *The Changing Face of Tibet*. Lexington: University Press of Kentucky.

Lhalungpa, Lobsang P. 1983. *Tibet: The Sacred Realm: Photographs 1880–1950*. Millerton, NY: Aperture.

Moraes, Frances Robert. 1960. *The Revolt in Tibet*. New York: Macmillan.

Patt, David. 1992. *A Strange Liberation: Tibetan Lives in Chinese Hands*. Ithaca: Snow Lion Publications.

Patterson, George N. 1960. *Tibet in Revolt*. London: Faber and Faber.

Rahul, Ram. 1969. *The Government and Politics of Tibet*. Delhi: Vikas Publications.

Richardson, Hugh E. 1984. *Tibet and Its History*. 2d ed. Boulder: Shambhala.

Schwartz, Ronald David. 1994. *Circle of Protest: Political Ritual in the Tibetan Uprising, 1987–92*. New York: Columbia University Press.

Shakabpa, Tsepon W. D. 1967. *Tibet: A Political History*. New Haven: Yale University Press.

Smith, Warren W. Jr. 1996. *Tibetan Nation: A History of Tibetan Nationalism and Sino-Tibetan Relations*. Boulder: Westview Press.

Stein, R. A. 1972. *Tibetan Civilization*. Stanford: Stanford University Press.

Strong, Anna Louise. 1976. *When Serfs Stood Up in Tibet*. 2d ed. San Francisco: Red Sun Publications.

U.S. Department of State. 1996. *Foreign Relations of the United States 1958–1960*. Vol. 19. Washington, DC: Government Printing Office.

■ 7 ■

International Relations
Robert E. Gamer

At the end of Chapter 6, we suggested that China is torn between its new desire to become a part of the world community and its traditional wishes to establish cultural and political dominance over its surrounding territories. The notion of being part of a world community composed of sovereign nations is something that has come into focus in China only during your lifetime. For most of its long history, China had little contact with the outside world. Its southern coastal communities developed trading contacts through the South China Sea. Its northern capitals sought to conquer, or protect themselves from conquest by, groups in the regions on China's borders. Abruptly and unexpectedly, all that changed in the nineteenth century when Beijing was brought to its knees by a small fleet of British ships. China spent the next century trying to free itself from domination by countries about which it had little prior knowledge and with which it had little prior contact. Then it spent three decades trying to reestablish rule without outside domination. Now, suddenly, during the last decades of the twentieth century, China has emerged as a premier participant in world trade and a player in regional crises of importance to the major powers; it is surrounded by small, newly independent nation-states dependent on its economic output and competes with Taiwan for seats on international bodies and the investments of enormously wealthy overseas Chinese families. It is scrambling to take full advantage of those opportunities while maintaining unity and stability at home. Those goals sometimes conflict, especially in a nation so recently thrust upon the world stage.

■ CHINA'S FOREIGN RELATIONS BEFORE THE OPIUM WARS

Throughout most of its history, China's leaders had little contact with regions beyond those on the western borders. Largely isolated from the rest of the world, it had much reason to think of itself as the "Middle Kingdom" in the universe. But, as Chapter 6 indicated, long before the time of Christ, its merchants began trade with Java (in the Indonesian archipelago; see Map 2.1), Europe, India, and points between. In the twelfth century B.C., towns stretching from Guangzhou (Canton) to Fuzhou began extensive sea trade with Southeast Asia (see Maps 2.1, 2.2). In the fourth century B.C. a kingdom along China's southern coast, and during the third century B.C. the Qin dynasty (Chapter 3) sent out fleets of rafts full of settlers who might even have reached North America (Needham, 1971). Early in the Han dynasty, Chinese garrisons began to protect traders along the Silk Roads into inner Asia (Map 2.1). In the sixth century A.D., Arab, Jewish, Christian, and Turkish merchants started settling in China's coastal cities. Chinese ship captains (most notably, Admiral Zheng He's expedition into the Indian Ocean early in the fifteenth century, discussed in Chapter 3) accepted gifts from local rulers that they passed on as tribute to Chinese emperors. Merchants coming overland brought the emperors tribute, as did emissaries from some kings of bordering states. As we saw in Chapter 6, China sought to control the administration of Tibet. Beyond this, China had no formal relations with foreign governments.

Like those of Siam (Thailand), Tibet, Japan, and Turkey, traditional Chinese leaders received tribute from lesser kingdoms around them. This solemnized their trade and foreign relations (Fairbank and Teng, 1941). Emissaries or merchants from the lesser kingdoms brought gifts to the leader of the dominant one; the leader of the dominant kingdom reciprocated with gifts of greater value. China's emperors assumed these gifts were an indication that the kingdoms sending them recognized China's cultural superiority. To emphasize this, emissaries carrying the gifts were required to kneel before the emperor, hit their heads against the ground three times, and then lie flat (prostrate themselves) on the ground nine times. This was called the "kowtow." After that, the emperor would hold a banquet for the emissaries, give them gifts of greater value than those they had brought, and accord them the right to trade with China. The emperors interpreted this to mean that the barbarians who brought this tribute had "come to be transformed" and were recognizing China as the center of world civilization. The emperors believed any kingdom sending such gifts was a "vassal" recognizing China's "suzerainty" (dominance) over it. Korea, the kingdom of Melaka (Malacca) on the Malayan Straits (near the southern tip of peninsular Malaysia; see Map 2.1), Siam (Thailand), Burma, and Vietnam (all in Southeast Asia; see Map 2.1), Japan, the Ryukyu islands (stretching between Taiwan and Japan, containing Okinawa), and bordering kingdoms of central Asia all sent emissaries to China's emperors bearing tribute; in exchange, China traded with them. Several ports were open for this trade; foreigners had to reside and stay within neighborhoods reserved for them. Ships came from as far as India and Arabia.

The sixteenth century brought major challenges to this system; new outside forces, coming by sea, challenged China's suzerainty. In 1511 Portuguese ships took over one of China's vassal states, the kingdom of Melaka, and then established a fort on an island off southern China. The emissary they sent to Beijing was rebuffed and jailed. By 1557, in the Pearl River delta below Guangzhou (see Map 2.2), the Portuguese had established the colony of Macao that was sending emissaries to Beijing with tribute in exchange for trading privileges. In 1555 Japanese pirates sacked the city of Nanjing, near the mouth of the Yangtze River (Map 2.2). In 1592 and 1597, the Japanese emperor Hideyoshi invaded China's vassal Korea and some Chinese ports; the threat subsided with Hideyoshi's sudden death. These provocations caused China's emperor to close most ports to trade. Macao became the principal port for China's trade with Japan, until Japan closed its ports to Portugal in 1639. In 1637 a British flotilla shot its way up the Pearl River toward Guangzhou, hoping to open the port. Then in 1685 China decided to open all its ports to foreign trade, and they remained open until 1757.

During the seventeenth century, the expanding Russian empire arrived at China's eastern border; the Ming emperors granted trading rights. When the Mongols, whose territories had bordered those of Russia, took Beijing and established the Qing dynasty in 1644, they created the Lifan Yuan, an agency (staffed entirely by Manchus and Mongols) to deal with Russia. The Russian emperors were not comfortable having their embassies prostrate themselves before the Chinese emperors; they preferred a relationship between empires of equal stature. After some protracted wrangling over kowtowing and some border skirmishes, Jesuit court advisers helped the Lifan Yuan negotiate a treaty—China's first—to demarcate China's western boundaries and stabilize China's relations with Russia. It was signed in Nirchinsk in 1689 and followed by another at Kiakhta in 1729. The treaties prescribed that, in exchange for kowtows in Beijing by Russia's emissaries, China's emissaries would kowtow at the czar's court in St. Petersburg. The trade missions that crossed the borders in increasing numbers would simply exchange gifts without court appearances. In a great break from precedent, Russia was allowed to send a permanent emissary to reside in Beijing, but it was not allowed to trade by sea.

As the volume of outside trade began to expand rapidly during the eighteenth century, China's government found it necessary to create new ways of dealing with the outside world. In 1720 Guangzhou merchants formed the first of the trading organizations *(cohongs),* which became the official points of contact between China and European merchants. After 1757 Guangzhou (Canton) became the only port legally open for foreign trade. But no foreigners were allowed to live there; the employees of their firms had to reside in nearby Macao. By 1784 Americans began trade with Guangzhou.

The *cohongs* had to pay government officials large sums of money from their profits; they recovered this by demanding bribes and arbitrary fees from the foreigners. And the Chinese government kept creating new regulations to control the personal behavior of foreigners, restricting their movement outside Macao. In 1741 a disabled British ship pulled into Hong Kong harbor and was refused assistance. In 1757 the emperor restricted all foreign trade strictly to Guangzhou; women were not to be allowed in the foreigners' warehouses (confining women to their residences downstream in Macao) and men could leave the warehouses, for an escorted walk in a park, only three times a month. Complaints about unfair trade practices had to be mediated by the very merchant associations with which the foreigners were trading. In 1759 Britain's East India Company sent an emissary to the emperor to complain about trade restrictions with the *cohongs*; he was imprisoned. With Britain now the largest seafaring trader in China, King George III sent an expedition to Beijing in 1793 to complain about these conditions and ask for the right to exchange ambassadors, let British live in Guangzhou and create warehouses to trade in other ports, allow missionaries to preach Christianity, and establish an outpost on an island near the mouth of the Yangtze River. Its leader, Lord Macartney, came laden with tribute consisting of Britain's latest manufactures. Qianlong, China's longest-serving emperor and one of its greatest, greeted him warmly (dispensing with a kowtow) and sent him home with many boxes of gifts and a long letter addressed to King George (Schurmann and Schell, 1967:104, 113; Cameron, 1975: 22–45), turning down all his requests. It explained the following:

• All foreigners living in China live in special neighborhoods that they cannot leave wear Chinese garb, cannot open businesses or interact with Chinese subjects, and are never permitted to return home. Ambassadors could not function that way, and China does not need other religious doctrines. The letter adds, "The distinction between Chinese and barbarian is most strict" (Cameron, 1975:33).
• Europeans are permitted to reside in Macao and trade through Guangzhou *cohongs*. They can buy what they want there and are making large profits. Provisions have been made for settling disputes to the satisfaction of Europeans. Rules forbidding Europeans to set foot in Guangzhou and other parts of China cut down on the chance for disputes between Chinese and barbarians and give foreign trading organizations control over their own people.

■ FROM THE OPIUM WARS
TO THE PEOPLE'S REPUBLIC

These rules prevailed until the British fleet forced the Chinese to sign the Treaty of Nanjing in 1842, ending the first Opium War, which is discussed in Chapter 6. During the subsequent half-century, European powers invaded China on numerous occasions; after the peace negotiations that followed, China signed twenty more treaties reinforcing the new rules created by the Treaty of Nanjing and extending them to interaction with Japan, the United States, Peru, Brazil, Russia, and all the major European nations (Tung, 1970:19–31; Bau, 1921:93–180; Cameron, 1975:45–52). Though it was greatly weakened, none of these countries acquired China as a colony. But its sovereignty and interaction with foreign lands had been completely transformed. Suddenly foreigners were able to reside in special neighborhoods in a variety of "treaty ports." They were able to learn Chinese, dress and behave as they pleased, open businesses, trade with anyone, travel in other parts of the cities where they lived, interact with Chinese subjects and propagate their religion, and travel to their homelands whenever they wished. They built industries and railroad lines and hired Chinese workers for jobs at home and overseas. Their boats plied inland waterways. Consuls appointed by foreign governments communicated directly with Chinese officials. Under new rules of "extraterritoriality," foreigners accused of crimes were tried under their own laws.

The new rules required China, for the first time, to establish a national customs office and foreign affairs ministry (in 1861) and to open a school (soon transformed into a college) to train interpreters for Chinese officials dealing with foreigners. By the 1870s China was sending ambassadors abroad and no longer requiring ambassadors received by the emperor to kowtow (Hsu, 1980:81–82). Smarting from its military defeats and loss of sovereignty, the Qing government took steps at "self-strengthening" by acquiring a modern navy, establishing naval and military academies, and sending students abroad to learn about modern technical subjects (Liao, 1984:21–37; Wang, 1966:41, 99; Schurmann and Schell, 1967:206–248; Cameron, 1975:95–111).

Meanwhile (as Chapters 3, 4, 6, and 8 explain), China faced civil wars, disintegration of Beijing's control from the center, extensive migration by many able people, and social and economic problems caused by rapid population growth and economic change. Seeing its weakness, foreign powers took control of countries that had once been China's vassals and of territory within China.

- As we discussed in Chapter 6, the Japanese took Formosa (Taiwan), the Ryukyu Islands (Okinawa), the Pescadores Islands, and the Liaodong peninsula in Manchuria.
- The French took control of Vietnam. They also demanded and received a lease for a port on Hainan Island (Map 2.2).
- The British took Burma. They also leased a port city on the north side of Shandong (Map 2.2) and Kowloon and the New Territories on the mainland opposite Hong Kong.

- Germany forced the Qing to lease it the port of Qingdao (now famous for its beer) and surrounding territory on the Shandong peninsula (Map 2.2).
- Nearby in Manchuria, the Russians received a lease for Port Arthur
  (Lushun, on the southern tip of Liaoning; see Map 2.2).

In retaliation for some missionaries killed during the Boxer Uprising
(see Chapter 12), foreign troops actually occupied Beijing's Forbidden
City from 1900 to 1901, forcing the emperor and empress dowager to flee.
Supported by France and Germany, Russia used the chaos to occupy
Manchuria (Heilongjiang, Jilin, and Liaoning; see Map 2.2), which
prompted an alliance between Britain and Japan to protect their interests
(Hsu, 1980:115–138; Tung, 1970:51–56; Liao, 1984:40–52; Cameron,
1975:163–186).

In 1905 Japan defeated Russia in a war; the two signed a peace treaty
in Portsmouth, New Hampshire, mediated by President Theodore Roosevelt. Roosevelt and the European powers were concerned about protecting the territorial integrity of China. The treaty acknowledged that Korea
was under Japan's sphere of influence and agreed to the withdrawal of all
foreign troops from Manchuria, except for some territory containing railway lines whose lease Russia was to transfer to Japan. Both Russia and
Japan were to be allowed to station some troops in Manchuria to protect
the railway. The Japanese received Port Arthur. This set the stage for forty-
five years of conflict (Hsu, 1980:138–141; Schurmann and Schell,
1967:249–260; Cameron, 1975:201–231) in which Japan would play a
major role (see Table 7.1).

In 1910 Japan annexed Korea. For supporting Britain in World War I
(and despite China's strong objection), the 1919 Treaty of Versailles gave
Germany's land leases in China's Shandong peninsula to Japan, kicking
off the May Fourth Movement of protest discussed in Chapter 13 (Tung,
1970:154–190; Wang, 1966:306–361; Bau, 1921:181–283). To counter the
Soviet takeover of Russia, Japan occupied land bordering Manchuria. The
Soviets kept claim to Russian railroad lines running through Manchuria,
which angered Japan. In 1931 Japan occupied Manchuria and set it up as
the puppet state of Manchuguo. In 1937, Japan attacked China and occupied large portions of it (as Chapter 4 discussed) until Japan's surrender
to the Allied Forces in 1945.

■ FOREIGN POLICY UNDER MAO

During the "united front" between the communists and Chiang Kai-
shek's Nationalists, which lasted from 1936 until the end of World War II,
the United States and the Soviet Union could deal with the communists

Table 7.1 Important Dates in China's Foreign Policy

1842	Treaty of Nanjing ends first Opium War
1861	Founding of Customs Office and Foreign Affairs Ministry
1895	Treaty of Shimonoseki cedes Formosa to Japan
1900	British occupy Forbidden City after Boxer Uprising
1905	Treaty of Portsmouth allows Japanese troops in Manchuria
1919	Treaty of Versailles gives Japan Shandong land leases
1931	Japan occupies Manchuria
1945	End of World War II brings KMT-communist combat
1950	Start of Korean War and U.S. Seventh Fleet in Taiwan Straits
1953	Korean War armistice
1955	Bandung Conference of "nonaligned" states
1956	Tibetan rebellion
1960	Break in relations with USSR
1962	Sino-Indian border war
1964	China explodes atomic bomb
1965	United States enters Vietnam War
1970	China takes Taiwan's United Nations seat
1972	U.S. President Richard Nixon visits China
1975	End of Vietnam War
1979	United States and China establish diplomatic relations
1987	Tibetan rebellion
1989	USSR General Secretary Mikhail Gorbachev visits China
1997	Hong Kong joins China

and the Nationalists at the same time. Even when the united front broke down, both gave technical and military assistance to the Nationalists while maintaining friendly contact with the communists (Sheng, 1998). As the Japanese surrendered, the Nationalist and communist armies turned to fight one another for control of China. The United States assisted only the Nationalists, while Joseph Stalin attempted to play both sides. He turned over control of enormous arms stockpiles and the city of Harbin to the communists and trained and supplied Mao Zedong's troops; he gave the Nationalists command of all the other Manchurian cities (after dismantling many industries and seizing many assets for shipment to the Soviet Union) and maintained good relations with Chiang Kai-shek. Thus, once he captured Beijing and the KMT fled to Taiwan in 1949, Mao felt uneasy taking on Stalin as an ally, but he had nowhere else to turn because he found himself isolated diplomatically (see Hunt and Niu, 1995, for revealing insights into his foreign policy during this period). Britain quickly recognized the People's Republic of China (PRC) (Jain, 1976:24–47) but also continued to recognize the legitimacy of Chiang's regime in Taiwan. Though he made overtures to President Harry Truman, the United States did not respond (Garver, 1993:40). The spread of communism in Eastern Europe was making the United States hesitant to carry on further relations with communist regimes. Therefore, needing foreign assistance, Mao accepted aid from the Soviet Union; this uneasy relationship lasted until 1960, when Premier Nikita Khrushchev withdrew Russian advisers from the PRC. Two days after North Korea attacked South Korea in June 1950, the U.S. Seventh Fleet moved into the Taiwan Straits to protect the Nationalists from invasion by Mao's forces; the United States would not recognize the PRC until 1979. We shall say more about all this in a moment, but first we should assess Mao's strategic considerations as he assumed power.

After 100 years of division and foreign intrusion, Mao sought to reestablish China's traditional borders and to reassert influence over all the regions that once paid tribute to China. That tribute had recognized China's moral and cultural superiority as well as its physical dominance. As a communist, Mao wanted to rid China and its neighbors of imperialist masters and to persuade its neighbors of the superiority of China's communist system. At the same time, he wanted to continue to attract capitalist investment so as to rebuild China's economy and to develop friendly trade relations with foreign nations. That combination of goals called for a delicate balancing act that involved several elements.

• The 11 million overseas Chinese, mostly residing in Southeast Asia, might provide technical skills and investment capital. But as their countries received independence from the colonial powers, they wished to incorporate their Chinese populace into their own citizenry. If the PRC were to continue treating these overseas Chinese as its own citizens, it risked alienating the governments of these new nations.

• Guerrilla movements were challenging the legitimate governments in many of these countries. As China's leader, Mao realized they could help him assert China's dominance over the region. As a communist, he was sympathetic to their revolutionary aspirations of returning power to the exploited lower classes, but he also wanted peace on his borders while he consolidated power and fought outside challengers. He did not want to force neighboring governments into treaties that would give the United States bases on China's borders or into retaliation against their Chinese communities. He wanted the support of the wealthy Chinese living in those countries, who hated the guerrillas and were also being wooed by Chiang Kai-shek to support the Kuomintang in Taiwan. And the guerrillas also had loyalties to their own countries and might not ultimately side with China.

• The PRC wanted admission into the United Nations and other bodies that could provide it with access to world markets and participation in international decisionmaking. But it was determined to defeat Chiang Kai-shek's Nationalist forces that had fled to the island of Taiwan while insisting (as Chapter 6 explained) that they were still the rightful government of all China. Only one could hold China's United Nations seat, and both had supporters there.

• Mao wanted to abrogate "unequal treaties" drawn up between imperial powers and former Chinese governments, but he also wanted trade, investment, and assistance from those imperial powers.

Overseas Chinese stood squarely at the center of all those concerns, so
Mao's government could not walk away from them. More overseas Chinese had contact with the Kuomintang and other parties in China than with
the communists; both sides needed their money and support to continue
fighting one another. Many overseas Chinese were facing political repression and finding it hard to get education or employment; some were joining guerrilla movements in their own countries. The new communist
regime initially responded with a simple offer: Come back home and help
rebuild China. It offered them inexpensive education if they stayed to become residents of China and higher salaries than locals. It created special
banking arrangements, housing, shops, grain allotments, and travel privileges for overseas Chinese and for local relatives of overseas Chinese receiving monetary remittances from them. It urged them to create enterprises in China. Nearly half a million Chinese came back (Fitzgerald,
1972:33). In addition, the government encouraged Chinese families with
relatives abroad to write them soliciting money. It still looked upon all
these overseas Chinese as China's citizens; they could become citizens of
other nations and still retain (dual) citizenship in China.

By 1957 the People's Republic had discovered the amount of technical talent and money and political support it could attract through these
policies was limited, and many Chinese who had stayed home resented the
special privileges accorded those who had left, so it reversed course, un-
leashing a rectification campaign (see Chapter 4) to limit the rights of
these returnees and urge Chinese to cut off their contacts with overseas relatives. By then, it also was negotiating agreements with Burma and Indonesia, the only Southeast Asian countries with which it had diplomatic
relations, allowing (for the first time in history) overseas Chinese who became citizens of those nations to break their affiliation with China, if they
chose to do so. Those choosing this course would no longer receive favors
or protection from China and no longer be considered Chinese citizens.
Furthermore, China now encouraged schools built for Chinese students by
wealthy Chinese in Southeast Asian countries to teach local languages and
history and skills that would prepare them for local employment.

Events in Korea and Vietnam made this normalization possible. North
Korea invaded South Korea in June 1950. Until then, Mao's government
had shown little interest in Korean affairs; the Soviet Union was North
Korea's principal ally. China had been informed by those two countries
shortly before the invasion took place and let North Korean troops stationed on its territory return home to participate. But the entry of United
Nations forces on the side of South Korea and the U.S. Seventh Fleet into
the Taiwan Straits as well as imposition of a trade blockade roused China's

concern (Chen, 1994; Garson, 1995; Cumings, 1981, 1990). In August, the United Nations proposed to China that it mediate a truce in exchange for a United Nations Security Council seat. However, in October General Douglas MacArthur's troops crossed into North Korea and headed toward the Yalu River (the same river the Japanese had crossed when they invaded Manchuria). Beijing lies within 400 miles of that border. China immediately mobilized troops and sent them secretly into North Korea; they succeeded in pushing the United Nations forces back into South Korea (Hinton, 1972:40–49; Garver, 1993:285–286; Gittings, 1974:181–184; Jain, 1976:49–70). A truce was signed three years later, leaving Korea divided. The United States suffered 160,000 casualties and China nearly a million (including one of Mao's sons), leaving deep antagonism and suspicion on both sides. The United States was now firmly committed to "containing" China, holding it within its boundaries and isolating it diplomatically. But China was also angry at the Soviet Union for starting a war on its borders in which China—not the USSR—suffered deep casualties. Hence China now made an all-out effort to improve relations with smaller neighboring Asian countries.

In Vietnam, Ho Chi Minh began guerrilla warfare against the French at the end of World War II. In 1949, Chinese Red Army troops moved to the Vietnamese border to chase remaining Kuomintang Nationalist troops from China (Chen, 1969:212–278). In the next few years, China's government gave Ho's forces small amounts of technical assistance. After the Korean War armistice was signed in 1953, this aid grew dramatically. Ho was attacking governments supported first by the French and then by the Americans, who now were moving to encircle China. Though many leaders of newly independent nations had themselves begun by resisting colonial rulers and therefore might have sympathy for Ho's attempts, they also were wary of attempts by the Soviet Union, the United States, or China to involve them in the Cold War. And communist guerrillas threatened their regimes as well. So China was careful to restrict its support to the Viet Minh in Vietnam, declaring that communist forces in Laos (an area of interest to India) and in Cambodia, where China lent support to Prince Sihanouk, should seek separate settlements. Meanwhile, remnants of Kuomintang troops remained in those areas, supported by the United States.

In 1955 China agreed to end support for communist guerrillas operating in Burma (which, in 1949, had been the first Asian government to recognize Mao's regime); China gave little support thereafter (Tung, 1970:357–62; Gurtov, 1971:89–118; North, 1974:93–96). During talks in 1960 Burma and China agreed to some concessions on territory they claimed. When a more radical socialist government gained power in Burma in 1963, defeating the Maoist guerrillas, it took a harder line against China.

In 1955, leaders of African and Asian nations held a conference in Bandung, Indonesia, to declare a neutral path toward "peaceful coexistence," avoiding alliance with either the Soviet Union or the United States. Zhou Enlai (Shao, 1996), representing China, was a major presence at this conference, declaring China's intent to sign agreements with these nonaligned nations to settle differences over dual citizenship by overseas Chinese, guerrilla warfare waged against independent nations, border disputes, and other contentious issues. As part of these efforts, China distributed hundreds of millions of dollars in aid to developing nations (Garver, 1993:221; Hinton, 1972:248–262; Jain, 1976:112–156; Ojha, 1969:174–209). Zhou Enlai was also competing for allegiance of these nations with India, which also declared its neutrality while seeking aid from the Soviet Union.

Taiwan's continuing insistence that foreign governments allow Chinese residents to fly Nationalist flags and obey their policies strengthened the PRC's position on normalizing relations. Even today, Taiwan's legislature contains seats representing overseas Chinese. As late as 1970, the Kuomintang kidnapped two Manila newspapermen of Han ancestry in the Philippines who did not consider themselves citizens of Taiwan and placed them on military trial for violating Taiwan's emergency regulations (Fitzgerald, 1972:76). Many Southeast Asians saw these assertions and actions as interference with the sovereignty of their own nations. By taking steps to break off ties with overseas Chinese, the PRC was attempting to distance itself from this approach (which had been habitual with Chinese governments during the past century) and thus gain more confidence among governments that feared subversion by overseas Chinese. In addition, few Chinese were now emigrating from the mainland into Southeast Asia.

Acts by surrounding countries made the PRC's attempts at normalization more difficult. Thailand had outlawed separate educational institutions for overseas Chinese (Gurtov, 1971:5–48). Many Southeast Asian countries suppressed Chinese newspapers. The 1955 nationality treaty with Indonesia allowed Chinese who had accepted Indonesian citizenship to regain Chinese citizenship by moving out of Indonesia, leaving many Indonesians wondering whether naturalized Chinese would remain loyal to their adopted country. In 1956 South Vietnam forced all Chinese to declare Vietnamese citizenship and excluded them from Chinese education and most retail trade. In 1960, Indonesia also banned Chinese from retail trade, their principal source of livelihood, and closed many Chinese schools and newspapers. The heat over this controversy sparked riots; the Chinese government sent ships to carry 100,000 refugees to asylum in China. After 1963, China also extricated refugees when repression in India followed the Sino-Indian border skirmishes (discussed in the last section of Chapter 6).

To quell these fears about the loyalty of overseas Chinese, Zhou Enlai announced that Chinese everywhere were free to choose their own citizenship;

he encouraged them to become citizens of and obey the laws of the lands where they resided and to marry local people. Overseas Chinese who chose to retain Chinese citizenship would be expected to obey the laws of the lands where they resided, but ultimately they were subject to the jurisdiction of the PRC and not of Taiwan. And no Chinese should be forced to accept citizenship against their will (Fitzgerald, 1972:112–114, 140–161).

In 1960, China and the Soviet Union broke off relations (Hinton, 1972:205–230; Ojha, 1969:111–145; Jones and Kevill, 1985:17–25; North, 1974:109–127). The Soviet Union, concerned about China's Great Leap Forward (see Chapter 4) and development of an atomic bomb, refused it further aid. Seeking to gain influence in South and Southeast Asia under its own policy of "peaceful coexistence," Khrushchev supported Indonesia and India—which was also developing atomic weaponry—in their disputes with China (see Chapter 6 on the dispute with India). Cut off now from all the great powers and arguing with its neighbors, China gave even higher priority to becoming a nuclear power (Lewis and Litai, 1988; Lin, 1988; Ryan, 1989). By 1963, the Soviet Union had moved troops to protect the Outer Mongolian border (see Mongolia on Map 2.1) from uncertainties in China; meanwhile, it was airlifting supplies to North Vietnam and Laos. An increasingly militant China was sending aid to forces fighting white colonialists in Rhodesia and Mozambique, to Albania, and to the neutral Sihanouk regime in Cambodia (Gurtov, 1971:49–82). In 1964, China exploded an atomic bomb. This helped it restore dignity and greatness in the eyes of smaller countries of the region but heightened the determination of the United States to halt its projection of power and caused some Americans to regret not invading China when they had the chance.

In the fall of 1964, Khrushchev was removed from office in Russia; his successors returned to a militant communism closer in spirit to that of Mao. The new leaders invited Zhou Enlai to see whether relations could now be improved and to enlist China's support in the Soviet Union's new resolve to substantially aid North Vietnam, but Mao remained suspicious. Soviet troops remained on the Mongolian border. In the summer of 1965, regular U.S. forces entered the Vietnam War for the first time. Once again, the United States was actively countering an invasion backed by the Soviet Union in a country on China's border. Hard lines were being drawn.

■ THE CULTURAL REVOLUTION

In 1966, Mao launched the Cultural Revolution (Hinton, 1972:127–162; Chapter 4). For a time in 1967, elements of the extreme left within the Red Guards took over the Foreign Ministry. By the end of that year, Zhou Enlai reemerged as a conciliator to begin restoring order, but for much of the next decade, China's domestic and foreign policy had to accommodate the wishes of the extreme left (Barnouin and Yu, 1997). This brought mistrust even among nations who had begun to feel more comfortable with China's policies. The radical elements were holding rallies and pillorying officials throughout China, talking about extending permanent revolution to all the rest of the world. Pol Pot in Cambodia, Sendero Luminoso guerrillas in Peru, and the Naxalite rebels in India sent emissaries to Beijing.

Such militant behavior and rhetoric helped the United States amass more support in the region for fighting the Viet Minh in Vietnam. Ironically, China was trying hard to stay out of the Vietnam War. Having sustained enormous losses in Korea, fearing an attack by the Soviet Union on its western border, and facing disruption at home from the Cultural Revolution, Mao hoped to avoid sending in Chinese troops (Karnow, 1984: 452–453). The main proponents of greater intervention were professional elements of the military displeased that their troops were bogged down at home carrying out public works and propaganda. They advocated spending more on weapons and equipment that could be used for armed conflict.

The radicals' desire for worldwide revolution caused problems for the Chinese in Indonesia. In the confusion surrounding a 1965 military coup in Indonesia, local inhabitants in many places slaughtered Chinese neighbors. Initially, refugees were welcome in China; China's policy was to repatriate Chinese rather than encourage them to revolt. After the 1967 seizure of the Foreign Ministry, however, this policy changed (Liao, 1984:169–188; Gurtov, 1971:113–124); the radicals now encouraged overseas Chinese to rebel. This only increased resistance abroad. By the end of 1967, Outer Mongolia was expelling overseas Chinese. Chinese in Burma, Cambodia, Penang, Macao, and Hong Kong clashed with authorities. Red Guards harassed overseas Chinese visiting China from abroad on trade missions and wrote to some of them, informing them that their houses and property in China were being seized. Letters and parcels from abroad were confiscated, and Chinese were discouraged from writing to relatives abroad. By 1969, suspicion of China in Indonesia grew so great that its government declared the 1955 nationality treaty null and void.

The radicalization of China's Foreign Ministry was short-lived, however. By late 1967 Mao was calling upon Zhou Enlai and the army to reestablish some order and restrain the Red Guards (Gurtov, 1971:125–158). Overseas Chinese engaged in rebellion would not receive material support from China. A 1969 border incursion by radical Chinese troops was decisively trounced by Soviet troops (Jones and Kevill, 1985:92–96). Slowly, China sought to restore normal relations with the outside world. In 1970, Mao asked U.S. journalist Edgar Snow to stand with him on the reviewing stand for National Day. The following year, Zhou Enlai met secretly with Henry Kissinger; in October, China took Taiwan's seat in the United Nations. Richard Nixon's visit to Beijing in 1972 dramatized the changing relationship. Soon Japan and a host of other nations established diplomatic relations. Japan was especially well poised to take advantage of the new era. Ever since the end of World War II, it had quietly resumed trade and diplomatic contacts with China. Now those relations were legitimized, and Japanese businessmen had a head start on setting up new enterprises in China.

In 1975, North Vietnamese troops entered Saigon, and the last U.S. troops were airlifted out. The following year, both Zhou Enlai and Mao passed away. On January 1, 1979, the United States and China established full diplomatic relations. Weeks later, relations between Vietnam and China were in disarray. China crossed the border with troops; within a month, their poorly equipped and trained troops were beaten back by superior Vietnamese forces. This was the ultimate proof of how weak Mao's policies had made China. After three decades of hostility, China and the United States were renewing relations, both smarting from defeat by a nation that had long pitted them as adversaries (Ross, 1995). Ironically, the United States had fought North Vietnam as part of an effort to stop China from extending its political power into Southeast Asia; now Vietnam was holding back China's troops from entering Vietnam.

■ JOINING THE WORLD COMMUNITY

Chapters 4–6 discussed the enormous economic growth China has experienced since Deng Xiaoping took the reins of power by 1980. Deng brought an end to the Cultural Revolution within China, freeing it to try his economic reforms. China's new position in the international community also facilitated reform. It was now a member of the United Nations Security Council and had diplomatic relations with the United States. And the Cold War was coming to an end. China was free to assume a normal position in world affairs (Liao, 1984:211–233). It could press aggressively to establish trade ties for its reforming economy. With the Soviet Union disintegrating, large numbers of traders were crossing the borders of its former republics to buy goods for their depleted economies. China set out to ease trade across the borders with Nepal, Mongolia, Burma, Laos, and Thailand (bringing a flood of unwelcome opium along with other goods). In 1989 Soviet leader Mikhail Gorbachev visited Beijing, and in 1992 China settled part of a border dispute with Russia (which resulted in the signing of a formal border agreement in 1997) and started importing Russian technology. China helped Thailand fight Moscow-backed Vietnamese and Cambodian forces until a Cambodian peace settlement in 1991 allowed it to withdraw support from Khmer Rouge guerrilla forces there and cut all ties with Thai communists. No longer a military ally or adversary,

Vietnam gradually emerged as a trading partner with China and the West; China opened trade across its border in 1990. In 1989 China ended support for Malaysian communist guerrillas, and in 1990 Singapore and Indonesia established diplomatic relations with China. Businesspeople from around the world began to explore the "China market."

The military intervention at Tiananmen Square in 1989 brought a chill to China's foreign relations for a time. But after Deng toured the Pearl River delta region early in 1992 and announced that in the new "socialist market economy" the reform efforts would be speeded and that China's people should explore capitalist techniques, investment began to pour in (see Chapter 5). Now China carries on trade and diplomatic relations with virtually every foreign nation. It belongs to the World Bank and signed the nuclear nonproliferation treaty in 1984 (though it still works behind the scenes increasing its own nuclear capacity and selling nuclear materials abroad).

Only North Korea remains a hard-core communist nation. China treats it with respectful reserve, urging restraint when South Korea (which established diplomatic relations with China in 1992) or the United States has sought serious retaliation against its nuclear program or military threats. It has cut off aid to North Korea and has not impeded U.S. efforts to inspect nuclear facilities there. It is disturbed by the disorder but does not want to see total collapse of North Korea as a buffer state against South Korea. In 1997, China joined with the United States and South Korea in formal negotiations with North Korea to bring a formal end to the Korean War. China's continuing support for the repressive military junta in Burma remains its only close formal tie with a bordering nation still cut off from normal relations with the rest of the world.

As we saw in Chapter 6, Hong Kong and Taiwan have become China's biggest partners in investment and trade. Japan, the United States, Western Europe, and Singapore joined in more slowly but have grown into sizable partners as well. By the mid-1980s, China's gross national product was growing at a double-digit pace, and this continued in the 1990s. That growth depended on maintaining good relations with these new partners, but three unusual factors threaten these good relations: the "most favored nation" clause and China's approach to international law; the status of Taiwan; and China's ongoing propensity to maintain traditional tributary relations with some border regions.

☐ Most Favored Nation Status

The "unequal treaties" imposed on China during the nineteenth century by the European powers contained clauses indicating that any privilege granted any other foreign power (i.e., the power "most favored") in another treaty should extend to the nation signing this treaty. Since China was forced to sign many treaties, the privileges extended were considerable. Since the U.S. Congress still had strong reservations about extending diplomatic recognition to China in 1979, it created another kind of most favored nation clause, indicating that the United States would extend the same trading rights to China as it did to any other nation. This meant the United States would treat China as it did all nations except those with whom it had a trade embargo—Cuba, North Korea, Libya, Iraq, and (until 1994) North Vietnam. But the United States added a stipulation that made China an exceptional case: China's most favored nation status was to be reviewed each year. If its treatment of its own people or its behavior in the international arena was deemed unacceptable to the president of the United States this "most favored" status would be withdrawn. This has never happened, even after the crackdown at Tiananmen Square in 1989, but each year the president must formally declare that the status continues, putting pressure on China to release occasional prisoners and initiate small changes in domestic policies. China strongly resents being singled out for this treatment. Trade relations have grown so enormously between the two nations that the threat implied—withdrawal of trading privileges—has ceased to seem realistic. Both sides have too much at stake.

However, many behaviors that prompted the clause continue. China signs agreements promising not to sell certain arms abroad or goods made in prisons or goods violating copyright laws; then it appears to wink as these practices occur. Many in the West are disturbed by crackdowns on political expression, treatment of children in orphanages, official corruption, and other domestic activities. The increased flow of tourists, press coverage of high-profile events like visits by foreign heads of state designed to promote normalized relations with the outside world, China's bid for the Olympics, and hosting the United Nations Conference on Women often draw attention to those abuses and fuel calls in the United States for restricting trade with China. So do news reports about the death of Haitian babies from mislabeled health products produced in China, the mislabeling of textiles to circumvent trade quotas, restrictions on foreign companies, or restrictions on U.S. imports to China.

China has discovered that the benefits of such independent behavior may not always outweigh the costs. Iraq found out, and surrounding nations noticed, that arms supplied by China were ineffective during the 1991 Desert Storm operations against sophisticated U.S. weaponry. This poor performance hurt China's arms sales in the Middle East and Algeria. China strongly desires to join the World Trade Organization (WTO) so it can benefit from the reciprocities members share with one another on trade allowances, credit terms, and the like. But the WTO also demands that China abide by some of these agreements and terms. And India and other countries are competing for business investment; with so many countries wooing investors, China's corruption, violations of copyright laws, uncertain legal protections on contracts, and threats of political instability can cause business investors to shy away. The uncertainty that gripped Asian markets in the wake of 1997 currency crises in Southeast Asia caused a decline in Asian investments and markets, which underscores the importance of maintaining a favorable domestic investment climate and opening markets fully on the basis of international rules.

□ Taiwan

Taiwan remains a puzzling foreign policy challenge, as Chapter 6 explained. China's government insists Taiwan is part of mainland China; Taiwan's government insists it is the rightful ruler of China. Though Britain recognized the PRC in Beijing early on, its simultaneous recognition of Taiwan's government prevented it from exchanging ambassadors with China for many years. Countries establishing diplomatic relations with China are forced to end relations with Taiwan. Taiwan is a disputed and disputatious border region displaying many ironies. It is the largest investor in China, and its trade volume with the United States matches that of China.

In 1996, the island held its first presidential elections. Both the leader of the Kuomintang, Lee Teng-hui (who won), and the leading opposition party proposed ending that claim on the mainland. The island has been independent and free from outside intervention for half a century. There is growing support, especially among younger generations, for simply declaring Taiwan an independent nation prepared to live at peace with China as a neighbor. China, however, continues to insist that it should rule Taiwan. It scheduled military exercises just before the election and renewed threats to invade the island. With communism fading as an ideology to cement China together, nationalist appeals like this gain strength, and China's military fuels such rhetoric, which provides a reason for higher military spending both in Taiwan and China.

□ Border Regions

China maintains a traditional concern about the regions to its south (in Southeast Asia) and west (in Central Asia; see Map 2.1). Since the second century B.C., some of China's greatest emperors have extended its borders in those directions. Its main traditional enemies—the Annamese and Champas (from Vietnam), Turks, Mongols, Manchus, Zunghars, Tanguts, Tartars, Russians, and Tibetans (from Central Asia)—lived in or invaded territory there. Those areas remain of great strategic concern to China. As just indicated, China has recently accommodated some of its disputes in

Southeast Asia, although its relations with Tibet remain tense (see Chapter 6). It also faces unrest among Muslims and other minorities in Xinjiang Autonomous Region, who are influenced by Islamic fundamentalists in regions to the west of China. China's sales of arms to Iran, Pakistan, and Iraq—which disturb many governments—are partly premised on keeping good relations with regimes in those territories in the hope that they can help China keep security on those borders. And China is outbidding U.S. oil companies for rich oil fields in Kazakhstan, which will take on increasing strategic importance when its new oil pipelines become operative.

Some of China's historical disputes with India in connection with Tibet were discussed in Chapter 6. The relations between the two countries remain tentative and complex. India and China have competed over control of strategic passes on China's western borders, dominance over Tibet and Nepal, and leadership among third world nations. While India was courting support from the Soviet Union, China was supplying arms to India's adversaries in Pakistan, Saudi Arabia, Iran, and Iraq and helping Afghan forces fight the Soviet invasion there (an incursion that also harmed Soviet-Indian relations). In 1986 India and China were once again engaged in a border dispute; Gorbachev (trying to patch Soviet relations with both countries) acted as mediator. When it became apparent in 1989 that China, in violation of the 1984 Nuclear Non-Proliferation Treaty, was selling Pakistan nuclear materials India stepped up its arms race with China. That same year China, breaking a treaty obligation with India, sold arms to Nepal; when India set up a blockade, China trucked in the supplies. In 1990, however, Nepal's government was overthrown by forces that capitulated to India. In 1994 India and China signed an agreement lessening tensions over (but not fully solving) border disputes. In 1997 China agreed to cut back on arms sales to Pakistan. But it still will not accede to U.S. and Indian demands that it sign a nuclear test ban treaty, and it remains angry that the Dalai Lama, along with many Tibetan refugees, has political asylum in India.

The South China Sea is dotted with many islands, which are potential launching points for military assaults and control of the petroleum reserves on the ocean floor. The Portuguese began the eventual European domination of China by occupying islands there. Both China and Taiwan lay claim to the Spratly and Paracel Islands north of Borneo and to the South China Sea surrounding them (including seabed near the Natuna Islands, where Indonesia is developing a huge natural gas project), in violation of the United Nations Law of the Sea convention, to which China is a signatory (Valencia, 1966). For the first time since the Ming dynasty, China has sent a navy into the open sea as part of its improved training and deployment of troops during the 1990s. Visits by those ships to the Spratly, Paracel, and Natuna Islands cause concern to the governments of Malaysia, the

Philippines, Indonesia, and Taiwan (Catley, 1997). Meanwhile, China, Taiwan, and Japan all claim ownership over the Diaoyu Islands in the East China Sea (Map 2.4). After a radical nationalist Japanese group erected a lighthouse there in 1996, Japan (declaring the islands their "exclusive economic zone") set up a coast guard patrol nearby, which in 1998 sank a vessel carrying twenty-five Hong Kong protesters who were rescued by accompanying Taiwanese protest ships ("China Warns Japan," 1998). To ease some of these concerns, in 1998 U.S. secretary of defense William Cohen signed an accord with the People's Liberation Army—the first between the two entities—designed to avoid naval and air conflicts at sea.

China has also worked to support other Asian countries that need help. In 1997 banking and investment deficiencies in Thailand, combined with speculation by foreign investors, caused a collapse in the value of its currency (see Chapter 5). Soon Malaysia, Indonesia, and other Southeast Asian countries had similar difficulties, and stock markets fell in Hong Kong, Japan, and other countries of the region. China rapidly stepped in to offer Thailand U.S.$1 billion in loans to help keep the value of its currency stable and promised aid to Indonesia as well before the International Monetary Fund stepped in with its many billions of dollars in loans.

Because of its large trade surpluses, China's government has extensive cash reserves. Its workers have long experience in producing textiles, shoes, toys, and other goods important to the international market, which gives it an advantage competing with Southeast Asian countries, even when manufacturing costs are lower there. But China's collective firms and township and village enterprises, which have accounted for much of China's growth, have slowed their output as international competition for markets increases (see Chapter 5). And China's banks, which have lent large amounts to inefficient state enterprises and real estate ventures whose property prices have tumbled and to now-bankrupt firms in Southeast Asia, have more bad loans than Southeast Asian banks. Furthermore, the value of real estate and the volume of tourism (heavily dependent on surrounding Asian countries experiencing tightened economies) in Hong Kong dropped precipitously. And the value of Japan's yen, the other major currency of the region, also plunged. If China and Hong Kong continue their resolve to maintain the value of their currencies while others stay deflated, investors may take their money elsewhere. All this tempted China and Hong Kong to lower the value of their currencies so the price of their goods on world markets would drop to compete with those of the region and tourists could afford to return. Knowing, however, that devaluation might further deflate all the region's currencies and standards of living, they chose to raise interest rates and take other uncomfortable measures to hold the value of their currencies firm. Unlike Japan, they cooperated closely with the International Monetary Fund and other major powers to bolster Asia's currencies. That helped surrounding countries, along with overseas Chinese who invest heavily in China. Should China or Hong Kong find a need to devalue its currency so China's businesses (often partially owned by overseas Chinese from surrounding countries) can compete with lower-cost goods on international markets, it might further deflate all the region's currencies and lower the buying power and standard of living of everyone in those countries. And, with Chinese controlling much of the region's wealth—Chinese constitute 4 percent of Indonesia's population, for example, but control 70% of its private assets—economic downturn can provoke rioting and violence against overseas Chinese (Mydans, 1998). China cannot ignore these concerns at its immediate doorstep, even when its interests conflict with those in other parts of the world. It has every reason to cooperate with the International Monetary Fund and other major powers to bolster Asia's currencies. Its responses on some of the other issues discussed in this section, however, may be less universally acclaimed.

■ CONFLICTING PRIORITIES:
UNITY OR ACCOMMODATION

Beijing's government wants to restore unity and power to China, and it wants to make its people prosperous. The two objectives are hard to accomplish simultaneously. It wants its own populace to feel—after the era of "unequal treaties" and Japanese occupation—that their nation is strong and able to resist outside pressure. Yet it does not want to frighten overseas Chinese and European investors and traders. After the Korean and Vietnam Wars, and decades of U.S. military aid to Taiwan, it remains wary of U.S. military and political intentions in the region. Yet it wants U.S. economic and political support, and it benefits from selling to the U.S. market, which absorbs about a fourth of its exports. It wants to attract investment both from Taiwan businesspeople and from overseas Chinese investors elsewhere; at the same time, it does not want those investors to feel that an independent Taiwan would be a safe place to site their factories and export their goods.

When it threatens to invade Taiwan, China's government appeases officers in its own military who believe in unification or want a greater role for the military, appeals to the nationalistic sentiments of its people, warns Taiwanese who are tempted to support party factions advocating independence that this could bring serious consequences, warns the United States that it will not tolerate any warming of relations with Taiwan or new expansion of its military presence in the region, and warns overseas Chinese that if they side with Taiwan they are dangerously involving themselves in China's internal politics and upsetting economic stability in the region (Sutter, 1998). It also gives President Lee Teng-hui support against factions in his own party and the opposing Democratic Progressive Party who advocate that Taiwan become an independent nation separate from China; voters know that calls for independence might bring war.

However, threats to take over Taiwan or the Spratly Islands also tempt U.S. political leaders to call for restrictions on trade and cultural relations with China and greater military assistance to Taiwan. They bring caution to U.S., European, Japanese, and overseas Chinese investors in China; they complicate China's efforts to join and work with international trade and financial organizations; and they raise doubts about whether China can be trusted as a partner in international affairs. Will it use its trade to support subversive guerrilla or military actions against its trading partner? Might it even revert to the extremes of the Cultural Revolution?

Yet, if the United States and European nations were free to establish full diplomatic relations with Taiwan and freely supply it with arms, fears could be roused in the minds of China's citizens that their security is threatened. This could strengthen those who advocate once again closing China to outsiders.

Taiwan's split from the mainland contains many strange elements that differentiate it from situations like the division of Korea or Germany after World War II. The mainland has 1.2 billion inhabitants, Taiwan 20 million. Yet tiny Taiwan is now the largest foreign investor in China. China and Taiwan both export similar volumes of goods to the United States. Both have rapidly growing economies, which benefit from involvement with one another. Although China's army is now the largest in the region, the level of its technology still lags far behind that of Taiwan's, Japan's, and South Korea's military. (In 1996, North Korea spent U.S.$2.4 billion, China U.S.$8.4 billion, Taiwan U.S.$13.6 billion, South Korea U.S.$15.6 billion, and Japan U.S.$45.1 billion on defense; see Shinn, 1997:18.) The leaders of both countries can use hostile actions by the other as a means of gaining support from their own people and fighting off internal rivals for power who might be more isolationist and less interested in growth and investment. So, ironically, the hostility, combined with offers of conciliation each side knows the other will not accept, helps bolster economic development and wards off political extremism in both countries. This shadow boxing helps keep the two regions economically interdependent, but the danger is that it also fosters continuing distrust that could blow up into civil war and economic chaos, should China, Taiwan, or the United States spark it through a rash move. The shadow boxing could turn to real boxing.

It is important for Americans to understand what is and is not shadow boxing, and the dynamics of this game. The powers that played the most dominant roles in opening China to international relations—Portugal,

Spain, Britain, Japan, Russia, France, and Germany—have stopped exerting major military and political power in the region. Today, the United States is the principal player. Unless Japan takes on a greater military and political role, the United States stands as the principal power that can prevent China from dominating its own region because the United States controls China's entry into international trade organizations, access to technology, and acceptance as a part of the world community.

The United States distrusted China's motives in the Korean and Vietnam Wars, fearing it wanted to dominate the region. China, in turn, feared that the United States might invade it. Many Chinese now fear that calls upon China to behave in conformity with world standards are thinly disguised demands that China give up its traditional moral codes and adopt U.S. standards instead. During the periods of greatest tension, Americans have feared that China wants to impose its system on the world, and Chinese have feared that the United States wants to impose its system on China. Whenever the U.S. government speaks or acts to counter what it considers to be China's provocations, nuclear buildup, arms sales, infractions of contract or international law, or violations of human rights, it reinforces those fears. Many in the United States are under the impression that China's central government has extensive control over its people; they feel justified in threatening sanctions when China breaks treaties. China's government often cannot control the actions of its citizens. At a time when the United States was threatening to retaliate against Beijing's government because Guangdong manufacturers were producing goods in defiance of international copyright laws, a study in Guangdong's leading economic zone, Shenzhen, found that two-thirds of the 35,000 companies registered there lie to the government about their boards of directors and business activities ("China in Transition," 1996). Beijing must persuade foreign powers that it is trying to abide by its own agreements in a difficult situation and convince its own provinces that it is not caving in to foreign pressure to discontinue traditional practices when it asks local governments and businesses to abide by the law. Things get more complicated when local *guanxi* networks include members of prominent Beijing families. China is being asked to contravene an ancient standard in order to enforce a new and alien one; however much its leaders see the justification for this new behavior, they feel the pressure to continue in the old ways.

Confucian "rectification of names" calls for people to stay true to themselves by maintaining proper relationships. People do not maintain a proper relationship with someone to whom they owe deference if they challenge a direct order from them. In Western terminology, that would cause the person who issued the order to "lose face." This goes beyond machismo or personal hurt from being challenged; it puts the person issuing the order into an improper relationship with the person to whom the order was issued. They must reject the improper challenge to their authority in order to maintain a proper relationship with the person who is expected to obey them. A more proper way to redress grievances is to quietly send back word through third parties that you are unhappy; this gives your superior a chance to quietly issue new orders more acceptable to you. Those third-party messages are delivered formally through carefully coded language.

Open confrontation is generally reserved for top leaders fighting over who will control the nation—two men arm wrestling to show everyone who is boss. No top leader can allow ordinary members of society to openly challenge him because that would prove he was no longer capable of holding onto his rightful place in society. And there is no way to reach accommodation in such battles; either one individual wins, or the other.

But international diplomacy, which China has entered in such recent times, depends on nations, on a regular basis, issuing direct challenges to one another's policies before working things out behind the scenes. Much is accomplished through frank, quiet conversations among key participants. But first there is frank, open debate. Modern democracies work in this manner as well. China has the skills for negotiating behind the scenes (Blackman, 1997), but it has little familiarity with negotiating amid a sea of criticism. As a result, a threat by a foreign nation to impose trade sanctions if human rights violations do not cease may be met by a threat by China (now in arm-wrestling mode) to explode an atomic bomb or send troops somewhere for an exercise; to the outside world, this seems irrational at best and threatening at worst. To break this impasse, both sides must learn to adapt to the other's techniques of negotiating (Irwin, 1997). For example, the Western nations wishing to impose trade sanctions in response to human rights violations are learning to deliver those threats more quietly and indirectly, and the Chinese learn to ignore criticisms from Western media and public officials not directly involved in the negotiations. In an atmosphere inevitably breeding distrust, such adaptations in tactics by either side are hard to achieve. With neither side fully comprehending the rules of the other's game, the chances for conflict are great. The unprecedented live radio broadcasts of debates (and public expressions of mutual regard) between General Secretary Jiang Zemin and U.S. president Bill Clinton during the latter's 1998 visit to China may indicate that both sides are learning some of these lessons.

The great Tang emperors presided over an empire that extended, for brief periods during their reigns, from Vietnam to the Aral Sea. Caravans and ships brought them offerings of the greatest cultures and trade items of their day. Today, China's empire can be even more dramatic. It presides over a land mass rich with fertile fields and natural resources. Its populace is the largest in the world, highly resourceful and organized to sustain its needs and produce for the marketplace. Its leading entrepreneurs have the deepest investment pockets on the planet. And its people have migrated to every corner of the globe. China is faced with a great irony. To maintain its unity, it must continue to accommodate the needs of the planet, enriching its economy through its compatriots at home and abroad. A bad economy at home means dissatisfaction and disintegration. The recent era of good economic growth has been accompanied by a weakened center at Beijing as provinces gain more economic power. But ultimately Chinese know that their prosperity depends on holding their regions and resources together for physical security and economic strength. In fact, China's greatest foreign policy challenge is holding them together, and it will require a combination of ancient and modern skills. The challenge is much greater than keeping the sea lanes or the Silk Roads open and marauders away from the capital city or inspiring awe and fear among subjects. And it is much greater than learning the fundamentals of European diplomacy. China must learn more about the rest of the world, and the rest of the world must learn more about China.

President Theodore Roosevelt brokered the Treaty of Portsmouth because he felt it was not in the U.S. national interest for China to be divided up among Japan and the European powers. If that is the consensus within today's major foreign policy community, China's leaders in Beijing and Taipei (Taiwan's capital) can continue a working relationship; amid all the sound and fury, their actual policy demands on one another over investment, commerce, travel, and other important matters often are compatible. If, however, other powers want China or its government to disintegrate or change faster than it is prepared to, or if both sides distrust each other's fundamental motives, those capitals are on a collision course. Even if all major players agree on goals, danger lurks. Traditional posturing among China's leaders has crossed over into bloodshed in the past. So has modern diplomacy. When those two traditions meet, a misstep or misreading of body language can have disastrous results. This is why it is important for each side to learn the rules of the other's game.

■ BIBLIOGRAPHY

Barnett, A. Doak. 1985. *The Making of Foreign Policy in China: Structure and Process*. Boulder: Westview Press.

Barnouin, Barbara, and Yu Changgen. 1997. *Chinese Foreign Policy During the Cultural Revolution*. New York: Columbia University Press.

Bau, Mingchien Joshua. 1921. *The Foreign Relations of China: A History and a Survey*. New York: Fleming H. Revell.

Blackman, Carolyn. 1997. *Negotiating China: Case Studies and Strategies*. London: Allen and Unwin.

Boardman, Robert. 1976. *Britain and the People's Republic of China, 1949–74*. London: Macmillan.

Cameron, Nigel. 1975. *From Bondage to Liberation: East Asia 1860–1952*. Hong Kong: Oxford University Press.

Catley, Bob. 1997. *Spratlys: The Dispute in the South China Sea*. Brookfield, VT: Ashgate.

Chang, Gordon H. 1990. *Friends and Enemies: The United States, China, and the Soviet Union, 1948–1972*. Stanford: Stanford University Press.

Chen, Jian. 1994. *China's Road to the Korean War: The Making of the Sino-American Confrontation*. New York: Columbia University Press.

Chen, King C. 1969. *Vietnam and China, 1938–1954*. Princeton: Princeton University Press.

———— (ed.). 1972. *The Foreign Policy of China*. Roseland, NJ: East-West Who?

"China in Transition." 1996. *Far Eastern Economic Review* 159, no. 20 (May 16).

"China Warns Japan over Boat's Sinking." 1998. *Straits Times* (June 26).

Clark, Gerald. 1966. *In Fear of China*. Melbourne: Lansdowne Press.

Clubb, Edmund O. 1971. *China and Russia: The Great Game*. New York: Columbia University Press.

Cohen, Warren I. 1989. *America's Response to China: A History of Sino-American Relations*. 3d ed. New York: Columbia University Press.

Conklin, Jeffrey Scott. 1995. *Forging an East Asian Foreign Policy*. Lanham, MD: University Press of America.

Cumings, Bruce. 1981, 1990. *The Origins of the Korean War*. 2 vols. Princeton: Princeton University Press.

Deane, Hugh. 1990. *Good Deeds and Gunboats: Two Centuries of American-Chinese Encounters*. San Francisco: China Books and Periodicals.

Dikotter, Frank. 1992. *The Discourse of Race in Modern China*. Stanford: Stanford University Press.

Fairbank, John K., and S. Y. Teng. 1941. "On the Ch'ing Tributary System." *Harvard Journal of Asiatic Studies* 6:135–148.

Faure, David, and Helen F. Siu (eds.). 1995. *Down to Earth: The Territorial Bond in South China*. Stanford: Stanford University Press.

Faust, John R., and Judith Kornberg. 1995. *China in World Politics*. Boulder: Lynne Rienner Publishers.

Fishel, Wesley R. 1975. *The End of Extraterritoriality in China*. Berkeley: University of California Press.

Fitzgerald, Stephen. 1972. *China and the Overseas Chinese: A Study of Peking's Changing Policy 1949–1970*. Cambridge: Cambridge University Press.

Garson, Robert. 1995. *The US and China Since 1949: A Troubled Affair*. New York: Associated University Presses.

Garver, John W. 1993. *Foreign Relations of the People's Republic of China*. Englewood Cliffs: Prentice-Hall.

Gittings, John. 1974. *The World and China, 1922–1972*. London: Eyre Methuen.

Goh, Bee Chen. 1996. *Negotiating with the Chinese*. Brookfield, VT: Ashgate.

Goodman, David S. G., and Gerald Segal. 1997. *China Rising: Nationalism and Interdependence*. London: Routledge.

Green, Marshal, John H. Holdridge, and William N. Stokes. *War and Peace with China: First-Hand Experiences in the Foreign Service of the United States*. Lanham, MD: University Press of America.

Gurtov, Melvin. 1971. *China and Southeast Asia—The Politics of Survival: A Study of Foreign Policy Interaction*. Lexington, MA: Heath.

Gurtov, Melvin, and Byong-Moo Hwang. 1998. *China's Security: The New Roles of the Military*. Boulder: Lynne Rienner Publishers.

Han, Suyin. 1994. *Eldest Son: Zhou Enlai and the Making of Modern China 1898–1976*. New York: Farrar, Straus, and Theroux.

Harding, Harry (ed.). 1980. *China's Foreign Relations in the 1980's*. New Haven: Yale University Press.

Harris, Stuart, and Gary Klintworth (eds.). 1995. *China as a Great Power: Myths, Realities, and Challenges in the Asia-Pacific Region*. New York: St. Martin's Press.

Hibbert, Christopher. 1970. *The Dragon Wakes: China and the West, 1793–1911*. New York: Harper.

Hinton, Harold C. 1972. *China's Turbulent Quest: An Analysis of China's Foreign Relations Since 1949*. New York: Macmillan.

Holdridge, John H. 1997. *Crossing the Divide: An Insider's Account of the Normalization of U.S.-China Relations*. Lanham, MD: Rowman and Littlefield.

Howe, Christopher (ed.). 1996. *China and Japan: History, Trends, and Prospects*. Oxford: Oxford University Press.

Hsiung, James C., and Steven I. Levine (eds.). 1992. *China's Bitter Victory: The War with Japan 1937–1945*. Armonk, NY: M. E. Sharpe.

Hsu, Immanuel C. Y. 1980. "Late Ch'ing Foreign Relations, 1866–1905." Pp. 70–141 in John K. Fairbank and Kwang-Ching Liu. *The Cambridge History of China, Volume II, Late Ch'ing, 1800–1911, Part 2*. Cambridge: Cambridge University Press.

Hunt, Michael. 1996. *The Genesis of Chinese Communist Foreign Policy*. New York: Columbia University Press.

Hunt, Michael, and Niu Jun. 1995. *Toward a History of Chinese Communist Foreign Relations, 1920s–1960s: Personalities and Interpretive Approaches*. Washington, DC: Woodrow Wilson International Center for Scholars.

Irwin, Harry. 1997. *Communicating with Asia: Understanding People and Customs*. London: Allen and Unwin.

Jain, J. P. 1976. *China in World Politics: A Study of Sino-British Relations 1949–1975*. New Delhi: Radiant Press.

Jian, Sanqiang. 1996. *Foreign Policy Restructuring as Adaptive Behavior: China's Independent Foreign Policy 1982–1989*. Lanham, MD: University Press of America.

Johnson, Linda Cooke. 1995. *Shanghai: From Market Town to Treaty Port, 1074–1858*. Stanford: Stanford University Press.

Jones, Peter, and Sian Kevill. 1985. *China and the Soviet Union, 1949–84*. Harlow, Essex: Longman.

Karnow, Stanley. 1984. *Vietnam: A History*. New York: Penguin.

Kau, Ying-mao, and Susan Marsh. 1993. *China in the Era of Deng Xiaoping: A Decade of Reform*. Armonk, NY: M. E. Sharpe.

Kim, Samuel S. (ed.). 1984. *China and the World: Chinese Foreign Policy in the Post-Mao Era*. Boulder: Westview Press.

Kueh, Y. Y. (ed.). *The Political Economy of Sino-American Relations: A Greater China Perspective*. Hong Kong: Hong Kong University Press.

Lewis, John Wilson. 1994. *China's Strategic Seapower: The Politics of Force Modernization in the Nuclear Age*. Stanford: Stanford University Press.

Lewis, John Wilson, and Xue Litai. 1988. *China Builds the Bomb*. Stanford: Stanford University Press.

Liao, Kuang-sheng. 1984. *Antiforeignism and Modernization in China, 1860–1980: Linkage Between Domestic Politics and Foreign Policy*. New York: St. Martin's Press.

Lin, Chongpin. 1988. *China's Nuclear Weapons Strategy*. Lexington, MA: D. C. Heath.

Liu, Ta Jen. 1996. *U.S.-China Relations, 1784–1992*. Lanham, MD: University Press of America.

Medvedev, Roy. 1986. *China and the Superpowers*. New York: Basil Blackwell.

Murphey, Rhoads. 1970. *The Treaty Ports and China's Modernization: What Went Wrong?* Ann Arbor: Michigan Papers in Chinese Studies no. 7, University of Michigan.

Mydans, Seth. 1998. "Indonesia Turns Its Chinese into Scapegoats." *New York Times.* (February 2):A3.

Nathan, Andrew J., and Robert S. Ross. 1997. *The Great Wall and the Empty Fortress.* New York: Norton.

Needham, J. W. 1971. "Civil Engineering and Nautics." In J. W. Needham (ed.), *Science and Civilization in China.* Vol. 4, pt. 3. Cambridge: Cambridge University Press.

Nelsen, Harvey. 1989. *Power and Insecurity: Beijing, Moscow, and Washington, 1949–1988.* Boulder: Lynne Rienner Publishers.

Ning, Li. 1997. *The Dynamics of Foreign-Policy Decisionmaking in China.* Boulder: Westview Press.

North, Robert C. 1974. *The Foreign Relations of China.* 2d ed. Encino, CA: Dickenson.

Ojha, Ishwer C. 1969. *Chinese Foreign Policy in an Age of Transition: The Diplomacy of Cultural Despair.* Boston: Beacon.

Oksenberg, Michel, and Elizabeth Economy (eds.). 1998. *Involving China in World Affairs.* Washington: Brookings Institution.

Robinson, Thomas W., and David Shambaugh (eds.). 1994. *Chinese Foreign Policy: Theory and Practice.* Oxford: Oxford University Press.

Ross, Robert S. (ed.). 1993. *China, the United States, and the Soviet Union.* Armonk, NY: M. E. Sharpe.

———. 1995. *Negotiating Cooperation: The United States and China, 1969–1989.* Stanford: Stanford University Press.

Ryan, Mark. 1989. *Chinese Attitudes Toward Nuclear Weapons.* Armonk, NY: M. E. Sharpe.

Schurmann, Franz, and Orville Schell (eds.). 1967. *Imperial China: The Decline of the Last Dynasty and the Origins of Modern China.* New York: Random House.

Segal, Gerald, and Richard Yang (eds.). 1996. *Chinese Economic Reform: The Impact on Security.* London: Routledge.

Shambaugh, David (ed.). 1995a. *Deng Xiaoping: Portrait of a Chinese Statesman.* Oxford: Oxford University Press.

——— (ed.). 1995b. *Greater China: The Next Superpower.* Oxford: Oxford University Press.

Shao, Kuo-Kang. 1996. *Zhou Enlai and the Foundations of Chinese Foreign Policy.* New York: St. Martin's Press.

Sheng, Michael M. 1998. *Battling Western Imperialism: Mao, Stalin, and the United States.* Princeton: Princeton University Press.

Shih, Chih-yu. 1993. *China's Just World: The Morality of Chinese Foreign Policy.* Boulder: Lynne Rienner Publishers.

Shinn, James (ed.). 1996. *Weaving the Net: Conditional Engagement with China.* Washington, DC: Brookings Institution.

———. 1997. "Northeast Asia: Strategic Crossroads." *Great Decisions.* Washington, DC: Foreign Policy Association.

Spanier, John W. 1959. *The Truman-McArthur Controversy and the Korean War.* Cambridge: Belknap Press of Harvard University Press.

Sutter, Robert G. 1996. *Shaping China's Future in World Affairs: The Role of the United States.* Boulder: Westview Press.

———. 1998. *U.S. Policy Toward China: The Role of Interest Groups.* Lanham,

MD: Rowman and Littlefield.

Tan, Qingshan. 1992. *The Making of U.S. China Policy: From Normalization to the Post–Cold War Era*. Boulder: Lynne Rienner Publishers.

Teng, Ssu-yu, and John Fairbank. 1965. *China's Response to the West: A Documentary Survey 1839–1923*. Cambridge: Harvard University Press.

Tung, William L. 1970. *China and the Foreign Powers: The Impact of and Reaction to Unequal Treaties*. Dobbs Ferry, NY: Oceana.

Unger, Jonathan. 1996. *Chinese Nationalism*. Armonk, NY: M. E. Sharpe.

Valencia, Mark J. 1996. *China and the South China Sea Disputes*. Oxford: Oxford University Press.

Van Ness, Peter. 1970. *Revolution and Chinese Foreign Policy*. Berkeley: University of California.

Vogel, Ezra. 1990. *One Step Ahead in China*. Cambridge: Harvard University Press.

Waley, Arthur. 1958. *The Opium War Through Chinese Eyes*. Stanford: Stanford University Press.

Wang, Y. C. 1966. *Chinese Intellectuals and the West: 1872–1949*. Chapel Hill: University of North Carolina Press.

Westad, Odd Arne. 1992. *Cold War and Revolution: Soviet-American Rivalry and the Origins of the Chinese Civil War*. New York: Columbia University Press.

Whiting, Allen. 1960. *China Crosses the Yalu: The Decision to Enter the Korean War*. New York: Macmillan.

Wilson, Dick. 1984. *Zhou Enlai: A Biography*. New York: Viking.

Xiang, Lanxin. 1995. *Recasting the Imperial Far East: Britain and America in China, 1945–1950*. Armonk, NY: M. E. Sharpe.

Yang, Richard H., and Gerald Segal (eds.). 1996. *Chinese Economic Reform: The Impact of Security*. Boulder: Lynne Rienner Publishers.

Zagoria, Donald. 1962. *The Sino-Soviet Conflict, 1956–1961*. Princeton: Princeton University Press.

Zhang, Yongjin, and Rouben Azizian. 1998. *Ethnic Challenges Beyond Borders: Chinese and Russian Perspectives of the Central Asian Conundrum*. New York: St. Martin's Press.

Zhao, Quansheng. 1996. *Interpreting Chinese Foreign Policy: The Micro-Macro Linkage Approach*. Oxford: Oxford University Press.

Zhao, Suisheng. 1998. *Power Competition in East Asia: From the Old Chinese World Order to the Post–Cold War Regional Multipolarity*. New York: St. Martin's Press.

■8■

Population Growth and Urbanization
Ma Rong

Each of the prior chapters has dealt with some common themes that, taken together, provide a basis for understanding the growth and dispersion of China's populace. China has long been divided between more prosperous and populous coastal regions and interior regions with fewer people, harsher conditions, and vast untapped natural resources. It has long had entrepreneurs in cities and the countryside producing an abundance of crops and goods, mostly in those coastal regions. And the market economy they supply has been at its liveliest when effective rulers unify great portions of the country; since those rulers usually have emerged from interior parts of the continent, this creates both a tie and a tension between the interior and the coast.

China's prosperity has hinged on three balancing acts that I discuss in this chapter: between city and country, between population and food, and between regions of hardship and regions of prosperity. Many Americans have heard of China's spectacular building boom in its cities, its controversial "one-child" birth control policy, and the contrast between life in modern areas like Shanghai and Hong Kong and the more traditional life in minority areas of the interior. China had extensive urbanization long before the rest of the world; but cities have always depended on the countryside for their prosperity, and the line between city and countryside has always been blurred. One cannot thrive without the other. At the end of Chapter 5, John Wong indicated that China must grow enough food to feed its rising population and find ways to spread prosperity inland if its current boom is to continue. These are not new problems or new solutions, but the magnitude of both is far greater than ever in the past. Food production and population have long risen simultaneously, but ultimately they reach a point where they cannot sustain one another, bringing social crisis. And China has never been able to survive with two nations, one rich and one poor; it needs social service networks linking the capital and regional cities to keep that kind of polarization from occurring. China's future success depends on maintaining these fine balances, but it will not be easy.

■ CITY AND COUNTRYSIDE IN HISTORY

China has always been a country on the move. Its history brought a succession of droughts, floods, plagues, famines, rebellions, conquerors, and great public works projects. All of these involved movement of great numbers of people. Emperors and soldiers built cities, moving people by force for their construction and occupation; in times of rebellion, angry peasants burned those cities. People in leaner regions of the north moved south and west to seek greater prosperity, often creating new cities in the regions they entered or settling close to existing ones. Cities were generally built by soldiers and rulers, but they were sustained by commerce, which moved both people and goods.

In *The City in Late Imperial China* (1977), William G. Skinner makes the case that a principal role of cities in late imperial China was as commercial centers. In these cities, public officials and merchants interacted to tap and regulate markets and means of production, creating wealth both for citizens and government. However, the cities were not the only place that generated wealth. Many villages, in fact, produced goods in cottage industries along with raising crops and helped maintain canals, roads, and streams that served as transportation networks to move their goods to and from the cities. Nearly everyone in and around the urbanized areas helped supply, and purchased from, this trade.

Cities were often located along major canals or rivers. The short Miracle Canal *(Ling Qu)* linked the Xiang River, which flows into the Yangtze, with the Gui River that flows toward Guangzhou; it was begun in the third century B.C. The Grand Canal (begun much later, in the sixth century A.D., using two or three million laborers) linked the Yangtze River valley with the Yellow River and later Beijing. Over the centuries, these and other canals were frequently rerouted to fit the needs of commerce and conquest, and their maintenance required extensive labor (Van Slyke, 1988:69–72). Huge quantities of grain moved along these waterways, along with troops, all manner of manufactured goods, small merchants, and thousands of boatmen and their families. Officials extracted taxes and tolls, and merchants profits, from this trade. The roads and waterways helped rulers hold China together and conquer people along the periphery.

To keep their rule alive, officials also established towns in areas with less commerce to control the populace and maintain defense networks. In contrast to the commercial centers, many of these centers cost the government a good deal of money to maintain while generating little revenue. As one moved inland, the number of such cities tended to increase (see Skinner, 1977:221). It was not the case that these centers were associated with poverty and the commercial cities were associated with wealth. Many of the laborers who contributed to the prosperity of the commercial cities worked very hard for little income. Many of the clans living around the administrative towns engaged in little commerce beyond their villages but may have supported themselves adequately on their small farms. City inhabitants had to garner money either from the capital or from outside commerce to prosper. Threats of outside attack or social unrest could help attract such funds to cities that had little outside commerce; the capital might also send money if the town formed a useful link to control neighboring regions.

The role of cities as centers of trade and administration began very early in China's history. In Chapter 3 Rhoads Murphey discussed the rise of cities as early as the Shang dynasty (see Table 3.1); his mention of the battle for dominance between the commercial towns and cities of the state of Qu in the Yangtze River valley and the frontier feudal fiefdom of Qin, which finally unified China, highlights their dual role as political and commercial centers. Cities surrounded by tall walls and "defense-rivers" were the settlements for governmental offices and the army. Cities were built to protect both urban and rural residents during wartime. Towns with no significance in administration, whose main occupation was trade, did not have walls and large populations (Elvin and Skinner, 1974). Since the Qin unification of China in 221 B.C., the country has needed to establish a strong administration system to manage the large territory. Therefore, big cities developed in China much earlier than in Europe. In the Tang dynasty (A.D. 752), the population of the capital city Chang'an (present-day Xi'an; see Map 3.1) was around 2 million (Chao and Xie, 1988:191); it was a center of both governance and commerce. In comparison, big cities developed in Europe much later, and their main expansion occurred after the industrial revolution in the eighteenth century.

As Chapters 3 and 4 indicated, the Song dynasty was a period of great commerce, with a fifth of the populace moving to towns and cities to engage in these pursuits (Chao, 1987:56). In the centuries following, urbanization increased as overall population began to rise rapidly (see Figure 8.1). At the beginning of the nineteenth century, China had 1,400 cities of over 3,000 people; more than half of the cities with a population above 10,000 were the seats of prefectures and provincial administrations (Rozman, 1982:209). China's population exceeded 300 million people by 1800 (Chao and Xie, 1988:378). In western and northern China, where the economy is less developed and population density is low, the main function of cities and towns is still administrative (Chang, 1981). Manufacturing and services are limited there, and a large proportion of the urban labor force works in governmental institutions.

Figure 8.1   Historical Changes in China's Population

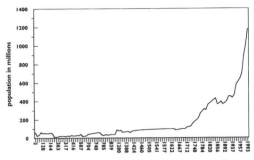

Source: Zhou and Xie, 1988; State Statistical Bureau, 1950–1995.

In contrast, many "market towns" in the coastal regions (especially in Jiangsu, Zhejiang, Fujian, and Guangdong provinces) have a more prosperous economy and high population densities. Trade, manufacture, handicraft, transportation, and services are important functions played by these "market towns." Some of them grew up rapidly and even became large cities. After the Opium Wars (1839–1842), the population of the treaty ports along the coast began to rise rapidly. Shanghai was only a country town with a few thousand people at the beginning of the eighteenth century, but it became the largest city in East Asia a century later since it served as the main trade center and transportation port between China and other countries. Today, although the general level of urbanization in China is lower than in most other countries, China has a number of big cities in its coastal regions. Among the seven cities in the world with a population over 10 million in 1975, Shanghai was the fourth largest, with 11.6 million (World Bank, 1984:68). By 1995, the population of Beijing exceeded 10 million, and Shanghai's population reached 13.3 million (Population Census Bureau, 1993:13). There were ten cities in China with a population over 2 million in 1993 (State Statistical Bureau, 1994:22).

■   **POPULATION AND FOOD**

It is well known that China is the most populous country of the world. On February 15, 1995, the government announced that its population had reached 1.2 billion—about one fifth of the total world's population, which stood at 5.5 billion in 1993 (World Bank, 1995:163). The population of China was greater in 1995 than the combined populations of the United States (258 million), Russia (149 million), Japan (125 million), and all of Europe and Middle Asia (495 million) (World Bank, 1995:163). The country with the world's second-largest population is India, with 898 million in 1993. Because of India's higher annual birthrates (twenty-nine per thousand versus nineteen per thousand in China), its population is expected to surpass China's during the twenty-first century.

Old city street in Chengdu, Sichuan.

By world standards, China's population has been high throughout recorded history; but its absolute numbers have been much lower than at present. A glance at Figure 8.1 will quickly show you that China's population exceeded 100 million in 1685, based on census and other records of population accounting during different dynasties for the purpose of tax collection and army recruitment, which are not entirely accurate but give some general sense of population sizes. From the first "census" (household accounting) in A.D. 2 to the one in A.D. 1400, China's population experienced a long process of instability. Sometimes the population increased at an annual rate of 4 to 5 percent under peaceful and prosperous social conditions, perhaps even exceeding 100 million during the twelfth century at the height of the Song dynasty; sometimes wars and famines decreased it by 30 to 40 percent. By the height of the Ming dynasty in the fifteenth century it had risen to 150 million, dipped again with the wars that brought it to office, and then moved into steady growth after those wars ended in 1681. It took seventy-nine years to exceed 200 million (in 1759), another twenty-eight years to exceed 300 million (in 1787), and another forty-three years to exceed 400 million by 1830—doubling in seventy-one years (Chao and Xie, 1988:378). Because of foreign invasion (such as the Opium War and the 1931–1945 Japanese occupation) and civil wars (the "Taiping Heavenly Kingdom," and the war between the Communist Party and Kuomintang; see Chapter 4), "the century between 1851 and 1949 was one of societal breakdown . . . an annual average population growth rate of only 0.3 percent" (Banister, 1987:3). Then China entered into a period of spectacular rise in population.

Food was a major factor in determining population. As Rhoads Murphey pointed out in Chapter 3, China's civilization was able to sustain itself because of the cultivation of rice and wheat. Wars, epidemics, and floods killed people directly. Along with droughts, they also destroyed fields and crops, leading to starvation, lowered fertility rates, and infanticide (killing babies at birth) to avoid having to share food with newborn infants. For many centuries, China's population rose and fell on the basis of how much grain it could grow and store. Then in the eighteenth century, new plants arrived from the New World and Europe: sweet potatoes, maize (corn), Irish potatoes, and peanuts—all of which could grow abundantly on previously unused terrain—along with new, more productive strains of rice from Southeast Asia. Especially in southern China, more people could marry at earlier ages and have more children, who had an increased chance to live because of better nutrition for both mother and infant.

One tactic used by armies in the civil wars and foreign invasions from which China suffered from the mid–nineteenth to mid-twentieth centuries was to break dikes and cause flooding. Bad weather also brought periodic droughts. Granary storage systems were emptied and extended families and communities scattered. Combined with the disease, direct killings, and other hardships brought by war and social disorder, these losses of crops brought great loss of life. Chapter 4 gave you some estimates of those losses. Yet despite all this hardship, China's population crept upward during this period, adding more people than all of China had supported before the seventeenth century. The new crops helped this to happen.

The arrival of the People's Republic of China (PRC) in 1949 brought peace, the economic stabilization measures discussed in Chapter 4 that ended the high inflation of food prices, the return of peasants to the land, and measures to provide basic medicine and hygiene. The first modern census, conducted in 1953, showed a population of 582 million. Twenty-nine years later, in 1982, it surpassed 1 billion.

From 1958 to 1961, there was a serious famine in China. Both natural disasters (drought) and policies of rural development (the "commune system" and the Greap Leap Forward) had impact on the famine and resulted in negative population growth rates in the early 1960s. The mortality rate was very high (Banister and Preston, 1981). The high birthrates in the late 1960s and 1970s are called "compensative births" by demographers, since many people who did not bear children during the famine wanted to have them right after (Tien, 1983:16). The total fertility rate (expected average number of children per woman at the end of her childbearing years) decreased to 3.3 in 1960 and jumped back to 5.8 in 1970.

Great regional variation in demographic dynamics exists among different areas of China. Table 8.1 shows the demographic indexes of several selected provinces and autonomous regions. For example, the birthrate was as high as 5.27 percent in Sichuan in 1970, but it was only 1.38 percent in Shanghai that same year. The death rate was very high in Sichuan in 1970 (1.26 percent), but it was as low as 0.5 percent in Shanghai. Variation also exists between urban and rural areas and between rich areas and poor areas within each province or autonomous region (Caldwell and Srinivasan, 1984). But the general trend is for the birthrate to exceed the death rate and for population to rise faster in rural areas than in urban.

There has always been a basic argument or debate within the government and among demographers in the PRC over whether family planning is necessary and what should be the "proper standard" or limitation in family planning programs. In other words, how many children should a couple have? The most famous debate was between the president of Beijing University (Ma Yinchu) and Chairman Mao Zedong in 1957.

Based on his study and population projections, Ma (an economist) called on China to control births and encourage family planning. At a meeting of the National People's Congress, he warned that China's population would reach 1.5–2.6 billion (at an annual growth rate of 2 to 3 percent) in fifty years and that such a huge population would become an intolerable burden preventing China from becoming a prosperous industrialized nation. To solve the problem, he suggested setting up a goal of two children per family (Ma Yinchu, 1957). His suggestion was supported by some senior officials, including Zhou Enlai; a movement was organized,

Table 8.1 Regional Variation in Demographic Indicators

Region	Crude Birth Rate (% increase)			Crude Death Rate (% decrease)		
	1970	1980	1990	1970	1980	1990
Tibet	1.94	2.24	2.76	0.76	0.82	0.92
Xinjiang	3.67	2.18	2.47	0.82	0.77	0.64
Guangdong	2.96	2.07	2.40	0.60	0.54	0.53
Jiangsu	3.07	1.47	2.05	0.69	0.66	0.61
Inner Mongolia	2.89	1.85	2.01	0.58	0.55	0.58
Sichuan	5.27	1.19	1.78	1.26	0.68	0.71
Heilongjiang	3.48	2.36	1.75	0.58	0.72	0.53
Beijing	2.07	1.56	1.34	0.64	0.63	0.54
Shanghai	1.38	1.26	1.13	0.50	0.65	0.64
China as a whole	3.34	1.82	2.10	0.76	0.63	0.63

Source: China Population and Information Research Center, 1985:848–850; China Population and Information Research Center, ed., 1991.

mainly to call people's attention to population issues without policy enforcement. This was the first family planning campaign, from 1955 to 1957, just before the terrible famine (Figure 8.2).

At the time, Mao was worried about the possibility of war between China and the United States. The Korean War was not formally ended, and the situation on the Taiwan Straits was hostile and fragile, as Chapters 6 and 7 explained. He believed China needed to maintain a large population to survive a nuclear war, since it had no nuclear weapon to deter such an attack. Mao said that even if nuclear bombs killed half of the population, China would still have millions left to continue fighting. Mao rejected Ma's suggestion on the basis of this strategic thinking. Then Ma was criticized very seriously as "the new Malthus" and lost his position and influence. Malthus was an eighteenth century thinker who gave a gloomy forecast that the world's population is destined to grow faster than food supplies.

But China was not involved in nuclear war with either the United States or the Soviet Union. As you can see from Figure 8.2 the birth rate shot up after the period of famine during the Great Leap Forward (1958–1960) and the government called for a second family planning campaign. Fertility rates declined again during the Cultural Revolution (1966–1976). After those periods of chaos they rose once more, as Ma Yinchu had predicted. The government announced the third family planning campaign with a new slogan: *wan, xi, shao* (late marriage, long birth intervals, and fewer births) (Lyle, 1980).

As the population pressure on land, urban jobs, housing, and social spending became more serious, it was clear that a rapidly growing population would make the "four modernizations" (of agriculture, industry, the military, and society and technology) announced in 1978 an impossible

Figure 8.2   Demographic Dynamics During China's Family Planning Campaigns

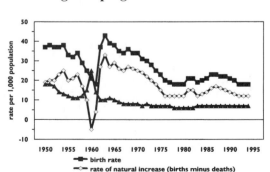

Source: State Statistical Bureau, 1950–1995.

dream. So in the 1980s, the Chinese government finally set up a more restrictive birth control policy, the one-child campaign (Tien, 1973, 1983). Under this policy, China's fertility rates and mortality rates both stablized (as Figure 8.2 shows), resulting in a low natural rate of population increase. Unlike the experiences of industrialized countries, where social and economic development gradually lead to low fertility, government policy and enforcement have played a key role in this transition in China (Aird, 1978; Chen and Kols, 1982).

Some argue that low fertility will be spontaneously adopted by people after economic and societal development and that no policy enforcement is really needed (see Beaver, 1975). But in China's case, the huge population and a high birthrate obviously hinder social and economic development. In 1982, 80 percent of China's population were traditional farmers and over 32 percent of the populace over the age of twelve illiterate. Such individuals are apt to have large families, straining food supplies and government support services at a time when resources need to be devoted to building an infrastructure for modernization that could bring societal and economic development.

Generally, urban residents accepted the one-child policy. First, equal education and work opportunities for women had already encouraged them to have fewer children. Second, the pension systems of governmental institutions and state-owned enterprises made people less worried about needing children to support them after retirement. Third, the expenses of kindergarten, schools, and other costs related to child raising increased very rapidly, and it became really difficult to raise more than one child if the parents wanted their offspring to enjoy satisfactory and competitive living and study conditions. In rural areas, however, especially poor ones where many farmers want more boys to carry on their family name, no pensions are available, and the expenses of raising children are still low, people want two or three children. Under the incentives of the household responsibility system, added offspring also provide field help to increase family income. So it is hard to enforce the family planning program in rural areas (Goodstadt, 1982), especially because local authorities in many rural regions are sometimes lax about doing so.

Since Han people, especially farmers, have a strong preference for boys, the sex ratio at birth (the ratio between males and females, with females as 100) increased from 108.5 in 1982 to 110.2 in 1990. One of the reasons is the higher possibility that couples will decide to have an abortion when they learn the new baby will be a girl. But it is also very likely that many rural households did not report the births of girls, which may in turn make the ratio more even (Zhen Yi et al., 1993). In regions where local administrators are more zealous about enforcing birth control, people often fail to report births of both sexes, and it is difficult to estimate the total number who were not reported to administration and registered by censuses.

Billboard promoting the one-child policy in Chengdu, Sichuan.

When the Chinese government recognized the difficulties in enforcing the one-child policy in rural areas, it made many local adjustments in birth regulations to allow farmers to have more than one child. For example, if the first child is a girl or has some disease or if the father is the only son of his family, a second child is allowed. By estimation, there are generally two children per family in most rural areas in China, whereas the one-child policy is generally followed in cities (Peng, 1991). In Chapter 11, Laurel Bossen discusses this topic further.

As you can see from Tables 8.2 and 5.2, the Chinese population has two major characteristics: large size and low education. Among the total population above age six in China in 1990 (994 million), 20.6 percent were illiterate and another 42.3 percent received only primary school education. Because many rural primary schools have very poor teaching conditions and many teachers only received primary school education themselves, the quality of education for a large proportion of graduates of rural primary schools is considered very low. With such a low quality in education, skill training, and social experiences, a huge population will have a more negative than positive impact on China's development.

The importance of family planning becomes even clearer if we carefully examine the connection between natural resources in China and population growth. Arable land in China covers less than 250 million acres (101.2 hectares) and has continually decreased because of urban expansion and construction of dams, roads, bridges, and new factories. The arable land per capita in 1991 was 0.27 acres (0.11 hectares) in China, one-ninth that of the United States, one-twentieth that of Canada, and one-thirty-four that in

Table 8.2 Selected Development and Demographic Trends in China

	1950	1960	1970	1980	1990
Total population (in millions)	552.00	662.00	830.00	987.00	1,120.00
GNP per capita (U.S.$)	—	—	—	290.00	370.00
% urban[a]	11.20	19.70	17.40	19.40	26.00
Infant mortality per 100 births[b]	13.80	8.56	5.15	3.76	3.70
Crude birthrate (% increase)	3.70	2.09	3.34	1.82	2.10
Crude death rate (% decrease)	1.80	2.54	0.76	0.63	0.63
Rate of population growth (%)	1.90	−0.45	2.58	1.19	1.47
Total fertility rate per childbearer[c]	5.80	3.30	5.80	2.20	2.30
Life expectancy (female)[b]	49.20	58.00	63.20	69.20	71.10
Life expectancy (male)[b]	46.70	56.00	61.10	66.20	67.80

Source: World Bank, 1982–1995.
Notes: a. Wang, 1986:284.
b. Lin, 1986:238.
c. Yan and Cheng, 1993; Huang, 1993.

Australia (Qu and Li, 1992:53). India, with 432 million acres (174.4 million hectares) of arable land, has fewer people than China. Therefore, the pressure of population on grain production is worse in China than in India. The Chinese government argues that, with 7 percent of the world's arable land and the need to feed 22 percent of the world's population, there was no other choice for China to maintain its social stability and proceed into modernization except practicing family planning.

The outlook for other natural resources in China is equally grim. Only 13 percent of China's territory has forest cover compared to 32 percent for the United States, 68 percent for Japan, 71 percent for Finland, and 31 percent for the world as a whole (Qu and Li, 1992:70). The indicator of forest area per capita is even lower for China: 0.27 acres (.1 hectares) compared with 3.3 acres (1.33 hectares) in the United States and 12.3 acres (4.97 hectares) in Finland. Water is one of the most important natural resources. The per capita surface water runoff—the amount of water that flows on the surface to use for drinking, agriculture, sanitation, and industry—is only one-fourth the world average and one-fifth that of the United States (Qu and Li, 1992:117). Furthermore, China's water resources are unequally distributed. Most of the cities in northern China experience serious water shortages, whereas southeastern China is often threatened by floods. (In Chapter 9, Richard Edmonds discusses all these problems in greater detail.) With such shortages and imbalanced geographic distribution between population and natural resources, birth control and family planning are necessary measures. In Chapter 5, John Wong discussed Lester Brown's concerns that China will be unable to feed itself and the growing consensus that although Brown's fears may be overblown, the difficulties of increasing food production for a growing population are substantial. Though ample food does not automatically bring population increases (Harris and Ross, 1987; Gates, 1996:54–60), history has shown that when the Chinese have enough food to eat, their population grows. If it keeps growing, food supply may not be able to keep up with population, and money would have to be diverted from other projects to import food.

Despite the one-child policy, China's population continues to grow and is predicted to become stable around 2033, after reaching 1.5 billion (Lu and Lin, 1994:104). Researchers in western China suggest that one of the most important reasons for the poverty problem there is the region's continuing high fertility (Zhou, 1994). China's population was 723 million in 1964; if the fertility rate, mortality rate, and natural growth rate had stayed the same as they were that year, China would have had a population of 2.075 billion by 1995. Even under the strongly enforced family planning program, the annual number of newborn babies in China (24.6 million) still exceeds the total population of Australia (17.6 million), which has a territory equal to 80 percent of China's territory.

■ CITY AND COUNTRYSIDE TODAY

Given the necessity of feeding its people, China must have enough people in the countryside to maintain the food supply while managing the gravitation to towns and cities that naturally accompanies modernization. Because of the geographic characteristics and distribution of natural resources, China's population is not equally distributed. The plateau and deserts in the western part of China can support only a very small population. As you can easily grasp by looking at Maps 2.2 and 2.3 and drawing a diagonal line from western Heilongjiang to western Yunnan, 94 percent of the total population lives in the southeastern part of China (about 36 percent of the total territory), whereas 6 percent live in the northwestern part (about 64 percent of total territory). This pattern has not changed for centuries. Furthermore, the most populous cities lie to the southeast. Although China's average density is 125 persons per square kilometer, its coastal regions are considered among the most crowded places in the world, with a population density of over 600–1,000 persons per square kilometer. Anyone who visits Beijing, Shanghai, or even rural areas in the coastal regions will certainly have a very strong impression about the high population density there. It is even difficult for urban people to move on streets and in shops in weekends and holidays, and there are very short distances between villages in rural areas.

In 1949, the PRC established a centrally planned economic system on the model of the then Soviet Union. In order to manage food and housing supplies, employment, education, and other public facilities under the

Shanghai's busiest shopping street, Nanjing Lu.

governmental plans, a residential registration system was created in 1953 to control the size of urban populations and the volume of rural-urban migration (Goldstein and Goldstein, 1985:9–12). Under this policy, the proportion of urban residents in the total population was kept around 20 percent for a long period of time, much lower than in other nations. The urban population of China reached 29 percent of the total in 1993, compared to 76 percent in the United States and 44 percent in the whole world (World Bank, 1995:222).

The Great Leap Forward, which began in 1958 (see Chapter 4), resulted in about 20 million rural people migrating into cities to participate in an urban industrial expansion. Since the factories were established in a hurry and there were many problems in management and the quality of the labor force, many new factories did not make profits and had to be closed. Then the government had to tell the 20 million new urban residents to move back to rural areas (Tien, 1983:28). After this crisis, the government set up a very restricted system of urban population control. Anyone who wanted to move from one place to another had to apply for an official transfer, and it was difficult to obtain approval for a move from the countryside into a town or city, especially into big cities. Kam Wing Chan (1994) argues that this system helped stabilize cities as they industrialized.

During the Cultural Revolution (1966–1976), the government arranged a special type of urban-rural migration for city middle school graduates. They were sent to rural areas in the periphery, army reclamation farms, and urban suburbs for "reeducation" (Banister, 1987:308). They were compelled to learn from farmers and herders and work as one of them. The total number of these students was around 1.2 million. After the Cultural Revolution, a large part of these students returned to the cities of their origin, resulting in a rural-urban return migration.

Following the new economic reforms in the 1980s, migration control has loosened. The grain coupons (which could only be used in each province) and hotel clerks' requests for "travel approval" for checking into hotels were abandoned. Now people may travel anywhere in the country, though official local residential status is still needed when applying for a formal job in governmental institutions. Migration abroad has also become more convenient if the visa is approved by foreign countries. According to the 1990 national census, 237,024 persons were living abroad and had temporarily canceled their local residential registration (Population Census Bureau, 1993:7). In 1994, 19,000 students went abroad for advanced study (State Statistical Bureau, 1995:589). Yet all this new freedom of movement comes with a price: the social guarantees and stability of neighborhoods and communities that the regulations helped establish are not as firm.

☐ Health Care

One guarantee under pressure is health care. Life expectancy at birth has increased significantly in China since 1950. At that time, life expectancy was only 49.2 years for women and 46.7 years for men; by 1990 this had risen to 71.1 years and 67.8 years (see Table 8.2). The improvements in income and housing have had a positive impact on people's nutrition and health. The general improvement of mass education has also had some indirect impact on reducing mortality. More children attend school; only 1.5 million children graduated from primary school in 1952, whereas 19 million did so in 1994 (State Statistical Bureau, 1995:588). Students learn about biology, nutrition, sanitation, infectious diseases, and simple medical treatments, which in turn help them to manage their life in a more healthy way.

The health care facilities managed by the government also play an important role in reducing mortality and increasing life expectancy. After 1949, university-educated doctors and nurses became available to urban workers. "Barefoot doctors," who received basic paramedical training and were supported by their local villages, proved very helpful in controlling infectious diseases and offering simple treatment of urgent cases in rural areas. But the gap between the quality of health care facilities in rural areas and cities remained wide. Before the reforms of the 1980s, there were two different health care systems in rural and urban China. In rural areas, a system called the "collective health care system" was in practice. At that time, all rural dwellers belonged to communes, which controlled management of the land; they were divided into brigades and finally into smaller production teams. Brigade members all contributed equal levies to a fund that supported their health care. When they became ill, the fund paid half their bill; they paid the rest. Urban workers had better coverage than that. The ministries, schools, and state-owned factories and shops for which over 90 percent of urban employees worked paid all their medical expenses and provided them with doctors and hospitals near their workplace. The work units also covered 70 to 80 percent of the health care expenses of their dependents. So urban workers had better access than rural dwellers to hospitals and fully trained doctors and paid few of their own medical bills.

Since the system reform in the 1980s, the collective health care system has lost its financial base because all lands and properties were redistributed among peasants. Now the peasants pay health care expenses by themselves. The former "barefoot doctors" now either open their own private clinics and make money from their services or have switched into other activities. These clinics are under the regulation of county bureaus of public health care. In some poor areas, local doctors with medical degrees left their villages and moved to rich regions and even cities in order to earn a

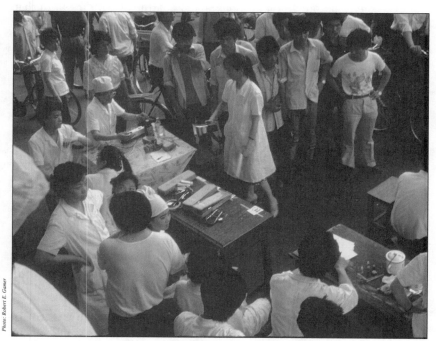

This day clinic set up on a busy street gave workers convenient access to health care. Hangzhou, Zhejiang, 1989.

higher income. Poorer regions are suffering from a serious shortage of doctors and health care services.

In urban areas, state-owned enterprises are now facing serious financial problems as they compete with private companies and joint ventures. Often they must cut back drastically on the health coverage they offer their employees. Fifty-eight cities have established health insurance programs, which they encourage all factories to join; their employees must pay monthly premiums in exchange for coverage. In rich regions along the eastern coast where township enterprises prosper, local health insurance systems are successfully established at town and even village levels. In other regions of China, the urban and rural health care facilities have been largely maintained by subsidies from central or provincial governments whose budgets are increasingly strained. Many individuals working for small cooperative enterprises have no medical coverage and must pay fees for medical care.

□ Housing

The housing system in rural China, like health care, differs from that in towns and cities. With the exception of a few private houses that residents built or bought before 1949, all houses and apartment buildings in urban areas have been managed by government institutions. These apartments are assigned to employees who need to pay only a small amount for rent. In rural areas, the peasants built their houses themselves after obtaining official permission from village, town, and county authorities for land use.

When the economic reforms were first instituted after 1978, this worked to the advantage of rural dwellers. Under the household responsibility system that let them lease land and sell crops in markets, many of them acquired savings that they used to build themselves houses; these are often quite large (especially in more sparsely populated areas like Yunnan). Meanwhile, urban dwellers remained confined to the apartments assigned them— often only one or two rooms for a family, with a tiny kitchen and toilet sometimes shared with another family. Since low rents cannot cover the expenses of maintenance, the buildings are often in poor repair. Sometimes young workers live in dormitories for several years, even after marriage, before they are assigned an apartment. Hence reform of the urban housing system became one of the key issues in the 1980s. During the 1990s, urban governments rapidly accelerated the building of tall housing blocks with larger, more modern apartments. Beginning in 1998, all workers moving to new apartments must purchase them, while rents will gradually rise for those in older apartments. The final goal of housing reform is to sell most apartments to the residents with subsidies from the institutions that employ them. Urban families have begun to buy air conditioning, carpets, kitchen appliances, and many other improvements for their apartments, and attempts are being made to improve maintenance of apartment blocks.

One of eight buildings in the housing compound of one rural minority-culture extended family, Yunnan province.

Public housing estates dominate this northern Beijing skyline.

Meanwhile, many villages located close to larger cities are creating new factories and other cooperative enterprises under the reforms. They, too, are using the income to build blocks of apartment buildings, along with schools, retirement homes, hospitals, and other amenities. Hence these rural areas are coming to look more like cities, and their inhabitants are being assigned housing in a manner resembling cities.

□ Blurring the Distinction Between City and Countryside

The relaxation of restrictions on travel from the countryside into cities and towns has resulted in large numbers of temporary migrants moving from villages into cities; these people are not counted as "permanent urban residents" (Goldstein and Goldstein, 1991:1–4). It is estimated that about 3 million temporary residents or migrants live in Beijing; Shanghai has about that number as well. Some of them have lived and worked in cities for several years and have no intention of returning to villages. Referred to by city folk as "peasant workers," they are hired for construction teams, by city factories, and as domestic servants in residents' houses, or they set up small shops and businesses. A proportion of these temporary migrants should be considered urban since they join the urban economy and urban life in many aspects.

These workers are not entitled to housing in the cities where they have come to work and must often live in makeshift housing they construct themselves or in dormitories provided by their place of work. Having grown up in the countryside, they may find it difficult to adapt to urban life. They often leave their families at home initially; if they bring or acquire spouses and children, they may not be entitled to full health care and education benefits. Some of them may engage in crime or even become involved in criminal syndicates. Resentments against them by long-term city residents sometimes leads to confrontation. When they travel back to villages for spring festival and then return to cities where they usually work, the trains and railway stations all around China become a mess. Studying these temporary migrants and their adjustment to cities is one of the hot topics in population studies in China today.

These "peasant workers" are part of even bigger changes in urban life. Wrecking balls and the tall cranes (often jokingly referred to as the "national bird") rising from construction sites herald a complete transformation in the way urban people live and the way cities blend with surrounding towns and villages. Unlike Europe or the United States, city planners need not contend with long legal battles to acquire property for development projects. Much of the land is not private and is available for conversion to public uses. So entire city streets and blocks are frequently torn down to make way for public development projects.

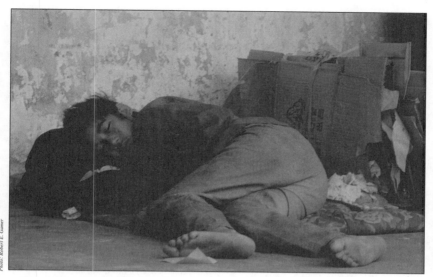

This temporary migrant laborer sleeps on a sidewalk in Xiamen, Fujian.

Many of China's ancient cities had walls, which were still in place in 1949. Most urban dwellers then lived in small low-rise houses within those walls. To make way for new roads, public squares, government buildings, factories, and high-rise housing, many sections of those walls were torn down, and building extended outward from the center. Still, many of the older urban neighborhoods remained. Today, such old-style buildings and houses are being rapidly torn down and replaced with modern high-rise offices, shopping centers, hotels, and apartment buildings. This has provided residents with better housing and hygiene, but it has also scattered the population and made it harder to maintain neighborhood activities. Often people are moved to an apartment miles from where they work, requiring them to use buses, bicycles, or subways to commute long distances. With new cars rapidly being added to the mix, traffic jams grow in intensity; extensive new construction of elevated highways, subways, and large bridges is seldom adequate to keep up with the rising demand. In Shanghai, the entire rural area to the east of the city is being converted into the Pudong Development Zone, transforming the farms that formerly occupied the land into industrial parks, apartment and office blocks, motorways, and port facilities; begun in 1990, this already covers an area as large as that occupied by Shanghai itself (Yeung and Sung, 1996; Gamer, 1998). The same phenomenon is occurring in all of the new special economic zones along the coast and inland and around all major cities (Davis et al., 1995). Workmen are constructing ring roads that are soon clogged with traffic and surrounded

Building one of Shanghai's many new elevated highways.

*One of the five new bridges linking
Shanghai with the Pudong Development Zone.*

Student parking at Nankai University, Tianjin.

by new high-rise buildings, airports, amusement parks, and other urban amenities.

Within this maze of construction may lie the outlines of older towns and villages, caught up in a megalopolis; surrounding the construction are villages a few miles away that are carrying out similar construction to support new township enterprises. Much of the development is, in fact, directed by local authorities rather than the national government. This can result in considerable confusion about what is local and what is metropolitan. There has been a debate on the strategy of future urbanization in China for several years. The official strategy put forth by the government in 1980 is to "control the population size of large cities, properly develop middle-sized cities, and encourage the development of small cities and towns" (Ma, 1992:141). Some experts emphasize the importance of small towns since they can absorb surplus rural laborers by developing township enterprises and can depend on their own revenues without much provincial or national governmental investment. Another group criticizes this strategy in favor of developing large cities. They emphasize the efficiency of large cities in management and land use.

Changes in the government's definition of what constitutes an urban area emphasize the difficulty of coming to grips with these problems. The definition may change to accommodate policy needs. For example, in 1963 when 20 million people were asked to return to rural areas after the failure of the Great Leap Forward, the criteria for setting up a "township" and a "city" became more restricted (to become a township, a village needed at least 2,100 nonagricultural residents, rather than the prior 750), so that villages could not declare themselves one of these to keep out migrants. Cities were required to have 100,000 inhabitants rather than the 20,000 needed previously, so that suddenly the portion of the populace officially living in towns and cities was radically reduced, showing "compliance" with the shift back to the countryside.

After 1980, however, the government wished to encourage the formation of townships so that they could set up township enterprises and take over responsibilities like education and health care, which were formerly handled by communes. Under the law implemented in 1984, any seat of county government could become a town, as could any former rural commune with a nonagricultural population over 2,000, and many border posts, mine settlements, tourist places, and villages in minority ethnic group regions. Under the new standards, the total number of towns increased from 2,781 in 1983 to 6,211 in 1984. And by 1986, towns with a permanent nonagricultural population over 60,000 and whose total value of annual domestic production exceeded 200 million yuan could apply for city status—down from 100,000 (Ma, 1992:120,128–129). Suddenly, many more people officially lived in towns and cities that could include them in plans for township and urban enterprises, health care, education, new housing blocks, and other initiatives.

In the 1980s, some provinces in China began practicing a new system called "city managing county." Then it became a trend to change prefectures (an administrative level between province and county) into "cities." Those new "cities" actually cover many rural areas and their population cannot be classified as urban residents. A parallel trend is to change *xiang* (former communes) into towns, and these towns also include a large number of rural people. If these "city" and "town" residents are classified as "urban," China's "urban population" would exceed 50 percent of the total.

Under the 1990 national census, only people in areas directly managed by town or city governments or under urban districts or street committees can be designated as urban—about 26 percent of the total population, or 211 million and 85 million for cities and towns respectively, which is closer to world standards for classifying urban population (Population Census Bureau, 1993:2, 14–17). But it is clear that cities, towns, and villages in China are increasingly intertwined in their governance, economies, and social connections. As cities grow out from their former boundaries, towns build modern buildings and amenities, and factories in the countryside produce expanding quantities of goods for the world market, the populations and social support programs of villages, towns, and cities will increasingly need to coordinate their efforts. Finding a balance here, like finding a balance between a rising population and food supply, will not be easy.

As urban construction covers arable land and new urban jobs become available, millions of agricultural workers are switching to urban pursuits; the government estimates there are 100 million migrant rural workers seeking such employment in cities ("China," 1997). Often they are leaving the land to work for cooperative enterprises that do not offer them health care coverage, housing, and other amenities available to settled rural or urban dwellers affiliated with state enterprises, neighborhoods, or most joint-venture businesses. This places great pressure on urbanized areas to provide them with housing, schools, health care, electricity, transportation, and other services. And migrations to towns and cities can leave villages with fewer resources to offer such services for those who remain, especially when they are far from urban markets where they can sell their produce and if they have marginal dry or hilly land. Since much of this migration involves movement from poorer inland areas toward the coast and since those most in need of such public services are those who have left the villages without regular jobs in state enterprises or the new joint ventures, failure to adequately address these problems can increasingly leave China polarized between rich and poor.

In 1997 Chongqing, situated within Sichuan province, joined Beijing, Tianjin, and Shanghai as a special municipality directly administered under the central government. It has 2.5 million inhabitants in this urbanized core, but 14 million with its surrounding rural territory.

■ ETHNIC MINORITIES

Deeply entwined in these attempts to find balance between urban and rural is the need to keep the less urbanized inland provinces, largely inhabited by ethnic minorities, from falling behind the more urbanized and prosperous coastal provinces as modernization continues. China is a multiethnic country. There are fifty-five ethnic groups in China (93 percent are Han and the rest are minorities), according to criteria established by the PRC (Dreyer, 1976, gives an excellent introduction to this topic). The central government of China established many autonomous areas for the different ethnic minority groups: five autonomous provinces; sixty-two autonomous prefectures (an administrative unit between province and county), and 659 autonomous cities and counties. These areas—mostly in inland areas away from the coastal plains—cover over 60 percent of China's total territory. Even in those autonomous areas, much of the population is from the Han majority group, who also tend to be among those in the most modernized sectors of the economy.

Ninety-one percent of China's total population in 1995 was Han; the non-Han portion of the populace grew from 6 percent in 1953 (35 million) to 9 percent in 1995 (108 million). In 1990 there were nine ethnic minority groups with populations over 4 million, as you can see from Table 8.3, while twenty-two groups contained fewer than 10,000 people. Table 8.3 makes it apparent that several groups had a very high growth rate between 1982 and 1990. This stems largely from the fact that ethnic minorities are exempt from the new family planning program. Not only are they having more children than the rest of the populace, but investigations have found that many individuals who had been classified as Han, but had a blood relationship with a minority, registered themselves as a minority (Manchu, Tujia, Miao, Mongolian, etc.) so as to be exempt from family planning and to take advantage of other special privileges enjoyed by ethnic minorities. The central government allows ethnic minorities to enter colleges and universities with lower scores, gives them priority for promotions in government institutions, and affords them other advantages to help them rise economically.

The central government and the National People's Congress established a basic law for the autonomy of ethnic minorities, which pledges respect for the language, religion, and traditional clothing of ethnic minorities and guarantees them equal rights. Among the fifty-five ethnic minority groups, two (Manchu and Hui) use the Mandarin language of the Han majority; fifty-three groups speak their own languages. Before 1949, only eighteen had written languages. In 1956, the government helped twelve groups create a new written language and helped three others revise their written language. There is also diversity of religion among ethnic minority groups in China. Of the fifty-five minorities, four are largely Tibetan Buddhists, another four

Table 8.3 Ethnic Minorities with a Population over 4 Million (in millions)

Ethnic Minorities	1982	1990	Growth (%)	Annual Growth Rate (%)
Zhuang	13.38	15.49	15.7	1.8
Manchu	4.30	9.82	128.2	10.9
Hui	7.23	8.60	19.0	2.2
Miao	5.02	7.40	46.9	5.0
Uygur	5.96	7.21	21.0	2.4
Yi	5.45	6.57	20.4	2.4
Tujia	2.83	5.70	101.2	9.1
Mongolian	3.41	4.81	40.7	4.4
Tibetan	3.85	4.59	18.6	2.2

Sources: Population Census Bureau, 1985, 1993.

Hinayana Buddhists, and ten are Muslim; others adhere to primitive religions such as shamanism. The government has also instituted programs to provide financial subsidies and investment to autonomous regions and to give more favorable consideration in education, housing, employment, cadre selection, social welfare, and childbearing to individuals belonging to ethnic minority groups.

Urbanization in minority regions developed rapidly after 1949. The population of Hohhot (the capital city of Inner Mongolia Autonomous Region) and Urumqi (the capital city of Xinjiang Uygur Autonomous Region) more than doubled as they became newly industrialized cities. In Inner Mongolia Autonomous Region as a whole, urban population was 15.1 percent in 1953 and increased to 28.9 percent in 1982 and 36.3 percent in 1990. The urban areas of Lhasa (the capital city of Tibetan Autonomous Region) expanded eleven times since 1952, when the Agreement on Measures for the Peaceful Liberation of Tibet (Karan, 1976:89) was signed.

The rapid growth of urban populations in ethnic minority regions is due partly to in-migration from Han majority regions, partly to natural increase of urban residents, and partly to rural-urban migration of local minorities. By moving into cities and living with Han urban residents—who have lived in cities and towns in many minority regions for centuries—these ethnic minorities gradually adapt to urban life and integrate with the Han (Mackerras, 1995). Their language, religion, culture, and customs are respected by others under the law, but when they adopt a modern urban lifestyle, some of their customs gradually disappear. Many of them now wear suits, use telephones and computers, listen to popular music, and believe that modernization is the only way for the future of their groups.

Some elderly people have difficulties adapting to urban life, and the generation gap that exists among all Chinese people extends to China's ethnic minorities as well.

Although the basic situation in coastal areas and cities has greatly improved with regard to income, housing, and public health care facilities, about 70 million people in China still live below the poverty line (annual per capita income of less than 200 Chinese yuan, or U.S.$25). These people usually have high birthrates, high mortality rates, and a low life expectancy. Many of them live in these autonomous regions, largely outside the monetary economy. Promoting the development of these "poverty regions" is a key issue in China today.

■ CHALLENGES

At the beginning of the chapter, I referred to three "balancing acts" China must perform—between city and country, between population and food, and between regions of hardship and regions of prosperity. By now it must be evident that these three issues are themselves interrelated. The main challenges faced by China in the twenty-first century regarding population and urbanization are as follows:

1. China's population will continually increase even under the one-child policy designed to keep it down, reaching 1.5–1.6 billion in the 2030s. These people must have food, jobs, housing, and social services.
2. Because of family planning and the one-child policy, China is facing the problem of dealing with an aging population. It is expected that 6.72 percent of the total population of China (about 87 million) will be 65 or older by the year 2000 (Li, 1993:107); increasingly, a single child will be responsible for aging parents.
3. About 250–300 million laborers will switch from agriculture into the nonagricultural sector in the next ten to fifteen years, which will result in a huge volume of rural-urban migration.
4. Because of the rapid growth in the urban population due to both natural increase and migration, the pressure on housing and public services (including health care, schools, transportation, the energy supply, etc.) will become very serious.
5. Since most human resources and capital move from the poor regions to prosperous regions under the market economy system, poverty in western China and ethnic minority regions will increase. Whether the national goal of modernization of China can be reached in the twenty-first century will largely depend on how successfully the Chinese government handles these challenges.

■ BIBLIOGRAPHY

Aird, John S. 1978. "Fertility Decline and Birth Control in the People's Republic of China." *Population and Development Review* 4, no. 2:225–253.
———. 1982. "Population Studies and Population Policy in China." *Population and Development Review* 8, no. 2:267–297.
Banister, Judith. 1984. "An Analysis of Recent Data on the Population of China." *Population and Development Review* 10, no. 2:241–271.
———. 1987. *China's Changing Population*. Stanford: Stanford University Press.
Banister, Judith, and Samuel H. Preston. 1981. "Mortality in China." *Population and Development Review* 7, no. 1:98–110.
Beaver, Steven E. 1975. *Demographic Transition Theory Reinterpreted*. Lexington, MA: Lexington Press.
Birdsall, Nancy, and Dean T. Jamison. 1983. "Income and Other Factors Influencing Fertility in China." *Population and Development Review* 9, no. 4:651–675.
Caldwell, John C., and K. Srinivasan. 1984. "New Data on Nuptiality and Fertility in China." *Population and Development Review* 10, no. 1:71–79.
Chan, Kam Wing. 1994. *Cities with Invisible Walls: Reinterpreting Urbanization in Post-1949 China*. Oxford: Oxford University Press.
Chang, Sen-Dou. 1981. "Modernization and China's Urban Development." *Annals of the Association of American Geographers* 71, no. 2:202–219.
Chao, Kang. 1987. *Man and Land in Chinese History: An Economic Analysis*. Stanford: Stanford University Press.
Chao Wenlin, and Xie Shujun. 1988. *History of China's Population*. Beijing: People's Press (in Chinese).
Chen, Pi-chao, and Adrienne Kols. 1982. "Population and Birth Planning in the People's Republic of China." *Population Reports* J-25.
"China on the Move." 1997. *The Economist* 342 (February 8):37.
China Population and Information Research Center. 1985. *Almanac of China's Population*. Beijing: China Social Science Press.
China Population and Information Research Center (ed.). 1991. *China's Fourth National Population Census Data Sheet*. Beijing: China Population and Information Research Center.
Clausen, Soren, and Stig Thogersen. 1995. *The Making of a Chinese City: History and Historiography in Harbin*. Armonk, NY: M. E. Sharpe.
Coale, Ansley J. 1981. "Population Trends, Population Policy, and Population Studies in China." *Population and Development Review* 7, no. 1:85–97.
———. 1984. *Rapid Population Change in China, 1952–1982*. Report no. 27 of the Committee on Population and Demography. Washington, DC: National Academic Press.
Davis, Deborah S., Richard Kraus, Barry Naughton, and Elizabeth J. Perry. 1995. *Urban Spaces in Contemporary China: The Potential for Autonomy and Community in Post-Mao China*. Cambridge: Cambridge University Press.
Day, Lincoln H., and Ma Xia. 1994. *Migration and Urbanization in China*. Armonk, NY: M. E. Sharpe.
Dreyer, June Teufel. 1976. *China's Forty Millions*. Cambridge: Harvard University Press.
Elvin, Mark, and G. William Skinner (eds.). 1974. *The Chinese City Between Two Worlds*. Stanford: Stanford University Press.
Fairbank, John K. 1979. *The United States and China*. 4th ed. Cambridge: Harvard University Press.

Gamer, Robert E. 1998. "The Continuing Transformation of the Welfare State: Planning and Funding Housing and Transportation in Shanghai, London, Paris, and Kansas City." *Political Crossroads* (Australia) 6:1.

Gates, Hill. 1996. *China's Motor: A Thousand Years of Petty Capitalism.* Ithaca: Cornell University Press.

Gaubatz, Piper Rae. 1996. *Beyond the Great Wall: Urban Form and Transformation on the Chinese Frontiers.* Stanford: Stanford University Press.

Goldstein, Melvyn C., and Cynthia M. Beall. 1991. "China's Birth Control Policy in the Tibet Autonomous Region: Myths and Realities." *Asian Survey* (March).

Goldstein, Sidney. 1985. *Urbanization in China: New Insights from the 1982 Census.* Papers of the East-West Population Institute no. 93. Honolulu: East-West Center.

Goldstein, Sidney, and Alice Goldstein. 1985. *Population Mobility in the People's Republic of China.* Papers of the East-West Population Institute no. 95. Honolulu: East-West Center.

———. 1991. *Permanent and Temporary Migration Differentials in China.* Papers of the East-West Population Institute no. 117. Honolulu: East-West Center.

Goodstadt, Leo F. 1982. "China's One-Child Family: Policy and Public Response." *Population and Development Review* 8, no. 1:37–58.

Graubatz, Piper Rae. 1996. *Beyond the Great Wall: Urban Form and Transformation on the Chinese Frontier.* Stanford: Stanford University Press.

Harris, Marvin, and Eric B. Ross. 1987. *Death, Sex, and Fertility: Population Regulation in Preindustrial and Developing Societies.* New York: Columbia University Press.

Henriot, Christian. 1993. *Shanghai, 1927–1937.* Berkeley: University of California Press.

Huang, Rongqing. 1993. "The Mortality of China in the 1980s." Pp. 137–143 in Chinese Association of Population Studies (ed.), *Selected Papers Presented at the Sixth National Conference on Population Science of China.* Beijing: Chinese Association of Population Studies (in Chinese).

Ikels, Charlotte. 1996. *The Return of the God of Wealth: The Transition to a Market Economy in Urban China.* Stanford: Stanford University Press.

Jefferson, Gary H., and Thomas G. Rawski. 1992. "Unemployment, Underemployment, and Employment Policy in China's Cities." *Modern China* 18 (January):42–71.

Karan, Pradyumna P. 1976. *The Changing Face of Tibet.* Lexington: University Press of Kentucky.

Li, Li. 1993. "The Present Situation, Characteristics of Aging in China and Countermeasures." Pp. 105–110 in Qu Geping (ed.), *Population and Environment in China.* Beijing: Chinese Press of Environmental Science (in Chinese).

Lin Fude. 1986. "An Analysis of China's Birth Rates." Pp. 237–246 in *Almanac of China's Population 1985.* Beijing: Chinese Social Sciences Publishing House (in Chinese).

Lu, Lei, and Lin Fude. 1994. "The Future of Population Growth with a Low Fertility Rate." Pp. 101–106 in Chinese Association of Population Studies (ed.), *Selected Papers Presented at the Sixth National Conference on Population Science of China.* Beijing: Chinese Association of Population Studies (in Chinese).

Lyle, Katherine Ch'iu. 1980. "Report from China: Planned Birth in Tianjin." *China Quarterly* 83:551–567.

Ma, L. J. C., and E. W. Hanten (eds.). 1981. *Urban Development in Modern China.* Boulder: Westview Press.

Ma Rong. 1992. "The Development of Small Towns and Their Role in the Modernization of China." Pp. 119–154 in Gregory E. Guldin (ed.), *Urbanizing China*. New York: Greenwood Press.

Ma Yinchu. 1957, 1981. "New Essay on Population." Pp. 174–195 in *Collected Works of Ma Yinchu on Economics, Vol. 2*. Beijing: Peking University Press (in Chinese).

Mackerras, Colin. 1995. *China's Minority Cultures: Identities and Integration Since 1912*. New York: St. Martin's Press.

Peng, Xizhe. 1991. *Demographic Transition in China*. Oxford: Clarendon Press.

Population Census Bureau. 1985. *Tabulation on the 1980 Population Census of the PRC*. Beijing: China Statistical Publishing House.

———. 1993. *Tabulation on the 1990 Population Census of the PRC*. Beijing: China Statistical Publishing House.

Poston, Dudley L., Jr., and David Yaukey (eds.). 1992. *The Population of Modern China*. New York: Plenum Press.

Qian, Wenbao. 1996. *Rural-Urban Migration and Its Impact on Economic Development in China*. Brookfield, VT: Ashgate.

Qu Geping, and Li Jichang. 1992. *Population and Environment in China*. Beijing: Chinese Press of Environmental Sciences (in Chinese).

Rozman, Gilbert (ed.). 1982. *The Modernization of China*. New York: Free Press.

Salaff, Janet W. 1973. "Mortality Decline in the People's Republic of China and the United States." *Population Studies* 27, no. 3:551–576.

Sanderson, Warren C., and Jee-Peng Tan. 1996. *Population in Asia*. Brookfield, VT: Ashgate.

Skinner, William G. (ed.). 1977. *The City in Late Imperial China*. Cambridge: Harvard University Press.

State Statistical Bureau. 1950–1995. *Statistical Yearbook of China*. Beijing: Chinese Statistical Publishing House.

———. 1995. *Urban Statistical Yearbook of China 1993–1994*. Beijing: Chinese Statistical Press.

Tien, H. Yuan. 1973. *China's Population Struggle: Demographic Decisions of the People's Republic, 1949–1969*. Columbus: Ohio State University Press.

———. 1983. "China: Demographic Billionaire." *Population Bulletin* 38:2.

———. 1984. "Induced Fertility Transition: Impact of Population Planning and Socio-economic Change in the People's Republic of China." *Population Studies* 38:1–16.

Van Slyke, Lyman P. 1988. *Yangtze: Nature, History, and the River*. Reading, MA: Addison-Wesley.

Wang Xiangming. 1986. "Urbanization of China's Population." Pp. 283–292 in *Almanac of China's Population 1985*. Beijing: Chinese Social Sciences Publishing House (in Chinese).

Wenlin, Zhao, and Xie Shujun. 1988. *History of China's Population*. Beijing: People's Press.

Wolf, Arthur P. 1984. "Fertility in Pre-Revolutionary Rural China." *Population and Development Review* 10, no. 3:443–480.

World Bank (ed.). 1982–1995. *Development Report*. Washington, DC: World Bank.

Yan, Rui, and Cheng Shengqi. 1993. "Age-Specific Death Rates and Life Expectancy in the Past 40 Years." In Chinese Association of Population Studies (ed.), *Collected Papers Presented at International Conference on Fertility Sampling Surveys of China*. Beijing: Population Press of China (in Chinese).

Yeung, Y. M., and Sung Wun-wing. 1996. *Shanghai: Transformation and Modernization Under China's Open Policy*. Hong Kong: Chinese University Press.

Zhao Wenlin and Xie Shujun. 1988. *History of China's Population.* Beijing: People's Press.

Zhen Yi, Tu Ping, Gu Baochang, Xu Yi, Li Bohua, and Li Yongping. 1993. "Causes and Implications of the Increase in China's Reported Sex Ratio at Birth." *Population and Development Review* 19, no. 2:283–302.

Zhou Qing. 1994. "Ideas of People About Births in Poor Regions and Countermeasures to Change Their Ideas." Pp. 70–73 in Chinese Association of Population Studies (ed.), *Selected Papers Presented at the Sixth National Conference of Population Science of China.* Beijing: Chinese Association of Population Studies (in Chinese).

■ 9 ■

China's Environmental Problems

Richard Louis Edmonds

Chapter 8 discussed human problems; this one discusses the environment in which humans live and their interaction with it. The quality of China's environment has deteriorated at an increasing pace since the founding of the People's Republic of China (PRC) in 1949. Doubling the population since 1949 has hastened deforestation, desertification, soil erosion, water shortages, and pollution. Pessimistic observers say that the current population of 1.2 billion already may have exceeded the number that the country can hope to support at a good standard of living. Negative predictions suggest that the population could reach a point above which minimal living standards cannot be sustained (1.5–1.6 billion people) as early as 2015 (Zhongguo Kexue Bao She, 1989:9, 17). Even the most positive observers see the combination of population and economic growth placing serious strains on China's geography.

Modification of China's environment, however, goes back a long way in time, as Rhoads Murphey explained in Chapter 3. When humans first arrived on the Loess Plateau in north-central China (see Map 2.4), this area, generally considered to be the earliest home of Chinese civilization, was probably covered with a mixture of forests and grasslands. Intensive use of some of these lands led to a reduction in vegetation and serious erosion on the plateau centuries ago. Similar problems occurred elsewhere as the proto-Chinese people proliferated, spread out from the Loess Plateau and the North China Plain, and incorporated other groups over the past 2,000 years (Edmonds, 1994:28–35). Even though the Han Chinese did evolve some ecologically sound agricultural practices that improved the quality of the soil, they stripped the land of forests as they spread southward (Ruddle and Zhong, 1988:14–17). As they spread to the north and west (at a much slower pace), they began to farm virgin land and substantially degraded many of these cool, dry, or fragile areas. Since the mid–eighteenth century, the pace of farming has intensified as the population grows. During the 1950s, the Chinese focused on reconstructing a war-torn country and devising means to promote rapid economic growth. Although these efforts led to better attempts at hygiene and health care, natural resources were generally viewed by the communists as a commodity to be exploited to create wealth for the state and, in theory, the Chinese people. After the creation of communes during the mid-1950s, many hillsides were cleared and wetlands filled to create new farmland. During the years of the so-called Great Leap Forward (1958–1961), huge numbers of trees were felled for fuel to produce low-quality steel in small, highly polluting home furnaces. From 1960 to 1962, China was hit with a drought that, combined with these policies, produced the so-called Three Bad Years (1960–1962) of widespread famine. In 1966, just as the country was devising policies designed to avoid recurrence of such a catastrophe, Chairman Mao Zedong proclaimed the Cultural Revolution. A decade of political unrest and lawlessness followed, during which ecological degradation became commonplace.

Recent efforts to deal with ecological problems began in a modest way around 1972 after the PRC sent a delegation to the First United Nations Conference on the Human Environment. In 1973 the government created the National Environmental Protection Agency, and environmental planning became included in national plans. Some Chinese academics and policymakers argued that economic development could not continue without considering its impact upon the environment; others argued that China must follow the "pollute first and clean up later" phase that the developed world had experienced before pollution control received high priority. In 1979 the government promulgated an Environmental Protection Law (for trial implementation). Under this law, the agency began to write environmental impact statements on proposed heavy industry, manufacturing, and infrastructure projects. However, the recommendations of these impact statements were often ignored.

From 1982, discussions began on a development strategy calling for low waste–high efficiency planning. The concept of harmonious development (*xietiao fazhan*), similar to the idea of sustainable development formulated by the Bruntland Commission, was adopted as official policy. It was supposed to increase efficiency by initiating recycling and pollution-abatement measures. However, the new small entrepreneurs who have flourished after economic reform have not complied with the plan, and it has been difficult to implement.

Poverty and the lack of education also make it hard for China to overcome its environmental problems. Half of China's counties still do not have rural extension services. This fact, combined with high illiteracy rates, makes it hard to teach the rural populace how to preserve the environment. A full-fledged Environmental Protection Law was adopted in

1989, but environmental policy decisions continue to be held back while the government attempts to reach consensus among various factions on how to proceed.

■ CONTEMPORARY ENVIRONMENTAL PROBLEMS

Pollution is growing rapidly in China, as we shall discuss presently. The most threatening environmental problems, though, are the reductions in water supply, vegetation, soils, and other natural resources. China already has only 36 percent of the land area, 13 percent of the forest cover, and 25 percent of the water resources per person found in the average country (Wang et al., 1989:1). Cropland accounts for only 10 percent of China's total area, and both the per capita level and the total quantity of arable land are decreasing despite some recent attempts to reclaim wastelands.

□ Water Shortages

China currently supports 22 percent of the world's population with only 8 percent of the world's water. Many rivers, lakes, reservoirs, and aquifers are shrinking or have dried up during the last quarter-century, and China has stopped expanding its irrigated area since the beginning of the 1980s. This problem is at its worst north of the Huai River (roughly, in a line due west along the mouth of the Yangtze River; see Map 2.4) where 64 percent of China's cultivated land has access to only 19 percent of the country's water, and there is considerable annual variation in precipitation. During the 1990s, the groundwater table in northern China has been dropping at a rate of 20 inches (50 centimeters) per annum, and in places it is 200 feet (70 meters) below where it was in the 1950s (Liu, 1993). Some eastern and northern cities such as Shanghai and Tianjin (Map 2.2) are sinking as the earth settles to adjust to this loss of water. In southern China, this reportedly is happening in forty-five cities. The subsiding can lead to floods during storms and can destroy building foundations.

The water supply problem is most acute around big cities in northern China, where precipitation levels are lower than in the south. Major efforts to save water by recycling or to increase water through diversion projects began only in the 1980s. Plans are under discussion to move water north via the Grand Canal or from the future Three Gorges (Sanxia) project discussed later. Northern China's water shortages, however, will worsen before these projects are completed. Conservation of existing water resources is of primary importance. Because irrigation water is often used in an inefficient manner, the government has modestly increased charges. Water quotas assigned to industries have resulted in some savings. Increased recycling of wastewater by industry should also help. So far, household water use has not been very wasteful. As incomes increase, however, and more people move from older housing into homes with modern plumbing, domestic water consumption will increase.

☐ Forest Loss and Recovery

Official statistics indicate that in 1994 China had forest cover equal to 13.39 percent of the country's total area, which was far below the world average of 31 percent. Vegetation cover has been decreasing since 1949, with occasional rises noticeable only since the 1980s. All major basins now experience annual floods and drought, in good part due to forest loss. By the 1980s, the average area affected by such disasters had increased by two-thirds compared with the 1950s (Han, 1989:804–805).

A Basic Forestry Law was ratified in 1986, but like other basic laws, this law still reads more like a wish list than concrete legislation. In recent years, planned cutting levels have been greatly exceeded. In some remote areas, lack of state control rules out enforcement of laws. Illegal logging activities have been widespread, especially as the market economy makes it easy to sell timber. The state wood-supply system has been excessively wasteful due to a lack of realistic pricing mechanisms. However, recent moves toward higher, more appropriate timber prices and other economic measures eventually may discourage such waste. Fire and disease also continue to seriously reduce vegetation cover.

Efforts since the 1950s to replant forests have not been very successful. Forest management has been corrupt and inefficient; the natural forests that remain today have been saved largely by inaccessibility. In the early 1980s, a complex forestry responsibility system was established, with individuals or households contracting to plant trees or manage a portion of forest. Several large projects are being implemented. The Three Norths Shelterbelt project *(sanbei fanghulin)* begun in 1978 is northern China's major reforesting project, expected to account for over a third of all trees planted during the 1990s. It is creating small tree belts, shrub plantings, grasslands, fuel wood forests, timber forests, and plantations of "economic" trees that produce fruit or nuts on 75,000 square miles (194,000 square kilometers) of land—38,500 square miles (100,000 square kilometers) by the year 2000—to halt soil erosion and to keep desertlike land from developing around Beijing. The Greening of the Plains project, administered at the county *(xian)* level, is doing similar planting on ten of China's major plains, river valleys, and deltas. The Greening of the Tai-hang Mountains project aims to plant trees on 1,500 square miles (3,900 square kilometers) of barren mountains and fields by the year 2000. The 11,000-mile-long (18,000-kilometer) Coastal Protective Forest project begun in 1988 covered an area of more than 26,000 square miles (67,000 square kilometers) by the end of 1992. Plans are in the works to create 13,750 square miles (36,000 square kilometers) of coastal forests by 2010. With these plans, China hopes to have 15 or 16 percent of its total area planted in trees by the year 2000, up from the 13.39 percent in 1994 (National Environmental Protection Agency, 1994:69).

China covers 3.69 million square miles (9.56 million square kilometers). It remains to be seen whether these projects meet their goals and whether they add more trees than those being cut down in the interim. China's Agenda 21 aims to have China's forests fully sustainable for production and ecosystem protection by the mid–twenty-first century. The Obligatory Tree Planting Program, adopted in 1981, requires all Chinese citizens above eleven years old to plant three to five trees each year or do other relevant forestry work. Most Chinese cities show the benefits of urban tree planting programs, many of which have been obligatory. However, the total area of public greenery in Chinese cities continues to decrease as building construction receives priority.

A shelterbelt project of 77,000 square miles (200,000 square kilometers) began in 1990 along the middle and upper reaches of the Yangtze River. This soil erosion control program, known as the Chang (Yangtze) River Middle and Upper Reaches Protective Forest Construction Project, is not due to be completed until the year 2030. By the mid-1990s, enthusiastic reports suggested that the project was enjoying high tree survival rates, improving microclimates, and generating timber revenue.

The Continual Production Timber Forest Base Construction Project was set up in 1988 to create 77,000 square miles (200,000 square kilometers) of timber forests over a thirty-year period. Efforts up to 2000 will concentrate on creating timber forests in the Lesser and Greater Hinggan Mountains of the northeast and in the hills of the southwest, as well as in the southeast, where possible. The government hopes that by 2010 these forests will be contributing enough timber to satisfy China's timber needs (National Environmental Protection Agency, 1994:70–73). In addition, four reforestation projects are planned to begin during the Ninth Five-Year Plan (1996–2000) in the Yellow River valley, the Huai River–Tai Lake area, the Pearl River valley at the mouth of the West River, and the Liao River valley ("Programme," 1996:6). You can find most of these rivers on Map 2.4.

☐ Soil Erosion and Nutrient Loss

China has one of the most serious soil erosion problems in the world. Conservative estimates suggest one-sixth of the nation's arable land is affected. Between 5,000 and 10,000 million metric tons of soil are washed down rivers each year. The loss in fertility is about equal to that supplied by the 40 million tons of chemical fertilizer China produces each year (Wang et al., 1989:ii). Rapid soil erosion has contributed to China's overall environmental degradation in several ways. Riverbeds, lakes, and reservoirs are silting up and have had their hydroelectric and flood control storage capacity reduced. The loss of good-quality topsoil has reduced arable land and threatens to cause serious food shortages in the near future.

Some of the most severe erosion occurs in northern portions of the semiarid Loess Plateau of north-central China (see Map 2.4). According to some reports, the plateau loses about a third of an inch (0.838 centimeters) of topsoil each year. The Yangtze River valley in central China and Heilongjiang and eastern Inner Mongolia in the north are other badly affected areas. Even areas in the far south that once had little erosion—like Yunnan, Hainan, and Fujian—have had severe soil erosion in recent years.

China has made considerable effort to stem the flow of topsoil. Over half of the 210,000 square miles (544,000 square kilometers) of eroded land that has been improved since the mid-1950s has been planted with trees, and another fifth has been terraced. In addition, about 30,000 check dams have been built across small gullies to control erosion. In recent years, the planning focus has shifted from individual plots to entire river basins and from central to local government. The problem is the massive scale of the effort required. As the erosion is being checked in one area, it may be increasing in another.

The increased erosion has largely resulted from policies implemented during the 1950s that opened steep slopes, formerly forested areas, and wetlands to farming. Now many of those areas must be returned to forests and herding, which affects the peasants using the land. The household responsibility system gives individual households control of land management. Enforcement of regulations to take steep slopes out of cultivation, replace crops with privately managed forests, and introduce new conservation techniques requires their cooperation. However, the areas in which the policy needs to be carried out are generally poor and hard to reach with grain shipments during the transition from agriculture to forestry or herding. Therefore, it is hard to persuade peasants to change or to enforce policies.

Even where they are not yet degraded to a point that crops will not grow, China's soils are of poor nutrition. For example, the rich yields of southern China have been obtained only through heavy labor inputs and the widespread use of manure and composted matter. The natural organic content of China's soil averages less than 1.5 percent. It has been estimated that if China adds no fertilizer to its soils, nitrogen would be exhausted in twenty to forty years, phosphorus in ten to twenty years and potassium in eighty to 130 years (Zhao, 1990:155).

The second national soil survey undertaken in the 1980s found overall soil fertility dropping, partly because farmers were leaving fewer fields fallow for shorter periods as they sought to maximize output and increase their incomes in the marketized rural economy. Today, particularly in eastern provinces, some peasants are beginning to practice "ecological agriculture," combining farming, animal husbandry, and forestry with local food processing and reuse of residual materials.

On Hainan Island (Map 2.2) and nearby regions of the south, peasants grow three rounds of crops a year in a field. When the only crop they grow is rice in flooded wet-paddy fields and drainage is poor, gleization (depletion of oxygen from iron compounds in the soil) can reduce the land's ability to grow rice or other crops. Approximately one-sixth of China's paddy lands suffer from this. In addition, the majority of soils in the populous southeast are acidic, rendering crops susceptible to acid pollution, more commonly known as acid rain. This possibility is increased by large amounts of industrial pollutants in the atmosphere. In some cases, the drop in soil fertility has been accompanied by desertification or by severe waterlogging and secondary salinization.

□ Desertification and Salinization–Alkalinization

Each year, the Chinese estimate from aerial photographs taken in 1975 and 1986, 800 square miles (2,100 square kilometers) of arid to semiarid land becomes "desertified," degraded into a desertlike barren landscape; this is a faster pace than in prior years (Zhu and Wang, 1990:431–433). Approximately 1.7 percent of China's total land area can be considered human-induced desertified land. An almost continuous belt of degraded land stretches for 3,400 miles (5,500 kilometers) from northwest to northeast China (see Map 2.4). Desertification already affects nearly 55 million people and nearly 40,000 square miles (104,000 square kilometers) of pasturage while threatening 15,000 square miles (39,000 square kilometers) of cropland, 19,000 square miles (49,000 square kilometers) of rangeland, and railway lines as well as roads (Guo, Wu, and Zhu, 1989:790; Han, 1989:805). Sandstorms related to desertification caused about 4.5 billion yuan (about U.S.$750 million) of direct economic loss per annum in the early 1990s ("1992 Report," 1993:5).

Desertification over the past decade has largely occurred on agricultural land that can be restored. However, the northwest arid region is also showing a modest increase in desertification that will be hard to rectify. By 1991 the State Council felt that desertification, particularly in the zone where pastoralism and agriculture meet in northern China, was damaging enough to call for the establishment of a National Sand Control Aid Group. In 1992 the Ministry of Forestry began a National Sand Control Ten-Year Plan, and in 1994 China signed the United Nations Convention on Combating Desertification.

Although China has improved an estimated 15,000 square miles (39,000 square kilometers) of salinized-alkalinied land since 1949, problems of salinization and alkalinization are getting more serious due to inefficient drainage and excessive irrigation, which have increased the levels of salts in the soil. Various estimates indicate a fifth of China's irrigated cropland has become salinized. Crops sensitive to salt cannot grow on this land. It appears that the total area affected by salinization is continuing to grow. Overpumping in coastal areas has also allowed saltwater to seep into the groundwater supply. The major land reclamation projects carried out during the Great Leap Forward in the late 1950s destroyed many wetlands, which had helped dissipate excess water during flood periods. This led to increased flooding and salinization of flooded areas. Today, more wetland areas are being filled for industrial development and housing, making this problem worse.

□ Pollution

China's industries are major polluters. By 1992, just under half of the total length of China's seven major river systems was categorized in the lowest two grades of water quality, the worst rivers being the Liao, Huai, and Hai ("1992 Report," 1993: 5). Approximately 15,000 miles (25,000 kilometers) of rivers fail to meet standards for fishing, and the fish catch for four major fish types in the Yangtze River declined from 20 billion in the 1970s to 1 billion in 1992. Pollution of surface water in the cities is serious and continues to worsen. Some rivers are getting warmer from all the wastewater dumping.

Water pollution is more serious in populous eastern China than in the west. In general, only lakes and reservoirs that provide drinking water have been protected, and even some of these, such as Guanting Reservoir near Beijing, have levels of ammonia nitrogen higher than the national standards. About a quarter of lakes surveyed are assessed as seriously or moderately polluted, and another quarter lightly polluted. Pollution is especially severe in lakes near urban areas such as Jinan, Nanjing, Shanghai, and Wuhan.

There have been some alarming recent cases of pollution of the coastal seas and some estuaries and bays. Pollution from organic chemicals and heavy metals has been serious in places, although heavy metal pollution has been reduced in recent years. Inorganic nitrogen and phosphorus generally exceed the Chinese maximum limit in coastal waters. Oil concentrations above fishery standards have been found in coastal waters like the Pearl River delta area around Guangzhou, Dalian Bay, and Jiaozhou Bay. In 1994 the Laizhou Bay and Zhoushan fishing grounds were deteriorating, with some aquatic organisms reportedly on the verge of extinction (National Environmental Protection Agency, 1995:6). Red tides, which refer to seawater discolored by certain types of marine plankton that feed on pollution and are fatal to many forms of marine life, also have been on the increase along China's coastline.

The groundwater around some cities has been found to contain phenols, cyanides, chromium, chlorides, nitrates, sulfates, and an increasing degree of hardness. Wells have had to be shut down. In recent years, this pollution has improved in some cities and grown worse in others. Lowered water tables around some coastal cities have added to salinization of groundwater.

Water pollution problems are by no means confined to urban areas. In suburban and rural areas with relatively high densities of farm animals, an increase in nitrates can be detected in the soil and water. Many small rivers have become anoxic—no longer able to sustain aquatic life. During the 1980s and 1990s, many highly polluting small industries have been created by township enterprises in rural areas. Because enterprises in the densely populated lower Yangtze River valley and the Pearl River delta are often located in small towns and villages with rivers or canals connecting them, the water pollution from one town often affects the drinking and irrigation water supplies in nearby villages and the surrounding farmland. Although China has undertaken many efforts to improve soils in a wide range of environments, soil pollution has negated much of this initiative. The Ministry of Agriculture estimates that nearly 40,000 square miles (104,000 square kilometers) of good cropland is polluted, eliminating from production enough grain to feed 65 million people, the current official number of Chinese not being adequately fed.

Increased and improper applications of chemical fertilizers, coupled with growing livestock production, have also led to degradation of soil quality in rural areas. China's average annual fertilizer usage is estimated to be 1,130 pounds per acre (208 kilograms per hectare), twice the world average (Han, 1989:806). Peasants often use nitrogen-rich human and animal wastes as fertilizer. Combining human and animal wastes with fertilizer made of plant and rock materials results in balanced enhancement of crop output, but when human and animal wastes are combined with nitrogen-rich chemical fertilizer, the soil receives too much nitrogen and crop yields drop (Liang, 1989:254). When chemical nitrogen fertilizer became available, many simply added it to the mix, actually reducing yields and sometimes caking the soil. Since the mid-1980s, such peasants have been encouraged not to mix chemical fertilizers with human and animal waste.

Although the production of organochlorine pesticides was banned by the government in 1983 and the percentage of cereal grains with residues exceeding permissible limits went down by the second half of the 1980s, overall pesticide use is still increasing. In recent years, cases of illness and death caused by eating vegetables treated with large doses of the chemical methamidophos have been reported. The extensive use of pesticides in the past also means that pests have developed stronger resistance to chemicals.

During the period of communization, the Chinese had considerable success using various combinations of plants and animals as a method of integrated pest management instead of pesticides. Such integrated pest management can only be effectively practiced over a wide area; by 1979 they were using this method over a larger area than any country in the world. With the demise of communes and the return to family farming, however, individual farmers have reverted to using pesticides. Research into pest control is advanced in China, although practice in the field lags behind the model research stations.

When chemical fertilizers became more available around 1980, many peasants stopped using human waste as fertilizer, and "night soil" collection became a problem in cities used to disposing of waste by carrying it out to the fields. The use of manure and human wastes as fertilizer has increased again since the mid-1980s, but there are worries that now more industrial wastes from the increasing number of rural enterprises are mixed in. Moreover, the consumption of imported and domestic chemical fertilizers roughly doubled between 1980 and 1990.

A partial solution to both the solid waste and the energy shortage problems in rural China has been biogas. Biogas, also known as marsh gas or gobar gas, is methane produced by the decomposition of organic matter. The gas can be generated in reactors into which crop waste, animal and human excrement, and a fermenting agent are placed. The residual sludge from this process is organic and makes an excellent fertilizer.

In 1978, the Chinese said there were 7 million biogas reactors in use, mostly in southern China. These reactors, while important locally, produced less than 2 percent of China's total energy supply (Glaeser, 1990: 262). The transformation to family farming generally has hurt the production of biogas, since the communes provided a larger scale operation for reactors, and the labor force needed to maintain them. Although biogas has made a small comeback in the early 1990s, in 1992 the number of reactors in use was still below the totals for the late 1970s, and it is not likely ever to play more than a minor role in China's total energy production.

As the economy expands, so does the amount of household rubbish. Trash in Shanghai and many other urban areas contains almost as much heavy metals and other inorganic matter as that found in the cities of developed countries. Around mining sites in rural areas, tailings of milled ore residues create reservoirs of polluted water. A considerable proportion of the urban waste released by large industry is dumped directly into rivers and streams. To counter this, the National Environmental Protection Agency began trial solid waste licensing in 1991 and has now begun to enforce a solid waste licensing system throughout China.

China's urban refuse also contains a large amount of coal ash. Although some of this is being put to use for paving roads, more is generated than can be used. A shift from solid fuels to gas would reduce daily per capita rubbish output significantly. About 60 percent of China's urban population now has access to gas. However, domestic natural gas production has stagnated.

Kitchen wastes make up about 31 percent of China's total urban refuse, creating high humidity that makes it difficult to transport and to incinerate. Most urban refuse is removed to farms or rural dumping sites at ever-increasing distances from cities by truck or boat; very little of it is sorted or treated. Plastic containers and other nondegradable forms of refuse are increasing; one positive step has been the decision of the railways to start using biodegradable packaging for foods sold on trains. China has a serious shortage of incinerators and of systems for lining dump sites to prevent polluted water from the trash seeping into the surrounding groundwater. Research into how to bury rubbish in lined landfills began only in 1986. Recently China completed its first garbage treatment plant using fermentation technology to produce energy and reduce the bulk of trash. In Jiangsu, a new method of incineration is now reducing incinerator fuel costs and secondary air pollution (Gao, 1995).

About 2.5 percent of industrial solid waste in China is classified as "dangerous." China only recently began to set up toxic waste storage sites. In 1991, the Standing Committee of the Seventh National People's Congress approved a motion to adopt the Basel Convention on the Control of Transboundary Dangerous Wastes and Their Disposal, and in 1992 the State Council promulgated the "Environmental Policies on the Disposal of Medium- and Low-Level Radioactive Wastes." It could be some time, however, before these measures take hold. One report suggests that people living within 95 miles (150 kilometers) of a nuclear testing site in Xinjiang (Map 2.2) are showing symptoms of radiation pollution similar to those found among Japanese near Hiroshima and Nagasaki at the end of World War II (*Zhongyang ribao*, 1991:4). A nuclear power station became operational at Qinshan in Zhejiang Province during 1991, a station at Daya Bay in Guangdong is now running, and several in Liaoning are scheduled to be completed during the 1990s (Map 2.2). The proximity of the Daya Bay plant to Hong Kong is a sensitive issue in the special administrative region because the PRC lacks experience in nuclear power generation and has not had a good safety record in many other industries. So far the Chinese say that monitoring at Qinshan and Daya Bay has indicated no perceivable impacts on the surrounding environment. In 1997 China signed an agreement with Russia to build a nuclear power station north of Shanghai.

Air pollution plagues most urban areas, although the types of pollutant and their sources vary from region to region. It is estimated that industry accounts for over 80 percent of China's total waste gas emissions. In recent years, some state-controlled enterprises have improved their gas cleaning. However, since growth of the state sector has stagnated while nonstate enterprises expand rapidly, such improvements do not necessarily indicate reductions in air pollution.

Particle levels in Chinese cities are far worse than in most urban areas in industrialized countries. The push for industrial development has caused China's coal consumption to rise steadily throughout the 1980s. As of the

These factories in the Yangtze's Three Gorges spew out air pollution.

Household stoves generally burn coke.

late 1980s, over 76 percent of China's energy was produced by burning coal. This ratio is not likely to go down much until at least 2025. In addition to the sheer quantity of coal burned, China's severe particle pollution problem is in part due to the fact that less than 20 percent of the coal undergoes washing to remove particle impurities, and most coal is burned in small to medium-sized furnaces, often with rather poor efficiency. Progress made in particle control has been largely offset by increased coal consumption.

The percentage of particles emitted from household chimneys that is recovered by pollution control devices is much lower than in industry. Most homes in Chinese cities use coal, and coal combustion is responsible for 69 percent of China's particle emissions (Cao, 1989:763). Lung cancer rates among housewives are higher than in any other occupation, with the small coal stoves found in most kitchens and the heavy use of hot oils for cooking the most likely causes. The low smokestacks on household stoves further intensify the street particle problem, with combustion efficiency in nonindustrial uses running as low as 20 to 30 percent (versus 90 percent in a U.S. high-efficiency furnace).

Particle levels are particularly high in the cities of the north. In 1994 the average daily particle levels in northern Chinese cities were 407 micrograms per cubic meter ($\mu g/m^3$), with levels in southern cities around 250 $\mu g/m^3$. The worst annual daily average urban particle level in China during 1994 was 849 $\mu g/m^3$; London normally has 48 $\mu g/m^3$, and the World Health Organization (WHO) recommends 90 $\mu g/m^3$ as the maximum particle level for safety. As China continues to industrialize, various elements have been added to the particle pollution. Dust in urban air exceeds permitted levels in over half of Chinese cities surveyed in 1994 and has been found to contain benzene soluble matter, lead, zinc, copper, arsenic, manganese, iron, cadmium, and molybdenum.

China is the third-largest emitter of sulfur dioxide (SO_2) in the world after the former Soviet republics and the United States. Sulfur dioxide, like particulate, is closely connected with coal smoke. Estimates suggest that China's sulfur dioxide emissions doubled between 1975 and 1990. As with particles, levels of sulfur dioxide are more severe during winter in the northern Chinese cities than in the south. Beijing, Xi'an, and Shenyang (all on Map 2.2) are among the world's ten worst cities for sulfur dioxide concentrations. However, in the summer months, certain southern cities such as Chongqing, Guiyang, and Changsha (also on Map 2.2) can have higher SO_2 levels than northern cities. Northern China urban SO_2 daily average levels were 89 $\mu g/m^3$ and southern China 83 $\mu g/m^3$ in 1994, with the highest urban daily average level being 472 $\mu g/m^3$. The WHO's safe level for SO_2 is 60 $\mu g/m^3$. All Chinese city centers have SO_2 emission levels that exceed the Chinese legal limits. There are plans to bring SO_2 levels in the worst northern cities below 130–150 $\mu g/m^3$ by the year 2000. In line with this, fines were initiated for SO_2 emissions on a trial basis in late 1992.

Coal combustion is also responsible for two-thirds of the nitrogen oxides (NO_x) emitted in China. Nitrogen oxide pollution is not yet serious when compared with particles and sulfur dioxide. In 1994 the urban daily average nitrogen oxide level for a sample of northern cities was 55 µg/m^3, and southern cities had 39 µg/m^3. Those levels are roughly the same as in recent years and in the early 1980s and are close to Chinese safety standards. Use of gasoline for cars and industry is increasing rapidly, so emissions of carbon monoxide, hydrocarbons, and nitrogen oxides will grow during the 1990s. Traffic congestion in cities has created levels of NO_x at intersections that often exceed the safety level. Preparing for an increasing number of photochemical smog problems and ozone alerts, the National Environmental Protection Agency and the police put together regulations for managing the supervision of auto emissions in 1990.

China is one of the few areas in the developing world with a major acid pollution problem. Nearly 30 percent of the country's total area is subject to acid rain. Acid pollution in China is caused largely by high levels of domestic sulfur dioxide emissions from burning coal. The problem is most serious in the area east of the Qinghai-Tibetan Plateau, including the Sichuan Basin and south of the Yangtze River (see Map 2.4). It is particularly serious in the far south because the high temperatures in the atmosphere there help sulfur dioxide convert to acid faster than in most northern industrial countries; indeed, the areas with the most severe acid pollution—Changsha, Nanchong, Ganzhou, Huaihua, and Wuzhou—are all in the south (National Environmental Protection Agency, 1995). More than half of the rainfall in southern China is now overly acidic. The situation became so serious in the Pearl River delta that the government decided to build no more thermal power plants there after 1995 (Ke, 1995). Chlorine and hydrogen fluoride pollution as well as sulfur dioxide have been found to be seriously affecting vegetation. By one estimate, in the second half of the 1980s, over 10,000 square miles (27,000 square kilometers) of crops are polluted by sulfur dioxide, and 5,000 square miles (13,500 square kilometers) were polluted by fluoride (Cao, 1989:772). Serious corrosion of metal and damage to concrete also has been thought to be caused by acid pollution. The Chinese have been trying to combat the impact of air pollution on vegetation cover by testing various plant varieties for resistance to specific compounds.

Until recent years, noise has received low priority compared with other forms of pollution. Prior to 1975, China produced virtually no noise testing equipment and had no factories producing noise control equipment. Before 1982, there were no standards set for construction materials. Many buildings were built with steel-reinforced concrete panels only an inch (3 or 4 centimeters) thick. When one walks on the stairs in these buildings, the noise produced sounds like drumbeats. In 1979 the Sanitation Ministry and the National Labor Bureau decided on 85 decibels on the A scale (85 dBA) as the workplace standard, with 90 dBA the absolute permissible high. At constant exposure, the level considered damaging to the ear is 75 dBA; serious hearing impairment can occur after eight hours of exposure at 100 dBA (Jones, Forbes, and Hollier, 1990:107–108, 300). Machine-sound levels in Chinese factories have often exceeded 90 dBA (Fang, 1989:177), and noise in most Chinese cities exceeds the suggested Chinese standards, with the 1994 area weighted average for thirty-nine cities at 57.4 dBA and road traffic noise between 68.7 and 75.7 dBA.

The pollution problem is compounded by the favoritism that many industries receive from the government, which allows them to operate inefficient equipment without scrubbers or sewage treatment. In China's paper-making industry, for example, average output of wastewater is six times the international average. Official statistics suggest that some progress was made in the treatment of industrial wastes during the 1980s and early 1990s and that levels of air, water, and noise pollution in many major Chinese cities dropped between 1989 and 1994. Most official statistics, however, are not likely to include pollution from rural small-scale industries.

Official statistics suggest that industrial waste levels generally stabilized during the second half of the 1980s, and real progress has been made in controlling waste from large and medium-sized urban enterprises. As it appears that rural industrial wastes are not included in these official numbers and many waste-producing industries have been relocated from the urban areas to the countryside over the past decade, these estimates could be overly optimistic. There has been some moderate success in the control of rural pollution, particularly water pollution, in recent years. Many rural areas, particularly along the prosperous east coast, have employed complex and intensive waste-recycling systems to produce high-value products such as silk and freshwater fish. In some cases, pollution in rural areas has been reduced by consolidating small plants so their wastes can be treated and minerals recycled. However, the number of serious cases of untreated rural wastes being discharged is still growing. Estimates from 1994 suggest that rural township industries account for 16 percent of China's industrial wastewater and solid wastes and half of industrial dust—all of which represent substantial proportional increases compared with a similar survey in 1989 (National Environmental Protection Agency, 1995:2).

Monitoring has increased but is still inadequate. Since 1982, 296 acid precipitation monitoring stations have been established throughout China, which is commendable but still not up to par. By the end of 1988 there were only 220 municipal-sewage-monitoring stations, and the local industrial waste monitoring network was not completed until 1990 (Vermeer, 1990:40–41). However, overall monitoring has been expanding rapidly, with 2,172 monitoring stations established at various levels by 1992.

As we have seen, pollution problems continue to grow in China despite significant efforts in recent years to address them. The costs of pollution have been tremendous in economic terms. The message that pollution control can be profitable as well as healthy got home to the Chinese leadership during the 1980s. The task for the future is to experiment with methods to regulate emissions effectively and to get the government to raise its investment in pollution control to a higher proportion of gross domestic product (GDP) than in the late 1980s. Between 1980 and 1992 the amount of GDP spent on pollution control already increased from 0.40 percent to 0.67 percent (World Bank, 1994).

■ NATURE CONSERVATION

China is known as a treasure house for many rare species of wildlife. The first nature reserve and laws directly dealing with nature conservation appeared in 1956; by 1965, several more reserves had been established. In the early 1980s, the government set up a wildlife protection bureau, an office to control import and export of endangered species, and the China Wildlife Conservation Association. By 1987 the State Council was alarmed enough about the hunting and smuggling of wildlife to issue a directive to local governments admonishing them to increase their surveillance and punishments. In 1988 the government devised China's first wildlife protection law, which stipulated details of administration and punishments. In 1992 the State Council promulgated Regulations on the Protection of Terrestrial Wild Fauna of the People's Republic of China, and the government published the first volume of China's *Redbook on Flora: Rare and Endangered Flora*. Local governments have followed suit with similar laws and regulations, but many species continue to dwindle. At the end of 1993, there were 763 nature reserves in China covering about 6.8 percent of China's national territory, with plans to increase the number to 1,000 and their area to nearly 9 percent by the year 2000, and then to 1,500 and over 13 percent by 2050. By the end of 1994, there were also 640 forest parks, 234 of which were national-level forest parks. In addition, nearly three-fourths of the territory in Hong Kong SAR remains forested, with twenty-two national parks.

The administration of nature reserves in China is not uniform, however. Ninety of mainland China's nature reserves are considered national nature preserves, and 332 are classified as provincial. Different reserves are often administered by different organizations and at different government levels. On the whole, the forestry bureaus tend to dominate because nature conservation work began in the Ministry of Forestry.

Approximately 379 vertebrate species are protected in the PRC at first-class or second-class levels of protection (Zhu, 1989:829–831). China has 389 protected species of plants, protected in three categories. Animals and plants receiving first-class protection are those that are endemic, rare, precious, or threatened. Those accorded second-class protection are species whose numbers are declining or whose geographical distribution is becoming more restricted. The third-class species are plants of economic importance, and thus harvesting is to be limited. In general, the method for preserving wildlife has been to establish nature reserves in the areas where they live and breed or to establish artificial breeding centers. Certain endangered species are recovering.

However, some animal populations continue to remain low or decrease. For example, birds tend to be scarce in China. Explanations for their disappearance include the destruction of their habitats for agriculture, industry, and housing; government eradication policies for certain species; excessive hunting; and pollution from pesticides and industry. Likewise, increased nutrient loading and industrial pollution in lakes along with the construction of dams and weirs have led to reductions in fish and crustacean yields and species. Often, in order to increase food production, crab and carp eggs have been stocked in lakes, leading to a reduction of indigenous species.

International wildlife organizations have been interested in working with China because of its varied environments as well as their concern that many aspects of nature conservation in China could be better managed. In 1979 China became a member of the United Nations Educational, Scientific, and Cultural Organization's (UNESCO) Man and the Biosphere Program, and ten Chinese nature reserves are now part of the Man and the Biosphere Program Network. In 1981 China signed the Convention on International Trade in Endangered Species (CITES) of Wild Fauna and Flora. Of the plant and animal species protected under this treaty, over 640 are found in China. China also has ten sites on the UNESCO World Heritage Commission's list, and six nature reserves were included on the International Important Wetlands List. In 1992 the China Council for International Cooperation on Environment and Development was established, and in 1995 a nongovernmental organization, the International Association of Artificial Plant Life Community and Biodiversity in Tropical Regions, set up its headquarters in Kunming, capital of Yunnan province (Map 2.2). Many of the larger reserves have research organizations attached, sometimes with international cooperation.

In 1981 an agreement was signed with the World Wildlife Fund to protect and study the giant panda, with an initial project completed in 1988. Although archaeological evidence indicates that pandas once were distributed widely over southern China, their range now has shrunk to small areas in southern Shaanxi, Gansu, and Sichuan. During 1975 and 1976, 138 giant pandas were found dead along the Sichuan-Gansu border (Map 2.2). The cause of their death was the deterioration of the arrow bamboo and square bamboo groves that provide their food (Enderton, 1985:13). This panda famine stimulated a series of attempts to preserve the animal's habitat. However, in 1983 about 965 square miles (2,500 square kilometers) of arrow bamboo groves (47 percent of the total arrow bamboo groves along the same mountainous border) again started to die out, and several dozen pandas died from starvation. The total giant panda population of China is now estimated to be about 1,000.

As of 1992 there were thirteen nature reserves that protect the giant panda. Of these, the Wolong Nature Reserve in Sichuan is by far the largest, occupying one-third of the total area of the panda reserves and containing perhaps one-seventh of the total number of giant pandas found in China (Estácio, 1989:56–57). At Wolong there are two major studies of the giant panda currently being undertaken—one related to their breeding in captivity and the other to their behavior in the wild. Keeping track of this solitary animal is a difficult task, even though the panda's food range is limited in the Wolong area. Pandas are difficult to capture, and identification of individual animals is not easy. The work is made more difficult by the 4,000 farmers and lumberjacks who live within the nature reserve and sometimes deliberately harm pandas. In 1987 two groups of people were caught and punished, some with life imprisonment, for killing pandas and trying to sell the skins. Panda killings are still being reported—the number lost in some districts has exceeded those saved despite the fact that Sichuan provincial authorities say they saved 128 giant pandas between 1980 and 1995. The range of the animal has continued to decrease from about 7,500 square miles (20,000 square kilometers) in 1970 to half that in 1990. The Chinese government has announced plans to establish another fourteen panda reserves to help preserve the panda's habitat.

Cooperation between China and other countries in conserving animals other than the giant panda also increased throughout the 1980s and 1990s. For example, in 1983 the Japanese joined efforts to protect birds; construction on a Sino-Japanese Friendship Center for Environmental Protection began in 1992. China, Nepal, and Pakistan have discussed establishing "international parks," and in 1994 China signed an agreement to establish joint nature reserves with Russia and Mongolia. However, as ecotourism grows, the desire to bring in tourist revenue could compromise the conservation aspects of such parks. Cases of national parks being turned into tourist spots are now all too common (Dangerfield, 1995:10–11). The effects of tourism on China's nature preserves have rarely been positive. For example, some protected areas were opened to foreign hunters in the mid-1980s for a fee. Even though China is a signatory to CITES, which gives all wildcat species protected status, quotas of skins are regularly set by the Chinese Ministry of Trade. Wealthy Hong Kong and Taiwan citizens pay large amounts for tiger bones, elephant tusks, and parts of other endangered species, risking these species all over Asia.

Most environmentalists would argue that China's efforts at nature conservation are too little, too late. The total area for nature reserves is still

Photo: Robert E. Gamer

Giant panda, Wolong, 1989.

not what it should be. Other types of nature reserves beside those already in existence are necessary. Also, the distribution of nature reserves is out of balance. Two areas are critically short of nature reserves: the densely populated eastern portions of the country and the Qinghai-Tibetan Plateau, where leopards, bears, wolves, wild asses, deer, mountain sheep, monkeys, and other wildlife—protected by the Buddhist respect for life—roamed freely before people immigrated there from other parts of China.

The Chinese admit that administration of their nature reserves is uneven. The various units that administer the nature reserves have a tendency to look for short-term economic advantage or protect only those aspects of the environment beneficial to their bureau's interests. The Wolong Nature Reserve in Sichuan established its own special district government, which has proved helpful in facilitating management of the reserve. However, even in the showcase Wolong reserve, one author found widespread evidence of illegal tree felling (Richardson, 1990:107). In 1989, Robert Gamer found unattended pandas locked in their cages at the Wolong breeding station, echoing observations by George Schaller (1993). These discoveries raise questions about the management of other reserves. In addition, the scale of some of China's nature reserves is too small to be effective.

Often, state forests or forest parks are located next to nature reserves; joint management of these could bring increased conservation benefits. Sometimes reserves are zoned for various revenue-generating or productive purposes, compromising their conservation role.

The lack of laws relating specifically to nature reserves prior to 1988 created confusion. Now that laws standardizing procedures for establishing nature reserves, management procedures, and penalties for violations have appeared, there is a need for clear enforcement of local versions pertinent to specific circumstances. Serious instances of killing and smuggling endangered species still occur. A case in point was the mid-1990s discovery in the northeast of a large shipment of frozen bear paws for export.

For laws and their enforcement to be successful, the nature reserve managers must consider solving the economic and social problems of the local inhabitants. Attempts have been made in some of the nature reserves to compensate local dwellers. At Wolong, farmers have resisted relocation to nontraditional village housing. The government has been trying to solve employment problems for some local people by training them as forest rangers or nature reserve staff.

Enforcement problems are compounded by the low level of environmental education among the inhabitants of areas surrounding the reserves. Low levels of education also make it very difficult to find well-qualified staff to manage the reserves. Under such circumstances, some nature reserves are reserves in name only. In many cases, logging and hunting are still going on in areas where such activities are prohibited by law.

Although nature reserves are now a part of China's national annual plans, their overall finance is not included in the annual national or local budgets. Nature reserve officials are expected to maximize income from the reserve lands while preserving their function and character. However, because there has been very little economic assessment of Chinese nature reserves, activities aimed at exploiting renewable resources within reserves, such as forestry, often become excessive.

Most Chinese environmentalists point to the long-term economic value that improved management of nature conservation brings. This is the only argument that will attract the attention of a government intent upon rapid economic development. China's policymakers must come to understand that nature conservation is a necessity for the country's long-term survival.

■ THE THREE GORGES DAM

The most environmentally controversial project in China today is the construction of the Three Gorges (Sanxia) Dam on the Yangtze River in western Hubei province. The Sanxia area, which extends for 125 miles

(200 kilometers) along the river, is rich in historical sites and evokes many ancient Chinese legends (see Hengduan Shan on Map 2.4). It contains six historic walled cities, ancient plank roads cut in cliffs, Stone Age archaeological village sites, many old temples and burial sites, and miles of spectacular caves. It is also home to a multitude of plants and animals. The sublime beauty and strategic significance of the three gorges have been celebrated for centuries in the works of China's poets and travelers. Today a boat trip through the gorges still offers one of the most breathtaking journeys in China. To build a dam in an area of such cultural and natural treasures is bound to cause irredeemable damage.

The proposal for building a dam at Sanxia dates to the 1920s, and arguments for and against the project have persisted among various ministries and provinces since the 1920s (Edmonds, 1992; Luk and Whitney, 1993). The climate of repression in the aftermath of the Tiananmen demonstrations in 1989 helped to stifle public opposition. The 1991 Yangtze and Huai River floods brought the issue to the fore; since a principal objective of the dam was flood control, the stance of proponents was strengthened. Defiant gestures in the National People's Congress during formal approval in the spring of 1992 over the dam issue included a

Photo: Robert E. Gamer

Wu Gorge, the center of the Three Gorges.

record-breaking number of delegates voting against the project or abstaining and an unprecedented walkout by two delegates.

Formal official construction began in December 1994, and the Yangtze River was formally severed in November 1997. The contracts are being awarded on a bidding system, and foreign companies have been invited to bid. In 1994 the State Council also approved establishment of a Sanxia Open Economic Zone with all the policies and priorities given to special economic zones. The city of Chongqing, standing at the western end of the proposed reservoir, has been separated from Sichuan province and given the same national municipal status as Beijing, Tianjin, and Shanghai. The cities of Yichang (Hubei), Wan Xian, and Fuling (Sichuan) have been designated as "open cities," and a large number of projects have begun. China hopes to use this opportunity to bring coastal prosperity inland. Arguments as to whether the dam should be constructed at all concentrated on several key questions: flood control, water supply, navigation, energy supply, safety, human dislocation, and ecological damage.

A dam at Sanxia would control about half of the Yangtze River valley's annual volume of flow. The 12 million people and 2,000 square miles (5,200 square kilometers) of good fields in the Jianghan Plain just below the dam site will receive the greatest flood protection. The dam supposedly will give the Jianghan Plain 100-year flood protection instead of the forty-year flood protection calculated to be the optimum obtainable from further investment in existing dikes. In addition, water will be diverted to water-deficient northern China.

With construction of the Sanxia Dam, 10,000 dead-weight-metric ton (dwt) vessels will be able to get as far as Chongqing for more than half the year, reducing present river freight costs from Wuhan (Map 2.2) to Chongqing by approximately 36 percent. Without the dam, no vessels larger than 2,000 dwt can make the voyage (Wang, 1990:95).

The Sanxia Dam is expected to have an 18,200-megawatt generating capacity, making it the world's largest hydroelectric generating plant (and the world's largest in terms of tons of concrete). When completed, it would supply an estimated one-eighth as much electricity as was generated in China during 1991. Proponents stress that building a large dam at Sanxia would be more cost-effective than building a series of small dams on tributaries upstream or constructing coal-fired plants, and that the site is best for distributing electricity up and down the Yangtze River valley as well as north to Beijing and south to Guangzhou. Proponents estimate it will cost about U.S.$8.7 billion, although some specialists project the costs as being up to 50 percent higher. Once generating electricity, the dam supposedly should pay for itself with fees from its electricity, which will be supplemented by revenues generated by the Gezhouba hydropower station just downstream.

Proponents say the dam would be safe from military attack, deny it lies in an earthquake zone, and assert it would not burst in case of an earthquake.

They also argue that construction will not involve large-scale human dislocation. Resettlement costs will be low because more than half those displaced come from small towns, and their incomes are skyrocketing through the sale of goods and services to construction workers.

Proponents also feel that ecological damage will be minimal. Because only 4 percent of the land to be flooded consists of plains, the loss of good agricultural land will not be serious. Moreover, paddy land for rice is irrigated during the summer, when nutrient-rich silt loads would be least affected by impounding water at the dam. Air and water pollution that would have been generated by coal-fired power plants would be avoided, and there is also little evidence to suggest that the reservoir would create breeding grounds for disease-carrying parasites. The reservoir would have great fish-raising potential and a positive effect on local microclimates. Some historical artifacts currently sited below the new water level can be moved to higher locations before the reservoir fills.

Opposition to the Sanxia Dam from within China has persisted, though with little airing in the press (for one rare airing by scientists, see Chen and Chen, 1993). Overseas opposition has been considerable. Opponents argue that flood control would only be relevant to the area directly below the dam. Major rainstorms upstream could flood areas there, and clear-water releases from the dam could lead to undercutting of dikes downstream. Some suggest that dikes already being raised in height on lower portions of the river combined with several dams on tributaries would be a far more effective and less expensive means of controlling flood control, with less aesthetic and environmental harm. For the first time in the history of any hydraulic project, manila grass is being grown on Sanxia project dike banks to stop erosion—a cheap and simple solution that opponents say should be used more widely before more drastic solutions as this dam are attempted. They also point out the mutually exclusive functions of a flood prevention dam and a power-generating dam: a dam used for hydropower generation should have its reservoir largely full of water, whereas one used largely for flood control should be kept almost empty.

Others argue that building a series of small dams along the Yangtze, using smaller ships, and extending hours of navigation would increase efficiency without as big a risk. Opponents also suggest that the buildup of silt upstream (accelerated by the loss of vegetation there in recent years) could lead to increased flooding above the dam or actually burst it. Considerable amounts of electricity could be lost in transmission over long distances, and there are questions about the efficiency of such large generators. Critics cite past big dam construction experiences that do not inspire confidence. Gezhouba Dam just downstream took eighteen years to finish at a cost close to four times the original estimate. Its locks have been experiencing serious failures that appear to be due to basic design flaws and lack of maintenance. In early August 1995, a passenger vessel

A dam project in Fujian province flooded many villages.
Here the village below is flooding as the water rises
and is being replaced by a new village above.

nearly smashed through a lock gate. If this happened at the future Sanxia Dam, with water depths of over five times more on either side of its locks, such an incident could result in a great disaster.

Some 1.13 million to 1.6 million people living in the area that will be flooded will have to be relocated by the year 2009, costing up to a third of the total estimated budget; compensation costs will rise along with rural incomes and inflation (though a third of the people who have been relocated for dam construction in China since 1950 are still extremely poor and short of food, and another third are no better off than they were before). Over 150 towns and a portion of Chongqing will be flooded. Furthermore, the land being submerged is more productive than the land being proposed to compensate peasants being moved; they undoubtedly will be farming on steeper slopes with more potential for soil erosion.

Construction of the Sanxia Dam means there will be little funding left to carry out any other water-management projects. Opponents point out that the official cost analysis does not include change in the future value of China's currency or certain social and environmental costs. Some also suggest that during the long construction period, disruption of navigation could have serious economic consequences.

Some postulate that the reservoir might cause the water table to rise and trigger landslides (Lin, 1989). Opponents also point out that there are three geological fault belts near the reservoir area. Earthquakes greater than 4.75 on the Richter scale have been recorded, and increased pressure upon the bottom of the new reservoir could cause stronger earthquakes in the future.

Up to 800 historical sites will be inundated by the new reservoir. There are worries about the effect of the dam on climate, the creation of disease-fostering habitats, pollution from submerged mines, impacts on downstream ecosystems, and the future of some forms of wildlife. A slowed flow rate may reduce the ability of the river to flush out pollutants. It could also result in land being lost along the coast because the balance between silt being deposited from the river and wave erosion will be altered.

The political situation in the PRC is such that domestic public opinion cannot block a project so long as the leadership is in favor of it. This project seems to be yet another attempt by China to catch up to developed nations and solve problems with grand projects, as occurred during the Great Leap Forward, which was disastrous in terms of human suffering and ecological damage. Statements by proponents of the dam acknowledging that there are problems with the project do not inspire confidence. Less spectacular measures such as preventing soil erosion by replanting forests, constructing reservoirs on tributaries, dredging the river and adjoining lakebeds, improving the central- and lower-course dikes, expanding floodwater-retention districts, improving flood-warning systems, and educating the local populace are supposed to be included in the project. Although they might be more effective standing alone as elements of a sustainable river management program, their faithful implementation can help reduce the ecological, economic, and social costs of a super dam while improving flood control, rapidly generating hydroelectric power, and facilitating navigation.

■ PROSPECTS FOR CHINA'S ENVIRONMENT

The Chinese government's stand on international environmental cooperation can be summed up by the Chinese delegate's speeches at the United Nations Conference on Environment and Development, held in Rio de Janeiro during June 1992. In his view, poverty is the main cause of environmental degradation in developing countries, and thus it is not reasonable to expect these countries to maintain lower emission levels or install expensive equipment to control emissions on their own. Instead, the developed nations should transfer funds and technology to help poorer countries reduce emission levels. It is thought that by 2050 global warming may submerge all of China's coastal areas, which are currently less than 13 feet (4 meters) above sea level, forcing relocation of about 67 million people. Rather than talk of shared responsibility for global warming, the Chinese government argues that it is up to the developed nations to acknowledge that they emit the majority of greenhouse gases (though, as I indicated, the former Soviet republics and China have the world's first- and third-largest sulfur dioxide emissions). This viewpoint echoes the position China took at the 1991 environmental conference of developing countries hosted in Beijing and in all environmental conferences since then. It is part of a foreign policy initiative to assume leadership of developing countries' environmental bloc. At the same time, China has joined in global environmental change programs and set up its own organizations (National Research Council, 1992:23–36). The State Council rapidly approved its own Agenda 21 (emulating the objectives issued at the Rio Conference) on March 25, 1994, making it one of the first developing countries to do so. China wants developed countries to contribute large amounts of money and technology to improve its environment. Such improvement will require both internal political stability and international support. Even then, it is unlikely that China will be able to reverse its ecological degradation within the next couple of decades.

As previously mentioned, the most threatening of China's environmental problems is the continuing destruction of resources, particularly in poor western and central areas. The fragile ecosystems of the western and border areas are under great strain. Since the 1950s, considerable numbers of Chinese have been relocated westward in order to develop poor areas and reduce population pressure in the east. The expansion of settled agriculture and industry in traditional herding pastures and oases of the west has led to serious degradation. These areas must no longer be seen as destinations for surplus population. Instead, population densities in parts of the west must be reduced and emphasis put on animal husbandry and forestry where possible.

Although resource degradation also is serious in the east, the immediate problem facing the better-off population of eastern China is pollution. As small-scale township and village enterprises rapidly proliferate with virtually no government regulation, pollution is becoming widespread in rural areas. Most rural enterprises use outdated equipment, cannot afford to spend money on pollution abatement, and are inefficient energy users. In particular, rural industries have caused serious water quality degradation. The central government can only guess at the seriousness of the total picture. Not until 1989 did any province complete a basic survey of the levels of pollution from rural small-scale industries. Dealing with the rural industry pollution problem will require a tremendous investment by the Chinese government, as well as strict enforcement of regulations.

The best that can be hoped for China as a whole is that the pace of water depletion, deforestation, soil erosion, and desertification will slow in coming years. If efforts at reforesting and population control during the 1980s and 1990s prove successful, we can expect to see benefits sometime after 2010. Efficient management also would help reduce environmental problems. Pollution abatement equipment is often not installed properly or regularly maintained, and pollution-related accidents are common, with over 3,000 serious incidents reported between 1989 and 1992 ("1992 Report," 1993:5). The Environmental Protection Law calls for environmental assessments as part of construction projects. However, such assessments are often not carried out for small-scale projects, and until the mid-1990s their results often were ignored in large-scale projects. In addition to more funds and personnel, there is need for more public openness to assessment information.

Many analysts feel that raising prices of polluting fuels and industrial inputs will increase economic efficiency and improve China's environmental problems (Ross, 1988:132). Such pricing policies have helped to control some forms of degradation, such as pollution by the state-run industries, and have aided in the promotion of environmentally friendly products. Although an array of price reforms has been introduced during the past decade, pressure from government nonetheless remains the main force regulating investment in environmental control since many inputs, such as water, timber, and coal, are still artificially underpriced.

Ultimately, though, China's environmental problems cannot be solved solely through price reform or regulatory policies. If the country is to feed and clothe all its people and provide a good standard of living in the next century, China needs strict population control, extensive environmental education, increased wealth and infrastructure, political stability, and a more open society where information can be obtained and opinions freely expressed. The degree to which these goals are met in the coming decade will have far-reaching implications not only for China's environment but for the whole earth.

■ BIBLIOGRAPHY

"1992 Report on the Environment in China." 1993. *China Environment News* (Beijing). (June):5.

Cao Hongfa. 1989. "Air Pollution and Its Effects on Plants in China." *Journal of Applied Ecology* 26:763–773.

Chen Guojie, and Chen Zhijian. 1993. *Sanxia gongcheng dui shengtai yu huanjing yingxiang de zonghe pingjia yanjiu* [Research into comprehensive assessment of the ecological and the environmental influence of the Sanxia Project]. Beijing: Kexue Chubanshe [Science Publishers].

Dangerfield, Lara. 1995. "Growing Treasures." *China Now* 153:11–12.

Edmonds, Richard Louis. 1992. "The Sanxia (Three Gorges) Project: The Environmental Argument Surrounding China's Super Dam." *Global Ecology and Biogeography Letters* 4, no. 2:105–125.

———. 1994. *Patterns of China's Lost Harmony: A Survey of the Country's Environmental Degradation and Protection*. London: Routledge.

Enderton, Catherine Shurr. 1985. "Nature Preserves and Protected Wildlife in the People's Republic of China." *China Geographer* 12:117–140.

Estácio, Antonio Julio Emerenciano. 1989. "Na Terra do Panda Gigante (2): o Panda em Liberdade" [The land of the giant panda (2): the panda in freedom]. *Macau* 15:56–57.

Fang Danqun. 1989. "Woguo zaosheng kongzhi jinzhan" [Noise pollution control and prospects in our country]. Pp. 171–180 in *Zhongguo Huanjing Kexue Xuehui* [China Environmental Science Institute] (ed.), *Zhongguo huanjing kexue nianjian* [China Environmental Science Yearbook]. Beijing: Zhongguo Huanjing Chubanshe [China Environmental Publishers].

Gao Jie. 1995. "A New Incinerator Achieves Success in Jiangsu Province." *China Environment News* (Beijing). (June 15):3.

Glaeser, Bernhard. 1990. "The Environmental Impact of Economic Development: Problems and Policies." Pp. 249–265 in Terry Cannon and Alan Jenkins (eds.), *The Geography of Contemporary China: The Impact of Deng Xiaoping's Decade*. London and New York: Routledge.

Guo Huancheng, Wu Dengru, and Zhu Hongxing. 1989. "Land Restoration in China." *Journal of Applied Ecology* 26:787–792.

Han, Chunru. 1989. "Recent Changes in the Rural Environment in China." *Journal of Applied Ecology* 26:803–812.

Jones, Alan Robertson, Jean Forbes, and Graham Hollier. 1990. *Collins Reference Dictionary: Environmental Science*. London and Glasgow: Collins.

Ke We-hong. 1995. "No More Thermal Plants for Delta." *China Environment News* (Beijing). (June):1.

Liang, Xiaoyan. 1989. "Analysis of the Stability of the NPK Effects on Rice in Guangdong Province." Pp. 249–254 in E. Maltby and T. Wollersen (eds.), *Soils and Their Management: A Sino-European Perspective*. London: Elsevier Applied Science.

Lin, Chengkun. 1989. *Chang Jiang Sanxia yu Gezhouba de nisha ji huanjing* [Sediment and environment in *(sic)* Three Gorges and Gezhouba of the Yangtze River]. Nanjing: Nanjing University Press.

Liu Changming. 1993. "Underground Water Table Under Heavy Pressure." *China Environment News* 44:6.

Luk, Shiu-hung, and Joseph B. R. Whitney (eds.). 1993. *Megaproject: A Case Study of China's Three Gorges Project*. Armonk, NY: M. E. Sharpe.

National Environmental Protection Agency. 1995. *Report on the State of the Environment in China 1994*. Beijing: National Environmental Protection Agency.

National Environmental Protection Agency; National Long Range Planning Institute. 1994. *Zhongguo huanjing baohu xingdong jihua 1991–2000 nian* [China's Environmental Protection Activity Plan 1991–2000]. Beijing: Zhongguo Huanjing Kexue Chubanshe [China Environmental Science Publishers].

National Research Council. 1992. *China and Global Change: Opportunities for Collaboration*. Washington, DC: National Academy Press.

"Programme Makes Country Greener." 1996. *Beijing Review* (Beijing). (March 25–31):6.

Qu, Geping, and Woyen Lee (eds.). 1984. *Managing the Environment in China*. Dublin: Tycolly International.

Richardson, Stanley Dennis. 1990. *Forests and Forestry in China: Changing Patterns of Resource Development*. Washington, DC, and Covelo, CA: Island Press.

Ross, Lester. 1988. *Environmental Policy in China*. Bloomington and Indianapolis: Indiana University Press.

Ruddle, Kenneth, and Zhong Gongfu. 1988. *Integrated Agriculture-Aquaculture in South China: The Dike-Pond System of the Zhejiang Delta.* Cambridge: Cambridge University Press.

Schaller, George. 1993. *The Last Panda.* Chicago: University of Chicago Press.

Smil, Vaclav. 1993. *China's Environmental Crisis.* Armonk, NY: M. E. Sharpe.

Vermeer, Eduard B. 1990. "Management of Environmental Pollution in China: Problems and Abatement Policies." *China Information* 5, no. 1:34–65.

Wang, Xianpu, Jin Jianming, Wang Liqiang, and Yang Jisheng. 1989. *Ziran baohuqu de lilun yu shijian* [Theory and practice of nature reserves]. Beijing: Zhongguo Huanjing Kexue Chubanshe [China Environmental Science Publishers].

Wang, Zuogao. 1990. "Navigation on Yangtze River and the Three Gorges Project." *Bulletin of the Permanent International Association of Navigation Congresses/Bulletin de l'Association Internationale Permanente des Congres de Navigation* 70:86–96.

World Bank. 1994. *China Urban Environmental Service Management.* Report no. 13073-CHA. Washington, DC: World Bank.

Yuan, Guolin. 1995. "Sanxia gongcheng de xingjian dui Changjiang liuyu jingji fazhan de ladong zuoyong" [The push effect of construction of the Sanxia Project on regional economic development for the Chang River valley]. *Zhongguo Sanxia jianshe* [China Three Gorges Construction] 5:5–7.

Zhao, Qiguo. 1990. "Woguo de tudi ziyuan" [Land resources of China], *Dili xuebao* [Acta Geographica Sinica] 45, no. 2:154–162.

Zhongguo Kexue Bao She (ed.). 1989. "Shengcun yu fazhan" [Survival and development]. Beijing: unofficial report of the Chinese Academy of Sciences.

Zhongyang ribao [Central Daily News, international edition, T'ai-pei]. 1991. vol. 6, no. 4 (November).

Zhu, Jing. 1989. "Nature Conservation in China." *Journal of Applied Ecology* 26:829–831.

Zhu, Zhenda, and Wang Tao. 1990. "Cong ruogan dianxing diqu de yanjiu dui jinshiyunian lai Zhongguo tudi shamohua yanbian qushi de fenxi" [An analysis on the trend of land desertification in northern China during the last decade based on examples from some typical areas]. *Dili xuebao* [Acta Geographica Sinica] 45, no. 4:430–440.

▪ 10 ▪

Family, Kinship, Marriage, and Sexuality

Zang Xiaowei

The family is a fundamental social unit in every society. In no aspect of culture are the diversities of human societies more striking than in the institutions of the family and marriage. Families meet basic human needs of mating, reproduction, the care and upbringing of children, care for the aged, and the like, but families in different societies meet these needs in differing ways (see, for example, Goldthorpe, 1987:163; Goode, 1963). Likewise, families across societies vary in their responses to new trends in employment, education, recreation, travel and relocation, contraception, housing, child care, and labor saving devices.

For example, a majority of Americans begin sexual activity before marriage—a radical change from the past. In a 1988 study, half of fifteen- to nineteen-year-old females reported having sexual intercourse (Brook-Gunn and Furstenberg, 1989:249–259; Day, 1992:746–749; Small and Kerns, 1993: 941–952). The number of unmarried couples living together has tripled in less than two decades (Giddens, 1992). The divorce rate in the United States is believed to be the highest in the world, with about half of recent marriages expected to end in divorce (Moore, 1989, 1992). New alternatives to traditional marriage, such as single parenthood, are becoming commonplace.

In China, too, premarital sex, divorce, and staying single are also on the increase—but at a much slower rate. Hollywood, rock music, and individual paychecks sing their siren songs there, too, but have been slower to disrupt family life. Loyalty to one's family takes precedence over all other obligations, perhaps more than in any other culture.[1] Even China's constitution contains detailed provisions about the family, discussing the care of the elderly and the upbringing of young children. In doing so, it echoes the emphasis of Confucius on the primary role of the family. That emphasis is weakening in China's culture, but its roots are so deep that the changes are likely to remain gradual.

■ FAMILY STRUCTURE

Sociologists usually divide families into four basic structural categories: the first category is single men and women living alone, including those who have not married and those who are widowed or divorced. The second category, the nuclear family, consists of a couple and their unmarried children. It also includes childless couples or one of the parents (the other either dead or divorced) living with one of their married or unmarried children. The third category is a stem structure of an extended family, containing an aged parent or parents, one married child and his or her spouse, and perhaps grandchildren as well. Finally, the extended family differs by having two or more married siblings living together with their children and a grandparent or two.

In traditional China, the ideal family was an extended family consisting of five generations living together under one roof, sharing one common purse and one common stove, under one family head. Confucianism expressed a preoccupation with familial relations and ethics. Families organized on the basis of "proper" relationships were considered by Confucian scholars to be fundamental to the maintenance of social harmony and political stability in China. The younger generation was ethically bound to support, love, and be obedient to their seniors.[2]

The Chinese imperial state, which relied on Confucianism as its ideological foundation, strongly supported the traditional family institution. A local magistrate, for example, might erect a large memorial arch testifying to a widow's virtue for her refusal to remarry or give an extended family a placard of honor to promote the ideal of five generations living harmoniously under one roof. Dividing the extended family, especially when aging parents were still alive, was strongly discouraged because it went against Confucian ethics (Mann, 1987).

Parents arranged marriages for their offspring, sometimes before they were old enough to live together and consummate the marriage. When a boy married he brought his bride to live with his parents. When the father died, he divided his estate equally among his sons. Thus marriage did not lead to the creation of a new household. Usually, new families were created through partition of the family estate after the death of the father. Each son might use his share as the economic foundation for a new, smaller family he now headed, moving out of the parent's house to establish a nuclear family. One son might stay with or take in the widowed mother to create a stem family. Because of this cyclical process, at any given time most families were small. Some included parents (or one surviving parent) living with one or more married sons and perhaps their children. Others were limited to parents and their unmarried children and were thus similar to many present-day Western families in size and composition.[3] Extended families with five generations living together were rare.

Family size was restricted not only because of divisions but also because of high infant mortality rates in imperial China and low life expectancy. However, rich families were more successful than the less well-to-do in raising their children to maturity. Rich families also tended to have higher birthrates than the less well-to-do because of better nutrition and the practice of polygamy (i.e., a man having two or more wives at the same time); the presence of additional women greatly increased the likelihood of more children. Although polygamy was generally acceptable in precommunist China, rich families were far better able to afford it. Consequently, rich families were larger than average in size; many of them were extended families including several generations and could be extremely large. For example, in 1948 two U.S. scholars claimed after their fieldwork in a Chinese village that "the Kwock and Cheung families are very nearly of equal size, having an estimated 500 to 750 members each, while the smallest unit is Choy, with about 200 to 300 members" (Baker 1979:1).[4]

In the late nineteenth century, because of Western penetration into China, new bourgeois and working classes emerged in Chinese coastal cities along with a new intellectual elite. Since they obtained their incomes through employment outside the family, these individuals were freed from control by family elders. They were exposed and receptive to the new cultural and intellectual forces entering China from Japan and the West. Hence they agitated for legal and cultural reforms to promote the ideals of marriage based upon free and romantic attachments and equality of men and women with respect to marriage, property, and inheritance.[5] The reforms led to an increasing trend in urban China toward smaller nuclear family units and growing freedom of choice for men and women in choosing marriage partners. Since the 1930s, most urban Chinese have resided as nuclear families (Zang, 1993; Tsui, 1989; Whyte and Parish, 1984: chap. 6). Tables 10.1 and 10.2 show that by 1900, over half of urban Chinese families included in those surveys took the nuclear form.

Chapters 4 and 8 discussed the increasing urbanization and rapid industrialization that followed establishment of the People's Republic of China (PRC) in 1949. Those trends contributed further to the separation of nuclear families from control by their elders, especially in cities. There nuclear families tend to make decisions about and engage in reproduction, residence, food preparation, consumption and expenditure, and child rearing with little involvement by their elders (Parish and Whyte, 1978; Whyte, 1992:317–322; Whyte and Parish, 1984:chap. 6).

The stem family structure has not disappeared in urban China, however. Young couples may choose to live with their retired parents for free child care; housing shortages may force young couples to live, at least for a few years, with their parents who have housing units. These considerations may stabilize or even increase the number of stem households temporarily (Riley, 1994:798–801; Tsui, 1989).

Table 10.1 Family Structure of Grooms' Families

Family Structure				Year of Marriage				
	1900–1938	1939–1945	1946–1949	1950–1953	1954–1957	1958–1965	1966–1976	1977–1982
Single family (%)	14.9	18.3	15.5	20.9	18.5	20.0	16.2	6.0
Nuclear family (%)	50.8	49.3	50.5	50.3	48.3	51.5	59.3	66.6
Stem family (%)	17.6	17.8	18.9	17.8	17.8	18.0	16.3	19.0
Joint family (%)	8.9	7.2	8.8	4.0	6.1	2.7	3.5	2.4
Others (%)	6.7	6.0	5.6	6.6	7.3	5.9	3.2	4.6
N.A. (%)	1.1	1.1	0.6	0.4	2.0	1.9	1.5	1.5
Number of cases	563	612	465	473	493	629	869	879

Source: Zang, 1993:42.
Note: N.A. = no answer; respondents did not answer question.

Table 10.2 Family Structure of Brides' Families

| | Year of Marriage | | | | | | | |
Family Structure	1900–1938	1939–1945	1946–1949	1950–1953	1954–1957	1958–1965	1966–1976	1977–1982
Single family (%)	5.7	6.9	7.7	8.6	7.8	7.0	4.3	1.7
Nuclear family (%)	54.7	55.5	53.0	48.6	51.2	56.2	65.9	67.5
Stem family (%)	25.3	21.1	23.5	27.8	22.1	21.8	19.6	20.5
Joint family (%)	8.4	6.9	8.5	6.7	9.4	7.2	4.2	3.7
Others (%)	4.2	7.9	5.8	7.6	7.4	4.8	4.1	4.1
N.A. (%)	1.6	1.8	1.5	0.6	2.0	3.0	1.8	2.6
Number of cases	570	622	468	475	498	641	877	889

Source: Zang, 1993:41.
Note: N.A. = no answer; respondents did not answer question.

Photo: Robert E. Gamer

Early morning dancing and mahjong in the park.

In rural areas, families continued to be organized along traditional lines until 1949. This is not surprising, given that the rural Chinese economy before 1949 was overwhelmingly based on traditional technologies and organizations. Traditional family forms were changed after 1949 (Fei, 1962; Stacey, 1983; Wolf, 1985). An important factor causing the change in rural areas was the long period of collectivization (1955–1980). Prior to

■ 12 ■

Religion

Chan Hoiman
and Ambrose Y. C. King

Chinese religion is not a subject that can be approached in any straightforward or uncontroversial manner. Chinese society and culture were rarely if at all dominated by any state religion or an associated order of church and priesthood worshipping a supreme godhead; yet its religious orders have generally been dominated by the state, and the state has been operated in accordance with religious precepts. The social order of the Chinese people has long been permeated by ritual practices with clear supernatural overtones, giving propitiatory ritual offerings to ancestors or idols; yet Chinese have seldom belonged to organized religious bodies. Scholars can therefore alternatively maintain that the Chinese are not a very religious people at all and that they are permeated with superstition of a magical, "prereligious" kind. Chinese scholars of a "New Confucian" bent retort that Chinese culture is verily "beyond belief," with spiritual reaches and depths that cannot be contained within the usual institutional or intellectual frameworks of religions. Even at the end of the nineteenth century, the missionary scholar Arthur Smith would still characterize the religious life of the Chinese people as simultaneously "pantheistic, polytheistic, and atheistic" (Smith, 1894:chap. 26).

Scholars have taken many approaches to the study of China's religions. In the late nineteenth century, the great German sociologist Max Weber (1864–1920), undertook his famous study of China's religion (1964 [1922]) as part of his much broader examination of capitalism and comparative civilizations, approaching Chinese civilization from the perspective of two major "homegrown" religions, Confucianism and Daoism. He sought to demonstrate that the social structure of China contained components that can contribute to the growth of capitalism. But Confucian orthodoxy emphasized above all a "rational adaptation" to secular life, generating in the people a traditionalist and conservative propensity that

became the decisive obstacle to the growth of aggressive modern capitalism. Daoism gave people some outlet from this conformity by promoting
personal values, which also did not support capitalism. The so-called
Weber thesis on Confucianism and the underdevelopment of capitalism in
China has since become the subject of heated scholarly debates.

The Dutch sinologist Jan de Groot (1854–1921) conceived the ambitious vision of a comprehensive and detailed study of Chinese religion,
which was published three decades earlier (1972 [1892]) than Weber's
work. He was interested in Chinese religion as laid out in textual canons
and as actually practiced in the religious life of the people. He richly detailed such topics as "the burial of the dead," "ancestor worship," and
other ritual practices and advocated China's religion as a field of scientific
study (Freedman, 1979).

Coming to the field a generation later than either Weber or de Groot and
following Emile Durkheim's quest to unravel the "collective consciousness,"
Marcel Granet's seminal work (1975 [1922]) suggested that in China "peasant religion" was the foundation of the religion of the literary class—a point
Charles Laughlin makes about China's whole literary tradition in Chapter
13. Granet (1884–1940) looked to archaic history for the "essence" of Chinese religion. Later an urban populace would develop a "feudal religion,"
and kings created an "official religion" to support their sovereignty. All this
subsequently diversified into specific religious currents or doctrines.

More recently, a U.S. sociologist of Chinese descent, C. K. Yang
(1961), noted the contrast between "institutional" and "diffused" religions:
"Institutional religion functions independently as a separate system, while
diffused religion functions as a part of the secular social institutions"
(Yang, 1961:295). This basic distinction may be employed in addressing
some of the alternative explanations we mentioned in the opening para-
graph. Confucianism, by and large a diffused religion, functions through
such secular institutions as the state, the family, and the education system.
Only in the cases of Buddhism (imported from India) and, to a lesser extent, Daoism can one speak of proper institutional religion with its monastic order and specialized priesthood. Diffused religion is inevitably a less
powerful form of religiosity, merely providing spiritual rationale to secular institutions. Yang concluded that though Chinese religions were rich
and dynamic on the surface, they were at heart restricted.

In this chapter, we want to give you an overview of how China's religions evolved and how they cover both the spiritual and secular realms of
life. We shall examine the development of China's religions in terms of the
interplay between diversity and syncretism—how religious streams alternatively diversified and converged in China's history. At each stage in the
unfolding of the Chinese religious universe, new impetus and horizons
were opened up and then reconciled with existing beliefs. From this
perspective, the development of Chinese religion remains an ongoing

story, an ebb and flow between diversity and syncretism. We are suggesting that China has experienced three great historical periods or configurations of divergence and syncretism, when competing rites and doctrines (some "institutional" and some "diffused," in Yang's terminology) were juxtaposed and reconciled. The resulting syncretism, in time, would be broken up by the introduction of yet other beliefs. Those three historical configurations are summarized in Table 12.1. As you can see, the table leaves us with a question. The first coming together of diverse religious streams began to take place in the twelfth century B.C. The second began in the third century B.C., and the third in the tenth century A.D. As we approach the twenty-first century A.D., is a fourth syncretism emerging?

■ FIRST CONFIGURATION: THE RISE OF HUMANISTIC RELIGION

We begin with the legendary, Neolithic origins of Chinese religion. Marcel Granet would readily point out that much that is unique about the orientation of China's religion can be traced to that era. And Hans Kung and Julia Ching (1989) maintain that elements of those ancient beliefs and cults persist even to this date, still retaining their archaic, primitive mode.

Table 12.1   The Development of Chinese Religions

First Configuration (to 256 B.C.)	Ancient Cults (2000–1123 B.C.):
	  Totemism
	  Animism
	  Occultism
	Zhou Syncretism (1122–256 B.C.): The Rise of Humanistic Religion

Second Configuration (to A.D. 220)	Axial Diversification (772–481 B.C.):
	  Confucianism
	  Daoism
	  The Yin-Yang School
	Han Syncretism (206 B.C.–A.D. 220): The Canonization of Confucianism

Third Configuration (to A.D. 1279)	Foreign Impetus (1):
	  Indian Buddhism
	  Near Eastern Nestorianism, Manichaeanism
	Song Syncretism (A.D. 906–1279): The Rise of Neo-Confucianism

Fourth Configuration (to A.D. 2000)	Foreign Impetus (2): Christianity Marxism-Maoism as Antireligion Toward a New Syncretism?

As Table 12.1 indicates, ancient Chinese religious beliefs go back at least to the Neolithic and Bronze ages and were widely practiced during the first, archaic dynasties in classical China (Eliade, 1982:3–6). During the Zhou dynasty, between 1122 and 256 B.C., they merged with some new ideas in a syncretic reconciliation of beliefs. The archaic gestation period of Chinese religion shared traits of primitive religions elsewhere. People became aware of and curious about nature and made crude, halting attempts to justify human social life on the basis of larger-than-life forces and ideas; especially relevant for the case of China were aspects of totemism, animism, and occultism.

□ Totemism

Totemism is a familiar elementary form of religious belief, identifying human groups with species of animals, birds, or even plants from which they presumably descended. A group sharing the same totemic ancestor bonded together for community and warfare against groups sharing other totems. Scholars like Emile Durkheim and Claude Lévi-Strauss point out that this classificatory system based on common descent of a group from the same mythic animal, bird, or imaginary monster helped set people apart in their own minds from other groups sharing a different totem, providing them with a rich sense of prehistoric genesis based on legend. The proliferation of totemic groups generated dynamics of war and alliance. The first step toward a unified Chinese culture was allegedly achieved when the mythical Huang Di (the Yellow Emperor) fostered a federation of totemic groups powerful enough to sustain control over what became the heartland of China. Down to the times of the Xia, Shang, and Zhou (see Table 3.1), the ruling dynasties and the kings were mainly the great chiefs who held the totemic alliances together. The passage into history took place at the point when totemic alliances were formalized into government and totemic groups became clans. Even today, Chinese often designate themselves "descendants of dragons," if not because they actually believe in it, at least because they still want to.

□ Animism

Animism forms the other major strand of ancient Chinese beliefs. Again, it is a mentality widely shared among peoples of the ancient world. Animism is belief in the omnipresence of spirits, that other living creatures and even inanimate objects or phenomena also possess spiritual essences that can impact the lives of humans. It is usually regarded by anthropologists as the most basic form of religious belief, based on the inability to distinguish between objective reality and the fantasy world of spirits. Yet as the case of China demonstrates, animism can far outlive its ancient origins. Animism is well documented in the archaeological finds of the Shang dynasty, mainly in sacrificial inscriptions on tortoise shells and animal bones (Keightley, 1978). These inscriptions indicate that people believed in and made offerings to spirits of natural phenomena like thunder and rain, of natural objects like mountains and river, of beasts and birds, and especially of deceased humans. Many of these practices were to continue in the folk religions of China in later times.

□ Occultism

Occultism is closely connected with animism and has to do with how the supernatural influence of spirits can be detected or even changed for human purposes. In the mind of believers, spirits were usually given form and character closely resembling human beings and shared our temperaments as well. It is therefore logical to assume that human beings can communicate with these spirits and in the process perhaps take advantage of their power. This may be achieved by specialized religious personnel obtaining blessings from these spirits and foretelling the future through their power. And in archaic China, these religious personnel often held political roles as well, serving as the foundation of kingship. The Shang dynasty indulged extensively in occultist practice and also embraced the notion of the supreme lord *(di)*, the personified supernatural overlord of all beings, toward whom acts of offerings and divination were ultimately directed (Eliade, 1982:7–9). The worship of *di* can be interpreted in a polytheistic mode, where the all-powerful *di* presided over the spiritual pantheon of the animistic world and answered to the pleadings and inquiries of the people.

The three themes of totemism, animism, and occultism formed the religious scaffolding of remote, archaic China. In the passage from the Xia and Shang dynasties into the Zhou dynasty—and from prehistory into documented history—two important strands of prehistoric beliefs would be assimilated into and continued in the religion of Zhou. These beliefs were the worship of heaven *(tian)* on the one hand and ancestral worship on the other. Both of these motifs were to exert heavy influences on the religious life of China to come. The worship of *tian* is essentially the depersonalized version of the former worship of *di*. In the transition from Shang into Zhou, the personified supreme deity of *di* was to be gradually metamorphosed into an impersonal, transcendental force. Although this ultimate force was no longer cast in a humanized mode, it nonetheless had purpose and direction. Comprehending and abiding by the will and mandate of heaven *(tianming)* would be among the key religious principles in Chinese culture, as you saw in Chapters 3 and 4. And the worship of *tian* would in later days converge with the imperatives of the *dao* (the way), whether defined in Confucian, Daoist, or Yin-Yang terms. As for ancestral worship, this is a heritage from totemism for which China has become particularly famous. It makes little difference that the early totemic ancestors were mainly legendary animals or even hybrids; they kindled a religious sentiment that constantly beckoned to the ancestral fountainhead, which would continue to oversee the conduct and welfare of the latter-day descendants. The impersonal, immutable *tian* and the highly personal, affectionate ancestors *(zu)* would form the two essential axes of supernatural beliefs, handed down as they were from the prehistoric past first to the Zhou civilization and in turn to Chinese culture as a whole.

□ Zhou Syncretism and Humanistic Religion

During the Zhou dynasty, these beliefs were assimilated and consolidated, especially in the Western Zhou. The individual traditions did not disappear; but society and scholars drew together important elements from all of them to bolster secular institutions along with religious ideas and practices (Eliade, 1982:9–13). Divination and other animistic, magical practices continued, as you also will see in Chapter 13; but at the same time, thinkers and religious practitioners combined them with other religious traditions, picking what seemed best from each to form a new body of doctrines and rituals. It was truly a syncretism—a generally contrived, strained sense of integration that would last for a few centuries and finally begin to fall apart under that strain. Then new diverse religious strands would unravel, to be brought back together in a second syncretism we discuss in the next section. This is how China's religious traditions have evolved amid the diversity and immensity of the Chinese religious universe—an interplay of unity and difference.

The Zhou syncretism emerged because, after a long prehistoric childhood, Chinese society had reached a stocktaking threshold requiring a more stable and "rational" framework of social life. As Chapter 3 explained, the Zhou people of the west toppled the Shang dynasty, which had grown corrupt and obsolete. They sought to create the underpinnings of a new social order. Although construction of the Zhou order was generally accredited to the Duke of Zhou, the younger brother of the founding emperor, it must also be seen as a product of its time (cf. Creel, 1970).

The Duke of Zhou presided over construction of a strong program of humanism, centering primarily around humanistic interests and ideals, that was to permeate all subsequent evolution of the Chinese religious world. The personified godhead of *di*—the closest that China ever came to professing a supreme, monothestic deity—became the abstract, ramified force of *tian* and of nature, no longer intervening directly in the mundane details of social life. *Tian* was a "hidden god." Although *tian* and nature had purpose and will, they were part of bigger cosmic dynamics that had no use for divine design or intervention. And if human affairs must nonetheless abide by heavenly principles, they do so mainly for the sake of harmony and felicity in social life. In this way then, the rise of Zhou humanism signified an essential new twist in the religious consciousness of the Chinese, in which both the sacred and the profane derived their defining meanings from within the concrete operation of the secular, human world (Nakamura, 1964:chap. 15). This would be the all-important leitmotiv that both Confucianism and Daoism took up in later times.

Starting with this basic propensity toward a humanistic religion, Zhou syncretism placed dual emphases on rites and ethics that (in the absence of divine decrees) together set the standard of proper behavior. The notion of, and the word for, rite *(li)* had its origin in the archaic ritual of making offerings to the gods. People were instructed to participate in rites with sincerity and care, just as their ancestors had done when worshiping their pantheon of animistic spirits and *di,* the mandate of gods and heaven. In addition, practice of rite evolved into social institutions and ideological doctrines. Rite as social institution defined proper behavior in different social occasions—celebrations, initiations, mourning, interaction, and so on. Rites would shape the elementary social structure of the community, visually demonstrating the sovereignty and power of the rulers and the rights and responsibilities of different social roles. Philosophical and ideological frameworks justified and codified the practice of rites, ensuring their continuity even beyond the reign of Zhou. That codification was partly recorded in the canonical *Book of Rites*, the compilations of ancient documents broadly related to this movement.

In lieu of divine decrees, the intellectual foundation of *li*—and of Zhou humanism in general—was primarily ethical in character. At the heart of this ethic was the use of blood ties and kinship dynamics as the foundation of values and standards of social relationship. In the absence of divine ordinance, blood ties were to become the most sacred organizing principle of society. The Zhou dynasty presided over a feudal social order, with peasants bonded to the estates of noblemen. Feudalism was founded upon the lineage rule *(zhongfa)* system, which determined rights and duties on the basis of blood ties. This *zhongfa* system also prescribed the distribution and inheritance of family resources from one generation to another. It raised familial and filial values into "social absolutes," serving as the ethical cum sacred foundation of Zhou humanism.

Instead of following a more familiar pattern of religious movement from animism into polytheism and then into monotheistic religion, Zhou syncretism generally sought to break with theistic religion altogether. Henceforth, the "great tradition" of Chinese religion would be characterized above all by what Max Weber called "this-worldly religion"—religious beliefs having little to do with transcendental order and divine godheads (Weber, 1964:1–3). Already in the time of Zhou, an "enlightened" outlook had developed, affirming the primacy and autonomy of humanity as the sole source of both existential enigma and fulfillment and asserting that humanity remains truly autonomous only when ritually bonded to the community and its rulers. Thus the rise of Zhou syncretism set the distinct temperament of Chinese religious beliefs, marking the master trend that later stages continued to deepen and enrich but never did abandon or supersede.

■ SECOND CONFIGURATION: THE AXIAL AGE AND THE RISE OF CONFUCIANISM

During later centuries, the Zhou syncretism broke down and contending schools of thought emerged. This lively stage of development, when such prominent schools as Confucianism and Daoism came into existence, is by far the most celebrated among observers. Beginning around 1000 B.C., India, Greece, Mesopotamia, and China all experienced major advances in their civilizations, independently of one another; scholars think of these civilizations as occupying several parallel lines or planes, each serving as axis to subsequent progress of their civilizations, and call this period the "axial" age (see Chang, 1990; Roetz, 1993). In China these advances occurred during the so-called Spring and Autumn and Warring States periods and extended into the short-lived Qin dynasty (see Table 3.1). The Han dynasty would then seek a synthesis among these contending schools. This second syncretism, building upon but moving beyond the first syncretism created earlier in the Zhou dynasty, stands unmistakably at the heart of cultural China. Even to this day, Chinese culture is identifed as Han.

First we will focus on three schools among the many contending during the axial age: Confucianism, Daoism, and Yin-Yang. Then we will examine how the Yin-Yang cosmological framework was deployed as the scaffolding upon which Confucianism and Daoism acquired tenuous syncretic unity during the Han dynasty.

□ Confucianism

Confucius lived from 551 to 479 B.C. (see Table 3.1). He sought a return to the humanist emphasis on rites and ethics found in the earlier Zhou syncretism. His, too, is essentially a "secular religion," founded upon beliefs about proprieties of human conduct: social values, social practice, and the image of the ideal person. In society and the individual, the ultimate ends of life coincide with the worldliness of the mundane here and now (see Fingarette, 1972).

The social values associated with Confucianism center around the cardinal notion of *ren*, rendered variously by sinologists as "benevolence," "humaneness," and "compassion." In the *Analects*—the record of Confucius's teachings—*ren* is made the foundation of social life. Divine authority should be respected but is generally irrelevant. *Ren* literally means "two persons"; it is not just a set of ethical rules but an inalienable inner necessity, a moral imperative for human personal and social existence. It cannot be approached as an individualistic ethic because human nature itself is inherently social; social interaction and relations between men will take priority over personal interest and experience. We have an innate moral mandate to show affection, sympathy, compassion, and benevolence toward our fellow humans by conforming to specific conventions of social behavior. Instinctive consciousness of that mandate sets humanity apart from other living beings. The value and goodness of *ren* is not something that should be validated by reason or logic. *Ren* is both higher and deeper than the mere exercise of intellect. In the end, mutual affection and sympathy—emotional bonds—best validate and vindicate its primacy. The individuals who exemplify these ideals by properly performing rites and social conventions are literally defining who they are, demonstrating their humanity.

The celebrated Confucian obsession with *li* (ritual and propriety) can be properly appreciated against this backdrop (Eliade, 1982:22–25). The elaborate and meticulous rituals governing social interaction are the practical articulation of the cherished ideal of *ren*—personal actors defining their own worth by the collective sentiment they show toward social solidarity (cf. Eno, 1990). Art, literature, and moral discourse must help individuals cultivate these social proprieties.

The Confucian distinction between gentleman *(junzi)* and commoner *(xiaoren)* also becomes clear in this context. Although achieving the remote ideal of becoming a Confucian sage is beyond the reach of most mortals, true followers of Confucianism can hope to become *junzi*. *Junzi*, or the Confucian gentleman, is someone who desires and is far advanced in the attainment and practical pursuit of *ren*. A gentleman is not merely someone generally righteous, honest, and knowledgeable. These well-accepted virtues must be assessed and related in terms of the core value of *ren*; a true Confucian gentleman is not motivated to attain individual success or precious assets but rather shows his benevolence to others by practicing the social rituals with propriety. In contrast, the *xiaoren* (literally, small-minded men, or commoners) are imperfect in attaining *ren*, or humanity. The *xiaoren* is the direct opposite of the *junzi* not because he is perhaps evil-minded or dishonest, but mainly because he is only concerned with his own interest and private desire. At their worst, such individuals ignore the cardinal value of *ren* by expressing frustration and social discontent; at their best, they show their respect for it by giving special deference to *junzi*. Chapter 4 has already explained how some of this works out in concrete terms. Confucianism intertwines ethics and religion to regulate social behavior. But it lacks a religious hierarchy to mandate its authority and is not inspired by divine authority from above, but rather by the inner benevolence of human nature itself (cf. Hall and Ames, 1987).

☐ Daoism

The other major indigenous religious tradition in China is Daoism, which (as Chapter 3 indicated) originated during the same period of axial diversification. The relation between Confucianism and Daoism is a contrast between orthodoxy and heterodoxy—a distinction made famous by Weber in his study of Chinese religion. Although Confucianism pertains overwhelmingly to the social aspects of human life, Daoism pertains more to nature and the individual. Although Confucianism gives primacy to asserting and striving for social values, Daoism gives primacy to tactically avoiding these allegedly superficial pursuits. Daoism rose as a contrasting parameter to assert the values Confucianism neglected. It was permissible and common for people to take on both Confucian and Daoist outlooks, letting each fill the void left by the other. The two together broadly demarcate the field of diversification in the axial age.

Standing at the heart of Daoism is the concept of *dao,* which can variously be understood as "the principle," "the way," and "the word." Thus, *dao* can be regarded as a mode of behavioral tactics, specifying the principles that are most closely compatible with the dynamics of human and natural affairs. Or *dao* is perceived in more philosophical rubrics as "the way," postulating the presence of a universal pattern or law that underlies the conduct of social and natural phenomena. And if *dao* is seen as "the word," it denotes the need for doctrines and codes to be formulated and espoused in words or utterances, for the articulation of the *dao*. These three aspects of the *dao* all revolve around the concept of virtue *(de),* suggesting that *dao* is by nature virtuous (Eliade, 1982:25–33). These multiple meanings explain why *dao* remains so much an enigma in Chinese thought, readily associated both with the crudest kind of magical practices and with philosophical enlightenment of a lofty order. As a metaphor or concept of truth, *dao* was commonly evoked even in doctrines outside Daoism. For example, the Confucian classics were replete with the use of the concept when discussing truth and its method, albeit with specific Confucian reference.

Whether according to Laozi (Lao Tzu) or Zhuangzi (Chuang Tzu), the two legendary founders of Daoism, the gist of *dao* lies not in human endeavor but rather in evading the futility of human endeavor. The universe is the totality of all being, generated from an unimaginable cosmic void, the omnipresent *dao*. *Dao* is emptiness, mystical and all-pervasive. The world derives from that emptiness. Humans can achieve a linkage with that emptiness by refraining from individual ambition and social activity and seeking oneness with *dao*.

The belief in *dao* naturally reinforces a passive attitude of retreat. Extreme Daoists preached a social doctrine calling for small social units, with minimal government structure and as little social interaction as possible. They saw the numerous moral values and ethical codes cherished by the Confucians as unwanted baggage; if social ties and interaction were avoided or minimized to begin with, most problems the Confucians set out to confront would not even exist. Resigning to the *dao* can create a very different kind of individual and social order.

Other Daoist schools believe that moving in accordance with the propensity and force of the *dao* would make the individual much more compatible and effective in the world, rather than in retreat from it. Correctly perceiving and abiding by the movement of *dao* actually strengthens one's potential and power. By this ironic twist, the passivity of Daoist tenets is transformed into tactical endeavor. This tempts one to channel the force of *dao*—by magical or physical means—to become a source of religious fulfillment. The tremendous hidden power of the *dao* can be manipulated to fulfill other personal needs as well. Practices such as macrobiotic diets and divination can be used to achieve such utilitarian ends. This utilitarian dimension receives prominence in the later development of Daoism. Its canonical doctrines emphasize a detached, spontaneous life attitude commensurate with the natural unfolding of the *dao,* even as one carries out social responsibilities. The institutional religion that came to surround these doctrines could point to utilitarian personal benefits to be gained from adhering to the religion—an effective way of persuading worldly believers.

□ The Yin–Yang School

The axial age in China boasted the blossoming of "nine currents and ten schools" *(jiuliu sijia)*. Among them, the Yin-Yang school is another current standing at the heart of religious formation in China, with important practical implications for both Confucianism and Daoism. The Yin-Yang school systematized some of the magical practices from earlier primitive religion. It is generally deemed less important than Confucianism and Daoism because it is less sophisticated, but it helped reconcile these more elaborate doctrines and became responsible for many of the more speculative, magical tenets of both Confucianism and Daoism (Schwartz, 1985).

Yin-Yang is represented graphically as the opposition and complementarity of light and darkness—expressing their inherent difference while suggesting that the essence of each is somehow related to that of the other (see Figure 12.1). The polarity of Yin-Yang also underlined part of Confucianism and Daoism. In addition, this polarity may be viewed as an ancient articulation of what later came to be known as binary thinking. The Yin-Yang dichotomy is the primordial impulse of classification—the very

Figure 12.1 Yin and Yang in Harmony

first act of intellectual classification that preceded all subsequent acts of intellectual operation. Other contrasts such as weak-strong, low-high, feminine-masculine, cold-hot, absorbing-penetrating, passive-active, darkness-light, earth-heaven, and so on can be defined by their juxtaposition as opposites—the master framework of Yin-Yang—irrespective of their actual substance or referents.

Yet the Yin-Yang school took this to much greater extremes. The manifestation and transformation in any phenomenon can be charted and even foretold in accordance with the interplay of Yin-Yang dynamics. The entire universe can become unified and understood under sets of Yin-Yang related principles or pseudo-theories. There are, for instance, the five elements *(wuxin),* which referred to the constitutive elements of the material world—fire, water, wood, metal, and earth. Each of these elements has different associations along the spectrum of the Yin-Yang principle, forming a unique system of checks and balances, harmony and conflict, diversity and unity. In addition, the four directions, four seasons, stellar configurations, aspects of human virtues, and so forth all attain similar cosmological and magical attributes that resonate above and beyond their natural and human forms (Schwartz, 1985:chap. 9). By weaving together a closed cosmology that attributes order to the world and a teleology that shows its design and ultimate ends, the Yin-Yang school developed its immense appeal. The Yin-Yang dynamics became, in effect, the articulation, perhaps even actualization, of both the elusive *tian* and *dao*—of heaven on high and the way of life on earth.

□ Han Syncretism:
The Canonization of Confucianism

The Spring and Autumn Period (771–476 B.C.) when Confucius, Laozi, and Zhuangzi lived was the last phase of axial diversification before the breakdown of the Zhou dynasty. The nine currents and ten schools of thought flourishing during that era shared some common traits with roots in the earlier Zhou syncretism. Such continuities led to the famous hypothesis that the diverse schools of the axial age all originated from the former imperial officials of the Zhou government. Like the preceding Zhou syncretism, none of these schools looked to a single divine being as the ultimate source of religious spirit. Magic, spirit, hybrids, and a metaphorical heaven were still regarded as normal parts of the world where humans live. And the cornerstone of Zhou humanism stayed in place, whether in the Confucian values of *ren* and *li*, the Daoist postulate of the all-pervasive *dao,* or the Yin-Yang resonance *(ganyin)* among humans, world, and cosmos.

In this light, the founding of the Han dynasty in 206 B.C. following the Qin unification of China acquired different levels of meaning. In terms of intellectual and religious development, the Han period became the second major movement of syncretism in Chinese religious thought. Unlike the epochal breakthrough in Zhou humanism, however, Han syncretism can boast of no similar fundamental innovation, at least not in intellectual terms. Han syncretism is significant mainly in its practical consequence for Chinese religion. It was during the consolidation of Han syncretism that Confucianism was first favored above all other competing doctrines, that the writings of classical Confucianism were canonized as the supreme source of authority. But this process brought into Confucianism important strands from those competing doctrines and provided ways for other religions to coexist with it (Kramers, 1986).

Han syncretism elected an orthodoxy only subsequent to the consolidation of a variety of thought currents. The dynasty opened on a Daoist note when the second emperor of Han, Wendi, chose to adopt a more withdrawn, noninterventionist approach to state administration, so that the country could recover from the protracted war of unification under the first Han emperor, Gaozu. Yet he did not attempt to privilege Daoism above other doctrines. It was the great Wudi (reigning from 140 to 87 B.C.) who instituted the Five Confucian Classics as the official syllabus of education. Dong Zhongshu (179–104 B.C.), the intellectual architect of this movement, advocated "dismissing the hundred other schools in respect of Confucianism alone." Dong was simultaneously the great advocate of Confucianism and its formidable revisionist, drawing into it Daoist and Yin-Yang themes and traditions of folk religion and magical practices.

Dong sought to reconcile heaven *(tian)* and humanity *(ren).* His formulation for this is *tianren ganyin*—resonance between heaven and humans.

From this perspective, human and transcendental realities are intrinsically linked. A primarily humanistic approach like classical Confucianism, which focuses solely on humanity, is too simplistic. The Yin-Yang school saw *tian* as essentially unchangeable, overpowering forces. Dong sought to revise that passive view by reintroducing the notion of supernatural forces that would oversee the conduct of men. This element, while not entirely absent in classical Confucianism, was greatly amplified by the hand of Dong. Confucius's humanism was too abstract and impalpable for common individuals. By making *tian* once again a supreme will accessible to human supplications through the intervention of supernatural forces, Dong gave Confucianism greater popular appeal. Heaven does not intervene directly into human affairs, yet heaven is responsive to human conduct. Misdemeanors and crime, beyond a certain threshold of seriousness and scale, would trigger signs from heaven, usually in the form of natural disasters and mystical omens. So humanity can decipher the way of heaven and build a moral social order on its basis. The purpose of life is not just harmony and well-being but ultimately to attain a state of unity with heaven *(tianren heyi)*; this ideal would make orthodox Confucianism more explicitly religious (Loewe, 1986, 1994:chap. 6).

The Emperor Wudi accepted not only Dong's version of Confucianism but also the proposal that Confucianism should be honored above all other schools of thought and beliefs. In subsequent ages, the Han syncretism came to be known as *Hanxue* (Han learning). *Hanxue* represented the first major reworking of Confucianism, not only by Dong but also through extensive exegetical works on the Confucian canon by other Han scholars. The Han syncretism, however, proved problematic for later Confucians; it was revisionist in spirit yet meticulously preserved the classical heritage. The Han dynasty collapsed at the end of the second century A.D., but it left behind an established Confucian tradition.

■ THIRD CONFIGURATION: FOREIGN IMPETUS AND NEO–CONFUCIANISM

The two syncretic stages configuring Chinese religion up to this point involved ideas and doctrines that may seem somewhat removed from the modern conception of religion. There was little by way of established religious institutions, worship of a specific deity, or the use of sacred texts for transcendental communication. Even magical practice and beliefs were found only among marginalized Daoist and Yin-Yang cults. Orthodox Confucianism never set up a priesthood or houses of worship. In contrast to other major world religions, Chinese religion did not seek immortality, inner ecstasy, or salvation for its adherents. Chinese religious development was to remain heavily intellectual, secular, and humanistic. The purest form of belief was ultimately in humanity as such, for all its virtues, follies, and possibilities. But the adherents of this belief could attain the same fervor, commitment, and faith common to all religious traditions.

The next two configurations of religious development in China would be more complicated and colorful. Though the humanism persisted, it was subjected to searching challenges, the latest episode of which is still going on today. These challenges came largely from outside, in the form of foreign religious traditions that either sought to take root in China on their own or to trigger transformations of the Chinese religions from within (Demieville, 1986). The religions involved are Buddhism from India, the three religions of Abraham from Europe and the Near East, and finally Marxism-Maoism, which figured as yet another thought system of heavy humanistic-religious bent. These will be the subject matter for the present and the next sections.

☐ Indian Buddhism

The great religious event dominating China's cultural landscape while Europe was experiencing its "Dark Ages" and medieval period was the introduction and expansion of Buddhism (de Bary, 1988:chap. 2). From that time forward, the tripartite epithet of Confucianism-Buddhism-Daoism *(ru-xi-dao)* would become the standard litany describing Chinese religion. In other words, Buddhism was the only foreign religion that has successfully taken root in China and exerted sweeping cultural and intellectual influence on mainstream religious belief. Buddhism is a highly institutionalized religion, with its own elaborate miscellany of sects and monastic orders, specialized personnel, institutional discipline, and theological doctrines. In contrast, Confucianism maintained a much more secular, moralistic outlook, precisely in its attempt not to separate social and sacred lives. And Daoism was largely split between its intellectual and institutional facade, with the Daoist institutions catering above all to the more magical, witchcraft-inclined aspects of religious life, whereas the loftier side of Daoist philosophy remained in the domain of intellectuals. Buddhism was the only "all-round" religion in traditional China, encompassing the full range of religious sentiment, forms, and levels of thought (Wright, 1977).

Buddhism seeks to "take flight" from the world, which allegedly only brings human suffering. It adopts a passive posture not unlike that of Daoism but seeks to extend this to its logical extreme, renouncing individual consciousness and cravings so as to better perceive the ontological abyss of nothingness (*sunya* in Sanskrit, *kung* in Chinese). Buddhism added new dimensions to indigenous Chinese religions.

Historically, Buddhism is another product of the world axial breakthrough, established in India around 600 B.C. by Siddhartha Gautama of the Sakya clan, who became Sakyamuni ("the sage of the sakyas"). Modern scholarship has come to the broad consensus that the earliest documented arrival in China of Buddhists and their canon was during the early Han dynasty (see Table 3.1). Although Buddhism had practically no role to play in Han syncretism, it was during the Han dynasty that institutional support for Buddhism was first secured—royal sponsorship, monasteries in the capital city, the beginning of scriptural translation, and so forth. And into the late Han and the subsequent era of political instability, Buddhism would greatly expand its influence, taking on first Daoism and then Confucianism to become a major religio-cultural force by the time of the Song dynasty (A.D. 960–1279), the other great era of syncretism in traditional China (Chen, 1964). Buddhism became assimilated as an indigenous part of Chinese religious traditions via a twofold process: the translation of concepts and the search for original texts and developments of sects.

The initial assimilation of Buddhism was greatly facilitated by emphasizing facile similarity and overlap between Buddhism and the indigenous Daoist doctrine. This strategy was formally known as "matching of meanings" *(keyi)*. The broad application of *keyi* served two purposes. On the one hand, it secured acceptance and even popularity for Buddhism without significant resistance from the Chinese populace. On the other hand, and more important, the method also ensured that Buddhism would soon shed its Indian outlook and become assimilated into the Chinese religious world—truly achieving *keyi* as a method of cross-cultural communication.

Keyi refers to the practice of translating Indian Buddhist concepts into Daoist categories, a method pioneered by Faya, a fourth-century Chinese monk. *Keyi* could range from translating particular concepts, like the Sanskrit *sunya* (emptiness) into the Daoist *wu* (nothingness) or Buddha into the Daoist *shensen* (deities), all the way to systematically rendering entire sutras (Buddhist classics) into Daoist idiom and analogy, even annotating sutras with Daoist classics. The worth of Buddhism was measured by its ability to hold its own in debates on Chinese culture and scholarship. During the four divisive centuries of post-Han China, many of the well-known Buddhist monks and masters earned their celebrity by demonstrating unexpected depths and insights in Daoist learning. In outsmarting the Daoist-leaning Confucian scholar-officials of the time—during sessions of idle talk *(qing-tan)*—famous monks like Daoan and Huiyuan gained respect and footing for Buddhism. *Keyi* would go a long way in transforming the foreign outlook of Buddhism into what would soon be regarded as properly Chinese.

The height of Buddhist influence came during the influential, unified Tang dynasty (A.D. 618–907). An imperial census of Buddhist communities counted 260,000 monks and nuns, 4,600 temples, and some 40,000 shrines altogether. Each temple and shrine owned land and other properties donated by believers, giving them great social and economic prominence. Clashes with local authorities and indigenous beliefs resulted in repression. This

Photo: Robert E. Gamer

One of the seated Buddhas carved into Feilai Teng,
"the Peak which flew over from India," outside Hangzhou, Zhejiang.

census, in fact, was compiled as a database for the short-lived official suppression of Buddhism in A.D. 845. During episodes of official repression, most temples and shrines were destroyed, their land confiscated, and their monks secularized (Chen, 1964:chap. 8).

During the Tang, Chinese Buddhism developed along two fronts—the accelerated assimilation of Indian Buddhism and the growth of native Buddhist sects. Famous Buddhist pilgrims went to India to systematically study Buddhist sutras and treatises *(lun)*. Moving beyond *keyi,* they felt compelled to explore these works at their source, taking on Indian Buddhism in its own terms. The most famous pilgrims were Yijing, Faxian, and especially the towering figure of Xuan Zang, who has become a rich source of inspiration and contribution not only to Buddhism but to Chinese culture in general (Wriggins, 1996). Xuan Zang left China for India in A.D. 629 and did not return until A.D. 645. During that time, he also visited Sri Lanka. He brought back a great number of original Sanskrit texts and spent the rest of his life rendering these Sanskrit canon into Chinese, a task continued by his disciples after his death. His is the best-known example of a Chinese pilgrimage seeking a more authentic understanding of religion in the world outside; Chapter 13 tells you more about him. This enterprise of scriptural translation would be among the most significant, catalytic events in the growth of Chinese Buddhism.

Formation of Chinese Buddhism in the Tang divided into two streams: "the three sects under the creed" *(jiaoxia sanzong)* and the "alternative teaching outside the creed" *(jiaowai biequan)*. The three sects were the more mainstream Tiantai, Huayen, and Faxian. The alternative teaching refers to the highly unique and controversial development of Zen Buddhism. Both streams sought to reconcile Indian Buddhism with Chinese sociocultural conditions and in that process contributed significant progress to Buddhism at large. The three sects focused especially on doctrines that implored people to treat their fellow humans properly and embark on various stages of enlightenment, by way of compassionate deeds to help others lead a better earthly life and to start their own paths toward enlightenment. Zen Buddhism, both in its moderate *(jian)* or radical *(dun)* version, sought spiritual liberation and enlightenment *(wu)* not through understanding doctrines and carrying out deeds, but by uncovering and acknowledging one's innate self *(jue)*, one's Buddhist nature *(foxing)*, trying to remove all thoughts and desires and connect with the universal mind during meditation. In thus breaking free from the constraints of culture or even of Buddhist doctrines themselves, this endeavor was the more extreme attempt to abandon the Indian roots of Buddhism altogether. This alternative stream of Buddhism and popular beliefs like the pure land *(jingtu)* sect that proposed down-to-earth doctrines and ritual practices for different social occasions would survive the suppression of Buddhism in the ninth century to become a part of Chinese culture. There was no perceived fundamental schism between such forms of Buddhism and Confucianism or Daoism. It was not unusual, in fact, for intellectuals or the lay public to adhere to parts of all these creeds. In essence and fundamental philosophy, all defied the notions of any ruling supreme deity or heavenly salvation for individual souls.

☐ Near Eastern Manichaeanism and Nestorianism

During the Tang dynasty, Manichaeanism *(molijiao)* and Nestorianism *(jingjiao)* came to China from the Near East (Gernet, 1982:281–289). Manichaeanism was associated with the Zoroastrianism of ancient Persia, whereas Nestorianism was a heretical sect of early Christianity. The Tang dynasty maintained close contact with many of the adjacent regions and cultures, and the imperial capital, Ch'angan (Xi'an), housed a sizable community of foreigners, known generally as *hu*. This general milieu greatly facilitated the introduction of these religions, and their initial spread was somewhat sheltered by the success of Buddhism. Yet, being much smaller in scale, they suffered heavily during the occasional crackdowns on Buddhism and other foreign religions during the Tang dynasty and after. The Nestorians were heavily subdued whenever nativism surged in China; they were also persecuted and denounced as heretical by the Christian church in the West. The Manichaeans went underground to associate with Chinese popular cults seeking "millennial" uprisings against the state, inducing further suppressions in subsequent dynasties. These intensely theistic and otherworldly religions never commanded the same respect and attention as Buddhism. And yet they completed the spectrum of foreign religious impetus that entered China during the medieval time and may be seen as preparatory moments for the next major stage of Chinese religious development, when Christianity and the Christian civilization would clash against the Chinese world in the most ruthless manner possible.

□ Song Syncretism

By the time of Tang, Confucianism, whether as state belief or moral philosophy, was by and large already part of the invisible, taken-for-granted ground rules of everyday life. Daoism was somewhat in the middle, straddling the gap between superstition and high philosophy. Buddhism, too, catered to more down-to-earth religious needs while standing its ground in intellectual terms. Like Daoism, the schism between its role as folk religion and as moral pillar for society rendered its reception among both literati and commoner often eclectic and superficial. Once again, there was a need to draw together strains of thought and belief.

The dynamic of this development set the backdrop for the new syncretism of the Song. This would be a syncretism operating at two levels of sophisticated religious ideas, and of folk beliefs and practice. Song syncretism reconciled both contending thought systems and the eclectic mosaic of folk beliefs and superstition. The Song dynasty saw the maturation of Chinese religious consciousness and its split into contrasting levels and aspirations (de Bary, 1988:chap. 3).

At the heart of the new syncretism was neo-Confucianism (see Figure 12.2). This is often referred to as the "second phase" in the development of Confucianism, the "first phase" being Confucianism in the time of Confucius himself. Neo-Confucianism accommodated the doctrinal challenge from Daoism and Buddhism in Confucian terms, but not without cost. By focusing more on inner religious experience and less on human relations, it may even have weakened the Song dynasty's defense against encroaching nomadic invaders and hence hastened its demise (cf. Liu, 1988).

There were, broadly, four celebrated schools of neo-Confucianism, the Lian, Lo, Guan, and Min, named after the home territories of their respective founders. These schools were not so much different "sects" of neo-Confucianism as different steps of development. They developed in nearly

**Figure 12.2   The Diagram of the Supreme Ultimate, Depicting the
Neo–Confucian Image of the Division and Unity of
the Yin–Yang Poles**

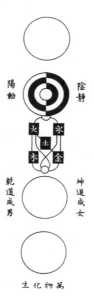

the chronological order given above, and their founders were often intellectual (and actual) kinsmen. The neo-Confucian schools all sought to strengthen, if not actually rebuild, the foundation that underlined the Confucian faith in morality, benevolence, and humanity. The rise of Buddhism and increasing popularity of Daoism rendered the emphasis on compassion or moral goodness no longer the prerogative of Confucianism alone. The same urge for virtuous conduct and mutual compassion figured prominently in Buddhism and even populist Daoism. The point was then both to reinforce and rebuild the foundation of the Confucian faith, so that the Confucian way could be demonstrated to be distinctive from and superior to other alleged champions of virtue and humanity. For this purpose, two general agendas emerged.

The first agenda, undertaken mainly by the Guan school, sought to reaffirm the necessity of morality and benevolence by a familial analogy binding humanity with the universe. This position was pronounced with great persuasiveness and clarity in the manifesto of the Guan school—the Western Inscription *(ximing)* by Zhang Zhai (Kasoff, 1984). As presented in the *ximing,* heaven *(tian)* and earth *(kun)* were but the benevolent universal parents of humans. Within this ultimate parenthood, every relationship—social, material, and natural—must accord with prescribed ethical (read filial) standards. The recognition of universal parenthood would render an ethical, benevolent worldview necessary and inviolable.

The second and eventually the more influential agenda was represented by Zhu Xi and the Min school. Instead of developing yet another set of beliefs like universal parenthood, Zhu Xi sought to create a more systematic metaphysical foundation for Confucianism. His elaborate intellectual construction explored the dichotomy between *li* (principle) and *qi* (expression) in order to demonstrate the unity and universality of principle as opposed to the multifariousness of expression. He deepened the rationale and assumptions behind the Confucian world of belief. Influenced by Buddhist and Daoist practices, he sought to relate human needs and feelings to doctrine and ritual behavior, sidestepping Confucian ethics in favor of seeking "higher" and ultimate metaphysical reality by incessant probing of inner experience. Zhu's approach brought a convergence in form and spirit (if not in doctrines) of the three religions but risked the danger of retreating into speculative musing and self-diagnosis. The subsequent development of neo-Confucianism into the Ming dynasty would be heavily tainted by the transcendental mood of a "Confucian Zen" (de Bary, 1975: 141–217).

At the other end of Song syncretism was the growing popularity of folk beliefs and magical practices borrowing indiscriminately from the systematic religions, whose insight and fine points often eluded the ability and concern of the general public. These folk beliefs were characterized by an abundance of gods, worshipped either as local deities or more universal idols. The figures popular among folk worship included historical figures, deceased local celebrities, and even Confucian sages, all of whom were turned into idols that, after proper sacrificial offerings, might bestow blessings and grant requests. They might simultaneously worship other deities like the Amitabe Buddha *(milafo)*, Kanon *(Guanyin*, a Buddhist Bodhisattva), the Jade Emperor *(yuhuang dadi)*, Gods of the Five Mountains *(wu yue dijun)*, and the Immaculate Lady of the Ninth Heaven *(jiutian xuannu)*. Confucianism, Buddhism, Daoism (see Figure 12.3), and popular legends all contributed to this pantheon. These deities and idols could be worshipped selectively or collectively, depending on the needs of the worshippers. They were also worshipped regardless of their religious origins. This is syncretism in the strong sense of the term, with an easy sense of unity gained by simply ignoring gaps and incoherence.

Syncretic folk creeds formed as well. Manichaeanism *(molijiao)* dressed itself as a kind of higher-order Buddhism. Its spread within the population was among the main contributing factors to millennial revolts against the dynasty. The well-known White Lotus sect *(bailianjiao)* also preached a form of simplified, eclectic doctrine advocating social reform. The White Lotus would lead a sustained underground existence into the early twentieth century.

Figure 12.3   A Traditional Representation of a Daoist Deity

After the Han dynasty, the development of Chinese religion became more complex. Daoism and Confucianism deepened their grasp on Chinese culture and society. At the same time, the outside world began to sink in. By the end of the Song dynasty, Chinese religious systems were generally confident of their own value and truthfulness. Assaults were, however, about to emerge that would call for even more profound and encompassing standards. After the Mongol kingdom overthrew the Song dynasty at the end of the thirteenth century, outside encroachment became broader and deeper; other exotic modes of faith, of religious sentiment and aspiration, asserted powerful new universalist claims.

■ **FOURTH CONFIGURATION:**
   THE FOREIGN IMPETUS OF CHRISTIANITY
   AND COMMUNISM

The next major movement in the development of Chinese religion was the head-on clash with outside religious precepts, especially Christianity and Marxism-Leninism. Ironically, the Christian faith would take on a strong and relentless political overtone, whereas the political ideology of Marxism-Leninism would be intensified into religiosity of the most fanatical kind. The resulting nexus of cataclysm and innovation looms over Chinese civilization even to this day.

□ Christianity

As noted above, Christianity was first introduced into China during the Tang dynasty, in the form of Nestorianism. At that time however, both Nestorianism and Manichaeanism were broadly lumped together with Buddhism, regarded as variations among exotic Buddhist currents. It was not until the sixteenth century, during the Ming dynasty, that the Roman Catholic Church began the full-fledged process of eastward expansion, first into Japan and then China. Many of the first missionaries were Jesuit priests, like the famous Matteo Ricci (Li Madou), who came to China in 1583, and Niccolo Longobardi (Long Huamin), who arrived in the late sixteenth century. From the beginning, both the missionaries and the Roman Catholic hierarchy made numerous blunders; the Christian faith had nowhere near the success of Buddhism in converting the Chinese population. But the broader impact of the Christian civilization on China has been immeasurable. China would be forced literally at gunpoint not only to accept the operation of the missionaries in its territory but also many of the values and principles central to Christian civilization. In his chronicle of these momentous developments, Jacques Gernet (1985) characterizes the situation not so much in terms of religious differences but as whole civilizations clashing. We shall approach these dynamics in terms of doctrines, politics, and native reaction.

The question of doctrine was a thorny one right from the beginning. Confucians were simply playing out the religious consequences that follow from their particular conception and understanding of the world. In contrast, Christianity was based on a transcendental leap of faith different from any China had confronted before—the unconditional belief in the reality of the biblical God, the Holy Trinity, and eternal life for individual souls. This voluntary surrender of the autonomy of humans to an abstract and unknowable deity could well be seen by Chinese as a phase of simplistic religious impulse that the Chinese civilization had long since superseded. Although the worship of one god or another was fully permissible, this was usually regarded in China as the less enlightened attitude of the masses. And in any case, none of these deities can claim monopolistic authority. Thus, although Christianity was at first accepted as perhaps one more addition to the pantheon of the people, much as Nestorianism and Manichaeanism were, the idea that this particular god must replace all others would be difficult to accommodate. At risk of oversimplification, one can say that according to the higher humanistic aspiration of the Chinese literati, all deities were equally suspicious, whereas for the Chinese followers of folk religion, all deities were equally real. The Chinese people would be ill-prepared for the kind of "unreasonable" leap of faith adhered to in the West.

Two strategies were adopted by the missionaries to break this bottleneck, both with little effect. One strategy was to camouflage or soften the tough fabric of Christian doctrines, embracing local tenets and precepts and explaining away doctrinal differences by pointing out common grounds—assimilating with local mentality as Buddhism had done with the use of *keyi*. This was the strategy of Ricci and his Jesuit colleagues and represented a first effort toward indigenization of Christianity in China. Ricci himself appeared openly to embrace doctrines of Confucianism. He wore Confucian garb, took on a Chinese name (Li Madou) and rendered Christian tenets into Confucian rubrics. He stressed his knowledge of science and astronomy in order to gain respect and admiration. This was a strategy to avoid conflict with local beliefs on grounds of doctrinal differences, but it was at best facile. The fundamental opposition in doctrines was put in the background but was far from resolved: True converts, once baptized, must adhere to the full the core tenets of Christianity. The second strategy, adopted largely as the official position of the Roman Catholic Church, was to insist on the hegemonic truth of Christianity right from the start. The church regarded the position of Ricci and other Jesuits as far too liberal. During the Qing dynasty in the eighteenth century, the Vatican officially denounced the Chinese worship of Confucian sages, ancestors, or local deities. This intolerant and impatient stance effectively made the first Chinese Christians into enemies in the eyes of other Chinese. The Qing government answered by expelling Christian missionaries.

From the nineteenth century onward, Christianity would be promoted on more than religious grounds. Together with a wide assortment of other values and institutions of Christian civilization as a whole, it would be forced upon China by military conflict and unequal treaties. The involvement of Christianity in the process provided a more high-minded alibi for what was clearly colonial exploitation. Backed by the full military strength of Christian nations like Britain, Germany, France, and to a lesser extent the United States, the increasing importance of Christianity was assured. The missionaries were aware of the human cost of colonial-style exploitation. The infamous Opium War of 1839 (discussed in Chapters 6 and 7), for example, had no better excuse than stark imperialist and commercial interests. The reaction of Christian churches and missionaries to the situation was two-pronged. On the one hand, if political sponsorship could ensure the expansion of Christianity in China, so much the better; in fact many of the Christian missionaries and their colleagues back home were not immune to ideologies of colonialism and racial superiority. Convinced of the prerogative of Christian faith, many missionaries were willing accomplices of politics. On the other hand, whatever the causes—or instigators—of China's social deterioration might be, this was a good opportunity for Christian churches to lend help. In the late nineteenth and early twentieth centuries, Christian churches in China set up welfare organizations of various kinds, running schools, hospitals, and even universities. Ironically, the Christian missionaries were determined to demonstrate their goodwill to a society devastated in its encounter with Christian civilization. The intertwining of Christianity with colonial politics reached its high point at the turn of the twentieth century, when the alleged protection of Christian churches served as pretext for a number of military interventions into China, most notably the *Tianjin jiaoan,* the religious crime of the Boxers in Tianjin, discussed shortly.

As a result, the Chinese people often accepted or rejected the Christian faith for nonreligious reasons: to receive welfare or an education or to achieve the same earthly power as the imperialist invaders. The native response to Christianity was hence widely divergent and erratic. Two examples can serve to illustrate: the Taiping and Boxer rebellions. The Taiping Rebellion (also discussed in Chapter 11) took place during the late nineteenth century; it lasted some fifteen years and laid waste to many of the southern provinces. Although it had all the trappings of Chinese peasant "millennial" movements of the past, it was also distinguished by its espoused allegiance to Christianity. The founder of the movement, Hong Xiuquan, actually claimed that he was yet another son of God and that Jesus Christ was his elder brother. Hong, as well as other leaders of the rebellion, also claimed to conduct direct communion with God (Spence, 1996). The movement, however, had little connection with or support from Western Christian churches, and the idea that Jesus could have a Chinese brother was not to be taken seriously by Jesus' Western followers. One can marvel at the extreme significance accorded Christianity, to become the ideological foundation of the *Taiping Tianguo* (Heavenly Kingdom of Eternal Peace). A different perspective is that perhaps Christianity had no special claim to supremacy—it was deployed as an expedient vehicle and pretext for articulating pent-up grievances, much as Manichaeanism and folk cults had been used in past rebellions (Shih, 1967). This mode of Christian fanaticism was clearly not what the Western Christian churches had in mind.

At the other extreme stood what might be seen as anti-Christian fanaticism, represented above all by the Boxer Rebellion *(yihetuan)* of 1900 (Esherick, 1987). The Boxer Rebellion was characterized by its all-out xenophobia. It was a state-sponsored populist cult, in the same folk-relogous order as the White Lotus sect, the *Mila* sect, and other sects that stood behind historical millennial uprisings. Strengthened by support of the empress dowager and her imperial officials, the *yihetuan* appeared ready to confront the Christian religion and civilization head on. Confident that through magical incantation, spells, and other rituals, the true believers could withstand firearms and other forms of attack, the Boxer sect set out to destroy Christian churches and Western embassies, mostly in Beijing. Although the movement was short-lived, at its height it won widespread admiration from common people. The Boxer's destruction was disastrous for China. Eight Western countries formed a military alliance to protect their churches and other interests in China, and the Boxers' magic proved no match against bullets. The Forbidden City soon came under Western control. More unequal treaties (discussed in Chapter 7) would have to be signed before the fiasco of the Boxer Rebellion could be settled. The incident was representative of the nativistic paranoia against Christianity and Christian civilization. The naivete of the uprising should not hide from view its deep-seated and widely shared objection against the imposition of a foreign faith and the world order that implied.

The drama of Christian impact continues unabated even now, and the fortune of Chinese Christianity fluctuates with the political climate. It has suffered whenever anti-Western sentiments surge in China. Even under the best of circumstances, Christianity still has a hard time resolving its theological position with the Chinese religious tradition. This major obstacle may have receded somewhat by the late twentieth century, when the Chinese religious traditions themselves are on the wane, after the intrusion of yet another foreign system of thought, Marxism-Leninism.

□ Marxism–Maoism

In many respects, Marxism and Confucianism are comparable in the positions they occupied in the Chinese religious life. Both are doctrines that concern the human order rather than transcendental reality. Both figure as the hegemonic thought system for China as a whole, yet neither can claim to be a religion as such. And both encompass the wide horizon between genuine humanistic sentiment and totalistic authoritarian propensities. These reasons help explain why, although the Christian challenge to Chinese culture was always looked upon with reservation, Marxism was more readily accepted as a viable alternative for China. Their assumptions and tenets may differ, yet at least Confucianism and Marxism operate on the some plane and address the same cluster of concerns. Of course, there are profound differences as well.

In contrast to the tangible humanism of Confucianism, Marxism as introduced to China by Mao Zedong is sweepingly utopian (Kolakowski, 1982:494–523). Confucianism emphasized the here and now, the "rational adaptation" to the world as the route of self-actualization and fulfillment. Utopian thinking was usually associated with folk cults or peasant movements. Marxism-Maoism is, however, forthright in postulating an ideal and inevitable future society, the realization of which is worth present material and human sacrifice. Based on this outlook, since 1949 the development of China has been conducted through a series of social experiments, designed to arrive at the ideal social form. Imitating the Soviet experience during the 1950s proved futile, leaving China to grope for its own way into socialism and thereby the communist utopia. The tremendous havoc and destruction brought on by the Great Leap Forward and the Cultural Revolution were understandable only in relation to their fundamental utopianism, which is very out of character with Confucianism but generally in keeping with the Taiping Rebellion and other millennial movements outside the mainstream of traditional Chinese culture. As in those movements, cultural and literary elites were marginalized. Instead, the society of socialist China would be founded upon the great alliance of the workers-peasants-soldiers *(gongnongbing)*.

The Marxian image of society also differs markedly from the Confucian one in its emphasis on conflict and contradiction as forces of history. This is totally incompatible with the Confucian vision of a harmonious, benevolent society. The Marxian conception of social structure is one of change, of differentiation, and of the scramble for social resources. In playing out this dynamic process, individuals join with others of the same social position and interest in a systematic conflict against other social classes. Traditional Chinese culture would have little of this. Conflict and tension were always exceptions to the norm and could be readily redeemed by invoking ethical dogmas. Human nature is, after all, formed of the same benevolent, virtuous essence. To claim as Maoism did that revolution is the highest vehicle for individual and societal purification is to be fundamentally wrong-headed. The Confucian ideal of harmony *(he)*, whether between two persons, person and society, or even person and cosmos, instead postulates a society that is intrinsically virtuous and benevolent, that minimizes the occasions of conflict and comes to resolution should these happen. And Daoism and Buddhism are by and large passive and withdrawn and certainly have not espoused conflict and destruction. One can see the extreme turnabout that took place in China with the holistic embrace of Marxism-Leninism-Maoism.

Should there still be any doubt regarding the religious—or antireligious—character of Marxism-Maoism, one need only consider that, whatever their substance and tenets, they were articulated above all as fanaticism and cult. The national malaise of the Cultural Revolution and the personality cult of Mao are cases in point. The religious overtone enters because the utopian promises of Maoism can never be sustained or validated by reason and evidence alone; they must be heightened by a state of mass elation.

□ Toward a New Syncretism?

After Mao's death in 1976, China entered a phase of fundamental reconstruction in all major arenas of society. Socialism is still official ideology, but other competitors are rapidly on the rise—capitalism, nationalism, even the newest fad of postmodernism. All these are but symptoms of the basic disorientation of China in the aftermath of disenchantment with Marxism-Leninism-Maoism. A new mode of faith and belief is being sought to once again provide society with a viable image of social order and with moral and behavioral codes for the social actors. The post-Mao transformation cannot be resolved simply on pragmatic grounds, as Deng Xiaoping suggested. China's leaders have always articulated its ethical standards; after a period during which all prior beliefs were stridently attacked, it needs new guidelines. If the elementary belief system in social reconstruction remains vacuous, much of society would be in limbo and nihilistic or disintegrate into groups with differing belief systems.

The present Chinese government is adopting a more lenient approach to religious belief. In line with current discussions of human rights, the right to religious belief is seen as part of this package. Both traditional and Western belief systems are in principle permitted, and individuals are free to choose, but such freedom has limits. Specific constitutional articles prohibit and even deem treasonous religious beliefs or activities that run counter to national interest. Religion must stay within the bounds of politics. Churches and temples—in keeping with long tradition—may function only with the approval of the state. Or more metaphorically, the City of God is subordinated to the City of Man. This is the flip side of the separation between church and state. Based on this principle, the Chinese government is deemed justified in its tightened regulation of, for example, Tibetan Buddhism (see Chapter 6). In this approach to religious policy, religions are not recognized as vehicles for any higher form of truth. They are rather tolerated as perhaps harmless pastimes for a worn-out nation. The fundamental enigma of society remains unanswered. As yet no belief system can serve as a source of meaning, direction, and identity for the already crises-laden society, let alone answer ultimate questions and needs of human existence (cf. MacInnis, 1989).

At present, a rough estimate is that one-tenth of the Chinese population (120 million) embrace religious beliefs of some form (Stockwell, 1993:31–55), that is, religions with formal institutions operating within allowed political confines. In this light, China is currently a country with few true believers; religions are allowed only a trivialized existence. Both believers and nonbelievers are equally paralyzed amidst the fundamental void of meaning and value. Only crude money motive, at present, seems to have given some momentum and purpose for those eager to upgrade their material life. One can hope that as material conditions improve, perhaps more attention will be given to elevating spiritual life as well.

How far this projection will come true is hard to tell at this point. Yet advocates for various belief systems are at least preparing for this possibility. Foremost among them are the New Confucians, who seek to revive

Confucianism as once again the belief system most appropriate for China. Of course, this cannot mean merely the reiteration of outdated tenets. Instead, New Confucianism would incorporate other ideological currents that played a part in the shaping of modern China and try to weave these different strands into the new syncretism of a Confucian "Cultural China" (Tu, 1991). The prospect of this drama is still being played out.

■ RELIGION AND CHINESE SOCIETY

Standing out in the sets of syncretism charted above is the secular, this-worldly character of Chinese religion. Each of the three great syncretisms in China's history—during the Zhou, Han, and Song dynasties—elevated a humanistic and collectivistic outlook above other competing theistic or pantheistic currents. It is in the final analysis this strongly practical, societal, and moral commitment to the here and now that distinguishes the spirit of Chinese religion. The answers to ultimate questions of existence and meaning are neither unknowable nor hiding in the transcendental beyond. They can be answered only by imputing the secular here and now with sacred authority and authenticity—by the clear-minded sacralization of the secular and mundane. The secret of Chinese religion does not lie in the quest for immortality, salvation, or ecstatic liberation. Rather, it is only in renouncing all these perhaps mystical ideals that the worldly reality would emerge as the only reality there is and hence the only source of meaning and value to questions both profane and sacred. In brief, the Chinese religious tradition renders the human order *(renlun)* itself sacred. If the social world is all that there is, then striving for social order and harmony would be the highest ideal that can be hoped for and the most sacred quest that human beings can conduct. Religious sentiment and commitment are defined above all by their focus upon the primacy of social relations, as the actual dynamics of the human order. Hence the celebrated Chinese emphasis on *guanxi* (relation) as the stuff that human order is made of (King, 1991). In the present context, this relationship may be taking on added importance.

There are two fundamental categories of *guanxi*, ascribed and achieved. In Confucian terms, ascribed relationships are the cornerstone of human order and more often than not have primacy over achieved relations. Ascribed relationships are part of the *wulun* (five orders), denoting the fundamental ties based on a priori principles like mandate of heaven and blood ties that the individual has no choice but to honor. These five orders include relations between emperor and ministers, father and son, husband and wife, one brother and another, and also between kin and friends. One is born or placed into the first four of these relationships, which are therefore ascribed. They help ensure that one's family and the country's leaders will command supreme loyalty. As to the fifth relationship, which is achieved, the relation between kin and between friends must also be conducted according to predetermined, proper principles and codes. These five relationships are the stable building blocks of human society and are the main obligations of every individual. In upholding these relationships, definite values and principles apply. The medium being exchanged in these relations must rise above the mundane concerns of economic or material benefit. It is essentially an exchange of goodwill, of human compassion *(renqing)*. In thus exchanging acts of goodwill—in the form of gifts, help, favor, understanding, kind words, and so forth—mutual compassion among individuals and toward society as a whole can be better consolidated. In this way, Confucian ideals such as loyalty, filial piety, honesty, and agnatic ties are articulated into concrete social dynamics.

In addition to ascribed relationships, into which you enter whether you like it or not, you can also achieve *guanxi* with people of your own choosing. These are usually classmates, fellow villagers, associates at work, or other people close enough to decide they will exchange *renqing* favors. In addition to a genuine sense of compassion, strategic calculation can come into play in the give-and-take of these achieved relationships. For example, you might use these exchanges to help get out of debt or put others in debt to you. Such subtle strategies evolved into elaborate power games in Chinese social life. Many of the techniques invoked are Daoist in origin, as clever adoption of cherished moral values or propensities of the situation to favor yourself.

The emphasis on *guanxi* and *renqing* are by no means a thing of the past, as Chapter 13 will also attest. Belief systems may displace one another, yet the same stress on human order persists. During the modern socialist era, the ascribed ethical ties have become weakened. Yet conversely, the obsession with achieved social relationships is on the rise as new market opportunities appear. It is well known that, nowadays in China, nothing much can be accomplished—regardless of the sphere of activities concerned—without getting in touch with the right person and setting up the right kind of ties. This network of social ties has in many respects replaced the open, institutional channels of social organization. That private network is an adaptation of Confucian ethics that has remained alive in spirit and practice today. Once again, the Chinese religious tradition gives shape to a society that focuses overwhelmingly on the personal affective side of social and cultural dynamics.

Chinese religion is essentially of this world, and it has withstood many of the forces that pull in other directions. Its emphasis on maintaining social order helps restore stability after periods of turmoil but also generally resists social change. Its emphasis on personal social relations also encourages people to tend to their own social circle at the expense of others to whom they do not owe direct obligations. This streak of conservatism can be both a blessing and a curse for China's enigmatic transition into the modern world and for its search for a new spiritual syncretism.

■ BIBLIOGRAPHY

Bays, Daniel H. (ed.). 1997. *Christianity in China: From the Eighteenth Century to the Present*. Stanford: Stanford University Press.

Bodde, Derk. 1991. *Chinese Thought, Society, and Science*. Honolulu: University of Hawaii Press.

Chan, Wing-tsit. 1953. *Religious Trends in Modern China*. New York: Columbia University Press.

Chang, H. 1990. "Some Reflections on the Problems of the Axial Age Breakthrough in Relation to Classical Confucianism." In P. A. Cohen and M. Goldman (eds.), *Ideas Across Cultures*. Cambridge: Harvard University Press.

Chang, Kwant-chih. 1963. *The Archaeology of Ancient China*. New Haven: Yale University Press.

Chen, Kenneth Kwang Sheng. 1964. *Buddhism in China: A Historical Survey*. Princeton: Princeton University Press.

Chuang Tzu. 1994. *Wandering on the Way: Early Taoist Tales and Parables of Chuang Tzu*. Trans. Victor H. Mair. New York: Bantam.

Creel, Herrlee Glessner. 1970. *The Origins of Statecraft in China: The Western Chou Empire*. Vol. 1. Chicago: University of Chicago Press.

de Bary, William Theodore. 1975. *The Unfolding of Neo-Confucianism*. New York: Columbia University Press.

———. 1988. *East Asian Civilizations*. Cambridge: Cambridge University Press.

———. 1991. *Learning for One's Self: Essays on the Individual in Neoconfucian Thought*. New York: Columbia University Press.

de Groot, Jan Jakob Maria. 1972 [1892]. *The Religious Systems of China: The Ancient Forms, Evolution, History, and Present*. 6 vols. Leyden: E. J. Brill Press.

Demieville, P. 1986. "Philosophy and Religion from Han to Sui." In Denis Twitchett and John K. Fairbank (eds.), *The Cambridge History of China*. Vol. 1. Cambridge: Cambridge University Press.

Eliade, M. 1982. *A History of Religious Ideas*. Vol. 2. Chicago: University of Chicago Press.

Eno, Robert. 1990. *The Confucian Creation of Heaven: Philosophy and the Defense of Ritual Mastery*. Albany: State University of New York Press.

Esherick, J. 1987. *The Origins of the Boxer Uprising*. Berkeley: University of California Press.

Faure, Bernard. 1997. *Chan Insights and Oversights: An Epistemological Critique of the Chan Tradition*. Princeton: Princeton University Press.

Fingarette, Herbert. 1972. *Confucius: The Secular as Sacred*. New York: Harper and Row.

Freedman, Maurice. 1979. "On the Sociological Study of Chinese Religion." In Maurice Freedman, *The Study of Chinese Society*. Stanford: Stanford University Press.

Fung, Yu-lan. 1952 [1937]. *A History of Chinese Philosophy*. Trans. Derk Bodde. Princeton: Princeton University Press.

Gernet, Jacques. 1982. *A History of Chinese Civilization*. Cambridge: Cambridge University Press.

———. 1985. *China and the Christian Impact*. Cambridge: Cambridge University Press.

Graham, Angus C. 1989. *Disputers of the Tao*. La Salle, IL: Open Court Publishing Company.

Granet, Marcel. 1975 [1922]. *The Religion of the Chinese People*. Trans. Maurice Freedman. New York: Harper and Row.

Hall, David L., and Roger T. Ames. 1987. *Thinking Through Confucius*. Albany: State University of New York.

Ho, Ping-ti. 1975. *The Cradle of the East: An Inquiry into the Indigenous Origins of Techniques and Ideas of Neolithic and Early Historic China, 5000–1000 B.C.* Hong Kong: Chinese University of Hong Kong Press.

Hsu, Francis Lan Kwang. 1971 [1948]. *Under the Ancestor's Shadow*. Stanford: Stanford University Press.

Hsu, Immanuel Chung-yueh. 1995. *The Rise of Modern China*. 5th ed. New York: Oxford University Press.

Kasoff, Ira E. 1984. *The Thought of Chang Tsai (1020–1077)*. Cambridge: Cambridge University Press.

Keightley, David N. 1978. *Sources of Shang History: The Oracle-Bone Inscriptions of Bronze Age China*. Berkeley: University of California Press.

King, Ambrose. 1991. "Kuan Hsi and Network Building: A Sociological Interpretation." *Daedalus* 120 (spring):2.

Kolakowski, Leszek. 1978. *Main Currents of Marxism: Its Rise, Growth, and Dissolution*. Vol 3. Trans. P. S. Falla. Oxford: Clarendon Press.

———. 1982. *Religion*. New York: Oxford University Press.

Kramers, R. 1986. "The Development of the Confucian Schools." In Denis Twitchett and John K. Fairbank (eds.), *The Cambridge History of China*. Vol. 1. Cambridge: Cambridge University Press.

Kung, Hans, and Julia Ching. 1989. *Christianity and Chinese Religions*. New York: Doubleday.

Liu, James T. C. 1988. *China Turning Inward: Intellectual-Political Changes in the Early Twelfth Century*. Cambridge: Council on East Asian Studies, Harvard University.

Loewe, Michael. 1986. "The Concept of Sovereignty." In Denis Twitchett and John K. Fairbank (eds.), *The Cambridge History of China*. Vol. 1. Cambridge: Cambridge University Press.

———. 1994. *Divination, Mythology, and Monarchy in Han China*. New York: Cambridge University Press.

Lopez, Donald S., Jr. (ed.). 1996. *The Religion of China in Practice*. Princeton: Princeton University Press.

MacInnis, Donald E. 1989. *Religion in China Today: Policy and Practice*. New York: Orbis Books.

Nakamura, H. 1964. *Ways of Thinking of Eastern Peoples*. Honolulu: University of Hawaii Press.

Overmyer, Daniel L. 1986. *Religions of China: The World as a Living System*. San Francisco: Harper and Row.

Robinet, Isabel. 1997. *Taoism: Growth of a Religion*. Trans. Phyllis Brooks. Stanford: Stanford University Press.

Roetz, Heiner. 1993. *Confucian Ethics of the Axial Age: A Reconstruction Under the Aspect of the Breakthrough Toward Postconventional Thinking*. Albany: State University of New York Press.

Schluchter, Wolfgang. 1981. *The Rise of Western Rationalism*. Berkeley: University of California Press.

Schwartz, Benjamin Isadore. 1985. *The World of Thought in Ancient China*. Cambridge: Belknap Press of Harvard University Press.

Shih, V. 1967. *The Tai Ping Ideology*. Seattle: University of Washington Press.

Smith, Arthur Henderson. 1894. *Chinese Characteristics*. New York: Revell.

Spence, Jonathan. 1996. *God's Chinese Son*. London: HarperCollins.

Stockwell, Foster. 1993. *Religion in China Today*. Beijing: New World Press.

Tu, Wei-ming. 1991. "The Living Tree." *Daedalus* 120 (spring):2.

Weber, Max. 1964 [1922]. *The Religions of China: Confucianism and Taoism*. Trans. Hans H. Gerth. New York: Free Press.

Wolf, Arthur P. (ed.). 1974. *Religion and Ritual in Chinese Society*. Stanford: Stanford University Press.

Wriggins, Sally Hovey. 1996. *Xuanzang: A Buddhist Pilgrim on the Silk Road*. Boulder: Westview Press.

Wright, Arthur F. 1977. *Buddhism in Chinese History*. Stanford: Stanford University Press.

Yang, C. K. 1961. *Religion in Chinese Society: A Study of Contemporary Social Functions of Religion and Some of Their Historical Factors*. Berkeley: University of California Press.

■ 13 ■

Literature
and Popular Culture
Charles A. Laughlin

As we approach the end of this book, I want to encourage you to include China in the poetry, short stories, and novels you read, the movies you see, and other aspects of your entertainment and sports. If you've read this far, you have enough knowledge about people, places, events, and traditions to enjoy both current and classic literature and popular forms of entertainment from China. The themes are universal—love, bravery, murder and intrigue, drunken reverie, jealousy, adultery, war, heroic men and women, moral uprightness, physical prowess. They also provide a lively and entertaining way to learn more about China, now that you have begun. Today we have evidence that Chinese classics derived from popular culture; contemporary Chinese thinkers and writers often challenge an age-old distinction between elite and popular culture, between the civilized and the "vulgar." Some of China's most exciting new writers, like the Beijing novelist and screenwriter Wang Shuo, or Lillian Lee, the Hong Kong writer who wrote the novel behind the Academy Award–winning film *Farewell My Concubine,* attract attention precisely because they blur or even demolish this distinction, mixing the sublime with the ridiculous until they become almost impossible to distinguish. This challenge to stuffy elitism is not a modern invention.

Today we associate popular culture with mass media, advertising, and high technology. To bring Chinese popular culture into focus, though, we must highlight the ways tradition lives and breathes in the contemporary imagination. Popular culture has always been the driving force, stimulus for change, and source of variety for Chinese literature. Fathoming just how much writing has been produced in China over the past 3,000 years is somewhat like imagining the distance to the nearest galaxy. That literature embodies seething, wrangling cultural diversity. Confucianism dominated but, as you saw in Chapter 12, many other traditions came into play as well. Over the long course of Chinese cultural history, writers and artists distilled into writing, visual arts, and drama a vast multiplicity of entertainment, religious, and everyday social practices.

I recommend Chen Shou-yi's *Chinese Literature: A Historical Introduction* (1961) and Liu Wu-chi's *An Introduction to Chinese Literature* (1966) as standard histories of Chinese literature. But the story is told from the point of view of the "literati"—the elite class of intellectuals who mastered the difficult Chinese written language. It is true that almost all we know about popular culture in ancient and early modern China comes through the prism of the writings and art of the literate elite, who capture only part of the richness of creative popular expression in their times. Nevertheless, looking through this prism, we can reconstruct the rich and diverse cultural panorama lying behind it.

■ WRITING: THE HUMAN PATTERN

It is often thought that the Chinese language is totally different from other languages because of its tonality (often misunderstood as "musicality") and its pictorial elements. Such notions, though inaccurate, were an important inspiration for modernism (particularly Imagism) in English and French poetry. The Chinese writing system lends itself to such theories because its characters look a bit like pictures, but by the time the earliest Chinese texts were written, the pictures in Chinese characters had long since ceased to be the primary means through which meaning was conveyed.

Still, the fact that written Chinese did not develop into a phonetic system like the Greek and Roman alphabets had far-reaching implications for literacy and literary expression. Because written Chinese involved learning tens of thousands of distinct characters, it was very hard to learn to read and write even in the earliest times—so hard, in fact, that the few who were able to manage it remained a small and closely knit group throughout the centuries. Indeed, the "literati" can almost be equated with the ruling class insofar as literacy was the sole avenue to power and responsibility. The written language was their stock in trade, and it made them socially indispensable.

The practice of divination, or fortune-telling, in the Shang and Zhou dynasty (see Table 3.1) royal courts was the foundation for the use of images in the Chinese language. As an official ritual with great political significance (see Chapter 12) divination was one of the activities that first required developing and preserving common symbols. By putting interpretation (and thus symbolic ambiguity) at the center of reading, divination, in a sense, produced some of China's earliest literary texts. In Shang times, divination often involved applying a heated metal pin to a predrilled hole in a tortoise shell or the shoulder blade of a sheep, and the cracking pattern determined the cosmic response to the question. The diviner's task, then, in addition to assuring the correct technique, was to interpret the cracks. The earliest examples of Chinese writing available to us today are the inscriptions on these "oracles bones" indicating the question asked and the significance of the response. The later (Zhou dynasty) technique of fortune-telling with milfoil or yarrow stalks relied on a standard manual of interpretation; responses fell into categories, each associated with a representative image that provided a context in which to interpret the situation of the questioner. The *Classic of Change (Yijing)* is the most famous such manual. In it, language provides indirect access to truth and cosmic forces through the ambiguity of literary images.

To the literate class of officials and diviners, language lay at the heart of relations between humanity and the natural world, the universe as a whole. In an early commentary on the *Classic of Change,* for example, the origin of human culture is associated with observation of natural patterns:

> When in ancient times Lord Bao Xi ruled the world as sovereign, he looked upward and observed the images in heaven and looked downward and observed the models that the earth provided. He observed the patterns on birds and beasts and what things were suitable for the land. . . . Nearby, adopting them from his own person, and afar, adopting them from other things, he thereupon made the eight trigrams in order to become thoroughly conversant with the virtues inherent in the numinous and the bright and to classify the myriad things in terms of their true, innate natures. (Lynn, 1994:77–80)

Later, the literary theorist Liu Xie expanded on this by conceiving of *wen* as "human markings," or the "pattern of humanity" in an organic world where everything has its own pattern:

> Dragon and phoenix show auspicious events in the brilliance of their design; the tiger by his brightness, the leopard by the tended lushness of his spots ever indicate a magnificence of manner. . . . If such things, unaware, possess the radiance of many colors swelling within, how can this human vessel of mind lack its own aesthetic pattern [*wen*]? (Owen, 1985:19)

Explanations like these show important assumptions that underlie use of language in early China: Writing preserves a symbolic connection between humanity and the universe, perceivable within specific concrete literary images that bring us closer to particular events and situations. Among ancient Chinese philosophers, the Daoists exploit literary techniques and images the most, but early Daoists were both imaginative and skeptical about the role of language. Daoist classics like the Lao-zi's *Dao de jing* and *Zhuangzi* question the ability of human language to transmit truths. The seemingly paradoxical opening line of *Dao de jing* (Lao-zi,

1963:57), for instance, states that "the way that can be spoken of is not the constant Way." *Zhuangzi*, one of the earliest repositories of narrative literature in Chinese, compares language to a "fish trap": Once you have caught the fish (meaning), the trap can be disposed of. The narrator Zhuang-zi yearns for a companion who, like him, has transcended the limitations of language to discuss the undiscussable (Zhuang-zi, 1981:140).

Confucius and his followers, though they had a very different worldview, shared with the Daoists a penchant for using analogy and metaphor. In contrast with Daoists, however, the Confucians' faith in the efficacy of language (and anxiety to apply it properly) made them fastidious editors, compilers, and interpreters of texts, with huge consequences for subsequent development of literature. They used writing to connect humanity with universal truths. Their compilation of the *Classic of Poetry (Shi jing)*, the earliest existing collection of Chinese poetry, gave political and moral interpretations of even the most ordinary-sounding folk songs, whether or not it was justifiable, creating a tradition of reading and writing that took such interpretive leaps for granted. Similarly, the earliest historical records and descriptions of archaic rituals and court music became centerpieces of Confucian classical tradition; Confucius declared their value lay in embodying the morally superior ways of ancient kings. In the Confucian tradition, reading and commenting on these texts centered on identifying and abstracting these moral principles and, through teaching and governing, putting them into practice in the contemporary world. The symbolic and interpretive functions of language come through also in Chinese philosophy of Confucius' time and the centuries immediately following. In the next section, we can see how Confucian attitudes toward literature and writing helped set the pattern for the relationship between elite and popular cultures.

■ SINGERS AND POETS

Singing has been the most widespread and lasting medium for expressing personal and collective emotions: love, social grievance, the joys and suffering of labor. These experiences, activities, and emotions are the constant subjects of song, from ancient millet fields and orchards to royal palaces, aristocratic residences, urban taverns, merchants' pleasure gardens, and even today's dance halls and karaoke clubs, and are the source from which all forms of Chinese poetry emerged. Confucians' obsessive interest in the moral powers of literature conditioned the selection, interpretation, and survival of historical, literary, and philosophical texts from the earliest times. For the moral edification of future literate generations, they preserved texts embodying the virtues and moral principles they held most sacred: humanity, decorum, righteousness, and respect for superiors. Poetry was no exception. The literati observed truth and feeling in the songs of the common people and committed some of these songs to writing. But the Confucian filter could never hide the fact that singing, chanting, and telling stories is not always motivated by Confucian virtues. It is said that Confucius compiled the 305 poems of the *Classic of Poetry* from a pool of over 3,000 folk songs chosen to assess the morale of each state, yet even those 305 rarely extol Confucian virtues explicitly. The first of the collection's four sections, the "Airs of the States" *(Guo feng),* makes up about half of the entire collection yet consists largely of love songs, harvest chants, and complaints about government harshness and corruption.

Literati poetry, though, largely moved away from popular themes, immersing itself in the exquisite extravagance of palace life or indulging in obscure metaphysical speculation, using strict complicated formal techniques of rhyme, assonance, alliteration, meter, and tone. After centuries of evolution, poetry was brought to its highest level of artistry in the Tang dynasty by vastly expanding subject matter and themes. Tang poetry was fresh in that it expressed profound insights and powerful emotions from an engaging, familiar perspective. Wang Wei's (699–759) poetry, for instance, embodies the Buddhist transcendence of the individual self through an impersonal immersion into peaceful natural landscapes; the poet literally loses himself in the environment:

> Empty hills, no one in sight,
> only the sound of someone talking;
> late sunlight enters the deep wood,
> shining over the green moss again. (Watson, 1984:200)

In this quatrain, the senses of vision and hearing indicate consciousness, but there is no self, no "I." There is also no sermonizing about the spiritual dangers of attachment to the self and the world.

Li Bai (701–762), whose extravagant, romantic poetic personality has made him a favorite among Western readers, blends the expansive imagination of the *Songs of the South (Chu ci),* a Han dynasty work rich with botanical images and cosmic journeys derived from liturgical shaman chants (Qu, 1985), the paradoxical Daoist wit of *Zhuangzi,* and the reclusive, wine-soaked nature love of Tao Yuanming (a fourth-century poet whose rediscovery was a major catalyst for the Tang dynasty poetic renaissance), with an almost effortless command of existing poetic forms and techniques. In "A Night with a Friend," Li exploits the comfortable roominess of the ancient style to subtly bring together the classic themes of friendship, moonlight, landscape, and wine:

> Dousing clean a thousand cares,
> sticking it out through a hundred pots of wine,
> a good night needing the best of conversation,

> a brilliant moon that will not let us sleep—
> drunk we lie down in empty hills,
> heaven and earth our quilt and pillow. (Watson, 1984:212)

Li Bai's major competitor in the popular imagination for the title of "China's greatest poet" is the slightly younger Du Fu (712–770), who has quite a different poetic voice. People generally first notice Du Fu's gloomy, severe themes and subject matter. But he is also one of the boldest technical innovators, accompanying this progressiveness with a highly traditional (Confucian) attitude about the mission of poetry. From sad narratives of abandoned women to critiques of official neglect of the people's suffering to expression of his personal woes, Du Fu's poetic vision was deeply committed to social aims. Du's "Dreaming of Li Bai" provides an alternative image of the latter poet, down to earth and entangled in the tribulations of society and politics:

> Parting from the dead, I've stifled my sobs,
> but this parting from the living brings me constant pain.
> South of the Yangtze is a land of plague and fever;
> no word comes from the exile.
> Yet my old friend has entered my dreams,
> proof of how long I've pined for him.
> He didn't look the way he used to,
> the road so far—farther than I can guess.
> His spirit came from where the maple groves are green,
> then went back, leaving me in borderland blackness.
> Now you're caught in the meshes of the law—
> how could you have wings to fly with?
> The sinking moon floods the rafters of my room
> and still I seem to see it lighting your face.
> Where you go, waters are deep, the waves so wide—
> don't let the dragons, the horned dragons harm you!
> (Watson, 1984:231)

Though their approaches differ considerably, the greatest Tang dynasty poets expanded the thematic scope of poetry, making it more emotional and personal. There are no Chinese, whether literate or not, who do not at least know who Li Bai and Du Fu are and few who have never heard of Wang Wei. Though these poets were basically refining a difficult, elite cultural form, their resulting renown also made them almost heroic figures, even in the eyes of ordinary people.

In Tang poetry and fiction, it is hard to confidently draw a distinction between popular and elite culture. Some poems of famous Tang poets circulated on all levels of society, even (orally) among illiterates. Especially popular was Bai Juyi (772–846), another teller of sad stories but with less of the sense of moral burden in Du Fu's work; Bai was interested in emotional effects brought about by a tragic story, particularly of a woman. The simplicity of his language, the ease of its rhythms, and his cultivated sensitivity to emotional suffering made him a medieval prototype of the modern singer-songwriter. By his own observation as well as that of his admirers (and detractors), Bai Juyi's poetry had penetrated the breadth of China at all social levels. In Bai Juyi's own words:

> In my travels from Changan to Jiangxi, over a distance of three to four thousand *li*, I have seen my poems written on the walls of village schools, Buddhist monasteries, and wayside inns as well as on the boards of passenger boats. And I have heard my songs sung by students, monks, widows, maidens and men in the streets. (Ch'en, 1961:314)

More interesting evidence of the popular attitude toward elite literature is provided by the huge collection of books and scrolls that were sealed up in the famous Dunhuang grottoes around the tenth century. Rediscovered in 1908, the Dunhuang manuscripts are a repository of Tang Buddhist and secular literature, much of it copied by common people not of the elite literati class. The manuscripts provide an alternative perspective on official literary history: There are texts in many non-Chinese languages and foreign narrative materials and forms even in the Chinese texts, and the collection gives physical evidence of a thriving, nonelite culture of writing and performance. Alongside copies of works by famous writers were found popularized tales from the Buddha's life or the lives of Buddhist saints that incorporate Chinese folklore and history and oral storytelling, as well as semiliterate attempts to imitate or parody elite forms. This is the beginning of a little-recognized trend of Chinese cultural history: From the Tang dynasty on, as the ability to read and write slowly seeped out of the literati's exclusive control, popular, folk, and foreign forms played a larger role in the elite culture itself. The line dividing "elite" from "common" was blurring.

By now it should be evident that I am using the term "popular culture" to refer to the full range of culturally oriented social activities from folk singing to religious ritual to secular performing arts, involving performers and spectators from all social classes. From the late Tang dynasty on, different forms of entertainment for city dwellers (including merchants, laborers, and artisans) as well as for literati begin to influence elite writing. Storytelling in the marketplace and at temple fairs, with its roots in Buddhist popular evangelism, influenced the emergence of written vernacular tales about ordinary people. And the literate class (including semiliterate merchants with highly cultivated tastes) began to develop its own distinctive forms of "popular culture."

Much of this leisure culture of the literate centered on collecting and appreciating exquisite objects (vases, tea bowls, ancient bronzes); fashioning carefully landscaped gardens within private estates; and enjoying various entertainments provided by talented, sophisticated courtesans. Many poems of the major Tang poets praise famous singing and dancing ladies who are no longer always the royal palace courtesans of previous dynasties but often "freelance" talents who might move from palaces to the entourages of rich merchants or officials and back again. Tang poets such as Du Fu, Yuan Zhen (779–831), and Bai Juyi were struck by the sadness of their unstable, transient lives in contrast to the joys and opulence of which and in which they sang. It was in this later part of the Tang that the radically new form of poetry called *ci* began to evolve.

The term *ci* refers to lyrics of popular songs. The art of *ci* consisted of writing new lyrics to familiar songs, usually love songs of central Asian origin that were part of the courtesan's repertoire and widely known at all levels of society. Since poems about professional entertainers began to appear in the high Tang, yet *ci* itself was not commonly used until a century or so later, literati officials of the highest rank seem to have been enjoying performances of the courtesans for some time before becoming artistically interested in the songs being sung. The practice of providing new words was probably widespread long before *ci* were written and included in the corpus of major poets. The "original" lyrics of these songs relating to the song's title are often forgotten. Some of the most famous *ci* written to a given tune have nothing to do with the song's title.

Although in the late Tang *ci* poems were something of a novelty, by the Northern Song dynasty (960–1126), the *ci* form dominated poetic expression. The *shi* forms of regulated verse and quatrain that began during the Han and reached their peak in the high Tang, though still widely practiced (people still write *shi* today), were looked upon as stodgy, old-fashioned, and lifeless. At this point, popular forms successfully invaded the culture of writing, affirming their own style and content; they tolerated less elite distortion, and elite literary forms would never again monopolize writing. Elite writers shifted their emphasis from poetry to fiction and drama.

■ STORYTELLERS AND NOVELISTS

□ Classical Tales

The roots of Chinese fiction are numerous and complex; although vernacular fiction can be confidently traced to oral storytellers manipulating an originally Buddhist tradition of popular evangelism (see Chapter 12), written fictional narrative had already existed in various forms in all kinds of early texts, including poetry, philosophy, and historical and geographical records.

History provided the most powerful narrative models for fiction; ancient works like the Zhou dynasty "Zuo Commentary" on the Spring and Autumn Annals *(Zuo Zhuan)* and the Han dynasty "Records of the Historian" *(Shi Ji)* by Sima Qian were revered throughout Chinese history as models of beautiful writing as well as sources of historical and moral knowledge. Interestingly, though people doubted the existence of ghosts and other supernatural beings as early as the Han dynasty, fictional and factual narrative were not separate categories, and thus narratives of the superhuman and supernatural were viewed as a special type of history. In ancient times, whether a story was true was much less important than whom and what it was about. Such unofficial chronicles included legendary stories about historical figures as well as tales of visitations by ghosts and deities.

However, the narrative is not limited to historical records; some of the most charming and fantastic early stories are retold in the works of Warring States Period philosophers, especially the Daoists (Zhuang-zi, 1981; Lie-zi, 1990). Even more informative about early folk beliefs is *an Account of Emperor Mu's Travels (Mu tianzi zhuan)*. This Zhou dynasty emperor's journeys through his empire, encountering and exchanging poems with the mythical "Queen Mother of the West" (Cheng, 1933–1934). Though unusual in poetry, Qu Yuan's "Encountering Sorrow" from *Songs of the South* in the Han dynasty is another extended narrative of a cosmic journey (Qu, 1985).

Another narrative genre that stressed creativity was imaginative geography. The best-known and perhaps oldest of this latter category is *The Classic of Mountains and Seas (Shanhai jing)*. This work preserves ancient lore about foreign lands organized into a kind of schematic map around the outskirts of the known world (China). *The Classic of Mountains and Seas* and works like it are more descriptive than narrative, but their vocabulary and imagination set the tone for later narrative treatments of fantastic events and journeys. The worldview that underlies *The Classic of Mountains and Seas* clearly reflects China's self-perception as a core of civilization surrounded by frightening, inscrutable, and barbaric peoples and also projects other fears and anxieties suggested by, for example, the frequent mention of fireproof materials and elixirs of immortality in exotic lands.

Within the written traditions, then, the origins of imaginative narrative can be identified with the ancient practice of chronicling the strange and wonderful *(zhiguai)*. Zhiguai emerged during and after the Han dynasty as generally biographical material based on popular accounts that was considered unsuitable for official histories. Such material included fantastic stories of historical figures, biographies of superhuman beings (especially Daoist immortals), and records of miraculous or astonishing events. In the context of popular culture, the *zhiguai* can be viewed along with the *Classic of Poetry* as being one of the earliest existing adoptions of popular or folk materials in the form of writing. But *zhiguai* were often ignored and suppressed by historians concerned with the purity of the textual legacy, and it was not until centuries later that collections like these were actively unearthed and reintroduced into the literary corpus.

An interest in the wondrous mixed with a fascination with love themes and legendary beauties led Tang dynasty literati to experiment with writing more self-consciously crafted tales in classical Chinese modeled on Han dynasty prose. This trend arose not only because of increasing interest in fictional narrative as a form of creative expression but also as a reaction against the stilted, artificial form of "balanced prose" writing *(pianwen)* that prevailed until the late Tang in the civil service examinations discussed in Chapter 4 (Ch'en, 1961:285–317). This can be compared with the attraction to *ci* as a new form of poetry after centuries of overdevelopment of the *shi*. The classical prose movement provided a medium better suited than the ornate, symmetrical *pianwen* to naturalistic expression of emotions and narration of events. Literate gentlemen who converged on cosmopolitan Chang'an (Map 3.1), whether successful in official careers or not, brought with them from their hometowns or from the streets of the capital itself personal experiences and popular tales that helped them produce eerie, moving stories. Despite the formal classicism and political conservatism of the classical prose movement, many of the stories created or passed along by Tang writers like Yuan Zhen and Bai Xingjian (Bai Juyi's brother) became staples of popular literature and performing arts for centuries to come.

Like the *zhiguai*, these "romance tales" *(chuanqi)* included elements of the supernatural and the fantastic; more importantly, they embodied the more personal and realistic emphasis of the Tang dynasty poet-officials. The exploration of emotional and moral dilemmas—represented perhaps best by Yuan Zhen's masterpiece, "The Story of Yingying" *(Yingying zhuan,* Ma and Lau, 1978:139–145)—guaranteed that the narrative material of *chuanqi* would continue to be a major resource for both elite and popular literature in centuries to come. "The Story of Yingying" narrates a chance love affair between the ambitious student Zhang and Yingying, a talented and beautiful young woman languishing in her widowed mother's house. Zhang, however, resolves to leave her and forget about her forever when he goes to the capital for the civil service examinations. The indignant Yingying resigns herself to bitterness and eventually marries someone else but never forgives Zhang for his faithlessness, refusing to see him when he visits her after he has married. "The Story of Yingying" is a classical and emotionally raw rendition of the conflict between the demands of social convention and emotional power that ends tragically, with social convention winning—a far cry from the amusing allegorical fables of the Warring States philosophers, or the strange supernatural chronicles and far-ranging adventures that were the earliest foundations of Chinese fiction.

Yuan Zhen and other writers of *chuanqi* accomplished in fiction what writers had been doing with poetry: exploring values that turned not on rigid or abstract moral principles but on emotional sensitivity and integrity, values that held their own claim to truth but might at times have come into dramatic conflict with the duty-saturated values of Confucianism that represented the mainstream ideology of traditional Chinese society. The artistic elaboration of an emotion-based value system is central to the Tang dynasty's contribution to Chinese literature, and it owed as much for material and themes to the thriving cultures of professional entertainment—singing courtesans, professional dancers—as to poets' and writers' own experiences and imagination.

☐ Vernacular Fiction

This new fashion in the Tang of telling strange, moving, and wondrous stories in terse, classical Chinese is only one strand of the development of Chinese narrative. Even more crucial to the later development of Chinese fiction and drama was the vehicle of oral storytelling (see Figure 13.1) with its roots in Buddhist popular evangelism dating back to the pre-Tang period. The contributions of Buddhism to Chinese literature were not limited to philosophical and spiritual themes but included the techniques and conventions of vernacular storytelling (the inclusion of a moral at the end of a tale, a mixture of poetry and prose, and an emphasis on stories about anonymous, ordinary people) as well. For example, Buddhist source texts like the Sanskrit *Lotus Sutra* (of which Kuramajiva's popular translation appeared as early as 406 B.C.; Watson, 1993:ix) already possessed all these features.

The venue of such storytelling, widespread by the Tang dynasty, was the urban or suburban marketplace. This was the focal point of the Chinese community, the hub of often multicultural commercial transactions, the meeting point of all walks of life from travelers to merchants, farmers, public officials, prostitutes, entertainers. The entire cross-section of Chinese society converged on the marketplace or square, from the county seat to the large mercantile centers and the capital. The square is crowded, and the crowd is as diverse as can be—everyone drawn by the center, the marketplace itself, where everything happens, or where at least you can hear tell of everything. This is where the stories are told, of great sages or heroes real and imaginary, remote in history or just around the corner, full of ordinary people fighting or running from the law, of great generals annihilating their enemies or entangled in political intrigue, and of ghosts, fox-spirits, gods, talking animals, sniveling cowards, and heroic prostitutes. All of this is in the hands of a single storyteller competing for his or her street audience with acrobats, magicians, theatrical troupes, blind balladeers with three-stringed guitars, and other storytellers keeping rhythm with bamboo or metal clappers or drums.

Figure 13.1 Depiction of a Crowd Gathered Around a Storyteller (center right) in the Marketplace of Kaifeng, Capital of the Northern Song Dynasty

Narration as such was not alien to Chinese elite culture; because of the Confucians' obsession with significance and cultural value, some of the earliest historical texts preserved are also some of China's most compelling narratives, and in late imperial times Chinese history became one of the vernacular storyteller's richest resources of material. But the official histories as well as the more exotic materials already discussed could be read only by the literate minority, which was extremely small in ancient and medieval times, and it is difficult to tell whether the same stories were being told among illiterate people at the time. What Buddhist and Buddhist-influenced storytelling had to offer Chinese narrative, then, was a form that lent itself to public performance, thus providing a bridge between literati art and a much broader, illiterate or semiliterate audience. Chinese legends, mythology, and historical records provided the storytellers with new material and themes. One of the most attractive aspects of Chinese historical narrative to the storytelling, theatrical, and ultimately film and television audiences is the combination of moral character (loyalty in particular) and military or fighting prowess of the gallant or knight-errant. Stories of such exploits abounded in the official histories, legendary biographies, and oral tales in the marketplace. As they multiplied in the repertoire of storytellers, many such legends were grouped together in long series of tales, often loosely based on historical events.

One such repository for narrative and lore in Song and Ming dynasty storytelling was the famous story of the Tang dynasty monk Xuan Zang (596–664), who went to India to fetch the complete set of Mahayana Buddhist scriptures; his pilgrimage was described in Chapter 12. As in the past, the exotic foreign journey was a favorite subject of tale spinners with a taste for the bizarre and supernatural. The Xuan Zang narrative was gradually embellished by adding various pilgrim assistants to protect the priest from earthly and otherworldly dangers on the road. Somewhere along the line, this set of stories came into contact with the ancient Indian legends of a Monkey King of overweening ambition, and such a monkey became Xuan Zang's chief disciple.

The resulting story of *The Journey to the West (Xi you ji*, 1592), then, links dozens of existing tales of the fantastic, of overcoming and outwitting animal spirits and supernatural beasts, under the premise of this sacred pilgrimage (Wu, 1977). This chain of episodes is cemented by a common set of characters centering on the monk and the monkey and other pilgrim-guardians, including a gluttonous talking pig and a dragonlike water spirit. The adventures are placed, in turn, into a cosmic context in which the monkey's mission to assist Xuan Zang is understood as penance for his past outrageous acts of mischievous hubris (he tried to overthrow heaven) narrated in the novel's opening chapters. Although the novel maintains a folksy irreverence toward traditional hierarchy, orthodoxy, and morality, the Buddha and his pantheon come out essentially invincible, and the sacred necessity of Xuan Zang's mission is never questioned.

Similar to *The Journey to the West*'s snowballing of popular legends, stories of gallantry and heroism, particularly ones featuring rebellious, unorthodox figures, tended to attach themselves to the Song dynasty rebel uprising of Song Jiang (Hsia, 1971:76). Stories based on these events began to solidify during the Southern Song, gaining a wide audience for their patriotic appeal because of the Southern Song regime's status as almost a government in exile as northern China was overrun by foreign people. These legends associated martial prowess, superhuman physical strength, and an almost brutally straightforward loyalty with China's integrity and the Han race.

These swashbuckling stories coalesced in a sixteenth-century Ming dynasty vernacular novel, the *Outlaws of the Marsh (Shuihu zhuan)*, which narrates the gathering of 108 colorful, Robin Hood–like heroic outlaws through a variety of adventures, in which they ultimately lead a series of successful battles against the Song imperial troops and then surrender out of patriotism and turn their energies toward assisting the Song in suppressing the evil rebel Fang La (Luo, 1981). *Outlaws*, particularly through its contribution of heroic figures like the leader Song Jiang and the colorful heroes Wu Song and Li Kui, is seminal in its contribution to the tradition of martial arts fiction *(wuxia xiaoshuo)*, part of the lifeblood of Chinese popular culture to this day.

For the purposes of the *reading* audience of vernacular fiction, the mere transcription and clever rearrangement of popular oral stories were ultimately limited in their appeal. The Qing dynasty novel *Dream of the Red Chamber (Hong lou meng*, 1791), however, is by all accounts the masterpiece of the full-length, vernacular Chinese novel (Wang, 1992). What people cannot agree on is what makes it so, and an entire scholarly

A Beijing acrobatic performance.

Photo: Robert E. Gamer

tradition has been devoted to this one novel's study and interpretation. Although *Journey to the West* and *Outlaws of the Marsh* string together a vast number of almost unrelated episodes drawn from history, myth, and traditional storytelling material, *Dream* is completely original, with a series of interlocking plots revolving around the declining fortunes of the wealthy families Jia, Xue, Shi, and Wang who have ties to the imperial court. The novel is said to be largely based on the personal experiences of its principal author, Cao Xueqin (1715?–1763). The setting is during the eighteenth century in the final glow of China's last dynasty, the Qing. A grandfather clock in the Jia's mansion hints at China's contact with and the influence of European powers, whose missionary efforts by late Qing times were a conspicuous aspect of the Chinese countryside and port cities.

Dream of the Red Chamber is remarkable in its time for its lack of physical action, the narrative's almost complete confinement to the Jia mansion and the surrounding capital suburbs, and its concentration on the relationships among a core group of young men and women, at the center of which are Bao-yu, second son of the Jia's youngest generation; Xue Bao-chai, the charming, practical woman to whom he is eventually betrothed; and Dai-yu, an ill-starred, frail, and gloomy beauty to whom Bao-yu is more strongly attracted (though the two seem to be able only to make each other unhappy).

This triangle is nestled in countless other relationships and conflicts among these and other families, amid armies of servants, dozens of vividly realized, colorful characters, and lavish descriptions of costume, decorations, and genteel entertainments ranging from tea appreciation to poetry games and theatrical performances. The epic family saga is further placed within a cosmic frame constructed of equal parts of Buddhism and Daoism, in which Bao-yu is cast not only in his earthly form of the effeminate, hypersensitive, and eccentric boy with no scholarly (social, political) ambitions who only likes to be among women, but ultimately as a superfluous stone left over from the mythical goddess Nü Wa's restoration of the damaged masonry of the heavens. This stone is cursed by the gift of consciousness with the desire to experience life in the human world, a wish granted to him by a Buddhist monk and a Daoist priest. Once his fate is sealed, a further adventure on the stone's part forms the supernatural basis of Bao-yu's relationship with Dai-yu: As a Divine Stone Page in the otherworldly Garden of the Goddess of Disillusionment, he is moved by kindness to water a parched fairy plant with dew, which thus incurs a "debt of tears" that Dai-yu must repay in the human world. Most of the other major young women characters are also spirits burdened with debts in heaven or former lives, whereas all the male characters except Bao-yu himself represent the human world, the constricting influences of society, politics, money, and power.

Despite the development of the novel in late imperial China into increasingly unified and complex forms, the vitality of the oral short story was not exhausted by its absorption into novels like *The Journey to the West* and *Outlaws of the Marsh*. As late as the end of the Ming and through the Qing dynasties, prominent connoisseurs of popular literature like Feng Menglong (1574–1646), Ling Mengchu (1580–1644), and Pu Songling (1640–1715) preserved in written form oral storyteller's *(huaben)* tales that were by then as many as several hundred years old. They also offered many original stories. More than any of the forms of fiction discussed so far, these stories feature characters of illiterate classes: merchants, farmers, artisans, entertainers, and prostitutes, always placed in unlikely and awkward situations and often in compelling moral predicaments (Birch, 1958; Ma and Lau, 1978). The plots of such stories rely on multiple coincidences, often also using physical objects to string events together and dramatic, even shocking scenes.

Pu Songling's somewhat later creations, written in classical Chinese rather than the vernacular, are much more homogeneous than the late Ming *huaben* stories edited by Feng and Ling. They more generally reflect the experience and imagination of the young scholar on his way to the city or capital to take part in the civil service examinations, revealing a similarity to the Tang *chuanqi*. In *huaben* tales, scholars encounter beautiful courtesans or other women who make them forget their wives, harm their reputations, or do poorly on the examinations. Pu Songling's scholars, however, are beset by all manner of supernatural beings—ghosts, demons, and fox and snake spirits—who materialize as beautiful women but also somehow get in the way of or complicate the scholar's career or family life (P'u, 1989).

This consistency of plot and narrative perspective speaks to the combination of elements in the character of the Chinese novelist that caused him to fail the civil service examinations and yet become a fertile cultural resource in his own right. It also suggests the commonality of experience among writers and readers of this sort of writing, who were almost exclusively young examination candidates themselves. These elements are equally conspicuous in the Chinese drama, which is heavily reliant on the fictional tradition for narrative material; but this brings us to another strand of the story.

■ PRIESTS AND PLAYWRIGHTS

Until recent years, discussions of Chinese drama in English invariably stress the "belatedness" of its appearance in comparison with other literary genres and in comparison with other cultures. However, recent research on Chinese folk ritual and drama shows that this view uncritically privileges the written literary canon and disregards folk culture. We now know that

Traditional Song drama performed in modern Hangzhou.

the performance practices, modes of representation, and stage conventions on which Chinese theatrical performance is based can be traced far back into shamanistic rituals and exorcisms of evil spirits that continue to be practiced in their primitive form in many parts of China to the present day.

In addition to ritual and folk practices, the performing arts also drew on medieval palace entertainment and urban storytelling. As early as the Song dynasty, both Kaifeng and Hangzhou had bustling theater districts nicknamed "tiles" after their jam-packed audiences (Liu, 1966:162–163). Song "variety plays" opened with a medley followed by a number of short pieces that may not have been linked together by a single story or group of characters. Some of the differences between the northern and southern theater of the Yuan and Ming dynasties were already established.

The link between oral performance and full-fledged operatic drama is substantiated by the Jin dynasty work *The Romance of the Western Chamber (Xi xiang ji zhugong diao),* in which Yuan Zhen's above-mentioned 'Story of Yingying" is presented in "medley" *(zhugong diao)* format (Ch'en, 1994). That is, the story is told in the framework of a musical composition in which successive sections have different musical modes *(diao),* and each section is made up of poems that share a single mode interspersed with prose narrative passages. The reputed author, Master Dong, gave Yuan Zhen's story a happy ending.

Later in the thirteenth century, the *Western Chamber* story was adapted again by Wang Shifu to become perhaps the most famous work of

Chinese drama, the *Xi xiang ji (Romance of the Western Chamber)*, a northern *zaju*. *Zaju* (also called "northern drama") inherited from previous forms like the previously mentioned "medley" the alternation of prose and verse passages, the latter of which were sung to musical accompaniment. The sung parts were limited to a single actor, providing a unity to northern drama further enhanced by its tight, four-act structure. The other major contribution of the Yuan dynasty *zaju* to operatic theater and Chinese literature in general is its unique new form of verse, called *sanqu*. Like the Song dynasty *ci*, *sanqu* represented a further innovation in the coordination of verse with music, allowing for a certain amount of variation and the addition of grammatical particles and colloquial expressions (Liu, 1966:186).

Although the Yuan *zaju* was associated with the capital of Dadu (modern Beijing), the southern drama that had been in existence at least since Song times was associated with the opulent and culturally sophisticated southern cities of Hangzhou and Suzhou. These Southern dramas, also called *chuanqi* like the Tang tales upon which they were often based, were extraordinarily long (running to thirty or forty scenes). They did not rise to central prominence in the history of Chinese theater until the Ming dynasty. There are hundreds of *chuanqi* plays from the Ming and Qing dynasties, but the best known are Gao Ming's *The Lute (Pipa ji)* and especially Tang Xianzu's *Peony Pavilion (Mudan ting)*.

Gao Ming's (c. 1305–c. 1370) *Lute* is based on an old story of a brilliant scholar who, after achieving glory in the civil service examinations, is induced to marry the daughter of the prime minister, though he had left a wife at home and forgets about his ailing parents. After his parents pass away, the scholar is finally reminded of his neglect by his first wife, who slowly works her way to the capital by performing with her lute on the road. Tang Xianzu's (1550–1617) *Peony Pavilion*, also known as *Return of the Soul (Huan Hun Ji)*, is based on a vernacular story and incorporates a supernatural theme of love beyond death (Tang, 1980). It features the popular formula of a well-born young lady coming across a talented scholar, but with the twist that they only meet in their dreams: Before they can get together, the heroine Du Liniang's passion overcomes her and she dies. However, when the scholar encounters Liniang's buried portrait, the power of his love brings her soul back out of the underworld. Now united, they are confronted with the wrath of Du Liniang's incredulous father, but she persuades him the scholar is innocent, emphasizing the importance of feelings over reason. Music and stirring poetry enhance the potency of a whole series of climactic moments and confrontations. The play is a storehouse of lyrical allusions scouring the length of Chinese literary history, as well as a showcase for Tang Xianzu's gift for wordplay and symbolism.

Although later forms of theater, notably the well-known Beijing opera, are of less literary interest than these earlier masterpieces, they do give us valuable hints as to the unique stagecraft and dramaturgy of Chinese drama, of which the texts of the earlier plays give us little idea. For example, although we know that by the Yuan dynasty, dramatic roles had already been reduced into certain stock types—the "old scholar," the "clown," the "painted lady"—it is only by watching the Beijing opera that we can get an idea of how costume and make-up are manipulated to signal these roles (for example, a white spot or spots on the face to indicate a clown). We do not know for sure, but it seems safe to assume that like Beijing opera, earlier forms of theater used few props or scenic backdrops as in Western theater, relying instead on descriptive dialogue, stock gestures, and symbolic objects to suggest location and movement. Finally, the figure of the devoted opera fan, still in existence today, indicates the challenge posed by Chinese theater to the traditional literati's monopoly on literary culture: The visual spectacle of opera along with its acrobatics and musical accompaniment came together to form entertainment of great sophistication that was yet accessible to the illiterate or only partially literate. Oral storytelling, vernacular fiction, and the theater all represent the slippage over the centuries of elite culture from the hands of the literate minority. Modern technological advances were about to create the potential for even greater cultural engagement on the part of the population at large, but new forms of cultural elitism would still maintain a stubborn division between the educated and the "masses."

■ RESISTING MODERN ORTHODOXIES

☐ The May Fourth Movement: Modern Cultural Orthodoxy

The May Fourth Movement is named after a climactic student demonstration at Tiananmen Square (the Gate of Heavenly Peace in front of the Forbidden City in Beijing) on that date in 1919, passionately opposing the weak Chinese government's passive acceptance of humiliating concessions of Chinese territory to Japan in the Treaty of Versailles that concluded World War I (the references to this treaty and movement in Chapters 4, 7, and 11 can give you a sense of the importance of this date). For students and writers, the demonstration represented the culmination of a groundswell of youthful antitraditionalism represented by Chen Duxiu's popular magazine *New Youth (Xin qingnian),* and the literary revolution sponsored by Hu Shi, signified by his promotion of writing forcefully and directly in the modern vernacular.

As in ancient times, cultural progress was still being measured in terms of writing. However, there was a characteristically modern nationalistic side to the May Fourth Movement as well. After decades of humiliating military and diplomatic defeats at the hands of European countries, the United States, and Japan, both popular and elite culture in modern times was saturated by a feeling that these indignities were suffered in large part because China's political and military leaders were too effeminate, lacking in the essential qualities of the *nanzi Han* (loosely translatable as "the virile Chinese man"), the decisive, physically powerful, and charismatic leader for which Chinese history and literature provide numerous models.

May Fourth intellectuals, equipped with Western learning, knowledge of foreign languages, and an acute sense of historical crisis, were making a revolution from above by writing in a new vernacular much closer to everyday speech, using quite different techniques borrowed in part from European novelists and thinkers. They were also writing fiery essays about what the new literature was for—the destruction of old thinking and the construction of a clean, healthy, and fair new China.

The cultural agenda of the May Fourth Movement is well represented by the work of Lu Xun (1881–1936). Lu Xun's short stories represented a break from the past for the most part because they were written in the modern vernacular, a mode of expression until then alien to writing. The stories often tell of a young intellectual returning to his home in the countryside after receiving a foreign education and having being exposed to Western ideas, only to find that he can no longer fit in with the people and landscapes of his youth (Lu, 1990). Unlike most writers that followed him, however, Lu Xun was a master of irony and distortion, and his vision of the world, though stridently politicized, was nightmarish and often bordered on the absurd and sinister.

But instead of signaling a triumph for popular literature, the May Fourth Movement set up a New Culture in opposition to traditional orthodox culture. Thus by the 1920s a clearly defined cultural triangle appeared: (1) traditional Chinese culture, the educational foundation of even the most radical cultural revolutionaries and the target of almost universal and incessant attack by modern writers; (2) the modern New Culture orthodoxy, based on humanism, science, and democracy—all murkily defined—and foreign (largely European) behavior, dress, and thought; and (3) mass media popular culture embodied in newspapers and magazines, radio, and film that began to emerge in the nineteenth century. This third leg of the triangle, like the first, has been neglected and disdained by historians who identify with the May Fourth Movement.

The issue is further complicated by the fact that both theorists and practitioners of the modern "progressive" or "revolutionary" art and literature, particularly in the first half of this century, consciously aligned and identified themselves with "the masses," "popular culture," or "folk culture" even as they transformed and distorted it for their own artistic and ideological ends. Apart from this explicit lip service being paid to the "popular," elites appropriating and distorting some of the same popular forms they criticize should by now seem familiar; it is very much the traditional stance of the custodians of the written word in China.

Not that the May Fourth generation and their leftist successors did not innovate a great deal. The "serious" side of modern Chinese literature, including poetry and drama, ushered in phenomena rare or nonexistent elsewhere, including a universally adopted rhetoric of "cultural hygiene" (a 1983 government-led rectification campaign attacked "cultural pollution" from abroad); the merging of individual subjectivity with national identity; and the idea of art as a dangerous weapon that not only fueled artists' and writers' sense of self-importance but also got them censored, landed them in jail, and even got them killed at a higher rate than in most other parts of the world.

The importance attributed by historians to the May Fourth Movement tends to obscure the even more profound changes in China's cultural activity brought about by the emergence of mass media in the mid–nineteenth century; the literary revolution itself was to a certain extent indebted to these changes. Newspapers, telegraph, telephone, radio, and even the railroad made it possible for a much broader swath of the population to engage in the same cultural activities. Reading news and illustrated fiction in newspapers and magazines and watching motion pictures made available in Shanghai almost as early as in New York, Paris, and London drastically changed the cultural and social life of even the most conservative. Before radical students began to dominate mass media, the commercial print media's audience consisted largely of traditional urban sophisticates similar to the opera buffs discussed in the previous section. Printed advertisements in mass-circulation newspapers, often exploiting graphic images—even accessible to illiterates—as much as text, brought larger audiences to theatrical performances and larger markets to books and magazines. These eye-catching pictures (particularly in commercial print media, but also on billboards, shingles, and flyers) broadened the affected market substantially beyond the literate (Lee and Nathan, 1985).

In the meantime, the higher technology mass media provided more of what a broader audience demanded: not the epoch-making, brooding short stories of Lu Xun, but traditional-style vernacular novels of love, detective stories, fantastic journeys, and the exploits of superhuman martial arts heroes mixed with accounts of real journeys to Europe and the United States. Unfortunately, little of this is available in English translation, but Liu Ts'un-yan's *Chinese Middlebrow Fiction* gives an authentic taste of the miscellanies of the turn of the century and thereafter (Liu, 1984).

May Fourth thinkers associated mass media popular culture with traditional China; they were largely indifferent to or unaware of what was modern (i.e., nontraditional) about it, and so the rejection of traditional-style popular fiction became one of the cornerstones of the movement.

They could not see, for instance the Western influences on Zeng Pu in his *Flower in a Sinful Sea (Niehai hua,* 1905), on Xu Zhenya's *Jade Pearl Spirit (Yuli hun,* 1912), or on Zhang Henshui's *Fate of Tears and Laughter (Tixiao yinyuan,* 1930)—the latter one of the most popular Chinese novels of the twentieth century—because they were presented in the form and language of traditional vernacular fiction. However, just like the vernacular novel and oral storytelling in previous centuries, the very popularity of what Perry Link calls the "literature of comfort" (Link, 1981:196–235) worked against the self-important authority of New Culture and thus took on a progressive value.

This is borne out by the obvious ambivalence of modern writers and critics toward traditional popular literature: Although they call for something radically different to blow away the cobwebs of a morally bankrupt culture, they are at the same time some of its most avid readers and promoters. Lu Xun, one of popular fiction's most strident critics, by assigning grudging praise to late Qing dynasty satirical works like Li Boyuan's *A Brief History of Enlightenment (Wenming xiaoshi,* 1903) and Wu Woyao's *Strange Events Witnessed over Twenty Years (Ershinian mudu zhi guai xianzhuang,* 1907) in his *A Brief History of Chinese Fiction (Zhongguo xiaoshuo shilüe,* 1959), actually guaranteed the continued recognition of these works and others long after the cultural supremacy of the May Fourth Movement had given way to more radical visions. Zheng Zhenduo and Ah Ying (Qian Xingcun), two of modern China's most prominent leftist cultural activists, were also foremost scholars and enthusiasts of late imperial popular culture.

The New Culture movement's attitude toward popular literature was based in part on an unfortunate identification of seriousness with progressiveness: the more fun a work of literature or art, the more suspect its ideology. Underlying this was the prejudice that the practitioners and audience of popular literature were inferior in character and intelligence to the cultural revolutionaries of the May Fourth Movement. Moreover, existing mass-media culture was incorrectly identified with an ill-defined idea of "traditional China," which was overwhelmingly viewed as an evil order to be thoroughly uprooted and eradicated.

In contrast to the May Fourth generation's disdain for humor and frivolity, Lao She (1899–1966), one of modern China's most unique and prolific novelists, at least implicitly defied this disdain. In works like *The Two Mas (Er Ma,* 1931) and *Rickshaw Boy (Luotuo Xiangzi,* 1938), Lao She creates a humorous, satirical vision of modern Chinese society that nevertheless expresses a yearning for something better. Influenced by Charles Dickens among others, Lao She had a mastery of humor unusual for a modern Chinese writer, making readers laugh without trivializing his subject matter or his characters. He exploits the fine line between comedy and tragedy so one is constantly aware of the tragic implications of the comic situations he creates. In *The Two Mas,* he accomplishes this through the cultural and generational misunderstandings created by a Chinese father and son residing in London in the 1920s and the son falling in love with a British woman. In *Rickshaw Boy* he does so in the story of a simple, forthright laborer in Beijing who wants nothing more than to make enough money to buy his own rickshaw but is constantly thwarted by the dishonesty of those around him, the sheer scarcity of wealth, and the military instability of 1930s China.

☐ Leftist Mass Culture

Leftism and communism in China inherited the May Fourth Movement's awkward relationship with popular culture once the movement had passed its prime and the literary revolution gave way to revolutionary literature. By the 1930s, leftist writers and critics occupied important, arguably mainstream positions in the New Culture industry. Old-style popular novels and magazines continued to sell and be written, but their audience was dwindling due to a new generation of readers with Western-style education (whose teachers had often been May Fourth activists like Lu Xun) who inherited the May Fourth hatred for old China. Ding Ling (1904–1985) is representative of the shift from self to society that characterized the 1930s. Her *Diary of Miss Sophie (Shafei nüshi de riji*, 1927), one of the best-known works of modern Chinese literature, narrates through the protagonist's diary entries an ailing young Westernized woman's struggle between desire and reason as she alternately tortures, manipulates, and pursues different male friends. The work can be viewed as taking the innovations of May Fourth literature, already colored by self-obsession, sexuality, and despair, to (or beyond) their logical extremes. But only three or four years after writing this and several similar stories, Ding Ling's narrative personalities were dissolving into the masses, her febrile self-obsession transforming into enthusiastic engagement in social and historical change; she was attempting to align herself, indeed lose herself among, workers and peasants.

This shift need not be viewed as paradoxical: The writer's attempt to become one with the people saturates the fiction, poetry, drama and reportage, and even films of the 1930s. Chinese leftists were much more keenly aware than the May Fourth generation of the power of mass media and better acquainted with its mechanics as well, and this is particularly evident in 1930s Chinese cinema. In *Street Angels (Malu tianshi*, 1937), for example, the familiar entertainment, fun, romance, and sensationalism of Hollywood are all exploited to advance themes of social injustice, class friction, and economic crisis, calling to mind the efforts of Charlie Chaplin. But although leftists seemed at home in the modern mass media, like their predecessors and teachers from the May Fourth movement, they were ambivalent about traditional popular and folk culture.

The urban control over mass media communications and transportation put the countryside at a greater cultural disadvantage than before. This situation has not changed substantially to the present day; the pervasiveness of television has only guaranteed the dissemination of centrally approved information and material, while local popular forms have tended to die out.

Leftists, particularly in rural base areas like Mao Zedong's Jiangxi Soviet, in a desire to unleash the revolutionary potential of the masses, went beyond the limits of literacy and explored traditional performing arts forms as potential vehicles for political propaganda. Viewing Western-style spoken dramas, the legacy of May Fourth, as boring, they turned toward traditional dramatic forms like the *yangge*, a new year's variety show (largely song and dance) with roots in ritual performances like *nuo* exorcism and *Mulian* plays. But in their efforts to remold these forms and inject them with new moralistic content, communists failed to observe many of the features that made them work, from their coordination with the lunar calendar and characteristic bawdiness and irreverence to the formal aspects of performance and relationship between form and content. The "new *yangge*," by displacing the old and having little appeal in itself (being an incongruous patchwork quilt of the traditional and the modern), effectively wiped out *yangge* from the areas in which it was promoted (Holm, 1991). This is characteristic of the Communist Party's adoption of all kinds of traditional forms clear through the Cultural Revolution (1966–1976): from storytelling to comedic dialog, from music to drum singing to dance, the Communist Party had a tendency to ruin popular, traditional art forms in the attempt to make "modern" and useful.

□ Alternative Voices

There were at the same time modern Chinese writers not so committed to the social functions of literature as such. Shen Congwen and Xiao Hong, for example, brought to modern literature a lyrical vision of the rural countryside in which the familiar questions of national identity, ethnic outrage, and indignation at the Japanese invasions took a back seat to the vivid, subjective recreation of the rhythms and emotional structure of rural life. Both of these writers discovered and constructed a new aesthetic in the life of the Chinese countryside that had never existed in Chinese narrative literature before but also bore no close resemblance or debt to Western literary forms.

Meanwhile, particularly during World War II, popular fiction was making a comeback and achieved unprecedented success in the novels of Eileen Chang (Zhang Ailing). In a way, Eileen Chang was the first truly modern writer in her open defiance of one of the most sacred credos of Chinese literary culture, that literature must have a positive social function.

Chang's "modern *chuanqi*" take the mood of traditional romantic tales—conflicts between emotional fulfillment, social obligations, and material gain; the jealousy, manipulation, and open struggle among wives and concubines; love triangles; and so forth, bring them into the cultural soup of modern China and expand them into a psychological dimension replete with dark and unpredictable personalities and even insanity (e.g., "The Golden Cangue"). One of Chang's most innovative contributions to modern literature is dispassionate narration of the experience of revolution and agricultural reform (an unthinkable sacrilege for a leftist writer) in such works as *Love in a Barren Land* (*Chidi zhi lian,* 1954) and *Rice-Sprout Song* (*Yangge,* 1953). Eileen Chang's importance, ignored by leftist literary historians, has been vindicated not only through the influential assessments of C. T. Hsia (1971) and Edward Gunn (1980) but also through her inspiration of a whole generation of contemporary writers in all of the Chinas, from Wang Anyi in Shanghai and Lillian Lee in Hong Kong to Li Ang and Yuan Qiongqiong in Taiwan.

□ Contemporary Literature and Culture in the Three Chinas

Eileen Chang's predicament in 1949—whether to stay in China after the communist takeover and years of bitter civil war or go abroad and continue her career free of pressure from political persecution—was probably difficult only for personal reasons, but it was emblematic of the path of modern Chinese elite and popular cultures. Many gifted writers decided to stay; some, like Shen Congwen, sadly never wrote again, whereas others like Lao She adopted, willingly or not, a rhetoric and mentality vastly different from those of the works that established their reputations. Writing in the 1950s and 1960s, one was largely compelled to extol the new society, and even courageous criticisms were deeply entangled in the ideology of literature in the service of politics alone. Eileen Chang's vision would have been even less tenable than Shen Congwen's.

Modern Chinese literary history is generally marked out in terms of cataclysmic political or historical events. The importance of the May Fourth Movement to modern Chinese literature has already been noted, but there were to be many more such dates, including the anticommunist purge of 1927, the Japanese invasion of Manchuria on September 18, 1931, the outbreak of war with Japan in 1937, the rape of Nanjing in 1938, and the communist victory in 1949. When we get to 1949, we tend to think of things in more geographical terms, imagining completely separate cultures in contemporary mainland China, Taiwan, and Hong Kong.

This view, however, is becoming problematic. Transformation within the cultural scenes on both sides of the Taiwan straits complicates the issue, as does the give and take between both Taiwan and mainland China on the one hand and Hong Kong on the other. Moreover, both mainland China and Taiwan after 1949 had their own cataclysmic political events that are of comparable to those in the period before the civil war.

Taiwan's cultural scene throughout the 1950s, though perhaps less oppressive than that of mainland China, was still profoundly politicized. The Nationalist Party allowed and encouraged literary and artistic visions tied to the conviction that the civil war was not over and that those who fled to Taiwan and other places after 1949 would eventually return home (Lau, 1983:x–xi). But as the Nationalists' position in Taiwan solidified, a new generation of writers too young to remember the war grew up in the 1960s in a society oriented more toward economic development than military goals or political purity, a society much more saturated with mass media and popular culture, including television and a burgeoning film industry. The educational background of the newer generation of Taiwan writers (many of whom studied at the University of Washington or the International Writing Program at the University of Iowa) also led to a remarkable upsurge in the late 1950s through the early 1970s of modernist poetry and fiction in Taiwan.

The works of Ch'en Ying-chen, Huang Ch'un-ming, and Wang Chen-ho, all writers who in one way or another resisted the current of pro-American sentiment and feverish economic development, best represent this period in Taiwanese literature. These writers, whether consciously or not, preserve the modern Chinese tradition of literature as the voice of opposition to authority established by Lu Xun. They were against the status quo in Taiwan without being pro-Beijing—no small achievement under the near-totalitarian political atmosphere of Taiwan in the 1960s.

Li Yongping is often described as a conduit of "native soil literature" *(xiangtu wenxue),* which focused on themes of home, belonging, cultural identity, and the rural Chinese experience; Shen Congwen is in some sense the spiritual ancestor of native soil literature in Taiwan. Native soil writers resisted both the at-times-affected modernism of the previous generation and the more commercialized, movie- and television-drama script phase that many writers went into in Taiwan in the late 1970s and early 1980s. They attempted to create or preserve a culture that belonged to Taiwan above all, as well as the ideal of a socially engaged literature that seemed to be fading from the modern Chinese cultural horizon in the face of feverish economic expansion. However, the lifting of martial law with the death of Chiang Kai-shek in 1975, the deregulation of journalism in 1986, and the gradual implementation of general democratic elections throughout the 1990s have led to a slackening of political intensity in Taiwanese literature, and its displacement by the popular literary marketplace as an important factor in literary success.

In mainland China, the deaths of Mao Zedong and Zhou Enlai in 1976, punctuated with particular severity by the devastating Tangshan earthquake, marked the end of an era of apparently blind faith in communism, with profound effects on the cultural scene. In the ensuing years, the rise of Deng Xiaoping and a new vision of the mission of the Communist Party and the trial and imprisonment of the "Gang of Four" for crimes committed during the anarchic Cultural Revolution set the tone for the cultural scene of the 1980s, which ushered in the rehabilitation of cultural figures who had been persecuted since the antirightist campaign of 1958 and had been in and out of prison and labor reform over the ensuing twenty years. Some of the more prominent of these, like Wang Meng, were promoted to important posts, whereas others like Liu Binyan were, in part through the good graces of such appointees, enthusiastically promoted in the mainstream literary press and experienced a new surge of creative work (Link, 1983). There was an outpouring of "scar" literature, humanist literature, and literature of historical reflection that reaffirmed the importance of intellectuals and artists after decades of persecution and tried to derive meaning and spiritual comfort from the therapeutic act of *suku* (recounting bitterness).

However, the literature written during this stage (in the early 1980s) did not differ in any essential way from the familiar conventions of socialist realism: Writers seemed to still accept the premise that literature's highest aim is the realistic depiction of social reality in progressive transformation, as Mao Zedong had himself called for in his 1942 "Talk at the Yan'an Conference on Literature and Art." This was merely a more genuine and honest way of approaching the task than had been common throughout the 1960s and 1970s, in which the bleak truths of contemporary reality were concealed under a false mask of idealism.

Around 1985, a new generation of writers emerged, writers who were too young to have gone through and to understand the turbulent and bewildering persecutions of the older writers since the antirightist campaign. These writers, like Ah Cheng, Zheng Wanlong, and Zhang Chengzhi, were children or teenagers during the Cultural Revolution. Many had lost a good portion of their education and held a much different view of contemporary Chinese social and cultural reality than the older generation. This view is reflected in their works, which are much less confident in the literary mission of social reform taken for granted until then in mainland China.

One of the most conspicuous trends of these writers' first departures from socialist realism is a mainland Chinese version of native soil literature referred to as "searching-for-roots literature" *(xungen wenxue)*. Unlike the more innocently lyrical efforts of Shen Congwen and Xiao Hong, searching for roots involves a more pronounced metaphysical mission derived in part from translations of Western philosophy and literature and in part from the rediscovery of aspects of Chinese literati and folk culture that had been suppressed in the Chinese communist educational curriculum. These writers also share an interest in rewriting the rural experience without the formulas and heavy hand (with class villains and heroic work-ers) that was normal within the communist cultural milieu since the Yan'an days of the early 1940s. This cohort of writers inspired the resurgence of films in the mid-1980s, most notably with Zhang Yimou's debut film, *Red Sorghum*, based on the novella of the same title by Mo Yan, and Chen Kaige's adaptation of Ah Cheng's *The King of Children* in 1988.

The kind of critical retrospection represented by searching-for-roots fiction resonated with the concurrent appearance of Bo Yang's *The Ugly Chinaman* and Sun Longkee's *The Deep Structure of Chinese Culture* (Chinese works from Taiwan and the United States, respectively), adding up to a general mood of unstinting and even overwrought cultural self-criticism on the part of Chinese intellectuals. One of the lasting results of this trend was the reemergence of the intellectual as a cultural commenta-tor, even a judge of contemporary cultural phenomena and foreign intel-lectual and cultural trends, for the first time after decades of Maoist dis-dain for intellectuals. Today, although the institutional status of intellectuals is unstable, from underpaid university professors to publish-ing entrepreneurs to up-and-coming voices in North American and Euro-pean universities, their identity as spokespersons for, interpreters, and crit-ics of Chinese culture has become firmly entrenched. Beginning with *The Deep Structure of Chinese Culture* and the *River Elegy* television series discussed in a moment, one of the primary tasks of the latest generation of Chinese intellectuals has been to explore recent Western theoretical ap-proaches, from feminism to liberal Marxism to cultural studies, to shed new light on Chinese culture, both traditional and modern.

Another ingredient in the cultural brew that had been fermenting throughout the late 1980s was a confidence or hope that ascendancy of the relatively liberal Deng Xiaoping regime could end totalitarianism in China. This hope kept the literature of the mid-1980s pinned under the continuing moral burden of history inherited from previous generations of modern Chinese writers. The Tiananmen Square massacre of June 1989 put an end to that hope, at least temporarily, and indirectly cast doubt on the necessity of literature's moral burden in mainland China for the first time in the century. Post-1989 writings retained many aspects that had been developing before the suppression of the democracy movement, no-tably a multifaceted fascination with pre-1949 China, a taste for the exotic, and a burgeoning ethnic nationalism. Literature also became more play-ful, and clear lines between "serious" literature and art and television, ad-vertising, and entertainment film began to fade.

The shift of box office interest from the films of Chen Kaige *(Yellow Earth, The King of Children, Farewell My Concubine)*, whose path-break-ing reenvisioning of modern China is nevertheless committed to (at times painfully transparent or banal) historical moral themes, to those of Zhang Yimou *(Red Sorghum, Raise the Red Lantern, Ju Dou, To Live)*, wrapped up in engaging stories and extravagantly beautiful images and colors and in which moral concerns become just another ingredient in his fragrant cinematic soup, is emblematic of parallel transformations within the realm of literature. Like Chen Kaige, Zhang Yimou makes a special point of adapting the fictional works of contemporary writers, and his choices reflect changes in literary priorities after 1989, even when the works in question were from before that time.

It seems likely that the pop culture rediscovery of traditional and interwar China will continue for some time; there may even be a more genuine resurgence (rather than freeze-dried preservation) of traditional performing arts. However, the temptation to fall into ruts has already proven irresistible to some filmmakers. Take, for example, the formula of building a movie around a family or village that depends for its survival on a traditional craft: Already we have seen films about liquor brewers, cloth dyers, rice-tofu makers, ginseng growers, sesame oil squeezers, and even firecracker makers, not to mention Beijing opera actors. There is also a tendency like that of the traditional theater to consolidate characters into stock roles, particularly in films with rural settings: the ancient village elder, the often mute and always male village idiot, the tautly sexual young woman and her two or three virile suitors. It is not surprising, then, that a village has been constructed in barren northern Shaanxi province for the sole purpose of shooting these so-called Chinese westerns. Few people have caught the irony that this locale was the crucible in which the Chinese Communist Party established its political and social order in the 1930s and 1940s.

These developments in mainland Chinese film owe much to the formulas of Taiwan and especially Hong Kong entertainment film, which in turn descended from the lively Shanghai film industry of the 1920s–1940s. In keeping with the pulse of traditional Chinese popular culture, film in Hong Kong draws heavily upon traditional sources like gallant fiction or vernacular tales of love and the supernatural. Even when the setting is contemporary, plots often center around traditional martial arts, chivalric virtues and values, and outlaws and police work. Much short vernacular fiction since the Yuan dynasty consisted of detective stories, with wise magistrates like Judge Pao or Judge Dee as their heroes.

These tendencies also strongly influence television in the three Chinas, where long serial dramas reenact or completely rewrite familiar fictional or historical stories. However, contemporary domestic drama commands a much more conspicuous presence on television than in the cinema. In mainland China, such melodramas as *Yearning (Kewang)* and *Tales from the Editorial Department (Bianjibu De Gushi)*, though refreshingly free from the contrived moral teaching of earlier programming, often serve as barometers of sensitive social and cultural issues. Even more so was the ambitious 1986 documentary *River Elegy (He shang)*, which portrays the Chinese people's futile attempts across millennia to come to terms with the cruel whims of the Yangtze River as suggestive of the people's helplessness under communist rule.

In contrast, Wang Shuo, one of the chief architects of the contemporary Chinese soap opera, reintroduces humor and irreverence with no moral strings attached. Starting out as a screenwriter of ordinary television series gave Wang insight into mechanisms of melodrama that let him create outrageously humorous situations by thwarting audience expectations and embedding inconceivable surprises. But he is best known for his characters: cynical, lackadaisical Beijingers whose moral blankness and black humor are strangely refreshing (Barmé and Jaivin, 1992:217–247).

Closer to the streets, screenplays and novels by Wang Shuo, lurid detective fiction, film magazines, martial arts novels, sex manuals, tales of the paranormal or the superhuman feats of *qigong* (the art of vital force) masters, and English language textbooks and cassettes, all clutter the most reliable indicator of mainland Chinese consumers' cultural tastes—streetside bookstalls. Whether just a tarp laid out on the sidewalk, a folding table, or a full-fledged shack with yards of shelving, bookstalls are currently the backbone and richest source of information on contemporary popular literature. State-run bookstores, whose inventory is determined by the government's cultural policies, tell you very little about what Chinese people want to read, but the bookstall's very survival depends on its knowledge of the market.

Independent book and magazine peddlers often sell unauthorized printings, banned books like the sensual Ming dynasty novel *Plum in the Golden Vase*, previously banned collections of literary works like the 1930s essays of Liang Shiqiu and Lin Yutang, or books smuggled from Taiwan and Hong Kong. Biographies of famous historical figures sell very well, whether written by Chinese authors or translated from foreign languages. Certain books by Western authors about China, like Robert van Gulik's *Sexual Life in Ancient China* and Ross Terrill's biographies of Mao Zedong and Jiang Qing appear in usually unauthorized translations, selling many times better than the most popular books distributed through normal channels. Western literature, previously represented in Chinese almost exclusively by nineteenth-century classics and a handful of award-winning twentieth-century works, took on a more popular guise in the 1980s with the appearance of books by authors like Sidney Sheldon at about the same time as series like *Dynasty* and *Falcon Crest* appeared on television. This, of course, strongly influenced Chinese people's perception of the United States.

Teahouses are still fixtures in the cities and towns of southwestern China, set up with bamboo furniture in old pavilions or makeshift bamboo shacks with thatched roofs. In such places in the past, you would have enjoyed the entertainments of a storyteller or Chinese opera arias as you chatted with your friends, sipping a bowl of tea and eating melon seeds and other snacks. Now teahouses almost invariably play videotapes of

A streetside bookstall.

Hong Kong action films with the volume at the highest possible level. Another favorite entertainment is karaoke, a Japanese invention in which you sing along with popular recordings you select in a cocktail lounge setting. Karaoke bars, popular in Hong Kong and Taiwan for years, have now already taken mainland China by storm. Although it would be easy to criticize the violent action films blaring in teahouses and the wildfire spread of karaoke, one can also see the distinctive marks of traditional Chinese popular culture in these new high-tech guises. We like to imagine traditional Chinese entertainments as being refined and genteel, but there is no reason to believe that traditional teahouses, theaters, and brothels were any less boisterous and chaotic than modern ones. "Boisterousness" (*renao,* literally, "hot and noisy")—may be one of the defining characteristics and values of Chinese popular culture.

■ CONCLUSION

The apparent triumph of popular culture over the elite in contemporary China makes an apt ending to this account of Chinese literature and popular culture. Perhaps the most significant contribution of popular culture to elite (written) literature throughout the ages is its challenge to orthodox moral values and literary forms with an alternative set of values based on sensitivity and emotional response. This is the serious message underlying its comic subversions of or perfunctory nods toward conventional morality—alternative canons that extol not moral excellence (as did the *Classic of Poetry* for the Confucians) or technical artistry, but rather grace, generosity of spirit, a great capacity for love, and emotional integrity.

These values underlie, for instance, the alternate canon of Jin Shengtan, an influential seventeenth-century editor and literary critic who honored as the "Six Works of Genius" the masterpieces of their respective genres: Qu Yuan's "Encountering Sorrow," the *Zhuangzi, Records of the Historian*, the poems of Du Fu, *Outlaws of the Marsh*, and *The Romance of the Western Chamber*. The works in Jin's canon have in common— along with a marginal relation to the orthodox classics of Confucianism, which were the common denominator of everyone's literacy—values of emotional integrity, intuition, and experiential immediacy.

Feng Menglong, a late Ming dramatist and editor of vernacular short stories and an avid transcriber of popular tunes and folk songs as well, was perhaps one of the earliest figures in China to offer vocal defense of the unique values of popular cultural forms:

> In this world, the literary minds are few, but the rustic ears are many. Therefore, the short story relies more on the popularizer than on the stylist. Just ask the storyteller to describe a scene on the spot, and it will gladden and startle, sadden and cause you to lament; it will prompt you to draw the sword; at other times to bow deeply in reverence, to break someone's neck, or to contribute money. The timid will be made brave; the lewd chaste; the niggardly liberal; and the stupid and dull, perspiring with shame. Even though you would recite every day the *Classic of Filial Piety* and the *Analects,* you would never be moved as swiftly and profoundly as by these storytellers. Alas! Could such results be achieved by anything but popular colloquial writing? (Liu, 1966:216)

By emphasizing the popular underside of traditional Chinese culture on the one hand and the persistent traditional underside of modern Chinese culture on the other, I do not mean to claim that Chinese cultural forms are essentially unchanging; only that a large portion of cultural activity in China tends to flourish quite outside the power of cultural elites to channel, control, or appropriate it. Cultural orthodoxies are always built upon a dazzling profusion of cultural activity, commonly drawing material and techniques from it.

The idea of civil service as the only appropriate goal for the cultivation of literacy and knowledge remains prevalent in the various Chinas (mainland China, Taiwan, Hong Kong, Singapore, and the Chinese diaspora throughout the world), only partially displaced by the modern values of professionalism, science, individualism, and the autonomy of art. This is one reason the dialectics of popular and elite, entertainment and edification, common and sophisticated remain at the center of Chinese debates on culture to the present day (Zha, 1995), as they have throughout the ages. The current ascendancy of popular culture is cause for celebration only insofar as it can foster those aspects that made traditional Chinese popular culture both impossible to ignore and yet impossible for the literati to completely assimilate.

■ NOTE

I would like to express here the indebtedness of this chapter to my mentors in traditional Chinese literature: Victoria Cass, C. T. Hsia, and Paul Rouzer.

■ BIBLIOGRAPHY

□ Classical Literature and Poetry

Ch'en, Shou-yi. 1961. *Chinese Literature: A Historical Introduction.* New York: Ronald Press.

Confucius. 1979. *The Analects.* Trans. D. C. Lau. New York: Penguin Books.

de Bary, William Theodore, Wing-tsit Chan, and Burton Watson (eds.). 1960. *Sources of Chinese Tradition.* New York: Columbia University Press.

Forney, Matt. 1998. "People's Theater." *Far Eastern Economic Review* 161, no. 3 (January 15):48–50.

Lao-zi. 1963. *Tao Te Ching.* Trans. D. C. Lau. New York: Penguin Books.

Lie-zi. 1990. *The Book of Lieh-tzu: A Classic of the Tao.* Trans. A. C. Graham. New York: Columbia University Press.

Liu, Wu-chi. 1966. *An Introduction to Chinese Literature.* Bloomington: Indiana University Press.

Lynn, Richard John. 1994. *The Classic of Changes: A New Translation of the I Ching as Interpreted by Wang Bi.* New York: Columbia University Press.

Owen, Stephen. 1985. *Traditional Chinese Poetry and Poetics: Omen of the World.* Madison: University of Wisconsin Press.

Qu Yuan. 1985. *The Songs of the South: An Anthology of Ancient Chinese Poems by Qu Yuan and Other Poets.* Trans. David Hawkes. New York: Penguin Books.

Watson, Burton. 1971. *Chinese Lyricism: Shih Poetry from the Second to the Twelfth Century.* New York: Columbia University Press.

——— (ed.). 1984. *The Columbia Book of Chinese Poetry: From Early Times to the Thirteenth Century.* New York: Columbia University Press.

——— (ed.). 1989. *The Tso Chuan: Selections from China's Earliest Narrative History.* Trans. Burton Watson. New York: Columbia University Press.

Yu, Pauline. 1987. *The Reading of Imagery in the Chinese Poetic Tradition.* Princeton: Princeton University Press.

Zhuang-zi. 1981. *Chuang-Tzu: The Seven Inner Chapters and Other Writings from the Book Chuang-tzu.* Trans. A. C. Graham. London and Boston: Allen and Unwin.

☐ Tales, Storytelling, and Vernacular Novels

Birch, Cyril (ed.). 1958. *Stories from a Ming Collection: Translations of Chinese Short Stories Published in the Seventeenth Century*. New York: Grove Press.

Cao, Xueqin, and E. Gao. 1973–1986. *The Story of the Stone*. Trans. David Hawkes and John Minford. New York: Penguin Books.

Cheng, Te-k'un. 1933–1934. "The Travels of Emperor Mu." *Journal of the North China Branch of the Royal Asiatic Society* 64:124–142; 65:128–149.

Hanan, Patrick. 1981. *The Chinese Vernacular Story*. Cambridge: Harvard University Press.

Hegel, Robert E. 1981. *The Novel in Seventeenth-Century China*. New York: Columbia University Press.

Hsia, C. T. 1996. *The Classic Chinese Novel: A Critical Introduction*. Ithaca: Cornell University East Asia Program.

Johnson, David, Andrew J. Nathan, and Evelyn S. Rawski (eds.). 1985. *Popular Culture in Late Imperial China*. Berkeley: University of California Press.

Li Yu. 1990. *The Carnal Prayer Mat [Rou putuan]*. Trans. Patrick Hanan. New York: Ballantine Books.

Liu, Ts'un-yan (ed.). 1984. *Chinese Middlebrow Fiction from the Ch'ing and Early Republican Eras*. Hong Kong: Chinese University Press.

Luo, Guanzhong. 1981. *Outlaws of the Marsh*. Trans. Sidney Shapiro. Bloomington: Indiana University Press.

———. 1994. *Three Kingdoms: A Historical Novel*. Trans. Moss Roberts. Berkeley: University of California Press.

Ma, Y. W., and Joseph S. M. Lau (eds.). 1978. *Traditional Chinese Stories: Themes and Variations*. New York: Columbia University Press.

Plaks, Andrew H. (ed.). 1977. *Chinese Narrative: Critical and Theoretical Essays*. Princeton: Princeton University Press.

P'u, Sungling. 1989. *Strange Stories from Make-Do Studio*. Trans. Victor H. and Denis C. Mair. Beijing: Foreign Languages Press.

Rolston, David L. 1990. *How to Read the Chinese Novel*. Princeton: Princeton University Press.

Wang, Jing. 1992. *The Story of Stone: Intertextuality, Ancient Chinese Stone Lore, and the Stone Symbolism in Dream of the Red Chamber, Water Margin, and the Journey to the West*. Durham, NC: Duke University Press.

Watson, Burton (ed.). 1993. *The Lotus Sutra*. Trans. Burton Watson. New York: Columbia University Press.

Wu, Cheng'en. 1958. *Monkey: Folk Novel of China*. Trans. Arthur Waley. New York: Grove Press.

———. 1977. *The Journey to the West*. Trans. Anthony C. Yu. Chicago: University of Chicago Press.

Xiao-xiao-sheng. 1993. *The Plum in the Golden Vase, or Chin P'ing Mei*. Trans. David Tod Roy. Princeton: Princeton University Press.

☐ Mass Media and Popular Culture in Modern China

Ah Cheng. 1990. *Three Kings: Three Stories from Today's China*. Trans. Bonnie S. McDougall. London: Collins Harvill.

Barlow, Tani E., and Gary J. Bjorge (eds.). 1989. *I Myself Am a Woman: Selected Writings of Ding Ling*. Boston: Beacon Press.

Barmé, Geremie, and Linda Jaivin (eds.). 1992. *New Ghosts, Old Voices: Chinese Rebel Voices*. New York: Random House.

Barmé, Geremie, and John Minford (eds.). 1988. *Seeds of Fire: Chinese Voices of Conscience.* New York: Hill and Wang.

Berninghausen, John, and Ted Huters (eds.). 1976. *Revolutionary Literature in China: An Anthology.* White Plains, NY: M. E. Sharpe.

Chang, Yvonne Sung-sheng. 1993. *Modernism and the Nativist Resistance: Contemporary Chinese Fiction from Taiwan.* Durham and London: Duke University Press.

Chi, Pang-yuan (ed.). 1975. *An Anthology of Contemporary Chinese Literature: Taiwan, 1949–1974.* Taipei: National Institute for Compilation and Translation.

Denton, Kirk A. 1996. *Modern Chinese Literary Thought: Writings on Literature, 1893–1945.* Stanford: Stanford University Press.

Dolezelova-Velingerova, Milena (ed.). 1980. *The Chinese Novel at the Turn of the Century.* Toronto: University of Toronto Press.

Faurot, Jeannette L. (ed.). 1979. *Chinese Fiction from Taiwan: Critical Perspectives.* Bloomington: Indiana University Press.

Feng, Zong-Pu. 1998. *The Everlasting Rock: A Novel.* Trans. Aimee Lykes. Boulder: Lynne Rienner Publishers.

Goldblatt, Howard (ed.). 1995. *Chairman Mao Would Not Be Amused: Fiction from Today's China.* New York: Grove Press.

Goldman, Merle (ed.). 1977. *Modern Chinese Literature in the May Fourth Era.* Cambridge: Harvard University Press.

Gunn, Edward M. 1980. *Unwelcome Muse: Chinese Literature in Shanghai and Peking, 1937–1945.* New York: Columbia University Press.

Gunn, Edward (ed.). 1983. *Twentieth-Century Chinese Drama.* Bloomington: Indiana University Press.

Holm, David. 1991. *Art and Ideology in Revolutionary China.* Oxford: Oxford University Press.

Hsia, C. T. 1971. *A History of Modern Chinese Fiction.* 2d ed. New Haven: Yale University Press.

Hsu, Vivian Ling (ed.). 1981. *Born of the Same Roots: Stories of Modern Chinese Women.* Bloomington: Indiana University Press.

Hung, Chang-tai. 1994. *War and Popular Culture: Resistance in Modern China, 1937–1945.* Berkeley: University of California Press.

Kinkley, Jeffrey C. (ed.). 1985. *After Mao: Chinese Literature and Society, 1978–1981.* Cambridge: Harvard University Press.

Lau, Joseph S. M. (ed.). 1983. *The Unbroken Chain: An Anthology of Taiwan Fiction Since 1926.* Bloomington: Indiana University Press.

Lau, Joseph S. M., and Howard Goldblatt (eds.). 1995. *The Columbia Anthology of Modern Chinese Literature.* New York: Columbia University Press.

Lau, Joseph S. M., and Timothy Ross (eds.). 1976. *Chinese Stories from Taiwan: 1960–1970.* New York: Columbia University Press.

Lee, Leo Ou-fan, and Andrew Nathan. 1985. "The Beginnings of Mass Culture: Journalism and Fiction in the Late Ch'ing and Beyond." Pp. 360–395 in David Johnson, Andrew J. Nathan, and Evelyn S. Rawski (eds.), *Popular Culture in Late Imperial China.* Berkeley: University of California Press.

Leyda, Jay. 1972. *Dianying/Electric Shadows: An Account of Films and the Film Audience in China.* Cambridge: MIT Press.

Link, E. Perry, Jr. 1981. *Mandarin Ducks and Butterflies: Popular Fiction in Early Twentieth-Century Chinese Cities.* Berkeley: University of California Press.

——— (ed.). 1983. *People or Monsters? and Other Stories and Reportage from China After Mao.* Bloomington: Indiana University Press.

Link, E. Perry, Jr., Richard Madsen, and Paul G. Pickowicz (eds.). 1989. *Unofficial China: Popular Culture and Thought in the People's Republic.* Boulder: Westview Press.

Liu, Lydia He. 1995. *Translingual Practice: Literature, National Culture, and Translated Modernity*. Stanford: Stanford University Press.

Liu, Ts'un-yan (ed.). 1984. *Chinese Middlebrow Fiction from the Ch'ing and Early Republican Eras*. Hong Kong: Chinese University Press.

Lu Xun. 1990. *Diary of a Madman and Other Stories*. Trans. William A. Lyell. Honolulu: University of Hawaii Press.

Shen Congwen. 1982. *The Chinese Earth: Stories by Shen Ts'ung-wen*. Trans. Ching Ti and Robert Payne. New York: Columbia University Press.

Spence, Jonathan D. 1982. *The Gate of Heavenly Peace: The Chinese and Their Revolution, 1895–1980*. New York: Penguin Books.

Su Tong. 1993. *Raise the Red Lantern: Three Novellas*. Trans. Michael S. Duke. New York: William Morrow.

———. 1995. *Rice*. Trans. Howard Goldblatt. New York: William Morrow.

Tai, Jeanne (ed.). 1989. *Spring Bamboo: A Collection of Contemporary Chinese Stories*. New York: Random House.

Wang Anyi. 1989. *Baotown*. Trans. Martha Avery. New York: W. W. Norton.

Wang, David Der-wei. 1992. *Fictional Realism in Twentieth-Century China: Mao Dun, Lao She, Shen Congwen*. New York: Columbia University Press.

Wang, David Der-wei, and Jeanne Tai (eds.). 1994. *Running Wild: New Chinese Writers*. New York: Columbia University Press.

Widmer, Ellen, and David Der-wei Wang (eds.). 1993. *From May Fourth to June Fourth: Fiction and Film in Twentieth Century China*. Cambridge: Harvard University Press.

Wu, Dingbo, and Patrick D. Murphy. 1994. *Handbook of Chinese Popular Culture*. Westport, CT: Greenwood Press.

Wu, Dingbo, and Patrick D. Murphy (eds.). 1989. *Science Fiction from China*. New York: Praeger.

Xiao Hong. 1979. *The Field of Life and Death and Tales of Hulan River: Two Novels by Hsiao Hung*. Trans. Howard Goldblatt. Bloomington: Indiana University Press.

Zha, Jianying. 1995. *China Pop: How Soap Operas, Tabloids, and Bestsellers Are Transforming a Culture*. New York: New Press.

Zhang, Xudong. 1997. *Chinese Modernism in the Era of Reforms: Cultural Fever, Avant-Garde Fiction, and the New Chinese Cinema*. Chapel Hill, NC: Duke University Press.

Zhang, Yingjin. 1996. *The City in Modern Chinese Literature and Film: Configurations of Space, Time, and Gender*. Stanford: Stanford University Press.

☐ Theater and Performing Arts

Birch, Cyril (ed.). 1995. *Scenes for Mandarins: The Elite Theater of the Ming*. New York: Columbia University Press.

Ch'en, Li-li. 1994. *Master Tung's Western Chamber Romance*. New York: Columbia University Press.

Gao, Ming. 1980. *The Lute: Kao Ming's P'i-p'a chi*. Trans. Jean Mulligan. New York: Columbia University Press.

Gernet, Jacques. 1962. *Daily Life in China on the Eve of the Mongol Invasion, 1250–1276*. Stanford: Stanford University Press.

Liu, Jung-en. 1972. *Six Yüan Plays*. Baltimore: Penguin Books.

Tang, Xianzu. 1980. *The Peony Pavilion: Mudan ting*. Trans. Cyril Birch. Bloomington: Indiana University Press.

Wang, Ch'iu Kuei. 1995. "Studies in Chinese Ritual and Ritual Theatre: A Bibliographic Report." *CHINOPERL* 18:115–128.

▪14▪

Trends and Prospects

Robert E. Gamer

At Chinese New Year celebrations, parents deliver little red packets filled with coins to their children, eat noodles and dumplings, hang small wall signs, and shoot off firecrackers to beseech the gods for prosperity and long life as the future unfolds. Before we leave, we too should think about China's future; it is bound to have an enormous impact on the lives of China's populace and on the rest of the world as well. In our part of the world, discussion about that future tends to center around these questions:

- Will China stay unified?
- Will China's economy continue to boom?
- What will happen to Hong Kong, Taiwan, and Tibet?
- Will China become more democratic?
- Will China and its peoples blend in as responsible members of the world community?

Scholars like Edward Friedman (1994, 1995) and Baogang He (1996) foresee a divided but democratic China; they focus on factors that may transform China. Others like David Shambaugh (1995), Constance Lever-Tracy, David Ip, and Tracy Noel (1995), and Daniel Bell et al. (1995) focus on the prospects for a more united and less democratic China; they point to factors that promote continuity but may hold back change. Like all crystal balls, this one can provide differing scenarios depending on where you set your gaze. Although no one can predict China's future with any certainty, we can make some observations that at least indicate what to look for.

First of all, the authors of this volume join most other observers of China in their belief that it would be very difficult for China to withdraw from the world economy. All factions of China's leaders—even those most culturally and politically conservative and its army—are deriving extensive benefits from China's economic dealings with the outside world that began with the 1978 reforms. So are its people. Our chapters on family, women, religion, and popular culture all point to tremendous changes in habits and expectations as a result of the economic changes. As John Wong observed in Chapter 5, "China's dynamic economic growth can be slowed but not stifled." Mao Zedong's collectivization and Great Leap Forward institutions helped provide a basis for many of the cooperatives, village and township enterprises, and dependent *(guahu)* firms that are fueling China's economic advance, and these new companies can be seen as direct outgrowths and natural successors to rather than as rejections of Mao (Wei, 1998; Chan, Madsen, and Unger, 1984:213ff.; Zhou, 1996; Croll, 1994; Yang, 1996).

Furthermore, economic reforms simultaneously give the provinces incentives to break away from and remain within a unified China. In Chapter 1, I pointed to some "creative tensions" in China's society. Each of those tensions—between Confucianism and capitalism, Confucianism and Christianity and communism, popular culture and formal traditions, regions and the capital city of Beijing, inward and outward reaching—provide China with reasons both to stay unified and to fly apart.

Today, the snapping points on all those tensions are located in the vicinity of Hong Kong and Taiwan. Because Hong Kong and Taiwan are inherent parts of China's economic growth, its prosperity would be very hard to maintain without them; yet the leverage this clout gives them frightens many Beijing leaders and can lead to serious miscalculations. Likewise, calls for greater political openness by student activists and by Tibetans and minorities in the western provinces among some leaders rouse fears in Beijing that the country could break apart; that has resulted in stern measures against those activists and regions.

And finally, such moves in themselves and attempts to unify China through nationalist appeals can lead to sword rattling by China, investor withdrawal, and retaliation by foreign governments that endanger the economic growth. Growth will also be endangered if China does not tackle the serious macroeconomic, legal, demographic, social, and environmental problems it confronts. Yet China is developing within itself a new generation that wants China to tackle its domestic problems, become a responsible part of the world community, and allow it to pursue both money and culture imported from the outside world; Perry Link (1992), Nicholas Kristof and Sheryl WuDunn (1994), and Jianying Zha (1995) all offer highly readable introductions to this new mindset. As the old guard retires, this new generation—which is connected to the internet and increasingly conversant in English—is taking command of important institutional positions and generating a debate (discussed in Chapter 4) about how China can develop a "civil society" to tackle its problems. Furthermore, the overseas Chinese who are fueling the economies of China and the other countries of South and Southeast Asia have a strong vested interest in continued prosperity for China. Much depends upon whether these positive motives can be translated into creative solutions for China's problems.

The creative tensions that offer hope for China by counseling moderation at the same time make it difficult to solve problems. Hill Gates (1996) captures this dilemma succinctly. She sees part of China's strength deriving from a tension between what she calls China's petty capitalism and its tributary system. China's family-centered Confucian tradition gave families the incentive to set up small capitalist enterprises to support and enrich their members; it also gave state officials the ability to "capture" and exact tribute from those enterprises, but in a form that would keep the enterprises going and the money flowing. This spurred the economy and helped keep China unified. The arrival of Western capitalism threatened to upset this delicate balance. Its calls for open markets, contract law, and rewards for people on the basis of ability assaulted the "nepotism," relationships *(guanxi)*, layers of bureaucracy, and state controls on which the old system had been based for centuries. As author after author has indicated in this volume, those Confucian values are still alive and well. Ironically, they are also a strong part of the reason why China's economy is thriving as part of the world capitalist system. In Gates's words:

> East Asia is becoming Number One not because its social formations are becoming more capitalist but because the dynamic of a tributary mode that has captured a petty-capitalist one is geared up yet further by the capture of [world] capitalism. . . . The Chinese petty capitalist mode of production does not generate all the organizations and ideology necessary to extricate the Chinese from their persisting problems. But it contains some of them and is, in any case, the cultural raw material from which their future must, inevitably, be forged. The effort to achieve social justice and a human social formation there will not succeed unless and until the Chinese take seriously their own popular traditions. (1996:276, 280)

This is where the dilemma lies: The more seriously Chinese take their traditions, the less likely they are to accept democratic reforms like a fair and impartial judicial system, protection of patents and other intellectual property rights, or the removal of government controls on business or free speech. Yet those traditions are responsible for the thrift, hard work, and entrepreneurial acumen of tightly knit families capable of setting up small businesses that have been powering China's economic resurgence. Gates is pointing directly at the problem. The Chinese must hold on to those values while seeking solutions to problems that can potentially derail economic development. And the family businesses must be willing to pass decision-making into the hands of professional managers who can let them grow beyond their family roots. In its long history, China's ideology has absorbed many challenges and will try to do so again. But China will seek its own solutions to such problems; they cannot be imposed from the outside world. The question is whether free markets and safe commercial contracts can be combined with the demands of *guanxi* and devotion to state and family.

In Chapter 3, Rhoads Murphey pointed to traditions of technology, from irrigated paddy to bamboo carrying poles, that endure even after the technological and industrial revolution has swept in from the West. Likewise, in Chapter 12, Chan Hoiman and Ambrose King pointed to the resilience of Confucian *guanxi* relationships. They say, "this streak of conservatism can be both a blessing and a curse for China's enigmatic transition into the modern world." It is a selective conservatism, stressing traditions that best suit the moment. These "private networks" of "achieved social relationships" may be weakening the "open institutional channels of social organization" that are also part of the Confucian tradition, resisting social change and ignoring the needs of those to whom they do not owe direct obligations (and thus undermining efforts like those Gates describes to achieve social justice and a human social formation) even as their members rush to acquire the latest designer clothes, electronic gear, fast foods, and blue jeans to wear in trendy new karaoke bars. In Chapter 13, Charles Laughlin, noting that "boisterousness" may be one of the defining characteristics and values of Chinese popular culture, pointed to the current popularity of sex manuals, pornography, martial arts, chivalric mythical heroes, outlaws, police work, and action films amid literature and videos on popular street stalls—not the sort of fare that focuses on social change or obligations. These new freedoms may actually make it harder for "modernized" coastal urbanites to understand the concerns of inland peoples isolated from this economic growth by distance and poverty or to comprehend the spiritual aspirations of Christians, Muslims, and Tantric Buddhists whose religions have never been syncretized into Chinese culture. Laurel Bossen indicated in Chapter 11 that the clearest advances for women have been the chance to earn and spend cash income on "frenzied consumer choices" of cosmetics, clothes, and home appliances. In Chapter 10, Zang Xiaowei pointed out that having their own incomes gives women greater freedom to choose and divorce their mates. Yet both authors indicated that women remain heavily influenced by their fathers, husbands, and loyalty to patriarchal institutions and patrilineages. All these trends surveyed by these authors—the enduring technologies, continuing *guanxi*, consumerism, recreation, and loyalty to patriarchal institutions—keep alive small capitalist enterprises and the ability of officials to exact tribute from them. The question remains whether China also can transform into greater adaption to the outside world and take the steps toward democracy John Wong outlined.

Taiwan, Singapore, South Korea, Malaysia, and other Asian countries have made moves toward democratizing and modernizing their economies. These countries, however, do not face the task of unifying large and diverse populations and territories and defending a large land base against powerful foreign competitors, and they do not contain large numbers of people still largely out of contact with the outside world. Tibet and the inland areas are not alone in wanting independence from Beijing; many in coastal provinces pursuing economic reforms have thoughts about how nice life might be if they were no longer tied down by economic and political controls emanating from Beijing. But the thousand border disputes over mining rights and control of villages serve as a warning; over the millennia, China's economy, resources, water controls, transportation, and bureaucracies have become heavily intertwined. Increasingly, modern investments cross provincial boundaries. And the Cultural Revolution stands as a fresh reminder of the chaos that can ensue when order is disturbed. Those considerations caution conservatism when tampering with the institutional and ideological bases that have held China together.

Part of what has brought modernity to the smaller Asian states also supports solidarity of the larger whole: the role of the overseas Chinese. As Chapter 6 explained, China is the base from which their economic power evolved. Today, many of the *guanxi* connections that hold together their power revolve around China. A turbulent and divided China would disturb not only those connections but the stability of Asia's business climate. If problems of weak currencies, and insolvent businesses and banks, which have affected neighboring nations to varying degrees, were to bring a vast downturn to China's economy, the effect would be felt throughout the region. Of course, another factor that could disturb peace in Asia would be a militant China challenging Malaysia or the Philippines to control islands, India over Tibetan borders, or Vietnam and Burma over border smuggling or the status of ethnic groups. Other Asian governments may wish to see China unified but not too militarily powerful, a country devoted to peace and not to war. That, too, depends upon the continuance of its economic growth. If this growth continues, in fact, China can provide a vast market and investment target for the other countries of Asia and serve as the nucleus of a powerful Asian economy (Seagrave, 1995; Robison and Goodman, 1996; and Lever-Tracy, Ip, and Noel, 1996, all speculate on those prospects).

In the words of Ma Rong (Chapter 8), "China has never been able to survive with two nations, one rich and one poor." As Rhoads Murphey explained, when dynasties stopped addressing pressing social problems, revolt tended to ensue. The new economy is widening the gap between rich and poor. This provides grist for the mill of the conservatives in the Communist Party who want a reemphasis on themes of equality and economic controls; the fact that many of these conservatives have themselves been enriched by the reforms makes their position less tenable. If conservatism stifled the economy, large numbers of people would resist the moves, but if the new growth leaves behind millions of unemployed people without hope, no longer provided the "iron rice bowl" protections they enjoyed under Marxism-Maoism, rebellion could also emerge from below. Jobs for those millions and government funds to create social programs are more likely to result if reform is intensified than if it is curbed.

Nature may provide its own curbs to economic reform. China's people must eat, drink, breathe, and retain continued access to natural resources. Degradation resulting from economic development and the continuing rise in population endanger its ability to sustain adequate supplies of food, water, fresh air, and other staples—not to mention electricity, petroleum, timber, and other requisites of modern economic development (Schaller, 1993; Smil, 1993). Rhoads Murphey explained that degradation of the environment has always been a problem when population grows. With the unprecedented growth of population discussed by Ma Rong, will the new measures to protect the environment discussed by Richard Edmonds in Chapter 9 be adequate to bring that degradation under control (Lieberthal, 1995:276–291)? If not, agricultural yields may decline and—as John Wong explained—even world markets may not be able to supply adequate food for China's people. This possibility could result in starving children, lowered food consumption and resistance to disease (which can spread around the world during flu season), and diversion of economic resources away from growth activities. As he concluded, this makes it imperative that China join international organizations and help seek solutions to these pressing problems at international conferences. They are unlikely to be solved without cooperation at a worldwide level.

Hence China's prospects for unity, continued economic boom, movement toward democracy, and peaceful absorption into the world community depend on the policies its leaders will be willing to craft and on good fortune in carrying them out. A source of its strength lies in the interdependence of its regions. Rhoads Murphey pointed to the extensive cultural advances that emanated from the seagoing south while the inward-centered north imposed order; as Ma Rong said, the market economy those coastal people supply has been at its liveliest when effective rulers unify great portions of the country. The longer-term prospects for Tibet and the western provinces are more murky. Ma Rong, referring to the regions Stanley Toops introduced as China Proper and the Frontier, pointed to the "tie and tension between the interior and the coast"; although many in those regions have reasons to break away, it would be hard for them to advance economically on their own. And, with the extensive Han inmigration discussed by Rhoads Murphey, they are no longer entirely culturally separate. Yet, as Chapter 6 indicated, Tibet's religious traditions stand in contrast to those of China. Islam, the religion of many inhabitants of the vast western provinces, is even farther removed from Chinese culture; it does not even share any common Buddhist themes. Like Christianity, it believes in immortality, ecstasy, and salvation in heaven for individuals by an omnipotent supreme God, with punishment in hell for those who reject the appeal of his prophet on earth. In the words of Chan and King, such religions can be "tolerated as perhaps harmless pastimes for a worn-out nation" but not accepted if they "run counter to national interest."

It is unlikely that China will adopt Western-style democracy in any kind of foreseeable future. But it is also unlikely that China can again withdraw from the world; China and overseas Chinese have become too absorbed into the world economy to allow for retreat. China has the resources, human and natural, to sustain economic growth and political unity. And behind its diversity of interests and beliefs lies a widespread reservoir of commitment to sustain that growth and unity.

China's economy, like all others, will have periods when growth slows; those are the periods when conflict could easily flare. Therein may lie the biggest problem. Perry Link (1992:195–196, 221, 273, 295) quotes a Chinese literary critic saying that Chinese intellectuals "have inherited two modes of responding to the political world: the Confucian mode of offering service to the state and the Daoist mode of withdrawing into oneself." Link observes that students may be far more interested in entering into dialogue and official channels than with actually examining ideas and solutions. A Chinese literature professor commented: "Why do all Chinese scholars abandon their work because of crisis?" Such a frame of mind impedes the process of tackling these problems; it also breeds timidity that can exacerbate problems. Instead of warning officials about the dangers of foolhardy projects, this political quiescence may tempt them into such behavior. Link himself comments about the view of wealthy people in Hong Kong who feel that Hong Kong will get special consideration only because it is a "money tree." "Do they really imagine that their wealth—fantastic by mainland standards—would cause China's rulers to keep their hands off, rather than produce exactly the opposite effect?" If China is to achieve a civil society that can hold on to its strengths as its role in the global economy grows, education may be the biggest challenge of all. Can it develop a responsible commitment to truth seeking and problem solving and to confronting officials with forewarnings that their policies may be at variance with both? That is something for Chinese to ponder when they deliver their little red packets and eat their noodles at New Year's; if they can tackle this challenge, they have many reasons to look to a bright future.

■ **BIBLIOGRAPHY**

Bell, Daniel, David Brown, Kanishka Jayasuriya, and David Martin Jones. 1995. *Towards Illiberal Democracy in Pacific Asia*. New York: St. Martin's Press.

Chan, Anita, Richard Madsen, and Jonathan Unger. 1984. *Chen Village: The Recent History of a Peasant Community in Mao's China*. Berkeley: University of California Press.

Croll, Elizabeth. 1994. *From Heaven to Earth: Images and Experiences of Development in China*. London: Routledge.

Friedman, Edward. 1994. *The Politics of Democratization: Generalizing East Asian Experiences*. Boulder: Westview Press.

————. 1995. *National Identity and Democratic Prospects in Socialist China.* Armonk, NY: M. E. Sharpe.

Gamer, Robert E. 1991. "Helping History Find Its Way: Liberalization in China." *Crossroads: A Socio-Political Journal* (Jerusalem) 32.

————. 1994. "Modernization and Democracy: Samuel P. Huntington and 'Neo-Authoritarian' Debate." *Asian Journal of Political Science* (Singapore) 2 (June):1.

————. 1995. "The Changing Political Economy of China." Pp. 187–219 in Manochehr Dorraj and Albert Harris (eds.), *The Changing Political Economy of the Third World.* Boulder: Lynne Rienner Publishers.

Garnaut, Ross, Guo Shutian, and Ma Guonan (eds.). 1996. *The Third Revolution in the Chinese Countryside.* Cambridge: Cambridge University Press.

Gates, Hill. 1996. *China's Motor: A Thousand Years of Petty Capitalism.* Ithaca: Cornell University Press.

Goodman, David S. G., and Gerald Segal. 1994. *China Deconstructs: Politics, Trade, and Regionalism.* London: Routledge.

He, Baogang. 1996. *The Democratisation of China.* London: Routledge.

Jenner, W. J. F. *The Tyranny of History: The Roots of China's Crisis.* London: Penguin Books.

Kristof, Nicholas, and Sheryl WuDunn. 1994. *China Wakes: The Struggle for the Soul of a Rising Power.* New York: Random House.

Lever-Tracy, Constance, David Ip, and Tracy Noel. 1996. *The Chinese Diaspora and Mainland China: An Emerging Economic Synergy.* New York: St. Martin's Press.

Lieberthal, Kenneth. 1995. *Governing China: From Revolution Through Reform.* New York: W. W. Norton.

Link, E. Perry, Jr. 1992. *Evening Chats in Beijing: Probing China's Predicament.* New York: W. W. Norton.

Robison, Richard, and David S. G. Goodman (eds.). 1996. *The New Rich in Asia: Mobile Phones, McDonalds, and Middle Class Revolution.* London: Routledge.

Schaller, George. 1993. *The Last Panda.* Chicago: University of Chicago Press.

Seagrave, Sterling. 1995. *Lords of the Rim.* New York: G. P. Putnam.

Shambaugh, David. 1995. *Greater China: The Next Superpower.* Oxford: Oxford University Press.

Smil, Vaclav. 1993. *China's Environmental Crisis.* Armonk, NY: M. E. Sharpe.

Wei, Pan. 1998. *The Politics of Marketization in Rural China.* Lanham, MD: Rowman and Littlefield.

Yang, Dali L. 1996. *Calamity and Reform in China: Rural Society and Institutional Change Since the Great Leap Famine.* Stanford: Stanford University Press.

Zha, Jianying. 1995. *China Pop: How Soap Operas, Tabloids, and Bestsellers Are Transforming a Culture.* New York: New Press.

Zhao, Quansheng. 1996. *Interpreting Chinese Foreign Policy.* Oxford: Oxford University Press.

Zhou, Kate Xiao. 1996. *How the Farmers Changed China: Power of the People.* Boulder: Westview Press.

▪ The Contributors ▪

Laurel Bossen is lecturer in anthropology at McGill University, Montreal, Quebec.

Chan Hoiman is lecturer in sociology at the Chinese University of Hong Kong.

Richard Louis Edmonds is senior lecturer in geography and director of the Contemporary China Institute at the School of Oriental and African Studies, London, and editor of the *China Quarterly*.

Robert E. Gamer is professor of political science at the University of Missouri–Kansas City.

Ambrose Y. C. King is professor of sociology and pro–vice chancellor of the Chinese University of Hong Kong.

Charles A. Laughlin is assistant professor of Asian languages at Yale University, New Haven, Conneticut.

Ma Rong is associate director of the Institute of Sociology and Anthropology, Beijing University.

Rhoads Murphey is professor emeritus of history at the University of Michigan, Ann Arbor.

Stanley W. Toops is associate professor of geography at Miami University in Oxford, Ohio.

John Wong is professor of economics and research director of the East Asian Institute at the National University of Singapore.

Zang Xiaowei is assistant lecturer in sociology at Flinders University, Adelaide, Australia, and assistant professor at the City University of Hong Kong.

▪ Index ▪

▪ About the Book ▪

Understanding Contemporary China offers undergraduates a coherent assessment of the most crucial issues affecting China today. Designed as a core text for "Introduction to Asia" or "Introduction to China" courses, it can also be used effectively in a wide variety of discipline-oriented curriculums.

Assuming no prior knowledge on the part of the reader, the book begins with an overview of China's geography and cultural history. The authors then provide a thorough treatment not only of the country's politics and economy but also of demographic trends, environmental problems, family patterns, the role of women in development, and religion and cultural expression. Each chapter provides historical context, and each topic is covered with reference to the latest available scholarship.

Written in an engaging and accessible manner, *Understanding Contemporary China* reveals the complexity of China's challenges at the end of the twentieth century, their global impact, and the prospects for the future of the country.

Robert E. Gamer is professor of political science at the University of Missouri–Kansas City. His publications include *Governments and Politics in a Changing World* and *The Developing Nations: A Comparative Perspective*.